COALFIELD JEWS

Coalfield Jews

An Appalachian History

DEBORAH R. WEINER

UNIVERSITY OF ILLINOIS PRESS

URBANA AND CHICAGO

Supported by grants from the West Virginia
Humanities Council and
the Southern Jewish Historical Society

∞ This book is printed on acid-free paper.

Library of Congress Cataloging-in-Publication Data
Weiner, Deborah R.
Coalfield Jews : an Appalachian history / Deborah R. Weiner.
p.   cm.
Includes bibliographical references and index.
ISBN-13: 978-0-252-03094-9 (cloth : alk. paper)
ISBN-10: 0-252-03094-x (cloth : alk. paper)
ISBN-13: 978-0-252-07335-9 (pbk. : alk. paper)
ISBN-10: 0-252-07335-5 (pbk. : alk. paper)
1. Jews—West Virginia—History. 2. West Virginia—
Ethnic relations. I. Title.
F250.J5W45   2006
975.400492'4—dc22   2006000320

CONTENTS

ACKNOWLEDGMENTS

I could not have written this book without the cooperation of coalfield residents, past and current, who graciously let me into their lives. Their interviews constitute the heart and soul of my source material, and I cannot thank them enough for their honesty, thoughtfulness, and patience. They are all cited in the references; unfortunately, space limitations prevent me from naming each one here. I must mention a few, though, who went way out of their way to help me. Bertie Cohen, Edna Drosick, Ed Eiland, Milt Koslow, Marilou Sniderman, the Sopher family (Ira, Mary Jo, and Tom), Mel Sturm, and the late Manny Pickus have my deep appreciation.

This study delves into the support networks that coalfield Jews relied on, and I realize now that I have relied on such networks myself. Family and friends of Jewish coalfield residents helped me expand my contacts, lent pictures, shared stories, and much more. I am especially grateful to Gail Bank, Cindy Burgin, Tom Childress, Shirley Ofsa, Tom Pressman, Craig Shell, Randy Wasserstrom, and the family of David Weinstein.

My own networks sustained me over the embarrassingly long time span of this project. Mentors and friends at West Virginia University provided intellectual and moral support every step of the way. I owe much to Ron Lewis, Liz and Ken Fones-Wolf, Maryanne Reed, Bob Blobaum, Chrisse Jones, and Susan Lewis. Paul Rakes shared his singular perspective as friend, coalfield expert, and dyed-in-the-wool southern West Virginian. Colleagues from the fields of southern and American Jewish history were generous in their encouragement and sharing of ideas. In particular, I thank Mark Bauman, Hollace Weiner, Lee Shai Weissbach, Sherry Zander, Len Rogoff, Rachel Heimovics Braun, Fred Krome, Wendy Besmann, and Sonny Werth.

I was lucky to receive timely support in the final stages of this project. My coworkers at the Jewish Museum of Maryland were tremendously accommodating. Special thanks to Avi Decter for his consistent support and understanding and Erin Titter and Olivia Klose for critical help during "crunch time." I am grateful to John Inscoe and Jonathan Sarna for their detailed and encouraging comments on the manuscript. Judy McCulloh of the University of Illinois Press graciously put up with my numerous questions and concerns.

Fellowships from the West Virginia Humanities Council, American Jewish Archives, and Southern Jewish Historical Society aided my research. Several publications gave permission to reprint parts of previously published essays: "From Shtetl to Coalfield: The Migration of East European Jews to Southern West Virginia," in *Transnational West Virginia: Ethnic Work Communities during the Industrial Era,* ed. K. Fones-Wolf and R. L. Lewis (Morgantown: West Virginia University Press, 2002), 73–111; "Jewish Women in the Central Appalachian Coalfields, 1890–1960: From Breadwinners to Community Builders," *American Jewish Archives Journal* 52 (2000): 11–33; "The Jews of Keystone, West Virginia: Life in a Multicultural Boomtown," *Southern Jewish History* 2 (Fall 1999): 1–23; and "Middlemen of the Coal Fields: The Role of Jews in the Economy of Southern West Virginia Coal Towns, 1890–1950," *Journal of Appalachian Studies* 4, no. 1 (Spring 1998): 29–56.

Finally, I thank my family for their unwavering encouragement: Lauren, Vicki, Howard, and extended "family members" Jean Butzen, Jim Strickler, and Moses Lee. This book is dedicated to my parents, Ron and Phyllis Weiner, who have always believed in me.

COALFIELD JEWS

Introduction

Louis Zaltzman came to Keystone, West Virginia, in 1896 at age four with his Russian immigrant parents Bessie and Mose. "The community there was small and rough, no electric lights or water supply, dirt and unpaved streets and roads, and very little law," he later wrote. "It was a frontier town with fourteen saloons and about fifteen Jewish families."[1]

Zaltzman was not a writer by profession, but rather, "the only Jewish man in the entire . . . region who had a career with a railroad," retiring as head timekeeper of the Norfolk and Western Railway. Yet in a few brief words he managed to capture the origins of Jewish coalfield communities with fullness and insight—not to mention flair, with a juxtaposition in his second sentence guaranteed to arouse the reader's curiosity. What were these Jews, immigrants from Eastern Europe and their children, doing in a rough-and-tumble coal town deep in the heart of the Appalachian Mountains?

An exploration of this question leads in many directions, with Zaltzman's statement an excellent starting point. Scholars have indeed referred to the Central Appalachian plateau as "one of America's last frontiers," and throughout history, Jews have found opportunity in such places.[2] In fact, Jews happened to own several of the saloons that were such a prominent feature of life in Keystone during its heyday as a turn-of-the-twentieth-century southern West Virginia boomtown. They also established numerous other retail businesses that catered to a fast-growing population of coal miners and railroad workers. Keystone was, as the old saying goes, good for the Jews: by 1900, they made up more than 10 percent of the town's one-thousand-plus inhabitants.[3]

That fact might startle anyone familiar with Appalachian history, since very little has been written about the region to suggest that such a demographic make-up could have been possible. Meanwhile, most American Jews would be surprised to hear that not all the Jewish immigrants who came to the United States during the great migration of the 1880s to 1920s settled in large cities. Among other things, then, this study of Jewish communities in the southern coalfields aims to

unsettle commonly held views of both Appalachia and the American Jewish experience.

The story takes place at the intersection of two historical phenomena. From the
1880s to the 1920s, as the entry of railroads into the mountains instigated the large-
scale extraction of coal, the Central Appalachian plateau underwent sudden and
rapid industrialization. During the same time, Jews from Eastern Europe streamed
into the eastern seaboard in search of economic opportunity and freedom from
oppression. Some of the immigrants found their way to the newly opened coalfields
of southwestern Virginia, southern West Virginia, and southeastern Kentucky.
Drawing on a cultural heritage as "middlemen" in the European countryside, they
carved out a niche as retailers in the region's expanding rural-industrial economy.

Jews arrived at the dawn of the coal era: the first Jewish settler came to the New
River boomtown of Sewell, West Virginia, in 1871, even before construction was
completed on the railroad that would kick off the coal boom.[4] As rail lines advanced deeper into the mountains, coal development followed close behind and
people from all over the world poured in to become part of a growing industrial
workforce. Jewish entrepreneurs and their families settled in burgeoning towns
throughout the region, eventually concentrating in the county seats, which emerged
as the principal commercial centers. They became a significant part of the small
middle class in their towns, integrating to a high degree into the local social scene.
As merchants and as citizens, they contributed substantially to town development,
especially downtown business districts.

It must be noted that Keystone's demographics were not typical: Jews made up
a much smaller portion of the population in other coalfield towns where they
resided. Nevertheless, enough families settled in the southern coalfields to form
thriving Jewish congregations in nine towns. Their populations ranged from a
high of around seventy in the smallest Jewish community to more than two hundred in the largest.

Although its protagonists are Jewish immigrants and their descendants, this
book is as much about Appalachia as it is about Jews. The coalfield environment
loomed over Jewish economic activity, shaped the interaction between Jews and
non-Jews, and influenced local Jewish culture and communal life. In turn, though
Jews remained a small minority occupying an economically marginal position
outside the coal industry, they made a decided mark on the region's development.
The Appalachian context was more than simply the backdrop against which Jews
acted out their lives. Accordingly, their story is treated here as Jewish history *and*
as Appalachian history, in equal measure. The linkages that emerge between these
two seemingly unrelated fields help to illuminate both.

But what exactly can the story of coalfield Jews add to the respective narratives
of American Jewry and Appalachia, aside from the fact that Jews did indeed live in
this place? It turns out that the Jewish experience speaks to key aspects of the region's social and economic order. As retailers, Jews faced the daunting challenge

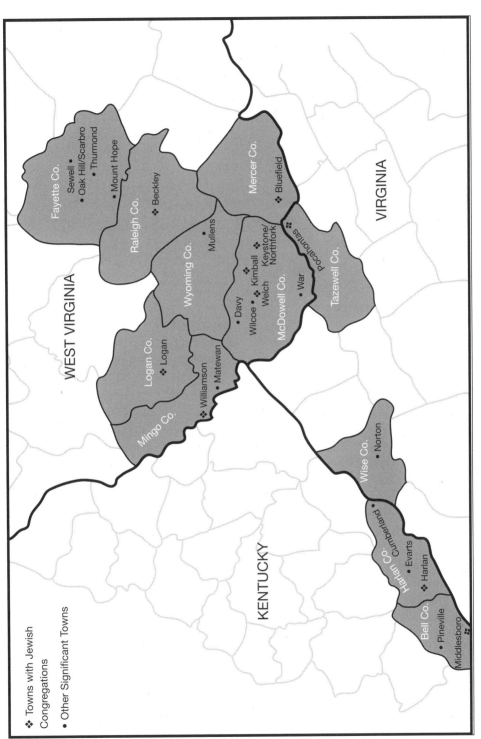

Jews in the Southern Coalfields. (Map by Amy Freese, Stonehouse Design)

of succeeding within the coal economy—an economy that initially offered tremendous opportunity thanks to an expanding population but also posed impressive obstacles to small businesses. The most important obstacles were the boom-and-bust nature of the coal industry and the institution of the coal company store. By analyzing how these forces affected Jewish economic life, this book portrays the coal economy from a point of view rarely considered in Appalachian studies: that of the independent merchant. An investigation into the position of Jews in the social order reveals how the region's population coped with the remarkable diversity of peoples brought together by the coal boom. Moreover, Jews acted on their class interests in the civic and political arenas. Their behavior—in particular, their ambivalent response to the labor conflicts that embroiled the region—sheds light on the attitudes of the middle class regarding critical issues of the day.

In general, Jews provide a window into the nature of the coalfield middle class. This in-between group has received little treatment in coalfield studies, and the independent towns where the middle class held sway have received far less notice than company towns. When the middle class does appear in the literature, it is portrayed, uniformly, as a "local elite" that acted as cheerleader for the coal industry.[5] This depiction is not inaccurate, but it is incomplete. In real life, members of the coalfield middle class and the towns they inhabited played a more dynamic role in the region's social, cultural, and commercial affairs. True, most of the population consisted of industrial workers and their families, while the economic decisions governing the region's fate were made largely by the corporate controllers of its land and resources. Yet the macro view does not necessarily reflect the day-to-day level where people lived out their lives, interacting with one another in neighborhoods, churches, schools, shops, and places of amusement as well as at the mines. Since coalfield Jewish communities were located solely in county seats and other independent towns, the study dwells on life in these towns, the region's economic and social centers.

Although it is easy to make the case that coalfield Jewish life offers a fresh perspective from which to view Appalachian history—after all, few studies of the region's ethnic groups have yet been produced[6]—it is somewhat more difficult to establish what the subject might contribute to the literature on American Jewry. Numerous works on small Jewish communities have been published dealing with every region of the country, though not specifically Appalachia. Their authors have established a basic pattern that the coalfield Jewish population did not depart from: these communities were merchant-based, usually starting with peddlers who gradually settled down to owning stores and raising families; they became fairly prosperous; they actively contributed to the civic life of their towns; and they formed congregations that might have started out Orthodox (especially if the membership was of Eastern European origin) but typically gravitated to Reform Judaism. Only on the matter of interaction with the surrounding society are there real disparities, with some studies reporting that Jews mixed easily with non-Jews and others suggesting that they remained socially segregated.[7]

As long ago as 1980, this uniformity led historian Howard Rabinowitz to question "whether or not scholars should be spending their time writing histories of individual Jewish communities. . . . After all, these studies simply fill in the details for an overall picture which already seems clear."[8] In large part, this book does provide one more variation on a theme. Yet within that familiar pattern, there are plenty of gaps remaining to be filled in order to understand how these communities actually functioned. For one thing, though many works on American Jewish women have come out in recent decades, rarely have issues of gender been integrated into a community study. The following pages include that half of the Jewish population usually left out of the peddler-to-merchant paradigm. Women in the coalfields made substantial contributions to the economic well-being of their families, and their efforts to sustain Jewish identity within the small community setting were too critical to be ignored.

Moreover, I take to heart Rabinowitz's protest against the upbeat tone of most community studies. "Surely," he stated, "there is more to [the American Jewish] experience than smooth assimilation, rapid economic progress, and noble behavior toward ourselves and others."[9] Coalfield Jews achieved economic mobility and integrated into local society while forming close-knit communities that helped them sustain their Jewish identity, but the process was far from smooth. This study chronicles a bumpy road to prosperity, acknowledging the people who fell by the wayside and showing that economic disaster lurked just around the corner for even the most successful family businesses. It explores the conflict as well as the camaraderie that marked Jewish communities. It considers the complex motivations that led people to become involved in communal activity and discusses the challenges posed by the position of Jews as a very small minority in a region where Christianity was a powerful daily presence.

Further, it delves into the less "noble" aspects of Jewish life in the region. Like everyone else who gathered in the towns that sprang up when the coal industry moved in, Jews became caught up in the boomtown atmosphere and engaged in behavior that could not always be described as kosher. By detailing their less respectable activities, I move away from the sedate depictions of most community studies and show that Jews living in the American hinterland had more in common with their counterparts in the rough world of the Lower East Side than has been generally recognized.

The boomtown milieu did more than give scope to the more unrefined tendencies among the region's Jewish (and other) inhabitants. It shaped economic life, ethnic relations, and even Jewish communal development. In fact, the concept of the boomtown turned out to be somewhat of an organizing principle for this book, connecting themes of American Jewish history and Appalachian history while enabling both to be considered within an international context. In the instant towns created by the coal boom, outsiders quickly overwhelmed the small local population, and a new social landscape formed that allowed for relatively fluid social dynamics. Although preexisting local elites remained a powerful force in this new society, they needed to seek allies among the newcomers, and so Jewish entrepreneurs found a greater welcome than they otherwise might have. The Jewish experience points to similarities between coalfield towns and boomtowns in other places around the world, where Jews found a comparable place in the social order.[10] The freewheeling atmosphere that prevailed throughout the coalfields—but found purest expression in non-county-seat towns such as Keystone—changed over time, as towns became more settled. But their boomtown origins continued to influence social interaction.

The boomtown concept not only provides a comparative framework within which to consider the history of a particular Jewish group but also offers a way to step back from the somewhat limiting view of Central Appalachia as a geographic entity to look at the region's place in the world. The boomtowns in various countries that welcomed Jews were located on peripheries, areas that were just beginning to be incorporated into the capitalist world system. So it was with Appalachia, its coal destined to fuel industrialization in distant lands. Resource exploitation led to the region's abrupt integration into the world market—a process that had begun over a century earlier but had stalled, awaiting the transportation networks necessary to complete it. This final transition to industrial capitalism was marked by social and economic upheaval that proved devastating to the agrarian-oriented people who lived in the mountains before the coal industry came. Ironically, many of the newcomers who arrived to participate in the new order, including Jews, were fleeing the same kind of transformation, then underway in Southern and Eastern Europe, that had eroded the place they had held in the precapitalist economy. The Jews who forged a commercial niche in the coal economy were fulfilling a role Jews had filled in Eastern Europe but could no longer maintain.[11]

The vibrant Jewish communities that thrived in the coalfields from roughly the 1890s to the 1970s have largely disappeared, victims of the drastic economic decline that hit the region starting in the mid-1950s. Only two of the nine congregations profiled in this study still exist, both in much reduced form. From today's standpoint, it is hard to believe that thousands of Jews lived in the coalfields during that eighty-year time span, that Jewish life once flourished there. Because of present reality, it is easy to look on their story as an oddity of history. It does not, somehow, seem possible that Jews really belonged in this place.

But they did. Jews were not out of place in the coalfields but were an integral part of the region's development, along with the many other ethnic groups brought by the coal boom. If their appearance seems anomalous, it is largely because definitions of Appalachia tend to either ignore or oversimplify the "industrial" part of its "rural-industrial" heritage. The Jewish presence was, in fact, the natural outcome of social and economic forces emanating from both within and outside the region, combined with the decisions of individuals who were parts of families and networks that influenced their choices. This book includes stories and anecdotes about some of these individuals in order to provide a sense of the coming together of personal choice and larger societal forces. The stories start in Eastern Europe and continue through the journey to the coalfields to the establishment of families and communities and careers in the region. They reveal that, in addition to belonging in Central Appalachia, coalfield Jews also belonged firmly within the pattern of small-town American Jewish life. Although they chose to settle in a seemingly unlikely place, they remained connected to their roots. They were both Appalachian and Jewish.

CHAPTER 1

From Shtetl to Coalfield: The Migration of East European Jews to Appalachia

In 1888, Sam and Herman Weinstein left their hometown of Raseiniai in central Lithuania. Although their father, a miller, had been "well-to-do for that country," their family's economic situation had deteriorated, leading the brothers to become early participants in the massive wave of Russian Jewish migration to America that occurred from 1880 to 1924. They landed in New York "penniless" and found work in a shirt factory where they earned $3.50 per week. Unable to support their mother and sister, who soon joined them, they resolved to seek new opportunities.[1]

Sana Moscovitch Pickus joined the immigration movement at the other end of its time span. She arrived in Baltimore in 1921, with her newlywed daughter and son-in-law, to unite with three sons already established in America. Her husband Mendel had died in 1909 "in his birthplace, the 'ancestral' home of the Pickus family, i.e. in the town of Uzda, province of Minsk, Russia." The Pickuses had been grain dealers, an occupation hard hit by changes in the Russian Empire's economy. A pious woman, Sana Pickus brought with her two prayer books with Yiddish commentary and a two-volume set of the *Tsenah Urenah,* a popular Yiddish rendering of the Hebrew Bible cherished by the common folk, particularly women (who, according to Jewish custom, did not learn to read Hebrew).[2]

The sagas of the Weinsteins and Pickuses closely follow the first half of the archetypal success story of East European Jewish migration to America: shtetl origins and old-country tribulations, early poverty in the new land, hard work and determination, family cohesion, and the piety of the elders. The second half departs from the conventional narrative, which usually unfolds within the confines of America's major metropolitan areas, from gritty ethnic neighborhood to middle-class suburb. Instead, the Weinsteins' search for economic advancement led them to southeastern Kentucky, where they became leading merchants in the town of Middlesboro. Sana Pickus joined her three sons in Beckley, West Virginia, and attended her first American high holiday services in a Presbyterian church the local Jewish community borrowed or rented for the occasion of her arrival.

Although atypical, the Weinsteins and Pickuses were hardly unique. A significant minority of East European Jews ventured beyond major U.S. cities to settle in towns and rural areas throughout the country—including the nation's southern coalfields, in the heart of Central Appalachia. To understand why Jewish immigrants journeyed to the mountains and how they adapted to their new environment, it is necessary to consider who they were and how they started. As with all immigrants, their old-country background combined with circumstances they encountered in America to shape their lives in the new land. The life experiences, skills, networks, and culture Jews brought from their place of origin profoundly influenced the communities they developed in southeastern Kentucky, southern West Virginia, and southwestern Virginia. For the vast majority, that place of origin can be traced to the Russian and Austro-Hungarian empires of Eastern Europe.

The Jews of Eastern Europe

By the late nineteenth century, Eastern Europe had long been home to the world's largest Jewish population. Jews had entered the region some six centuries earlier, a dispersed and landless minority that had developed skills and networks in commercial pursuits. Welcomed by the rulers of Poland, Hungary, and Rumania, they found a niche as traders and artisans in a premodern agrarian economy. The Polish gentry in particular, which came to control a vast territory that included Poland, Lithuania, Belarus ("White Russia"), and Ukraine, found Jews to be most suited to serve as the economic link between noble and serf, between the rural economy and the evolving international economy. As Poland thrived from the fourteenth to seventeenth centuries, so did its Jews, who filled all levels of commerce, from financiers, exporters, and estate managers to the much more numerous peddlers and shopkeepers, tavern owners and innkeepers, teamsters and artisans living in small towns and villages throughout the countryside.[3]

Like other ethnic groups within the greater Polish state, Jews enjoyed communal autonomy within their small towns, known as shtetls. A distinctive East European Jewish culture grew out of the interaction between age-old Jewish tradition and the influences of the local environment. The hallmark of this culture was religious observance: for centuries, Judaism regulated every aspect of life, so that it was "impossible to separate the religious from the secular—they (were) fused into one whole." The Judaic concept of *tzedekah* governed community affairs. Often translated imprecisely as "charity," its true meaning conveys a sense of communal obligation and social responsibility. Its imperative was "woven into the organization of the community," resulting in a web of religiously based charities and mutual-aid societies that, along with the synagogue, promoted solidarity despite palpable and often rancorous economic divisions among Jews.[4]

With its niche in the East European economy, the Jewish population served as a classic "entrepreneurial minority," or "middleman minority," terms coined by sociologists to describe a worldwide phenomenon: in many premodern agricul-

tural societies, religious or ethnic minorities have occupied the economic position, or "status gap," between the ruling elite and the majority peasant population, performing necessary distributive and managerial functions yet never losing
their standing as outsiders. The Chinese in Southeast Asia and Indians in colonial
Africa present two other prominent examples. In such cases, ethnic minorities
link local rural economies with markets near and far, while serving as "interme-
diaries between the ruling elite and the masses, . . . between the producers and the
consumers." Though mixing on a daily basis with the majority, they remain separate by virtue of their own desire to preserve their cultural heritage and by their
status as "out-castes," despised for their "otherness" and for their willingness to
take on tasks—such as trading or money lending—that agrarian societies often
consider lowly, dishonorable, even immoral.[5]

The middleman minority concept offers an intriguing cross-cultural perspective
on ethnic relations, though it can obscure important social realities. Even East
European Jewry, often seen as the quintessential middleman minority, does not
conform entirely to the model. The Polish lands of the medieval and early modern
period contained many ethnic groups; Jews were far from being the only minority.
This heterogeneity enabled Polish Jewry to flourish, because, as Gershon Hundert
observes, "the status of Jews was most favorable in states of multiple nationality in
which they were less conspicuous."[6]

Moreover, the concept of "otherness" can be taken too far. Centuries of daily
interaction and cultural exchange fostered a certain intimacy between Jews and
their Lithuanian, Ukrainian, Russian, and Polish peasant neighbors that encom-
passed shared folklore, superstitions, foodways, health-care and child-rearing
practices, and economic customs (such as a propensity to bargain). The marketplace served as their main point of contact and symbolized "the interdependence,
the reciprocity, the ambivalence that exist[ed] between Jew and Gentile." The
combination of everyday social interaction with deep cultural and religious disparities has led author Jack Kugelmass to use the paradoxical term "native aliens"
to describe the Jews of Eastern Europe.[7]

As agrarian societies move toward capitalistic forms of economic organization,
the niche occupied by middleman minorities enables them to play an important
role in investment, market expansion, and business innovation. As a highly visible
"other" involved in commercial activities, they prove ideal scapegoats to blame for
the disruptions caused by economic modernization. Despite their longtime place
in the rural order, they come to represent the embodiment of capitalist excess and
the antithesis of rural values and stability. Doubts and fears about socioeconomic
change are projected onto them, causing them to become targets of hostility for
those who suffer materially or socially in the transition to capitalism. The results
of such hostility have often been devastating—particularly for Jews, since this
scapegoating has been augmented by ancient religious myths and aversions that
surface during economically troubled times.[8]

With the rise of the modern era, Poland suffered a sustained political and economic decline, and as conditions worsened, Jews did indeed receive much of the blame. By the late eighteenth century, Poland was widely perceived to suffer from a "Jewish problem," which neighboring states inherited when they moved in to carve up the former great power. In the partitions of the Polish lands in the 1770s to 1790s, most of Polish Jewry suddenly became Russian Jewry, as the Russian Empire took over Lithuania, Belarus, most of Ukraine, and much of Poland itself. Prussia and the Austro-Hungarian Empire grabbed the western and southern portions of the Polish state, with Austria-Hungary acquiring a large Jewish population in Galicia, southeastern Poland.[9]

Eastern Europe's wrenching transition to capitalism caused economic and social dislocation for Jews and non-Jews alike. Competition from distant markets crippled small-scale agriculture and enterprise, encouraging the consolidation of land and commerce. While some people benefited from new opportunities, most were impoverished by the obliteration of their traditional role in the economy. Peasants, petty traders, and artisans displaced from the countryside sought work in urban areas, but the emerging industrial sector did not develop quickly enough to absorb them. As vast numbers of Jews—small-scale traders and skilled workers—lost their livelihoods, discrimination in many industries and a general dearth of capital pushed them into the low-capital, labor-intensive clothing industry.[10]

While Jews throughout Eastern Europe faced dire economic conditions, the situation in the Russian Empire became especially unbearable. Anti-Jewish violence rose as Jews found themselves blamed for a mounting social and economic crisis. Pogroms in 1881–82 traumatized their immediate victims and caused psychological distress for the entire Jewish population. The oppressive May Laws of 1882 ushered in an era of anti-Jewish legislation that, among other things, barred Jews from many occupations and caused frequent expulsions from the countryside. Their status as an officially despised group encouraged escalating harassment, from low-level, routine abuse to an outbreak of catastrophic pogroms between 1903 and 1906.[11]

Russian Jews proved receptive to the drastic solutions that emerged in the wake of violence and persecution. Urbanization and exposure to modern ideas, the rise of a Jewish proletariat, conflict between Jewish workers and Jewish employers—all had undermined societal norms and communal solidarity. Many Jews flocked to movements such as socialism, communism, and Zionism. For the masses who saw no future for themselves in Russia, the answer seemed more obvious: departure.[12]

Although the pogroms and May Laws spurred the emigration movement that gathered steam in the 1880s, the underlying push was economic. Jews began to leave Russia well before the pogroms: as early as 1869, a Hebrew-language newspaper declared that "the reasons for this emigration are the shrinking possibilities of gaining a livelihood and the fear of military service." An earlier tsarist policy of conscripting young Jewish boys into the army and forcibly converting them to Christianity had prompted a dread of conscription that lasted long after it was abolished. Military service also remained anathema because of the abuse Jewish recruits encountered and the near-impossibility of following religious rituals while in the army.[13] Moreover, Russian Jews were far from alone in their desire to leave their native land. Across Europe, economic change spread from west to east, leaving great migrations in its wake. The mid-nineteenth century saw a mass movement of Germans to America, including more than two hundred thousand German Jews who would pave the way for their eastern coreligionists. From the 1880s to 1920s, millions of Southern and Eastern Europeans migrated overseas. Because the Russian Empire's Jews had "double cause for emigration," though, they emigrated in much larger percentages than other East European Jews or other ethnic groups quitting Russia.[14]

Many factors influenced individual decisions to emigrate. For young men, Jews and non-Jews, the prospect of conscription into the Russian army often provided the immediate stimulus. Meanwhile, the "pull" of America combined with the "push" of local conditions. While rumor may have overstated the opportunities and life-style available to newcomers in America, the Jewish press and earlier migrants provided credible information on the booming U.S. economy, not to mention America's tradition of religious tolerance and freedom. Debates raged among Jews about whether Palestine or America should be their destination, but difficulties in reaching and settling in the Holy Land dictated that only the most ideologically committed would go there. Millions of ordinary people fixed their sights on the *Goldeneh Medinah* (Golden Land), America.[15]

The East European Legacy and Central Appalachian Jews

East European Jews who migrated to the United States emerged from a traditional way of life developed over centuries yet tempered by the modernizing trends of the late nineteenth century. Despite widespread urbanization, a close-knit, communally based culture continued to exert a powerful hold. Most people were not too far removed from their shtetl origins, while many clung tenuously to their rural niche. The tenets of Orthodox Judaism still permeated Jewish life, though the very fact of mass emigration showed the diminishing influence of religion. Rabbis had warned against America, calling it a heathen land where Jews turned away from their heritage; these admonitions gradually lost force as more and more people decided to leave. Although the most pious remained least likely to emigrate, the majority of those who ventured across the ocean, a diverse cross section of Jewish society, considered themselves to be observant Jews, and they brought their traditional practices with them.[16]

Their experiences had accustomed Jewish immigrants to lives of profound instability. Even those who achieved success knew their good fortune could be snatched away at any moment. Author Ewa Morawska cites two typical Yiddishisms that capture the chronic uncertainty of life: "Jewish wealth is like snow in March, here today, gone tomorrow" and "A Jew's joy is not without fright." The sense of unpredictability was paradoxically accompanied by a strong belief in human agency, derived from Judaic teachings on the importance of free will. In other words, though individuals may have no control over fate, they are nevertheless required to act to improve their lives, to strive toward a particular "end-goal," or *takhlis*.[17]

Traits forged within their precarious old-country role as "middlemen" would prove useful to East European Jews in America. They brought to their new homes the experience of being strangers in a strange land, despite their centuries-long presence in Eastern Europe. They were familiar with, and often adept at, cross-cultural communication. Many possessed a knowledge of different languages. Though the original meaning of *takhlis* applied to the religious realm (with Torah mastery as the highest goal), when carried into the outside world, *takhlis* encouraged the pursuit of "individual self-realization," which in turn promoted long-term decision making and striving toward success even under chaotic conditions.[18] Moreover, though most Jews arrived as skilled workers, they came from families and communities rooted in trade and were more prepared than other immigrants to make their way in an environment that rewarded market values and enterprising behavior. The very commercial traits for which they were denounced in Eastern Europe would prove advantageous in their new home.

The Jewish immigrants who arrived in Central Appalachia shared in the East European legacy. They came from Russian Poland, Lithuania, Belarus, Ukraine; from Galicia, Hungary, and Rumania; from the largest cities and the deepest countryside.[19] Their hometowns were buffeted by the social currents sweeping Eastern Europe, as traditionalism and modernity vied for the hearts and minds of ordinary Jews. Like the Weinsteins, the Totz family hailed from Raseiniai, Lithuania, a center of the Haskalah (Jewish Enlightenment), a movement that promoted the modernization of European Jewry. Israel Noah Spector and his brothers came from the Ukrainian city of Nezhin, a center of the ultrareligious Hasidic movement; he was named for Hasidic leader Israel Noah Schneerson. Their differences apparently were not irreconcilable since Totzes and Spectors intermarried in McDowell County, West Virginia.

Budapest sisters Charlotte, Pauline, and Gizella Wilczek married three friends from small Hungarian towns who brought them to Logan, West Virginia. Chaim Brownstein started out in a Jewish agricultural colony in Bessarabia and ended up in an unincorporated section of Logan County. The four Seligman brothers grew up in the Lithuanian hamlet of Ylakiai as sons of a Hebrew *maskil* (adherent of the Haskalah) who raised them to be fine scholars. A rabbi who served briefly in the coalfields remarked of these Northfork, West Virginia, merchants, "It was a revelation to me to find Jewish laymen in an obscure coal town who could read and understand modern Hebrew."[20]

The stories of coalfield Jews reveal the same economic distress, fear of conscription, and oppression that caused millions to emigrate. Mary Schwachter fled an impoverished farm and a "religious fanatic" husband in the mountainous Transylvanian region of Austria-Hungary, depositing two sons in Budapest until she could afford their passage. She moved to Pocahontas, Virginia, and her son Harry later became a prosperous merchant in Williamson, West Virginia. David Skot (later Scott) ran away from home at age fifteen, leaving Kolk, "a town of poverty" in Ukraine, for a land where "the streets were paved with gold"—Welch, West Virginia. When the tsar's troops came to eighteen-year-old Louis Fink's corner of Ukraine in pursuit of fresh recruits, he fled to the nearest port; Bernard Silverman, born in Kishinev in 1902, arrived in the United States with his family in 1904, soon after the infamous Kishinev pogrom. Both ended up in Beckley.[21]

Despite commonalities with the general Jewish immigration stream, Jews who settled in small coalfield towns exhibited distinctive characteristics. They tended to come from more rural backgrounds than most East European Jews, who had become heavily urbanized by 1900. Of coalfield Jews whose hometowns were identified, almost 60 percent came from towns of fewer than five thousand inhabitants and more than 70 percent came from towns of fewer than ten thousand. They fit a pattern identified by historians of American Jewry: those who ended up in small towns were more likely to have a background in rural petty trade than the general East European Jewish migration stream, in which urban skilled workers were overrepresented. They sought U.S. locales similar to the places they left behind so that they could draw on previously acquired skills to earn a livelihood. Thus the act of immigration, seemingly a radical step, had a conservative aspect, as immigrants found environments that would allow them to continue to do what they could no longer do in their homeland.[22]

The origins of coalfield Jews also reveal regional trends. Almost half of those whose origins were identified hailed from two places: Lithuania and Hungary. These immigrants also arrived in the coalfields earliest, accounting for more than half of those who came before 1900. Three factors contribute to their predominance: the overrepresentation of Lithuanians and Hungarians in the early stages of Jewish migration from Eastern Europe, the tendency of early Jewish immigrants to move away from U.S. port cities more readily than later immigrants, and the impact of chain migration.

Differences in migration rates reflected the uneven advance of capitalism through Eastern Europe. Austro-Hungarian Jews contributed about one-quarter of Jewish immigrants to the United States between 1881 and 1902, but only about 15 percent between 1903 and 1914. Lithuanian Jews emigrated in higher proportions than other Russian Empire Jews before 1900 because they suffered the worst poverty, unemployment, and overcrowding at that time. The overrepresentation of these two groups disappeared after savage pogroms struck southwest Russia in the first decade of the new century, sparking "emigration fever" in that region.[23]

By the time of the pogroms of 1903 to 1906, most of the Jewish immigrants who lived (or would eventually live) in the coalfields had already come to the United States. Fully 60 percent of East European–born coalfield Jews with ascertainable immigration dates had arrived in America (though not necessarily the coalfields) by 1903, whereas only one-third of all East European Jewish immigrants had arrived. It therefore makes sense that the coalfield Jewish population was weighted toward those groups that had a large presence early in the migration stream.[24] The relatively early immigration of coalfield Jews supports the theory of some historians that earlier Jewish immigrants moved away from their first homes in U.S. cities in greater proportions than later arrivals. It is unclear why this was so. Possibly earlier migrants came from more rural backgrounds, or perhaps economic opportunities in large U.S. cities increased as time went on.[25]

However, the pervasive phenomenon of chain migration provides the best explanation for the origins of Central Appalachian Jews. All great migrations have been heavily influenced by kin-based networks, and Jewish migrants to the coalfields offer no exception.[26] Most came not as isolated individuals but as parts of families whose members arrived together or, more commonly, in succession, with early settlers encouraging relatives to join them. Some may have had a predilection for small-town life because of their roots in the East European countryside—and the circumstances they encountered in the United States also helped lead them to the coalfields, as will be seen. Yet the concentrations from certain East European locales were largely the result of migration chains. The extended family of Ida Euster serves as a good example: she and her six sons, two daughters, their spouses, cousin, and a boarder all settled in Middlesboro and Pineville, Kentucky, between 1890 and 1920. Their presence accounts for the heavily Rumanian makeup of Jews in the southeastern Kentucky coalfields.

Encountering the American Reality

The journey from Eastern Europe to Appalachia began with a grueling passage out of the old country. Russian Empire Jews faced an especially difficult ordeal, since notoriously arbitrary laws made it "very difficult for a Russian subject to leave his native land in a lawful manner," as the 1911 U.S. Immigration Commission put it. Would-be emigrants often had to procure false passports, bribe officials or border guards, or steal across the border in the dead of night. James Pickus's trip from Minsk to his two brothers in Beckley started auspiciously, as he managed to obtain a passport to leave Russia. But he postponed travel when his mother's home was struck by fire. While he helped her recover, his visa lapsed. Unable to get it renewed, he had to be smuggled across the border.[27]

Pickus's woes continued during the ocean crossing. His son Manuel recalled his father's vivid description: "They were stuffed in like pickles in a jar." Steerage travelers spent the ten- to sixteen-day voyage in varying degrees of misery, plagued by overcrowded and unsanitary conditions, near-inedible food, and seasickness. But the buoyancy of youth helped some survive the trip. While his seasick brother huddled in a bunk, teenaged Harry Schwachter and a "slight, dark Rumanian girl" spent the evenings dancing to music provided by fellow steerage passengers. Onlookers from the upper decks tossed coins down to the entertainers, netting Schwachter $7.30 on the journey.[28]

Harry Schwachter may have demonstrated more entrepreneurial spirit than the average steerage passenger (or at least, superior dancing abilities), but everyone who landed in America during the era needed a certain amount of resourcefulness to find his or her way in the dynamic U.S. economy. Though the nation's industrial cities offered opportunities, rapid mechanization meant that jobs were increasingly unskilled and low paying. Immigrants with skills transferable to their new environment advanced faster than those—the vast majority—forced to seek work in the lower levels of the economy. Most immigrants relied on ethnic-based kin networks to ease their way into the job market and guide them to various parts of the country. These networks became the basis of the ethnic neighborhoods and institutions of urban America, providing invaluable support as immigrants adjusted to American life.[29]

East European Jews did have skills relevant to the U.S. economy. Almost two-thirds of working adults came as skilled workers, most with experience in clothing manufacture. In fact, some 30 percent of Russian Jewish working-age adults who immigrated between 1899 and 1914 were tailors or seamstresses. They found ready opportunity in the garment industry, which was not only expanding but also dominated by German Jews receptive to employing their newly arrived coreligionists.[30]

Like the Eastern Europeans, German Jews had filled a niche as petty traders and artisans in the old country.[31] Their arrival in mid-nineteenth-century America coincided with the birth of the ready-to-wear clothing industry. Lacking financial resources but experienced in trade, they entered all facets of the low-capital, wide-open new industry. Many started as lowly peddlers and became mainstays of downtown business districts in cities and towns across America. Others achieved success as clothing manufacturers in urban centers from New York to San Francisco. By the time the East Europeans arrived, the Germans had emerged as a fairly established and acculturated American Jewish community. Although tensions between Jews of German and East European descent would become legendary, the existence of an American Jewish population of German origin helped East European Jews get started by providing jobs, social services, and other kinds of support.[32]

Nevertheless, factors promoting their successful absorption into the economy did not save East European Jewish immigrants from the cruel and unforgiving nature of American industrial capitalism. Like other U.S. workers, they faced harsh and unhealthy working conditions, meager pay, and brutally long hours. Jews also experienced discrimination in some industries. In Pittsburgh, for example, one study found "rabid anti-Semitism which existed at the mills and the mines, both among the workers imported from Eastern Europe and among the employers." Living conditions offered little respite from economic woes: overcrowding, inferior housing, poor sanitation, and disease plagued immigrant neighborhoods across urban America.[33]

Jewish immigrants responded to the realities of American urban life with strategies to ensure their economic and spiritual survival. They circumvented discrimination by relying on networks in largely Jewish economic arenas such as the garment and cigar-making industries. Dense Jewish neighborhoods enabled many families to earn a living providing goods and services to fellow immigrants. Like other immigrant groups, Jews continued the old-country practice of involving husbands, wives, and children in work toward family subsistence. They also drew on their old-country experience to forge a dynamic labor movement that fought for, and often won, higher pay and better working conditions.[34]

Jews created a vibrant urban culture to sustain them, rooted in the Yiddish language and known as *Yiddishkeit:* a blend of old-country customs, urban American street life, religious observance, and labor solidarity, described by Irving Howe as "a way of life, a shared experience, which goes beyond opinion or ideology." Mutual-aid associations based on hometown origins provided everything from burial services to insurance to small loans to sociability. Some strategies could not be described as entirely positive; a significant number of Jews resorted to vice and crime to earn a livelihood, as an organized Jewish underworld took shape.[35]

As many as 30 percent of East European Jews devised yet another solution to the poverty and excess competition of America's urban centers: they left. Many of these immigrants sought opportunities for self-employment, an elusive goal in cities such as New York. Less populated locales held greater promise: while 60 percent of Jews in the nation's metropolises worked in manufacturing at the turn of the century, in small cities and towns, 70 percent were in trade and service. Like the German Jews before them, Eastern Europeans who journeyed beyond major cities often started as peddlers and then opened retail establishments. Their economic profile more closely resembled their German Jewish predecessors than their big city relatives.[36]

The literature on American Jewry gives little attention to the experience of East European Jews in small-town America. When small-town Jewry is acknowledged, its German roots are usually emphasized. But as a few historians have noted, East European migration chains bolstered German Jewish settlements across America while creating hundreds of new communities, thus becoming the critical demographic element in small-town Jewry and providing a counterpoint to the urban story of the majority of East European Jews in America.[37]

Among those struggling to earn a living in New York City's garment industry were the brothers from Lithuania, Sam and Herman Weinstein. As they later told it, they felt like "strangers in a strange land and suffered many hardships. . . . The men in the sweat-shops said to Herman: 'This is a big country. Get out of here, you can't do much worse.'" Fourteen-year-old Joe Lopinsky landed in New York "without a dollar, without language and without a known friend." He tried to survive on low-paying factory work before striking out for more promising territory. Sam Polon debarked in Baltimore, where "he got such jobs as he could pick up, painted [railroad] cars, and did odd jobs such as loading drays, etc."—none of which satisfied his driving ambition. Annie Wasserkrug, daughter of struggling immigrants in Baltimore, left school in the sixth grade to work in the needle trade. She later married Louis Fink, and they opened a small grocery near the Baltimore and Ohio Railroad terminus, where they scraped together enough money to seek out a better opportunity. In Cincinnati, Russian immigrants Isadore and Lizzie Weiner clung to cigar-factory jobs in order to support their young family and yearned for something better.[38]

These stories typify the experience of Jewish immigrants who settled in the coalfields. Most landed in New York, though a large minority arrived at the port of Baltimore. Unless they already had connections in the coalfields, they generally lived and worked for awhile in the immigrant enclaves of those two cities before deciding to venture out. Some came to the United States as children and migrated to the coalfields as young adults. Interviews with descendants reveal that the desire for self-employment drove many to leave their first American homes. As more than one interviewee put it, their parents' "dream" was to own a store. Dissatisfied with their chances in the big city, they kept moving.[39]

Paradoxically, the southern coalfields attracted them because the region was undergoing a process similar to that which had prompted their departure from Europe: transition from a rural, locally based economy to an industrial capitalist economy fully linked with national and international markets. The "town of poverty" in Ukraine that David Scott fled had more in common with the American "streets paved with gold" than he ever would have suspected. But whereas the socioeconomic changes occurring in Eastern Europe boded ill for most Jews, the changes taking place in the Central Appalachian mountains would provide some with the opportunity they sought.

A Matter of Timing

Two overriding characteristics have shaped the history of the Central Appalachian plateau: its succession of steep, rugged mountains and its vast reserves of coal and timber. The mountainous terrain, by impeding the advance of transportation networks, ensured that full-fledged capitalist development would come relatively late. Coal and timber, abundant and lucrative commodities in great demand by a booming national economy, ensured that once railroads finally penetrated the region in the 1870s, development would occur fast and furiously. With coal as the driving force, the mountains of southwestern Virginia, southern West Virginia, and eastern Kentucky experienced rapid industrialization and precipitous growth from the 1880s through the 1910s.

This time period, of course, coincided exactly with the arrival of East European Jews to the United States. Thus it happened that some Jewish immigrants, having run up against the limitations of America's urban environment, found their way to the mountains to explore the opportunities that the coal and timber booms afforded. Their journey to the coalfields and the niche they developed once they got there resulted from a convergence of their own background with conditions in Central Appalachia at the time they appeared on the scene.

Those conditions emerged from the region's past. Preindustrial Appalachian society was dynamic and complex, neither the bucolic utopia nor the primitive wasteland of popular (if contrasting) myths. Not unlike later migrants to the region, the earliest European settlers, Scots-Irish and German farm families, arrived in the eighteenth century seeking opportunity after experiencing economic upheaval in the old country and restricted prospects on America's eastern seaboard. They were joined by prosperous Anglo-American landowners eager to expand their holdings. A diversified farm economy developed, with the rivers and turnpikes that traversed the mountains serving as trade routes that enabled farmers large and small to sell their surplus to outside markets.[40]

As in Eastern Europe, development did not occur evenly. Geography and topography led to the evolution of three distinct Appalachian subregions. The Blue Ridge and valley section, to the east and south, became connected to southern markets through settlement patterns and transportation routes. On the western and northern side of the mountains, the Ohio River and its tributaries linked the population to northern markets, enabled the early growth of industry, and gave rise to town life in places such as Charleston and Wheeling. Between these two sections lay the Central Appalachian plateau, "a wildly beautiful interior" of "peaks and ridges . . . rugged uplands . . . coves, hollows, and tablelands." In this most remote subregion, travel was difficult, settlements appeared later, and the population remained small and scattered. Without adequate means of importing goods or exporting agricultural surpluses, the economy revolved around self-sufficient farming, "domestic production for domestic use."[41]

While railroad lines spurred development in other parts of Appalachia before the Civil War, the lack of infrastructure stalled development of the plateau. Some mountain residents, those who valued a traditional agrarian way of life, were not bothered by this. Others yearned for economic growth but lacked the resources to transform the area by themselves. The subsistence-oriented economy stunted the accumulation of capital, leaving the region's leading families land rich but cash poor. The costly financing of railroad construction and industrial development would have to come from beyond the mountains.[42]

The plateau's family farming system inhibited the growth of another building block in the evolution of a more complex economic structure: towns. With the prevalence of home manufacturing and only a modest amount of staple crop production, there was little need for processing centers or specialization in trade—two key reasons for people and services to congregate in commercial hubs. A handful of general merchants spread throughout the region could easily market the surpluses produced by this system while also importing the small amount of goods that farming communities could not produce for themselves. What town life did exist grew up around the county seats, centers of local government dominated by the wealthiest and oldest-established families whose roots were in the surrounding countryside.[43]

The *West Virginia State Gazetteer* for 1882 reflected the self-sufficiency of the plateau's residents and their lack of need for towns or services unrelated to farming. The directory listed virtually no specialized stores in the six counties that would soon make up the southern West Virginia coalfields.[44] The sole exceptions were two purveyors of liquor in the newly developed coal shipping center of Quinnimont, in Fayette County, where the Chesapeake and Ohio Railroad (C&O) had recently made inroads. While Quinnimont and its liquor establishments would prove a harbinger of things to come, most commercial activity centered around county seats or small settlements clustered near grist mills. More people made a living as artisans or professionals than as traders: wagon-makers, blacksmiths, carpenters, lawyers, and physicians far outnumbered shopkeepers.[45]

Mercer County, where the regional hub of the coalfields would arise, boasted the single bank in the entire six-county area in the county seat of Princeton, population 150. Logan County had only thirteen general stores in 1882, with three of those stores and both of the county's hotels based in Logan Court House, the county's sole town, population 200. In a later time, a prominent Logan Jewish merchant would marvel that as late as 1896, before the railroad came, "Thomas Buchanan . . . of Logan County operated a mercantile establishment which sold everything from one-hundred-pound barrels of flour to axes." The least-developed county of all was McDowell, with the state's smallest population in 1880: a mere 3,000 residents. The 1882 directory listed only ten general stores and three hotels in the county. Four of the stores and two of the hotels were located in the county seat of Peerysville, population 60.[46]

Given Peerysville's tiny population, it is more than likely that its ability to sustain two hotels in 1882 was due to the increasing appearance of outsiders looking to use the courthouse to research land titles and record new transactions. In fact, interests representing the newly incorporated Norfolk and Western (N&W) Railroad, along with land speculators with advance knowledge of company's plans for the area, spent 1881 to 1882 frantically buying up land in what would shortly become the heart of the Pocahontas coalfield. By March 1883, the railroad would ship its first load of coal east from Pocahontas, Virginia, and after construction of the Elkhorn Tunnel in 1888 allowed the company to push across the state line and into McDowell County, southern West Virginia would be forever transformed.[47]

By the 1880s, the time had arrived when the urgent need for coal to fuel the nation's rampant industrialization finally made profitable the expensive and arduous construction of railroads through the mountains. Geologists had long been aware of the high-quality bituminous coal contained within the Central Appalachian plateau, and local elites had worked tirelessly to attract outside capital since the end of the Civil War. The C&O Railroad opened the New River coalfield when it built its main line through Fayette County in 1873, but development had slowed with the onset of a national economic depression. The recovery of the 1880s enabled the coal industry to take off. Coal surpassed wood as the nation's chief source of fuel by 1885 and filled 75 percent of America's energy needs by 1910—and a large portion of it came from Central Appalachia.[48]

Railroad building and coal land development took place interdependently, transforming local conditions as they advanced deeper into the mountains. Rail companies planned their lines along the most promising coal seams, while promoters and speculators from within and outside the region acquired huge tracts along proposed routes. These acquisitions often involved deceiving local farmers unaware of the coming railroad or the value to industrializing America of the minerals that lay beneath their property. Speculators engaged in legal manipulation—laying claim to obscure, long-forgotten land titles or using the infamous "broad form deed"—to wrest control away from owners. To ensure profitable coal traffic, railroad officials promoted the formation of large land corporations to purchase property from speculators and lease it to coal-mining operations. Thus land passed quickly from local families to enormous concerns based in Philadelphia, New York, and London.[49]

The particular form that coalfield development took would create lasting problems for Central Appalachia and its people. The "near-monopolistic pattern of land ownership," historian Jerry Bruce Thomas explains, meant that "the region's future was mortgaged to absentee owners whose sole interest was in seeing the timber and mineral wealth of the land removed." Their control over land and resources would stunt the diversification needed for a healthy economic system. Meanwhile, to succeed in a notoriously volatile national coal market, coal companies would fix on controlling labor costs as the key to underselling competitors. This strategy prompted a rabidly anti-union stance and determination to gain complete political domination of the region. Although they would largely achieve the hegemony they sought, their methods resulted in the violent labor conflicts that periodically wracked the coalfields. With a dearth of other industries and a low-wage workforce suppressing local economic growth, the region's fortunes would remain tied to the vagaries of the national coal market. During boom times, the coalfields bustled with activity; the busts had dire consequences. In either case, most of the profits would flow out of the region, as Ron Eller puts it, "into the pockets of outland capitalists and into the expansion of the larger industrial order itself."[50]

The region's first coal companies were operated by entrepreneurs, typically immigrants or sons of immigrants from Britain who had practical mining experience, drive and determination, but little capital. They arrived from overseas or from the Pennsylvania coalfields and began their companies on a limited budget, enlisting outside capital to bankroll start up and expansion. Eventually the coal industry, too, became dominated by large, non-locally-owned companies. Until then, the early coal operators were the "visible masters" of the region, given leave by the "real masters"—the holding companies whose property they leased—to develop the land as they saw fit. They promptly began to hire workers and build the mining infrastructure.[51]

The tiny preindustrial population and weak links to outside markets meant that coal companies would have to recruit much of their labor from outside the region, transport workers to the area, and provide them with houses, stores, and other necessities of life. Their efforts set off a population explosion and caused an entirely new civilization to spring up in Central Appalachia's coves and hollows, one of startling multicultural diversity. African Americans from the South and recently arrived immigrants from Southern and Eastern Europe joined the virtually all-white mountain population, and by 1908 the mining workforce was 41 percent native white, 31 percent black, and 28 percent foreign born. Hungarians made up the largest foreign group in the Pocahontas coalfield; Italians predominated in the New River area. Other immigrants included Poles, Slovaks, Germans, Austrians, "Bohemians," Lithuanians, Russians, "Slovenians," Croatians, Rumanians, Bulgarians, Greeks, Syrians, Lebanese, English, Welsh, Irish, and Scots. Between 1880 and 1920, southern West Virginia's coal counties grew from forty thousand to more than three hundred thousand inhabitants.[52]

Miners and their families moved into hastily constructed coal company towns and camps. In the early 1920s, three-quarters of mining households lived in company-owned towns, which remained a dominant feature of the landscape for decades. The quality of life they offered varied considerably. At the upper end, a few "model towns" provided decent homes, modern schools, and other amenities. At the lower end were numerous barely habitable camps with flimsy structures and unsanitary conditions. Most company towns had conditions somewhere in between; however, all company towns shared at least two basic features. First, they quickly formed into stratified societies. Class distinctions became evident in the layout of the towns: company officials lived along "Silk Stocking Rows," and miners, usually segregated by race and often by ethnicity, were relegated to less desirable locations. Second, and above all, the company towns existed for the sole purpose of extracting coal.[53]

The company-owned town has received much attention in literature on the coalfields, but it was not the only urban form to arise with industrialization. The

change from an agricultural economy to an economy based on extractive industry generated demand for "new kinds of centralized, specialized economic activities" that could be met neither by the single-minded company towns nor by
the few preexisting villages.[54] Though not as ubiquitous as company towns, the
independent towns that emerged during the coal boom played an important and
multifaceted role as centers of shipping and distribution, commerce, and social
life. Some grew out of once-sleepy county seats, others out of the tiny rural settlements that dotted the landscape. Still others sprang up around newly built rail
depots where no settlement had existed before. While some independent towns
rose and fell as raw boomtowns, others, particularly those that started out as (or
soon became) county seats, developed into small yet bustling commercial hubs.

Joining the local merchants, service providers, and workers who gathered in
the burgeoning independent towns were enterprising newcomers drawn by the
region's growing consumer market. As agriculture gave way to industry, the local
population became less self-sufficient, requiring outside imports to furnish the
necessities as well as the comforts of life. Certainly not all, or even most, of the
entrepreneurs who responded to this opportunity were Jewish immigrants. But
Jews emerged as a significant segment of the merchant class in many coalfield
towns. How did they find their way to the region, and what impact did their presence have? Answers to these questions illuminate an important aspect of the region's industrial transformation: the commercialization of the countryside.

The Role of Jewish Networks

Jacob Epstein probably never set foot in the southern coalfields, yet he was the
individual most responsible for the creation of Jewish communities there. A Lithuanian Jew who came to America in 1879 at age fifteen, Epstein started out peddling in Pennsylvania, northern West Virginia, and western Maryland. In 1881, he
settled in Baltimore where he proceeded to build a veritable wholesale empire, the
Baltimore Bargain House. "From the outset Jacob Epstein set out to do a jobbing
business with the peddlers who played such an important part in those days in
bringing needed wares, and entertaining stories, to rural housewives," states his
biographer. "Trusting the peddlers, he was willing to sell to a number of them on
credit, which was unobtainable from most of the larger wholesale houses. As a
result, his business prospered from the very beginning."[55]

But Epstein did not rely solely on farm women for his customer base. He apparently kept abreast of regional developments, because he steered more than a
few peddlers onto the newly built rail lines that reached into the lumber and coal
settlements sprouting up in Central Appalachia—the very same rail lines that
were just beginning to haul the treasures of the mountains off to distant markets.
This two-way traffic has not received much attention in historical accounts of
Appalachia, which focus on the removal of resources *from* the region but rarely

on the transporting of goods *into* it. Though the exporting was carried out by the coal industry, the importing, with the noteworthy exception of company stores, was carried out by an entirely different set of people: people who had their own commercial networks and were linked to different kinds of markets.

The crowds of young, penniless Jewish men arriving from Eastern Europe provided Jacob Epstein with a ready pool of would-be itinerants. Not content to wait for budding entrepreneurs to show up at his doorstep (though many did), he sent Yiddish-speaking agents to meet immigrants as they disembarked from ships at Baltimore's Locust Point. His offer of credit enticed many to pick up a knapsack and head into the nation's interior. Epstein took somewhat of a paternal interest in his peddlers, handing out advice on all manner of topics (to maintain health on the road, he urged, "eat prunes"). The solid relationship that developed between the Baltimore Bargain House and its retailer clients lasted for decades, as peddlers became small shopkeepers and successful merchants in small towns in Appalachia and throughout the South. Their business helped the Baltimore Bargain House become one of the largest wholesalers in the United States and enabled Epstein to become one of Baltimore's most prominent philanthropists, a major supporter of such institutions as Johns Hopkins University and the Baltimore Museum of Art.[56]

Some descendants recalled that the wholesaler directed their fathers and grandfathers to the coalfields even as the railroads were under construction. Peddlers would disembark "where the railroad ended" and immediately begin to trudge up the hillsides with their packs. Wolf Bank "chose to pick up some things from the Baltimore Bargain House and start peddling" a few years after coming to the United States from Lithuania, his son related. Wolf's brother Harry joined him, and the pair arrived in McDowell County in the mid-1890s. Fellow Lithuanian Jewish peddler Jacob Shore entered McDowell County around the same time. He apparently roamed through a broad swath of the coalfields, since according to family legend he developed a friendship with a celebrated customer in neighboring Logan County: "Devil Anse" Hatfield. Shore occasionally stayed at the home of the Hatfield patriarch, who warned his neighbors, "Don't bother Uncle Jake, he's all right."[57]

This stamp of approval from the famed feudist probably allowed Shore to feel more secure than most peddlers. The job involved considerable risk, as they traveled alone and were known to carry cash. Stories of the robbery and/or murder of foreign peddlers abound in American literature, and peddlers in the rough-and-tumble coalfields faced more danger than elsewhere. Saul Bernstein, who later became a respected Baltimore artist, peddled in various parts of Maryland and West Virginia in the 1890s, but felt most unsafe in the "bullet raining atmosphere" of the Pocahontas coalfield. "Many pistols I had in my face . . . but Jehovah stood by me all the time," he later wrote. Bernstein also pointed out a more prosaic occupational hazard: falling over when a pack became unbalanced, especially when descending steep hillsides. His semicomical account describes the tendency "to roll ahead helplessly, on account of the slippery fall leaves or grass. . . . My pack was always, when filled, heavier than myself, so I discovered myself contemplating the sky with closed eyes." Fortunately, "the head-over-heels seldom harmed me much. There was only once I had my left arm in a sling for a few days."[58]

It is often hard to tell fact from fiction concerning the oft-romanticized life of the peddler, especially in the oft-romanticized world of the coalfields. In the Shore family legend, for example, Hatfield's use of the term "uncle" raises some doubt, since it conforms more to stereotypes of peddlers—as stooped, frail old men— than to reality. Stooped the coalfield peddlers may well have been, carrying their heavy loads up steep mountains, but most were quite youthful. They saw peddling as a starting point, a necessary step on the way to their goal of operating their own store. Jake Shore's peddling days occurred in his twenties; Devil Anse was some thirty years older than he.

On the other hand, Anse Hatfield's penchant for consumer goods, documented by historian Altina Waller, suggests he was open to patronizing peddlers and lends credence to the tale. In fact, perhaps the story's real significance lies in Hatfield's positive response to the outsider, which contradicts the stereotype of mountain people as suspicious and hostile to strangers. Rural Americans welcomed these purveyors of products from far-off markets, and Appalachians were no exception. A woman from Greenbrier County, West Virginia (just outside the coalfields), vividly described the peddlers of her youth in the 1880s: "We . . . had Jewish peddlers that came occasionally and gave us something to look forward to. It was almost like having Santa Claus come, even if Mother couldn't afford to buy much. We loved to see the big bundle opened up, for we seldom saw new things."[59]

This warm reception occurred despite the peddlers' obvious foreignness. Most had lived in America only a short time and could barely speak the language. Herman Weinstein once admitted that he "scarcely knew the value of the goods" he had peddled through eastern Kentucky before becoming a leading Middlesboro merchant. Jake Shore, all his life, was more comfortable speaking Yiddish than English. (His dog responded only to Yiddish commands, his grandson recalled.) But to the peddlers' customers, the contents of their packs and the tales they told made up for their strange accents and broken phrases.[60]

While many Jews arrived in the coalfields directly from the Baltimore Bargain House, others took a more complex route. Some learned about the region while peddling Jacob Epstein's goods in other places. Jacob Berman peddled in Maryland about 1900. "When he had a little capital ahead," his son recounted, "then he went to Keystone and opened up his little clothing store." Not all peddlers got their start through Epstein; other wholesalers too realized the region offered a potentially lucrative new market. Peddlers in West Virginia's Williamson and Logan coalfields were outfitted by suppliers in Cincinnati, the western terminus of the N&W and a "center of German-Jewish clothing enterprise." Those in south eastern Kentucky had ties to Knoxville. The Weinstein brothers, after quitting New York on the advice of their fellow sweatshop workers, joined a friend in Tennessee. Herman went to Knoxville, whose German Jewish retailers had begun to send peddlers into the nearby coalfields. He "got hold of a pack of trinkets and goods" and headed for the mountains, which were "then being opened to the world." After peddling for awhile, he settled in Middlesboro with his brother Sam within a year of the town's founding in 1889.[61]

Communal and economic factors intertwined to bring Jews to the coalfields. Certainly the primary incentive of businessmen such as Jacob Epstein and the Knoxville retailers was a desire to benefit their businesses. Yet another motivation also pertained, rooted in the Judaic concept of *tzedekah*, the communal obligation to help others. By enabling a young man to get a start in life, they were performing a *mitzvah* (often loosely translated as "good deed," the term literally means "commandment," an act of righteousness commanded by God). That their good deed advanced their own business goals and strengthened the economic condition of the Jewish community as a whole simply confirmed the relationship between communal and individual good.[62]

As peddlers settled down and opened stores in the region, they became critical links in an ever-expanding network. By laying the foundation for small Jewish communities in the coalfields and across the nation, the peddlers, in effect, established "colonial outposts" of urban Jewish centers, in author Leonard Rogoff's words. The economic activities carried out by these outposts would continue to extend the ties between city and countryside. Meanwhile, small-town Jews would draw on the cultural resources available from big-city bases to sustain their communities.[63]

But peddling was only one way that Jewish networks drew people to the coalfields. Within predominantly Jewish industries in Baltimore and Cincinnati, rumors of the economic potential of the coalfields were evidently rampant. Ike Levinson, who toiled in Baltimore's garment industry, heard "in the trade, through rumors," that "there was a good opportunity for small merchants." He arrived in Welch about 1906 and opened a small clothing store, later sending for his sister and brother-in-law. Manufacturers and wholesalers employed drummers—traveling salesmen—who crisscrossed the land, selling their wares to small-town shopkeepers. "Those drummers were regular grapevines," asserted one former coalfield resident. Everywhere they went, they spread information about places they had visited: not only the climate for small business but also job openings. David Scott came to southern West Virginia after a drummer told him that a "horse trader" in Wilcoe needed help. The trader was Jake Shore, who by then owned more than one coalfield enterprise. Salesmen who called on Louis and Annie Fink at their Baltimore grocery store told Louis about "West Virginia and the black diamonds," his son recalled. "He became fascinated with that." So much so that he closed up shop to move to Beckley and start a clothing store.[64]

The first settlers to arrive through these networks encouraged many more to follow them, from immediate family members to distant relations. For several decades this chain migration brought a steady infusion of "fresh blood" that allowed Jewish coalfield communities to grow. Married men sent for wives and children once they became established. Joseph Cohen came to the United States at age thirty-four in 1898 and by 1900 owned a store in Norton, Virginia, where he boarded at a hotel. By 1902, he had brought his wife Anna and four children over from Russia, and by 1910, the couple and their six children resided in their own home in Norton. Single men went to Baltimore or New York to find a Jewish woman to marry. (As a Keystone native whose father did just that put it, "If you wanted to marry another Jew, New York was full of them.") Often they returned with their new spouse relatively quickly, suggesting they had recourse to the Jewish custom of arranged marriage.[65]

Some men went all the way back to Europe to find a bride. I. L. Shor, soon to become Keystone's most prominent businessman, returned to Lithuania in 1901 to wed a woman his parents had picked out for him. Sarah Benjamin was not thrilled with the match: since her family had a wooden floor in their house and Shor's parents did not, she thought she would be "marrying down." But she ultimately agreed, and after a hasty wedding, the couple came home to Keystone.[66]

Although Sarah Shor may have been mollified to find that "a six room house, fitted out previously," awaited her arrival, women whose marriages brought them to the region often had a difficult time adapting to an environment not entirely of their own choosing. Those from big cities had to get used to small-town life; those from Europe felt isolated in a foreign land far from family and friends, where they could not speak the language. (Fortunately for Sarah, I. L.'s sister came with her from Europe.) Men, too, who arrived straight from the old country to work for coalfield relatives faced a difficult adjustment. Just making their way to the region could be a challenge. James Pickus, who had had a hard enough time getting out of Russia, continued his misadventures in America as he traveled to his brothers in Beckley. An official at Ellis Island pinned a tag on him indicating his final destination, but he missed his train connection in Washington, D.C. Undaunted yet hungry, he ducked into the train station restaurant, where he "saw his first fried eggs, his first white bread, and his first black man"—the waiter. To his astonishment, the waiter directed the obviously confused foreigner to the Travelers Aid office in Yiddish. Pickus eventually made it to Beckley unscathed.[67]

Most members of coalfield migration chains, though, came from large American cities. In desperate need of a job, Louis Koslow journeyed from New York City to Kimball, West Virginia, about 1915 to work in a tailoring business owned by his brothers-in-law. His wife and baby daughter joined him a year later after an infantile paralysis epidemic struck New York. Teenager Harry Abel came from Baltimore about 1900 to work for his uncle Ben Hurvitz in Fayette County. He eventually opened his own store in Mount Hope, and in the early 1920s he sent for his brother-in-law Thomas Sopher, a Baltimore cigar shop clerk. Sopher, too, stayed on to open a store of his own. Isadore Gorsetman arrived during the Depression from Cleveland, where the steel companies "wouldn't hire Jews." He joined his brother-in-law in Charleston in 1935 and immediately headed into the coalfields, where he peddled household goods from his car.[68]

Clearly, the push of adverse conditions in the big cities combined with the pull of coalfield opportunities to stimulate Jewish migration to the region. Push factors were primarily job-related, though living conditions also played a role. Like the Koslows, Louis Sturm's parents fled New York because of an epidemic (in this case, typhoid) when he was a baby. They landed in Pineville, Kentucky, in the 1890s just as the railroad was being built, and the elder Sturm opened a restaurant for railroad workers.[69] Pull factors often included an already-established relative but in all cases revolved around a developing industrial economy that offered an opportunity for Jews to fill a niche providing retail services to a growing population.

There were some exceptions to the pattern of Jewish networks stimulating migration to the coalfields. Hungarian-speaking Mary Schwachter was recruited at Ellis Island to become a boardinghouse keeper for Hungarian coal miners in Pocahontas. Baltimore laborer Sam Polon responded to a coal company advertisement promising free transportation to the Pocahontas coalfield to work in the mines. Louis Schuchat first worked as a coal company bookkeeper in Northfork, West Virginia. Yet all three immigrants soon gravitated to traditionally Jewish occupations to advance up the economic ladder. Schuchat became a bookkeeper in a local saloon before starting his own saloon. Schwachter moved to Ohio, where she too opened a saloon. Polon ended up in the real estate business in McDowell County.[70]

The factors that drew Jewish entrepreneurs into the consumer goods sector, rather than the region's dominant industry, caused them to bear more than a passing resemblance to the hard-bitten early coal operators chronicled by coalfield historians. In both cases, immigrants with little capital but great determination drew on previously acquired skills, family backgrounds, and cultural resources to build businesses in the region.[71] Admittedly, the dramatically different nature of the two types of businesses makes it difficult to carry the comparison very far. The characteristically Jewish interpretation of the American Dream revolved not around standard formulations such as owning property or even gaining economic success but around achieving self-employment, and more specifically, owning a store. This somewhat modest goal would sometimes lead to considerable wealth, often to long hours of work and ongoing struggle.

Ironically, a Judaic concept, *takhlis,* motivated coalfield Jewish pioneers to venture far from the centers of Jewish life. One interviewee repeatedly offered a single phrase to explain why her father quit a job as a clerk to take up the much more difficult life of a peddler: "He couldn't see any future" working in someone else's store. Even artist Saul Bernstein chose slogging through the coalfields over slaving at a sewing machine in Baltimore: "I knew there was no future for art in tailoring while peddling seemed more like a business to me."[72]

In pursuit of the perfect chance, many followed a circuitous route, leaving numerous jobs and locales in their wake. Harry Schwachter wins the prize for most jobs before finding his coalfield niche. After landing in Baltimore, he joined his mother Mary in Newark, Ohio, where he worked in a glassworks, as a grocery store clerk, a clothing store clerk, and a court interpreter. He then clerked in stores in Cincinnati and Hamilton, Ohio. Finally he saved enough money to open his own store in Coke-Otto, Ohio, which promptly failed, at which point he signed on as a laborer in a Hamilton paper mill. After again saving money, he bought a dilapidated theater in New Richmond, Ohio, but could not make a go of it. This led him to work in his mother's saloon and then briefly as a furniture maker before he saw a want ad in a Cincinnati Jewish newspaper: a merchant in Williamson, West Virginia, needed a clerk. When he arrived there in 1909, he was all of twenty years old and had lived in America less than four years.[73]

The wholesalers, rumors, and migration chains that caused Jews to gather in various parts of the coalfields demonstrate that the process was far from random. The mythic story of the peddler-turned-shopkeeper, that he decided to settle in a certain town because "that's where the horse died," has little basis in fact, at least in this particular region. Not only did Jews enter into the broad territory of the southern coalfields for concrete reasons, but their settlement patterns within the region also followed a distinct logic. Two factors in particular determined where Jewish communities would arise: the timing of migration in relation to local developments and the railroad connections that led from U.S. cities to specific places within the coalfields.

The Geography of Jewish Coalfield Settlement

Just southeast of Charleston, West Virginia, the mountains make a sudden ascent into the rugged back country surrounding the New River Gorge. Before the industrial era, these mountains presented a formidable barrier to travelers and settlers. This began to change in 1873 when the Chesapeake and Ohio Railroad completed its main line between Richmond and the newly created Ohio River town of Huntington, West Virginia (named for C&O magnate Collis P. Huntington). As the railway snaked through the gorge, it opened the rich coal lands in Fayette County. Small coal mining settlements began to appear along the line, and in 1874 the C&O shipped more than 158,000 tons of coal. The New River coalfield thus became the first of the southern coalfields to develop.[74]

The New River Gorge had not been completely inaccessible before the railroad arrived. The "Old State Road" had traversed the mountains between Lewisburg and Charleston since 1790. Where the road met the New River deep in the gorge, a man named Peter Bowyer had established a ferry service and a tiny settlement known as Bowyers Ferry. In 1873, the C&O built a depot there and renamed the site Sewell Station, later shortened to Sewell. It became the first commercial center for the gorge's small mining communities, with a population of more than three hundred by 1880.[75]

According to local historians, "Entrepreneurs sensed business opportunities and migrated to Sewell as the C&O Railway was being completed. One of the first was Arnold Midleburg, who opened the first store at Sewell in 1871 after he had secured the ferry rights of the pioneer Peter Bowyer." Midleburg operated a water-powered sawmill and was "the first to ship lumber from the New River Gorge." He also built a row of twelve homes between the tracks and the river, known as "Red Row" because all the homes were painted red.[76]

Arnold Midleburg was, in all likelihood, the first Jew to settle in the southern coalfields. He came to the United States from Germany in 1866, offering an exception to the overwhelmingly East European background of the region's Jewish population. He lived in Charleston before relocating to Sewell, where, by 1880, he resided with his German-born wife Berta, three children, two servants, and two boarders (laborer Leopold Goldberg and clerk Frederick Schodel, German immigrants, both probably Jewish). Midleburg returned to Charleston by 1900, but his sons Ferd and Charles remained in Sewell to run the family businesses, which included dry goods, groceries, a saloon, and a bottling company that sold carbonated beverages. Ferd later became a prominent Logan theater owner and real estate developer. Charles followed the pattern of many rural merchants and became the Sewell postmaster and justice of the peace, as well as a member of the state legislature. By 1920, he had moved to Charleston, where he operated a coal mining supply business and remained active in local politics.[77]

The Midleburg story is one of "firsts": Arnold Midleburg built the first store in the first local hub of the first coalfield in the entire region, two years before completion of the first railroad. The pioneering Midleburg family would both reflect and depart from patterns exhibited by the Jews who followed them. German Jews would be a rarity in the region, and the family's connection to Charleston also was unusual, since most Jews arrived through networks emanating from well beyond the region. It is doubtful that any other coalfield Jew served as justice of the peace, since that role usually was filled by members of the region's small, long-established landowning class. Charles Midleburg's connection to the coal industry (and his father's lumber interests) would also deviate from the norm. Yet Jewish involvement in local politics would become, if not widespread, certainly not uncommon. And most of the family's commercial endeavors, from saloons to dry goods to theaters to residential real estate, were highly typical of the kinds of businesses coalfield Jews would establish.

Arnold Midleburg's arrival in Sewell even before the C&O finished constructing its railroad highlights another common phenomenon: in many coalfield towns, Jewish entrepreneurs were present from the very beginning as peddlers, small shopkeepers and clerks, or saloon owners. From their "ports of entry" within the coalfields, the immigrants or their grown children moved to other parts of the region as it developed, just as Ferd Midleburg did. Sewell attracted other Jews who operated stores there in the 1880s and 1890s before fanning out to nearby towns. Brothers-in-law Joe Lopinsky and Ben Hurvitz established the Great Eastern Bargain House in Sewell by 1900 and soon opened branches in several other Fayette County towns. William Schaffer and son Leo came from Austria in the mid-1880s. They conducted a store in Sewell and Leo went on to become one of the more colorful characters in the fabled New River railroad town of Thurmond. Other Jews who settled in the New River area before 1920 also had ties to the original Jewish families of Sewell, but they bypassed the region's first coalfield center, settling instead in small towns such as Mount Hope, Scarbro, and Oak Hill.[78]

These newcomers avoided Sewell because the town did not develop beyond its initial boom. In 1910, it contained 356 people, only a couple dozen more than it had in 1880. The topography and rail system of the New River area promoted the growth of several small mining centers rather than one regional center, until development shifted to the south bank of the river and the Raleigh County seat, Beckley, emerged as the area's major hub. Moreover, coal exploitation around New River stalled shortly after the C&O completed its rail line. The depression of the 1870s and the C&O's halfhearted promotion of coal development retarded industrial progress for at least a decade. By that time, another railroad company had entered the coalfields, and its owners' determination to base their profits on coal traffic greatly accelerated the transformation of the region. While Jews in the New River area remained scattered in small towns until coalescing in Beckley after 1910, the first actual Jewish community formed in the Pocahontas coalfield by the mid-1880s, in the same town from which the Norfolk and Western Railroad shipped its first load of coal in 1883: the boomtown of Pocahontas, Virginia.[79]

When people think of boomtowns in American history, the West comes immediately to mind. Yet boomtowns typically arise in frontier places undergoing incorporation into the capitalist system, and despite its location in the eastern United States, the Central Appalachian plateau at the turn of the twentieth century fit the definition of a "frontier."[80] Bypassed by the railroads until the late 1800s and then plunged into industrialization, the region offered perfect conditions for the rise of instant towns where newcomers and opportunity seekers of all sorts gathered, drawn from the local countryside as well as far-off lands—entrepreneurs large and small and, especially, multitudes of young, single male workers who lent a raucous character to the proceedings.

Not all the newly emerging coalfield towns took on the wide-open traits of a classic boomtown. County seats, as centers of local government, tended to undergo a somewhat less boisterous transformation even as they experienced precipitous growth. But the towns offering the earliest opportunities and the fastest early growth were not county seats. Rather, they were new towns that sprang up at strategic rail locations: places such as Sewell and Thurmond, Pocahontas, Middlesboro, and Keystone. All these towns gained reputations for hosting various types of disorderly behavior while also providing goods and services to surrounding populations. The latter three would become home to the region's first Jewish communities before the turn of the century.

The early coalfield boomtowns have taken on a legendary status happily promoted by local historians. The title of one recent book, *Thurmond, Dodge City of the East,* seems an apt description of the riverside rail town known for its saloons and brothels, killings that "were almost an everyday occurrence" (a major exaggeration), and the continuously running poker game at the splendiferous Dunglen Hotel. Thurmond's two most notable personalities were the fierce, gigantic police chief Harrison Ash, "a lawman of easy conscience," and "mayor" Leo Schaffer, an Austrian Jew described in one account as "one of the memorable and lovable characters of all Thurmond's romantic history" and in another as "not above interpreting the law in whatever manner was the most profitable." The most famous Schaffer story has the mayor fining a dead man "the contents of his pocketbook—eighty-one dollars and one gold watch" for, depending on the version, carrying a gun without a permit or committing suicide within the town limits (the man, apparently in a drunken stupor, had jumped into the river and drowned).[81]

However appealing (or appalling, depending on your point of view), Schaffer was one of only a handful of Jews to ever live in Thurmond. The real beginning of Jewish communal history in the coalfields occurred in southwest Virginia, where, states historian Jerry Bruce Thomas, "with the opening of the Pocahontas coal field, the Industrial Revolution . . . arrived in Central Appalachia." As the nation emerged from the depression of the 1870s, the time had come for the region's coal to establish a presence in eastern markets. In 1881, a group of Philadelphia investors incorporated the Norfolk and Western Railroad and laid out a route through prime coal territory. To maximize rail traffic along the route, N&W officials promoted massive coal development, supervised land acquisition throughout the area, and oversaw the creation of the Southwest Virginia Improvement Company, the region's first major land and coal development corporation. This company immediately commenced to build a town and mining operation at the mouth of a creek beside a promising outcropping of coal.[82]

Town building and coal mining took place concurrently at the newly named Pocahontas, Virginia, as the N&W constructed its railway into the region. Newcomers flooded into town, with African Americans and Hungarian immigrants arriving to make up much of the mining work force. In early 1883, coalfield promoter Jed Hotchkiss reported on the town's progress in his Staunton-based journal, the *Virginias:* "Last February its location was a tangled forest . . . now it contains nearly one thousand people, has seven mercantile establishments, a hotel, etc." With the arrival of the railway in March 1883, thousands of tons of coal waiting at the depot headed east.[83]

Just as at Sewell, the activities generated by the N&W attracted entrepreneurs before completion of the railroad. The Southwest Virginia Improvement Company owned half the land in the town of Pocahontas, upon which it constructed mine buildings, houses for workers and their families, and a company store. It allowed the other half to be developed by individuals such as Alexander St. Clair, who had been eagerly buying up property in the area since 1877. St. Clair sold parcels to newly arrived entrepreneurs, including one Michael Bloch, who in December 1882 purchased a town lot on St. Clair Street "under condition that no intoxicating liquors be sold." Bloch opened a general store that would evolve into the Bloch and Company department store, a fixture in Pocahontas for the next forty years or more.[84]

Like Arnold Midleburg, Bloch was a German Jew who had immigrated to the United States in the 1860s. By April 1883, he and his Pennsylvania-born wife were joined by fellow Germans Jacob and Lena Baach, who had resided in Virginia for some years. By 1887, a Baach daughter and son-in-law accounted for the third German Jewish family in town—and any future German Jews would be descended from the two families. In fact, almost no Jews of German descent entered the entire southern coalfield region after these early Pocahontas and New River pioneers until the 1930s, when some refugees from Nazi Germany settled in a few towns.[85]

The Jewish community of Pocahontas gained its members from the first wave of immigrants who arrived from Eastern Europe in the 1880s. The historical record reveals five Jews of East European descent living in town by the end of the decade. The actual number was no doubt a good deal higher, since by 1892 enough people had gathered to form the first Jewish religious association in the coalfields, an Orthodox congregation that reflected the traditional upbringing of its East European members. In 1900, at least 95 Jews lived in Pocahontas, and in 1910, the Jewish population reached a recorded peak of 149 people in twenty-nine households. Because Jewish households tended to be large (with many children and, often, elderly grandparents), whereas most other groups consisted of single coal miners, Jews constituted a healthy 6 percent of the town's 2,452 residents.[86]

The area's growing industrial activity enabled the Jewish community to thrive. Pocahontas coped with two early catastrophes: a massive mine disaster in 1884 that killed almost two hundred miners and the depression of the mid-1890s. But as a Tazewell County historian wrote in 1920, "In 1897 the rainbow of prosperity once again hovered . . . and its gracious influence has remained here until the present time." The business climate in Pocahontas was enlivened by the coalfield's expansion into neighboring West Virginia, as the town was situated practically on the state border. The town's Jews offered a variety of retail services to a burgeoning population, though in the first few decades, three types of enterprises predominated: dry goods, saloons, and liquor stores. Businesses respond to consumer demand, and in an area overflowing with single workingmen, the demand for liquor was sky high.[87]

The town began to lose its economic élan after prohibition came to Virginia in 1916. By then, Pocahontas was no longer—actually had not been for some time—the only commercial center of the coalfield that bore its name. It competed with newer coal towns in southern West Virginia, and with Bluefield, the region's rail hub, located on a grassy summit some ten miles beyond the coalfield in Mercer County, West Virginia. Founded when the N&W built its roundhouse and regional facilities there in the 1880s, Bluefield by 1900 was one of West Virginia's largest municipalities, a shipping and distribution center with a population of 4,600. Pocahontas Jews eventually gravitated to Bluefield, which by 1920 had the region's largest Jewish community, around 150 people. The Pocahontas Jewish population had shrunk to 71 by that time, less than half its 1910 count.[88]

But for some reason Jews were slow to make Bluefield their home. Most new arrivals from Baltimore passed through the new city on their way to smaller towns where the chief occupation was coal mining. In 1900, only forty-five Jews lived in Bluefield, while almost three times as many lived in McDowell County. The vast majority of the county's Jews resided in the most notorious boomtown in the southern coalfields: Keystone.[89]

The construction of the Elkhorn Tunnel in 1888 enabled the N&W to enter the mountainous terrain of McDowell County and spelled the end of an agrarian way of life for its residents. Within a few short years after the railroad's arrival, McDowell no longer had West Virginia's smallest population and no real towns. Now, having experienced the region's most rapid growth, it boasted several towns. Its 1900 population of eighteen thousand represented a 610 percent increase over twenty years. Formerly the most homogeneous county—no blacks at all appeared in the 1870 census—it became the most diverse county: its 1910 population was 31 percent black, 17 percent immigrant (or children of immigrants), and only 52 percent native white. A 1915 state handbook attested to a complete turnaround in the county's demographic profile when it proclaimed that "McDowell is one of the most densely populated of the West Virginia counties. From one end to the other one are prosperous towns and coal mining camps."[90]

The brothers Wolf and Harry Bank entered at an early stage of this transformation. Their own trip through the Elkhorn Tunnel around 1893 constituted the final leg of a journey made relatively easy by the rail system that now connected McDowell County to Baltimore. The pair probably started by picking up their packs at the Baltimore Bargain House and trudging the short distance to the B&O rail terminal. If they hopped on an 11:10 P.M. westbound train, they would have reached Shenandoah Junction in West Virginia's eastern panhandle within two hours. There they would have boarded a 1:15 A.M. N&W train. Traveling south on the Shenandoah Valley line, they would have reached Roanoke at 7:45 A.M., in time for their 8:00 A.M. transfer to the N&W main line. By noon they would have reached Bluefield, where the train might have paused before passing through the tunnel into McDowell County. The train would have traveled along Elkhorn

Creek until it met up with the Tug Fork and then followed the Tug into the next county, but the brothers would have disembarked by then, somewhere along Elkhorn Creek, where coal camps were starting to spring up. They each peddled for a while before settling down around 1894.[91]

Chain migration works only if the opportunity is there. In rural towns across the South, one or two "Jew stores" were sufficient; the local economy could not support any others.[92] The same cannot be said for McDowell County, which would, at its peak, boast three Jewish congregations, in Keystone, Kimball, and Welch. The Bank brothers would prove critically important to the growth of these communities. In a noteworthy example of chain migration, they were joined by a sister, two brothers-in-law, a friend, and two first cousins; one of those was joined by three more brothers-in-law—not to mention the spouses and children of all these people.

While Harry chose to locate at a sparsely inhabited spot along the railway called Norwood (soon to be renamed Kimball after the president of the N&W), Wolf selected a more immediately promising locale further east along Elkhorn Creek. Keystone, one of the first independent towns in the county, was the likeliest spot to offer a livelihood for small retailers. The town did not exist in 1890; the hamlet of Cassville occupied its site. In 1892, the N&W opened a depot there, and the Keystone Coal and Coke Company began operations, giving the town a name (derived from the Pennsylvania origins of the company's founders) and an impetus to grow. Within eight years, the town had a population of just over one thousand, the largest in the county. Remarkably, fully 10 percent of Keystone's residents in 1900 were Jews, giving Keystone a larger percentage of Jews than any major U.S. city outside of New York.[93]

Wolf Bank was not the first Jewish resident of Keystone. The year the town was founded, Kopel and Goldie Hyman and their grown sons arrived from Baltimore and Louis Morse came from parts unknown. Max Hermanson relocated from nearby Pocahontas. Former peddler Jake Shore and his cousin I. L. Shor (who dropped the "e" from his last name) also found their way to Keystone during the 1890s. Like the Banks, these early settlers encouraged relatives to join them, and by 1900 Keystone had 110 Jews: 54 adults and 56 children in twenty-five households. All but five of the adults were immigrants, 43 from Russia, 4 from Austria-Hungary, and only 2 from Germany. Sixteen Jews resided in other McDowell County towns in 1900, most of them related in some way to Keystone Jews.[94]

As a boomtown, Keystone's reputation soon rivaled, actually surpassed, that of all other towns in the region. While Thurmond may have been the "Dodge City of the East," Keystone became known as the "Sodom and Gomorrah" of the coalfields, its famous red-light district, Cinder Bottom, condemned as a "revelation of human depravity" in a well-circulated tract written by an anonymous "Virginia lad." Decent people lived in Keystone, the "lad" conceded, but "the percent of good ones is mighty low." A staunch white supremacist, he no doubt ruled out half the residents by virtue of their skin color. McDowell County received the largest influx of African Americans in the coalfields, and more blacks lived in Keystone than any other town, a fact that added to its dubious reputation among the region's whites.[95]

But economic potential is in the eye of the beholder, and to hard-scrabble Jewish immigrants looking for a start, the tough little town appeared to be a beautiful sight. They quickly made a commitment to Keystone, organizing a congregation before the turn of the century. In 1904, they built an Orthodox synagogue that would remain in use for the next half century.[96]

Like their neighbors in Pocahontas, Keystone Jews engaged in a wide range of retail activities, with the liquor trade as a key component. Liquor was the cornerstone of the town's commercial vitality, the staple that allowed it to stand out among the growing towns around it. And like Pocahontas, the town was damaged by prohibition, enacted in West Virginia in 1914. The end of legal liquor sales had a ripple effect on commerce: by 1915, real estate values had declined by half. Keystone's Jewish population underwent a shift that exactly mirrored the Pocahontas Jewish decline. In 1910, it reached a recorded peak of 147; by 1920 it was halved to 72, while the town's overall population dropped from 2,000 to 1,800. The Great Depression of the 1930s struck the coalfields hard, and Keystone did not rebound as well as other towns. The generation of Jews who grew up in the boomtown had to find economic opportunity elsewhere once they came of age.[97]

Most of them did so without having to leave the coalfields. The advance of the railroad deeper into the mountains opened up new areas of growth and new potential for small business. Young Jewish entrepreneurs did as their parents had done: they followed the course of coal and rail activity. More than seventy Keystone Jews relocated to newly developing coalfield towns during the 1910s and 1920s and started their own families. Several people simply moved to the adjoining town of Northfork, while others found opportunity in places a little more distant. Hungarian immigrant Rudolph Eiland, working as a Northfork clerk in the mid-1910s, heard about a promising locale one county away. According to his son, "They were just opening up the coal mines. Everyone said Logan was the place to go."[98]

Some pioneer Keystone merchants relocated with their families. Jake Shore moved to the McDowell County town of War just as coal mining took off there around World War I; he and his sons became the town's leading merchants. More commonly, the immigrant generation remained in Keystone while their sons and daughters dispersed throughout the region. Many Keystone Jewish children grew up to become the founders and mainstays of Jewish communities in the county-seat towns, which took over as leading coalfield centers during the 1910s.

The movement of Jews to county seats can be seen as the second phase in the development of Jewish coalfield communities, and not coincidentally, a second phase in the development of the coalfields themselves. But before turning to the county seats, it is necessary to consider the third major coalfield boomtown, a town whose almost mythical founding and dramatic history of booms and busts made it an extreme example of trends that occurred throughout the region. Middlesboro, Kentucky, was the brainchild of Scottish speculator and promoter Alexander Arthur, who toured the Cumberland Gap in 1886 and designed a grand plan to develop the coal-rich territory. With the backing of British capitalists, his company secured eighty thousand acres in the Yellow Creek Valley using highly dubious maneuverings to acquire the property from local mountaineers. At a site in Bell County, the company created a town to serve as a commercial hub for the anticipated coal boom. Town building was well underway before the railroad arrived in 1889. By 1890, Middlesboro had more than three thousand inhabitants, making it by far the largest town in the southern coalfields at the time. It had a link to Louisville and nearby Knoxville via the Louisville and Nashville (L&N) Railroad, a streetcar system, numerous businesses, six banks, seven churches, a library, and an opera house, and it would soon boast a lavish resort and one of the nation's first golf courses, built by displaced Englishmen.[99]

Middlesboro's bust followed almost immediately and proved as spectacular as its rise. Its hasty development caused immediate problems. During the first scheduled train ride in 1889, which departed Knoxville with much fanfare, the train wrecked in the mountains, causing the death of Knoxville's mayor and seriously injuring Alexander Arthur. A fire wiped out Middlesboro's business district in May 1890, the very month the town incorporated. That same year, the collapse of a British investment bank with financial interests in the region caused the speculative bubble to burst. As overseas bondholders demanded repayment, the town sank into default, and the financial panic of 1893 supplied the finishing touch. All the banks closed, businesses shut down, and "the citizenry left in droves," according to one account. Meanwhile, Middlesboro's creditors secured passage of a state law requiring that the town pay off its debts before paying for its municipal needs. This law, until its repeal in 1906, hobbled the town's ability to provide essential services and added to the raw boomtown atmosphere, especially in the "dark ages" before recovery began around 1897. A paucity of law enforcement officers enabled "vice" to flourish virtually unchecked; like other boomtowns, Middlesboro developed a reputation for less-than-respectable activities, violence, and general mayhem.[100]

Jewish merchants joined in the heady days of Middlesboro's founding, with some fifteen families reportedly living in town in 1891. Several remained after the crash, and perhaps their loyalty to their new home accounts for the effusive praise heaped upon Jewish merchants—especially Sam and Herman Weinstein—by the local press. One May 1900 article in the *Middlesborough News* recalled the Weinsteins' business activities "during the hardest times" and noted, "With the business and enterprise that has characterized the Jew merchants here their business grew rapidly." A local historian later asserted that the Jewish community had been "one of the main forces holding the town together during the 'bust' days of the '90s."[101]

It is unclear why Jewish merchants might have been more willing to gamble on the town's recovery than others who came to enjoy the boom. Perhaps these immigrants had less to lose than other entrepreneurs. They may have been able to tolerate a higher degree of financial uncertainty, since Jewish businesses in Europe and America had traditionally existed under conditions of instability and marginality. Merchants who hung on through the grim years aided the town's recovery as the nation rallied from depression in the late 1890s. Increased coal mining activity in the surrounding countryside stimulated a rebound and Middlesboro reemerged as the leading town of southeastern Kentucky, with a population of more than seven thousand by 1910. In that year, Middlesboro had eighteen Jewish households with around eighty people, most related to families who had arrived in the 1890s. Like the other boomtowns, however, this number fell by 1920, to around sixty.[102]

Despite Middlesboro's growth, the Jewish population of southeastern Kentucky never approached the numbers who settled in southern West Virginia. The reason was more geographic than economic: with the L&N as the rail route into the Cumberland Mountains, the area did not have a direct link to large Jewish populations on the East Coast. Middlesboro's proximity to Knoxville, only seventy miles away, also may have helped limit its Jewish population. While some early residents arrived from that city, in later years they were likely to move back so they could partake in a much larger Jewish community. Several Knoxville Jewish merchants operated businesses in the southeastern Kentucky coalfields without ever moving into the mountains.[103]

Nevertheless, Middlesboro and its environs managed to attract enough Jews to form an active congregation, which never built a synagogue but rented space in the local Masonic hall. Its far-flung membership came from coal towns within a fifty-mile radius on both sides of the Cumberland Gap. The Bell County seat, Pineville, contributed many members, mostly related to the Euster family. Like other coalfield county-seat towns, the number of Jews in Pineville jumped between 1910 and 1920, doubling from twenty to forty as the Middlesboro Jewish population declined. Eusters eventually spread to another Kentucky coalfield county seat, Harlan—and that town would later challenge Middlesboro as the center of Jewish life in southeastern Kentucky.[104]

As a web of rail lines spread through the coalfields and the mining industry placed its mark on the land, the human geography of the region began to take shape. Of the boomtowns described above, only Middlesboro advanced much beyond its raw beginnings. Its geographic position, rail connections, and extensive infrastructure enabled it to become a regional service center for the coal economy in the Cumberland region of Kentucky, Tennessee, and Virginia. Bluefield served the same role in southern West Virginia, and the two small cities became the gateways to the southern coalfields.[105]

By the mid-1910s, each coalfield had its own network of mining settlements,

Table 1. Total Population of Coalfield Towns with Jewish Congregations, 1900–1960

Town/County/Coalfield	1900	1910	1920	1930	1940	1950	1960
County Seat Towns							
Beckley, W.Va./Raleigh/New River	342	2,161	4,149	9,357	12,852	19,397	18,642
Logan, W.Va./Logan/Logan	444	1,640	2,998	4,396	5,166	5,079	4,158
Welch, W.Va./McDowell/Pocahontas	442	1,526	3,232	5,376	6,264	6,603	5,313
Williamson, W.Va./Mingo/Williamson	600*	3,561	6,819	9,410	8,366	8,624	6,746
Harlan, Ky./Harlan/Harlan	557	657	2,647	4,327	5,122	4,786	4,177
Regional Service Centers							
Bluefield, W.Va.**	4,644	11,188	15,282	19,339	20,641	21,506	19,256
Middlesboro, Ky.	4,162	7,305	8,041	10,350	11,777	14,482	12,607
Other Towns							
Keystone, W.Va./McDowell/Pocahontas	1,088	2,047	1,839	1,897	2,942	2,594	1,457
Kimball, W.Va./McDowell/Pocahontas	—*	1,630	1,428	1,467	1,580	1,359	1,175
Pocahontas, Va./Tazewell/Pocahontas	2,789	2,452	2,591	2,293	2,263	2,410	1,313

Source: U.S. Census Bureau.
* Unincorporated in 1900. Population figure is from *West Virginia Gazetteer*, 1900.
** Bluefield is not, strictly speaking, a coalfield town. Numbers are included for comparative purposes.

connected by rail to each other and to a local commercial hub. County seats had a built-in advantage in seizing this coveted position, as their governmental functions drew county residents into town for various purposes and required a permanent cohort of professionals, white-collar workers, and ancillary services. Some county seats were brand-new towns whose coal industry–based leaders had wrested control of local government away from older, agricultural-based county seats. In 1892, for example, the recently created town of Welch replaced Peerysville as the McDowell County seat "after a bitter election followed by court proceedings." Peerysville sank into obscurity; eventually coal mines opened in its vicinity and it took on a new name, English. Other county seats, such as Logan and Beckley, had been long established, and their embrace of the coal economy enabled them to continue as the focal point of their county, in new and greatly expanded form.[106]

Like the boomtowns, the county seats experienced rapid growth, though slightly later and under more controlled conditions (see table 1). County seats that would emerge to service the four southern West Virginia coalfields—Welch, Williamson, Logan, and Beckley—each had from 300 to 600 residents in 1900, while Keystone and Pocahontas had 1,088 and 2,789, respectively. With the first decade of the new century, the county seats took off: the total population of the four towns quadrupled between 1900 and 1910, then doubled the following decade. By 1920, each town had far surpassed Keystone and Pocahontas in population and, in fact, housed many former residents of the declining boomtowns. County seats in the eastern Kentucky coalfields also underwent rapid growth, although the

Table 2. Jewish Population of Coalfield Towns, 1900–1920

Town/County/Coalfield	1900	1910	1920
Pocahontas, Va./Tazewell/Pocahontas	95	149	71
Davy, W.Va./McDowell/Pocahontas	0	14	20
Keystone, W.Va./McDowell/Pocahontas	110	147	72
Kimball, W.Va./McDowell/Pocahontas	7	45	44
Northfork, W.Va./McDowell/Pocahontas	0	33	70
Welch, W.Va./McDowell/Pocahontas	9	31	98
Wilcoe, W.Va./McDowell/Pocahontas	0	23	8
Beckley, W.Va./Raleigh/New River	0	6	22
Mount Hope, W.Va./Fayette/New River	2	0	19
Scarbro, W.Va./Fayette/New River	0	13	16
Sewell, W.Va./Fayette/New River	13	8	0
Matewan, W.Va./Mingo/Williamson-Thacker	0	10	19
Thacker, W.Va./Mingo/Williamson-Thacker	4	11	0
Williamson, W.Va./Mingo/Williamson-Thacker	4	28	69
Logan, W.Va./Logan/Logan	0	7	40
Pineville, Ky./Bell/Cumberland	10	20	39
Middlesboro, Ky./Bell/Cumberland	18	79	62

Sources: U.S. Manuscript Census, Fayette, Logan, McDowell, Mingo, Raleigh, Bell, Harlan, and Tazewell Counties, 1900–1920 (birthplace, parents' birthplace, native language); Shinedling, *West Virginia Jewry*; Marino, *Welch and Its People*; Shinedling and Pickus, *History of the Beckley Jewish Community;* interviews; Harlan, Logan, Welch, Williamson congregation records.

Note: Includes towns that had a Jewish population of 10 or more.

process occurred later than in southern West Virginia because the L&N did not make significant inroads until the 1910s.[107]

Jewish families gravitated to the county seats, but not in a direct fashion (see table 2). After first concentrating in the boomtowns, they followed the rail lines to areas of new growth, often settling in small, newly created mining towns. By 1920, they had begun to reconcentrate, this time in the county seats.

The new county seats along the N&W main line developed earliest, as did their Jewish populations. Coal surveyor Isaiah Welch purchased land at the junction of Tug Fork and Elkhorn Creek fifteen miles west of Keystone in 1888. When the railroad arrived in 1891, his settlement had only ten houses. The following year, the town of Welch captured the McDowell County seat, its court convening in a former saloon building. Some sixty miles farther west along Tug Fork, local farmer and entrepreneur Wallace Williamson developed his town on land he acquired from relatives. A corn field in 1891, Williamson's site was reached by the N&W in 1892, and in 1895 the town of Williamson became the seat of newly created Mingo County, carved from western Logan County. As a divisional rail headquarters, Williamson became the most prominent town in the southern West Virginia coalfields until superseded by Beckley in the 1930s.[108]

Three Jewish families, all from Austria-Hungary, lived in Welch by 1900: merchant William Sameth and wife Lena, tailor Josef Herzbrun and wife Leina, and Leina Herzbrun's sister and brother-in-law Pauline and Herman Josephy, also a tailor. By 1910, Welch had thirty-one Jews in seven households, a pittance compared to nearby Keystone. But the number of Jews tripled to almost one hundred in the next decade as Welch passed Keystone as the Jewish center of McDowell County. Meanwhile, the county prevailed as the major Jewish population center in the coalfields into the 1920s, when it gave way to other areas. McDowell's Jewish population shrank from more than three hundred in 1920 to around one hundred in 1955, including seventy Jews in Welch.[109]

A handful of Jews resided in Williamson before 1900. Lithuanian-born peddler Jacob Levine settled in town in 1896 and opened a dry-goods store. In 1900, he and his wife Gertrude, their clerk-boarder Reuben Nathan, and ginseng dealer H. B. Green were the only Jews in town. But they were not the first to arrive in Mingo County. As early as 1895, produce seller Louis Shein, butcher Louis Crigger, and dry-goods merchant Isaac Weinstein lived in Thacker, an early mining settlement. By 1910, Mingo County had more than 50 Jews, some 30 in Williamson and almost all the rest in Thacker and Matewan. By 1920, most of the outlying Jews had moved to the county seat, along with many former Keystoners, increasing Williamson's Jewish population to 70. This number almost doubled by 1927 to around 130 and peaked in the 1950s at an estimated 180 people.[110]

The Logan, Beckley, and Harlan Jewish communities formed after those in Williamson and Welch, reflecting the later development of those towns. The C&O and N&W main lines had bypassed Logan and Beckley. In 1904, a C&O branch line reached Logan, causing the population to jump from four hundred in 1900 to sixteen hundred in 1910. When the C&O finally reached the Raleigh County seat of Beckley in 1906, its population explosion was even greater. The smallest of southern West Virginia's four future coalfield centers in 1900, Beckley was second in size only to Williamson by 1910, and in the 1930s it became one of the state's largest cities. Rail progress through southeastern Kentucky came later still. The L&N did not reach the Harlan County seat, Mount Pleasant, until 1911. Within a year the town had a new name, Harlan, and within a decade its population had quadrupled.[111]

The seeds of Logan's Jewish community were planted by 1910, when two Jewish families lived in town: tailor Jake and Anna Wells, their children, and Jake's brother Harry, also a tailor, and dry-goods merchant Morris Max and his wife Olive. By 1920, Logan had some 40 Jews in fifteen households, and by 1927 that number had tripled to around 120 Jews in forty households. Many came from Keystone and Northfork; others came from Cincinnati, New York, and Baltimore. Logan's Jewish community peaked in the late 1920s. In the 1930s and 1940s, some families relocated to Beckley, and others left the region. By the mid-1950s, only around twenty-five Jewish families lived in Logan.[112]

The first recorded Jewish family in Beckley consisted of hotel proprietor Samuel Fisher, his wife Agnes, and their three children, the only Jews in the 1910 census. The Fishers had come from nearby Fayette County where Sam had lived since 1901, clerking for merchant Ben Hurvitz. Beckley's Jewish population grew much more slowly than Logan's, reaching 50 by 1927, with most coming from Fayette County or Baltimore. It took off in the 1930s, increasing to around 140 by 1940. By then, Beckley had become a major population center in the state, and it soon had the largest Jewish contingent in the coalfields, estimated at 228 in the early 1950s. Many arrived from Logan and Welch, both towns, by that time, much smaller than Beckley.[113]

Because of the relative inaccessibility of southeastern Kentucky to Jewish population centers, only one eastern Kentucky coalfield county seat developed a significant Jewish population. By 1920, the town of Harlan had three Jewish households, all headed by Russian immigrants: dry-goods merchant Philip Sachs, his wife Rebecca, and their children, and merchants Samuel Michaelson and Ellis Wender. The Harlan County villages of Poor Fork (soon to be renamed Cumberland) and Evarts each had one Jewish merchant that year. By the 1930s, around sixty Jews lived in the county, with more than half in Harlan town and the remainder mostly in Evarts and Cumberland. Despite the county's notorious labor troubles, Harlan managed to support a small business district that included Jewish-owned clothing and department stores. Their owners formed the basis of a Jewish community that lasted into the 1970s.[114]

Communal activity began in each county seat once the Jewish population grew large enough to support it. All four West Virginia county-seat congregations built synagogues. The Harlan congregation never acquired its own synagogue but, like its Middlesboro counterpart, rented space in the Masonic hall. As in Middlesboro, the congregation included Jews from a broad area, including Cumberland, Evarts, Pineville, Hazard, Jenkins, Corbin, Neon, and Barbourville, Kentucky; Appalachia, Norton, Coeburn, and Pennington Gap, Virginia; and LaFollette, Tennessee.

Jewish county-seat communities were sustained by the economic prosperity their towns generally enjoyed in the first half of the twentieth century. "Bust" periods caused hardship and a temporary drop in the population, but lean times were much worse in the surrounding countryside. Although dependent on the coal economy, the county seats were shielded from its worst effects by their relative diversification compared to company-owned towns, their importance as regional centers, and the existence of a core of middle- and upper-middle-class merchants and professionals.

Notably active business districts reinforced the commitment of Jewish merchants to the county seats. On Saturdays, shoppers flocked in from the countryside and downtowns were packed with people. One Jewish merchant recalled that "the streets of Beckley were impossible to maneuver through" from the late 1930s into the 1950s. In his memoir *October Sky,* Homer Hickam relates the excitement of his family's weekly trips from tiny Coalwood to the nearest metropolis, seven miles away: "Welch was a bustling little commercial town set down by the Tug Fork River, its tilted streets filled with throngs of miners and their families come to shop. Women went from store to store with children in their arms or hanging from their hands, while their men, often still in mine coveralls and helmets, lagged behind to talk about mining and high school football with their fellows." The hustle and bustle was enhanced by constant railroad activity (Williamson, for example, hosted eighteen passenger trains a day in the 1920s) and, above all, the topography of the towns. Hemmed in by looming mountains, virtually all available space became built up, with solid brick edifices constructed along narrow downtown streets and residential districts rising in layers on the hills above.[115]

Unlike the boomtowns, the Jewish population never exceeded 3 percent of the total in any county seat (and more likely hovered around 1 or 2 percent). Nevertheless, Jews played an important role in commercial life, establishing a significant presence in downtown business districts. They owned more than half the clothing and department stores in Logan in 1927, at least half the clothing stores in Beckley in 1940, and 60 percent of the clothing, furniture, jewelry, and department stores in Williamson in 1952. On the Jewish high holidays, recalled one Logan merchant, "a good bit of the town was closed up."[116]

Coming, Going, Staying—and Forging a Familiar Niche

In her study of the Jews of Johnstown, Pennsylvania, Ewa Morawska found that her subjects had two major goals: to ensure the economic well-being of their families and to foster "a good Jewish environment to live in and raise children." The Jews of the southern coalfields shared these priorities. The two goals were not necessarily compatible, however. Financial success often depended on geographic mobility, and uprooting the family often meant leaving a Jewish community behind. But as one coalfield descendant succinctly put it, "You go where you can make a living."[117]

For people who had already traveled great distances in search of opportunity—first across the Atlantic and then from U.S. cities to the mountains—migrating within the coalfields must have seemed natural. A constant coming and going characterized Jewish communities. Sam Abrams came from New York to Scarbro to work for his Lopinsky cousins, then moved his family to nearby Oak Hill to start his own business. Later the family relocated to Beckley, where they remained thanks to the success of Abrams's department store.[118] Such stories are common throughout the coalfields, with three, four, even five or six moves within a short period not unusual. For many families, all this moving finally ended in a county-seat town, where they could participate in Jewish communal life. But some did not stop there. Dozens of people moved from a county seat to a different coalfield town (often another county seat), and others left the coalfields altogether.

Like the internal migrations of the region's coal miners, who shifted from coal camp to coal camp also searching for the right situation, the movements of Jewish merchants were not random but reflected ongoing regional development. Yet even as the relocation of Jews from boomtowns to county seats reveals the trajectories of these towns, patterns of persistence may be discerned, with certain families remaining in the same place for twenty years or more. Typically, the original founders of Jewish communities remained, with one or two members of the second generation staying on to take over the family business. Such patterns of transience and persistence are reflected in the larger American Jewish experience. As historian William Toll notes, Jewish peddlers "were accustomed to continual migration.... Nevertheless, their persistence rates in specific towns were high compared with gentiles.... Their propensity to remain in town rose dramatically with advancing age, which produced marriage and family, property holdings and accumulated wealth."[119]

Persistence in the face of strong migratory tendencies, coupled with the creation of communal institutions, provided the cement that held Jewish coalfield communities together. Geographic mobility complicated but did not preclude community. This was not unusual among immigrants; Caroline Golab, for example, refers to "community creation in the midst of hypermobility" in describing (non-Jewish) Polish neighborhoods in Philadelphia. Apparently, people who managed to make it across the ocean with group associations intact were not going to easily lose them during their wanderings around America.[120]

The impulse toward continuity amid rapid change not only had implications for Jewish communities but also guided the economic life of coalfield Jews. With networks and occupational patterns that extended back to the old country shaping their choices about what type of work to pursue and where to pursue it, they ended up filling the same kind of niche Jews had occupied in Eastern Europe: as commercial "middlemen" in a rural setting. All immigrant groups rely on premigration resources and networks in their new environment, and coalfield Jews were certainly not the only Jewish immigrants in the United States to forge a special niche in the local economy. Members of small American Jewish communities from the industrial North to the rural South and the frontier West did the same. While Jews in New York and other metropolitan areas drew on their previous experience as skilled workers to join the ranks of the garment industry proletariat, those who journeyed to smaller cities and towns found conditions that enabled them to draw instead on their commercial background.[121]

That the Jewish economic role in the coalfields conformed to a national small-town pattern runs counter to the theory of Appalachian exceptionalism—the premise that Appalachia developed in an anomalous fashion to the rest of the nation, with the anomaly often attributed to the cultural peculiarities of its people.[122] On the contrary, for Jewish immigrants whose ancestors had served as middlemen in European economies, the Central Appalachian coalfields provided one of many regions in the United States where they could attempt to duplicate that role. In a broader context, coalfield Jewish communities could be said to have filled a niche within a niche: their networks supplied consumer goods and services to the region, which was busy playing out its role supplying coal and timber to the nation.

Both Central Appalachia and Eastern Europe were introduced to the industrial era at roughly the same time. In both regions, the transition occurred unevenly but generally gathered force in the late nineteenth century, as shown by the movement of people, consolidation of land and enterprise, urbanization, and industrialization that each experienced then. As John Bodnar points out, immigrants to America during the era came from many backgrounds and responded to their surroundings in many ways. What they shared was the need to devise strategies to provide for their families when faced with "the common experience of confronting capitalism" on both sides of the Atlantic.[123] The migration of Eastern Europeans, both Jews and non-Jews, to Central Appalachia was one manifestation of the process. Future coalfield immigrant miners and shopkeepers had much in common: both left an industrializing Europe only to find their place in an industrializing Appalachia.

Ironically, occupying their traditional old-country position as traders enable coalfield Jews to Americanize quickly, as they became absorbed into the local socioeconomic structure and emerged as middle-class boosters with an intense if ambivalent relationship to the area's dominant economic power. The following chapters will explore the Jewish economic niche in the coalfields as well as the social and communal ramifications of that role.

BALTIMORE BARGAIN HOUSE

ONE OF THE
FOUR LARGEST
WHOLESALE
HOUSES IN
THE U.S

JACOB EPSTEIN
Proprietor Baltimore Bargain House

Jacob Epstein. From *Club Men of Maryland*, 1915, published by Roycroft Press. (Courtesy of the Jewish Museum of Maryland, JMM 1999.14.1)

Baltimore Bargain House catalogue, 1906. (Courtesy of the Jewish Museum of Maryland, JMM 1987.127.1)

The wedding of I. L. and Sarah Benjamin Shor, near Yelok, Lithuania, 1901. Shor traveled from West Virginia to Lithuania for an arranged marriage. He and his new wife are at rear, his parents are seated, and others pictured are his siblings. (Courtesy of Cynthia Burgin)

I. L. Shor dressed to return to Europe for his wedding, 1901. (Courtesy of Cynthia Burgin)

Sarah Shor and her children (*left to right*) Rosa, S. David, and Reuben, c. 1910.
(Courtesy of Cynthia Burgin)

Etta and Shirley Michaelson with an unidentified relative, Logan, West Virginia, c. 1920s. The extended Michaelson family made up a significant portion of Logan's Jewish community. (Courtesy of Randy Wasserstrom)

A coal-dust enshrouded view of Keystone, West Virginia, from *Sodom and Gomorrah of Today,* c. 1912. In the center is the Reynolds-Shor Company, owned by I. L. Shor. (Courtesy of West Virginia and Regional History Collection, West Virginia University Libraries)

Keystone, West Virginia, street scene, from *Sodom and Gomorrah of Today,* c. 1912. Katzen's Restaurant is just visible in the background. (Courtesy of West Virginia and Regional History Collection, West Virginia University Libraries)

CHAPTER 2

Middlemen of the Coalfields:
Jewish Economic Life

Esther Sherman Scott arrived in Poor Fork, Kentucky, with her two-year-old son about 1911, straight from her small Ukrainian hometown. Her first reaction was, to put it mildly, disappointment. After journeying across land and sea she had landed in a place that seemed even less refined than a shtetl. Upon seeing her husband's store, she commented, "In Europe, they keep their cows in a better place."[1]

Her brother Mike, a Baltimore businessman with wholesale connections, had sent his greenhorn brother-in-law David Scott (not to be confused with the West Virginia Jewish merchant with the same name) to the region and financed the store. Mike Sherman was no Jacob Epstein, but he did his part: blessed with five sisters, as each one married, he dispatched the newlywed couple to a different town in the southeastern Kentucky coalfields. For decades, the Middlesboro and Harlan congregations would be full of Sherman family members who came in from the surrounding area for the Jewish holidays. Sherman's inadvertent success as a community builder was not matched by his business prowess, however. Though many of his relatives stayed in the region, according to Esther Scott's daughter, "everything they did with my uncle flopped." The Scotts eventually prospered after acquiring their own store in the Bell County seat of Pineville. David Scott brought members of his own extended family from Europe, and they too found a place as merchants in the southeastern Kentucky coalfields.[2]

The Scott family's story—of family networks that undergird economic and communal life, of business failure as well as success—exemplifies the Jewish coalfield experience. It also points to continuities with the past: by comparing Poor Fork to a Ukrainian shtetl, Esther Scott was not so far off the mark. As in the Eastern European countryside, coalfield Jewish communities owed their existence to their ability to maintain an economic niche providing goods and services to a rural population. And, as in the old country, Jewish commercial activities had an impact on the surrounding society.

Many factors merged to encourage coalfield Jewish immigrants to enter into trade. Above all, fellow Jews provided jobs, credit, and guidance, while the coalfields provided opportunity in the form of a commercial gap that needed to be filled. Beyond this, young immigrants who lacked capital or even actual experience could draw on family resources that were cultural if not financial. European Jews came to the United States embedded in a culture molded by generations of commercial life, what historian Walter Zenner calls a "heritage of small business."[3] This legacy nurtured traits that included not only a desire for self-employment—the impetus that brought many Jews to the region—but also such intangible characteristics as economic adaptability, a high tolerance for financial risk taking, and ability to start a business on a shoestring. Such qualities would prove invaluable under the volatile conditions of the coal economy.

Profile of an Ethnic Economic Niche

Unlike most other newcomers to the region, Jews arrived via their own networks, not through recruitment by coal companies, and their initial independence from the industry would continue to set them apart. A survey of Jews who worked in the coalfields from the 1870s to the 1950s found less than 4 percent who had a direct connection to the coal industry at some point in their lives—a remarkable statistic, considering how coal so completely dominated the region's economy.[4] However, this does not mean they were the only ethnic group to occupy a particular economic niche. The varying skills and experiences that people brought to the region, along with the discriminatory practices of coal operators, promoted an ethnic division of labor within the coal economy. A non-Jewish woman from Pocahontas recalled that in her town, the Welsh were the mine bosses and engineers, blacks worked in the coke ovens, Hungarians and other Eastern Europeans mined the coal, Italians built the buildings, and the Jews were "purely business people."[5] Nor were Jews the only group to play a predominantly mercantile role. Middle Eastern immigrants (especially Lebanese and Assyrians) carved out a retail niche using the same kind of ethnic networks that Jews maintained. They too got their start as peddlers before opening stores in towns such as Beckley, Williamson, and Logan.[6]

The peddler-to-merchant paradigm occupies a central place in studies of small-town American Jewry. Indeed, the progression from lowly itinerant to respected store owner, civic leader, and Jewish community progenitor was replicated throughout the nation. But the paradigm tells only part of the story, because the retail niche forged by immigrant Jewish entrepreneurs varied with local circumstances. Historians of antebellum southern Jewry, for example, draw on images of European feudalism to depict a classic middleman minority situation, with German Jews filling the status gap between "genteel aristocratic" planters and the rural poor, white and black. In early-twentieth-century Johnstown, Pennsylvania, dominated by an old-stock commercial elite, Jewish immigrants formed a "(multi)ethnic economic enclave" serving their former old-country customers and fellow outsiders, the Hungarians and Slavs who predominated in the industrial work force. In the post–Civil War South, many East European Jews built a similar niche-within-a-niche, relying on blacks for their customer base rather than competing with the merchant elite for white middle-class trade.[7]

In the coalfields, the commercial gap arose not through the dictates of a caste structure in a semifeudal economy but through the sudden advent of industrial capitalism, with a burgeoning work force creating a retail market beyond the capacity of the small contingent of local merchants. Coalfield Jews cannot be described as a prototypical middleman minority. They did not stand out as the sole "foreign" element in society. They were not the only people who engaged in commerce or who occupied a middle position between the masses and the ruling elite. They did not find themselves at a competitive disadvantage with the undersized preexisting merchant class and had no need to develop a niche catering to black or Eastern European workers. Their situation more closely resembled that of the merchant-based Jewish communities in the nineteenth-century American West, where Jews participated, along with other groups, in a dynamic and expanding economy that offered opportunities for advancement within a framework of exploitation.[8]

Coalfield Jews did not "re-create" their old-country role but drew on resources derived from that role to find a place in the coal economy. The commingling of Jewish agency and coalfield reality resulted in an economic profile that remained well within the American Jewish pattern even as it retained its own character.

The occupational profile of coalfield Jews reveals just how thorough their retail orientation was.[9] In a sample of 950 Jews who worked in the region from the 1870s to 1950s, more than 85 percent held retailing jobs as peddlers, proprietors, or employees (including managers, salespeople, tailors, bartenders, bookkeepers, and clerks) (see table 3). The actual percentage of Jews employed in retail was even higher, since the figures do not include all wives and children who worked in family stores. Moreover, even nonretail jobs were often connected to Jewish businesses. Wives took in boarders, mostly single Jewish men working as clerks in the family store. Jewish-owned concerns employed Jews as teamsters or laborers. In fact, only 75 individuals showed no link to Jewish businesses, barely 8 percent of the sample (and many of them probably worked in a family store at some point).

Although Jews concentrated in a single sector of the economy, their activities within that sector were diverse. The mainstay of Jewish retailing was the clothing and dry-goods business, which occupied 64 percent of retail jobholders at some point in their lives—55 percent of all employed people in the sample. But since the major opportunity in the early years involved the sale of alcohol in coalfield boomtowns, over a quarter of those who worked before prohibition had at least one job as saloonist, liquor dealer, or bartender. The liquor trade virtually disappeared as a business option for Jews after it became illegal in the mid-1910s and

Table 3. Coalfield Jewish Economic Profile

Job Type	Number of Jobs (by Job Type)	Percentage of Total Jobs	Percentage of Employed People
Total Jobs	1,145	100	120
Retail	986	86	86
Proprietor	543	47	57
Retail employee	413	36	43
Peddler	30	3	3
Nonretail	159	14	16
Professional	54	5	6
Blue collar	30	3	3
Kept boarders	39	3	4
Miscellaneous nonretail	36	3	4

Sources: See chapter 2, note 9.

Note: Sample size: 950 employed people. Most people held more than one job during their years in the region. This survey counts the job types held by each person, not each separate job. For example, a person who worked as a clerk at three different stores and then owned two different businesses is counted once as retail employee and once as proprietor. In total, 821 people held at least one retail job and 156 people held at least one nonretail job. So 86 percent held retail jobs and 16 percent held nonretail jobs. Because some people held both retail and nonretail jobs, the combined percentage exceeds 100.

Job types: Proprietor: owned or co-owned a business offering goods or services to the general public; retail employee: worked for a retail business in a managerial, sales, or office role; peddler: itinerant trader who sold goods directly to the public; professional: includes lawyers, doctors, dentists, nurses, teachers, social workers, public accountants, engineers; blue collar: includes coal miners, laborers, teamsters, carpenters, plumbers, janitors, butchers, and bakers (non-owners); kept boarders: performed household duties for paying guests; miscellaneous nonretail: includes coal industry owner/managers, white-collar employees (bookkeepers, stenographers, radio announcers, telephone operators, hospital technicians, etc.), government clerks, and farmers.

did not recapture their attention after prohibition ended in the 1930s. By that time other types of businesses had emerged. Through the years, Jews owned furniture, jewelry, grocery, hardware, cigar, drug, and auto supply stores. They were tailors, milliners, butchers, bakers, confectioners, plumbers, carpenters, mechanics, and junk dealers. They operated hotels, pawnshops, theaters, billiard parlors, and restaurants. They sold insurance, real estate, stocks and bonds. As one Jewish man who grew up in the region put it, "They did anything to make a living."[10] Anything, that is, that involved offering goods and services to the general public.

Metropolitan-based Jewish distribution networks guided Jews into certain lines of business, and local conditions also shaped their retail activities. Early Keystone business directories illuminate the growth of coalfield boomtowns and how merchants reacted to the opportunities these towns provided. Half of the ten Jewish business owners listed in the 1898 directory operated saloons, while saloons constituted 40 percent of all businesses in town (Jews owned five out of the seventeen saloons listed). As Keystone grew, it could sustain more diverse enterprises. The percentage of Jews engaged in the liquor trade decreased steadily after 1898, as did the town's ratio of saloons to other commercial ventures. Meanwhile, the retail clothing sector grew: in 1898, Jews owned all three clothing establishments; in 1904, they owned all eight.

While their dominance of Keystone's clothing trade suggests the strength of their ties to Baltimore's clothing industry, Jewish merchants in Keystone and throughout the region pursued an ever-broadening range of retail activity. In the county seats, competition among merchants and an expanding local market encouraged specialization and diversification into new lines of business. By 1914, Jews in Logan, Williamson, and Welch were operating theaters; by 1927, Logan even had a Jewish-owned piano store. The most prominent retailers branched into residential and commercial real estate development. Meanwhile, specialties within the clothing and dry-goods trade helped merchants distinguish themselves from the pack. From general stores and clothiers came department stores, army-navy stores, credit clothing stores, men's and ladies' boutiques, discount or "underselling" stores, and children's clothing stores, to name a few.

Changing conditions also shaped retailing in less beneficial ways. Downturns in the coal economy, and especially the disaster of the Great Depression, caused businesses to contract, change form, or disappear. Leading McDowell County merchant Harry Bank lost department stores in Kimball and War in the early 1930s. He moved to Welch and opened an army-navy store, which he operated under much-reduced circumstances. The Depression saw the return of peddlers, as some young men resorted to this economical way to sell—though now they traveled by car, filling their vehicles with goods and making the rounds of the coal camps. Technological innovation filtering into the region brought both opportunity and adversity. Jewish-owned moving picture houses, appliance stores, and automobile-related businesses appeared, while businesses that offered outmoded merchandise had to adapt or fold. In the post–World War II era, new technology in the form of shopping malls and chain stores would help destroy the Jewish economic niche altogether.

Along with shifting external conditions, internal dynamics affected the economic profile of Jewish communities. Eli Evans's often-quoted pronouncement that "the story of Jews in the South is the story of fathers who built businesses to give to their sons who didn't want them" began to apply to coalfield Jews by the 1930s and became increasingly relevant for the generation that came of age around World War II. Aided by a lessening of discrimination in the corporate and professional worlds, many young people who had left the region for college or military service decided to seek careers elsewhere.[11] Some who opted to return to the coalfields joined a new professional cohort. Before 1920, only eight Jews in the occupational sample held professional jobs—six teachers, a lawyer, and a doctor. From the 1930s to the 1950s, at least forty Jewish professionals worked in the region, mostly doctors, dentists, and lawyers. Fifteen had grown up in the coalfields.

While some parents may have been disappointed by their children's rejection of retailing, others were not. A man raised in Northfork in the 1920s-30s noted that his parents expected him and his sister to attend college even though the cost "was a real economic problem" for the family. He explained, "That was their dream, that their children would make more of their lives than they themselves did." His sister became a McDowell County high school teacher and he became a Charleston lawyer. Yet most coalfield Jews continued to be employed in trade, signifying an enduring interest in the family store. As late as 1974, a study of Williamson Jews observed, "Their occupational involvements seem characteristic of an earlier era, when enterprises were small or at least family-owned. Moreover, [they] are . . . satisfied with the economic order and the place they occupy in it."[12]

To further revise Eli Evans's observation by adding the half of the population that he omitted, it must be noted that coalfield businesses were family operations, built by mothers as well as fathers. And at least a few daughters, as well as sons, faced the choice of whether or not to follow in their parents' footsteps. Ethel Catzen Cohen, for example, managed her father Aaron Catzen's considerable Northfork business and real estate interests after his death 1951. The generational shift to professional careers affected both men and women, though women tended to become teachers while men tended to become doctors and lawyers (with exceptions on both sides).

Coalfield retailing reached its peak from the late 1930s to early 1950s as wartime and postwar demand for coal brought vitality to the economic scene. Jewish residents fondly recalled that "it was a pleasure to shop down[town] then," as masses of shoppers and a plethora of stores lent an air of excitement to county seats.[13]

Starting in the mid-1950s, several developments brought about the end of the Jewish retail niche. Above all, coal industry mechanization transformed Central Appalachia's economy. The mining work force in this study's five southern West Virginia counties plunged 70 percent between 1950 and 1970. With few local employment alternatives, most people faced the choice of moving away or sinking into poverty. The population declined by 38 percent over two decades. In eastern Kentucky, the population dropped by one-third between 1950 and 1960 alone. Local businesses suffered as their customer base dwindled. Referring to the machine that replaced the most workers, a Logan interviewee succinctly summed up the situation, noting that "you can't sell a continuous miner clothes and food." Next came the nationwide transformation of retail shopping, as malls and chain stores devastated downtown business districts across small-town America.[14]

These blows not only decimated coalfield retailing but also dissipated the "critical mass" holding Jewish communities together. Even people who might have tried to maintain businesses saw the viability of Jewish life disappearing; for some, that became reason enough to leave. Additionally, many merchants began to reach retirement age, making the decision to close out the family business relatively easy. (The Williamson Jews surveyed in 1974, though satisfied with their own economic position, no longer expected their children to follow in their footsteps.) This convergence of factors meant that Jews joined the larger Central Appalachian diaspora in even higher percentages than the rest of the population. Only in towns that managed to diversify their economy did Jewish communities hang on past the 1970s, now dependent not so much on retailing as on newly emerging professional positions at hospitals and governmental facilities. In Williamson, Jewish doctors came to town with the opening of a union-sponsored hospital in the mid-1950s, while in Beckley, Jewish doctors arrived to work at the Veterans' Administration hospital.[15]

The story of the Fink family of Beckley dramatizes how economic forces and personal goals came together to shape generational trends. In the 1920s, Russian immigrant Louis Fink built up a successful retail business that was battered but not destroyed by the Depression. His son Sidney went off to college for one year but then came home to work in the family store, which, he stated, he "learned to love, and fared extremely well." He became a partner by 1940, during a flourishing time in the coalfields. "I always took to the fashion business and enjoyed it," he recalled. "I prospered to the extent that I could send my two boys to a prep school and my daughter likewise." One son returned from college to take over the business in the 1970s, but then, observed Fink, "began the exodus from downtown U.S.A. to the malls." The family recognized the difficulties and closed out their stores. Both of Fink's sons became professionals and moved away, while his daughter decided to pursue a retail career—though not in Beckley.[16]

Life within the Coal Economy

Coalfield merchants operated in an economic environment that, not unlike the air they breathed, was permeated by the presence of coal. The region's complete reliance on the industry caused national trends such as recession or wartime expansion to have an exaggerated impact. Developments directly related to the coal industry, such as fluctuating national energy prices, labor disputes, and mechanization, reverberated powerfully through the local economy. As one Jewish coalfield native explained, with the air of someone stating the obvious, "*Everybody* was dependent on the coal companies." Retail businesses sprang up with each jump in the world's demand for coal and disappeared with each recession or strike. A retired Beckley merchant observed that "it was a changing atmosphere, all the time," with Jewish families coming and going as stores opened and closed. Yet on the whole, he stated, "Beckley was a very good business town."[17]

Other Jewish county-seat merchants echoed his phrasing. Into the 1950s their towns had the reputation of being "good business towns" where commerce was lively and prospects were favorable. Families who persevered and weathered the downturns eventually prospered, they maintained. A Williamson merchant summed up their attitude when she asserted that "the people who stayed had thriving businesses. . . . Everybody made money here. Everybody did well." The ultimate source of economic prosperity seemed clear to all. As Logan merchant

Rudy Eiland wrote in his town's 1952 centennial booklet, "Quite naturally, as the coal business prospered, so did the merchants in general and the city of Logan in particular."[18]

But in reality, the coal economy contained highly *un*natural features that posed significant challenges for retailers. Its boom-and-bust nature led to frequent lay-offs, with no other industries to pick up the slack. Its propensity for labor turmoil made strikes bitter and lengthy. Such events translated into a customer base that was often unemployed, if not destitute. More than one interviewee noted that "strikes were disastrous for business." Relating how a coal operator in the New River field shut down his mines for a year rather than allow workers to unionize, a man whose family had owned a small store summed it up: "We went broke."[19]

The *Bluefield Daily Telegraph* emphasized the direct relationship between slowdowns in coal production and small business failures in 1915, reporting that "small businessmen had hard sledding at the beginning of the year [because of] bad conditions in the coal fields." Sixty-nine bankruptcy petitions had been filed over six months in McDowell, Mercer, and Mingo Counties, and the article's headline highlighted the marginal nature of these firms: "None Failed with Big Wad." Even during periods of sustained industry employment, cutthroat competition in the national coal market led coal operators to enforce the lowest possible labor costs, resulting in a generally low-wage work force whose purchasing power was limited.[20]

Meanwhile, the original dearth of merchants in the mountains had propelled coal companies into the retail business themselves: they had to provide a way for their employees to obtain basic goods and services. What started as a necessity soon turned into a profitable sideline, and company stores continued to proliferate after independent merchants appeared on the scene. The control that coal operators had over their workers, along with their domination of the social and political structure, gave them a commanding advantage over other retailers and distorted the retail picture throughout the region.

This portrait of harsh coalfield reality, well documented by historians, seems at odds with the glowing narrative of success recounted by Jewish business owners. How could merchants have prospered under such conditions? Generalizations on both sides give way to complexities when one takes a close look at the impact of the region's coal dependency on local commerce. Not all Jewish merchants prospered, as interviewees tacitly acknowledge. The "people who stayed" achieved economic mobility (to varying degrees, as will be seen), but there were plenty who did not—could not—remain in the region and maintain viable businesses. The retail niche remained small and, at times, overcrowded; the coal economy would allow it to expand only so much. And those who did stay endured a history of ups and downs that gave coalfield retailing the character of a wild roller coaster ride.

On the other hand, for many decades the coal industry did support a sizable wage-earning population that provided a ready market for goods and services. As a retired Jewish merchant commented, "*Everybody* wasn't poor." He offered this simple statement as both an explanation for retail viability and a commentary on the oversimplified image of the region. Boom times, when, as he put it, "everything was going great guns," offered merchants the opportunity to make up for down times. Coalfield newspapers trumpeted the success enjoyed by local businesses during such periods—though sometimes they took on a wistful tone. One 1915 article welcoming the region's latest economic recovery (courtesy of wartime Europe's demand for coal) concluded, "If it only will continue for awhile." The factors militating against an independent retail niche, though considerable, were not completely unyielding. There was some room for maneuvering—and Jewish entrepreneurs, accustomed to economic marginality and possessed of resources of their own, were perhaps better equipped to do so than others.[21]

To anyone with a rudimentary knowledge of coalfield history, one major challenge to independent merchants seems obvious. How did they compete with coal company stores? Indeed, the company store loomed large in coalfield life. A fixture in coal towns large and small, it frequently served as the focal point of the community.[22] It often provided essential retail services, especially in more remote locales. And it came to represent the vast power coal companies possessed to exploit their workers and extract profits from the region.

In both scholarly and popular accounts, the picture, broadly painted, looks like this: coal companies monopolized the trade of their employees. They compelled miners to shop at the company store by threatening to fire them or place them in the least productive areas of the mine (miners were paid by the ton) if they shopped elsewhere. They then charged their captive customers inflated prices. If that wasn't enough, they further ensnared workers through the use of scrip, coal company currency that workers could draw in advance of payday for use only in the company store. When payday came around, miners could find themselves in debt to their employer or, at best, would receive little pay since most of their earnings had already been spent. Either way, they were then obliged to draw more scrip, binding them further to the store and to the company as employer. Meanwhile, coal companies used their control over the land to keep independent merchants away from their work force.[23]

Given the volatility of the international coal market, it is not surprising that companies would use all the powers at their command to guarantee store sales. Many were driven by a compelling incentive: the need to make hefty profits in their stores to make up for losses from their coal operations. In 1915, for example, "not a few" coal operators asserted that coal business losses were "more than counterbalanced by profits from selling merchandise and renting houses," reported the trade journal *Coal Age*. A *New York Times* reporter discovered in 1931 that "many Harlan mines were turning their only profit at the commissary."[24]

As the very existence of an independent retail sector suggests, however, the company store's monopoly power was limited. In fact, not all companies under-took to drive off retail competitors, and not all coal miners "owed their soul to the company store." Nevertheless, the company store as a dominant coalfield institution imposed an inequitable and restrictive set of conditions that miners and their families (as employees and consumers) and local merchants (as com-petitors) were forced to confront. The tension between its monopolistic tenden-cies and the response of these consumers and competitors shaped the local retail economy.[25]

Coal companies pressured miners to use the company store with strategies ranging from subtle to heavy handed, with more blatant tactics applied before unionization began to reduce their control over their workers in the 1930s. A New River coalfield resident's comment about one local mine is typical: "Before the unions got so strong, if you worked there, you spent your money there. If they caught you spending your money uptown, they'd either lay you off or put you in a water hole—you couldn't make a living."[26] Employers freely acknowledged such practices among themselves. A 1915 letter in *Coal Age* noted that "all mine officials are expected to make their men realize, in some subtle but effective way, that the man who spends most at the company store will receive more favors than the one who buys elsewhere." A coal operator told journalist Winthrop Lane in the early 1920s that he formerly discharged men "for buying two dollars' worth of flour somewhere else," though Lane heard that most mines no longer compelled work-ers to trade at company stores. Perhaps not overtly, but in the early 1930s a com-pany bookkeeper slyly informed researcher James Laing, "We wouldn't fire a man for not trading at the store—but he could be let out for something else."[27]

But not all coal operators attempted to coerce their employees, and those who did didn't always succeed. In an often-tight labor market, dissatisfied miners could easily move to other mines (though there was no guarantee that their new employer would be any better). Some mining officials professed indifference as to where their workers spent their pay. A former company store manager recalled that his firm's miners often purchased groceries at a nearby independent store. "They thought they could get 'em cheaper. . . . It was all right. It didn't hurt us any." Meanwhile, some miners and their families refused to submit to pressure. A former coal camp resident recalled that her mother "declined to shop at the company store, and when the store manager tried to pressure her, she told him she would shop where she pleased."[28]

Intimidation practiced by company stores hampered independent retailers but did not necessarily prevent them from operating. A storekeeper in 1920s eastern Kentucky later asserted that the local mine superintendent would tell miners "it might mean their job" if they patronized his store, but they ignored the threat. Jewish residents expressed the view that miners were required to spend a portion, but not all, of their earnings at the company store. One interviewee stated that miners who were paid twice per month spent their first paycheck at the company store and came to town to shop with their second paycheck.[29]

Yet even if coercive policies were unevenly or halfheartedly applied, the relationship between coal companies and miners gave company stores an inherent edge. Author John Hevener, comparing three different mines in 1930s Harlan County, noted that one did not apply any pressure at all while at another, the superintendent "bluntly told his employees: 'If you trade at Piggly Wiggly's you can get your job at Piggly Wiggly's.'" The third company "sent its miners a letter that they interpreted as a warning" to trade at the company store or be fired. Indeed, the line between coercion and aggressive marketing could be fuzzy, as the U.S. Coal Commission noted in 1922: "The energetic [company] store manager desires to show good profits at the end of the year. . . . He has access to the mine company's pay roll and can find out which families do none or but part of their buying at his store. If he solicits the trade of these families . . . he is doing no more than any wide awake merchant would do. Yet he is exposing himself and his company to the charge of 'forcing purchasing.'" The coalfields' independent "wide awake merchants," of course, had no such access to their customers' payroll records and no such opportunities to "solicit" trade.[30]

A 1913 *Coal Age* article listed other advantages company stores enjoyed over independent retailers: they "pay no rent, do no advertising, should have no losses on bad credits and have small delivery charges, all of which cost usually from 8 to 10 percent of the gross profit." A 1915 article asserted that some operators faced "fierce" competition from independent stores, "and they frequently succeed so well . . . that they take away the bulk of the business from the local merchants, owing to the fact that they have a large trade absolutely secured from bad debts and of a volume which can be relied on." The author did not need to spell out the reason for this fortunate situation: their ability to deduct from their employee-customers' wages and to pressure employees to use the store.[31]

Access to the financial resources of their parent corporations enabled company stores to carry a larger stock than small, family-owned businesses. Their ability to buy in mass quantities allowed them to undersell competitors if they so chose. At least one company applied this strategy selectively. In 1909, a general store owner in Bramwell, West Virginia, complained in a letter to the governor that the Caswell Creek Coal Company was "soliciting business from this town, and selling goods, at ruinous prices" in order "to choke off the small local merchant." The prices the company offered townspeople for goods delivered were far lower than the prices it charged its workers in its store, the letter claimed.[32]

Their proximity to the bulk of the coalfield population gave company stores their most obvious advantage over independents. In 1922, for example, more than 80 percent of West Virginia's miners and their families lived in company towns. Until road improvements and the spread of automobile ownership starting in the late 1930s, company stores did indeed have a "virtual monopoly" (as Winthrop Lane put it) in the more remote coal camps.[33]

Some coal companies were determined to protect this geographical advantage by refusing to allow independent stores on their property and banning peddlers from their camps. A 1911 government study observed that "in most instances the companies own large tracts of land and keep out competitors very largely." Beckley Lebanese merchant Asaff Rahall recalled being chased away from coal towns by company police during his peddling days in the 1910s, while a West Virginia labor commissioner told Lane that "hucksters and peddlers" were prohibited from coal camps "in nearly every case."[34]

The commissioner overstated. While some companies enforced strict "no trespassing" rules, others were more lax. A Harlan County local historian writes that peddlers, mostly Jews and Assyrians, "sold in all the communities and the coal camps" in the 1920s and 1930s. "They were not welcome in some coal camps," he states, "but they did well and prospered." Moreover, there were limits to the coal companies' power to keep independent retailers out of their territory. Jewish merchant Rudy Eiland operated a small grocery store outside of Logan town and made deliveries into nearby coal camps in the 1910s. Company officials "weren't happy about his coming," stated his son, but they could not stop him because he owned the land on which his store sat. In 1915, Superior Pocahontas Coal Company superintendent George Wolfe sued a local firm, McNeal and Goodson, for trespassing when the firm tried to deliver goods to miners in one of his McDowell County coal camps. The suit caused considerable local controversy and, in a rare court defeat for coal operators, it was dismissed.[35]

This incident cannot be used, however, to conclude that coal companies did not routinely get away with such behavior. For years Wolfe had enforced a policy barring retailers from company property, as he noted in a 1913 letter to his employer, mine owner Justus Collins: "About once a year I have a round with these merchants at Davy, as there seems to be always some new one that has to be broken in." Several of the Davy merchants were in fact Jewish immigrants, newcomers unlikely to challenge their powerful neighbor. Only after McNeal and Goodson (a non-Jewish firm) began to ignore the rule did Wolfe bring his lawsuit. By taking a respected business to court instead of relying on his usual methods of intimidation, Wolfe apparently overreached his authority and raised the specter of bad publicity, as Collins pointed out to him: "You can see what a club you have . . . placed in the hands of the enemies of the coal industry." Collins, though a strong believer in authoritarian rule, recognized that "the Company's stores have every advantage in many ways" and there was no need for "coercion in any shape or form," which needlessly aroused antagonism. He preferred to save heavy-handed tactics for keeping out "undesirable people . . . during strike times."[36]

Collins's instincts were correct. Although public attacks on local merchants might backfire, coal companies could conduct their campaigns against unionism virtually unchecked. Conveniently, their no-holds-barred anti-union measures also had the effect, intended or not, of restricting interaction between their retail competitors and their workers. Jewish immigrant James Pickus, newly arrived from Minsk, entered a company town one day in the 1910s to post signs advertising his brothers' Beckley store. A mine guard attacked and beat him badly, leaving "a real deep scar" on his forehead, according to his son. This company's officials cared little about competition from independent retailers, or so they said; Pickus had been mistaken for a union organizer.[37]

Routine inquisitions carried out by coal industry watchdogs extended to any and all suspicious persons and had a chilling effect on trade. A 1920 Baldwin-Felts Detective Agency memo reported that one agency spy "has failed to locate any Union organizer . . . notwithstanding the fact that he has investigated dozens of miners . . . picture agents, peddlers, insurance agents, newspaper collectors, and others." Local authorities joined in the repressive measures that stifled commerce as well as union activity. A traveling salesman told a reporter in 1920, "Every operation has its armed guard—usually two. I was served with a little notice by a deputy sheriff in Logan . . . to not go up Island Creek any more, that it was dangerous and I was liable to get shot. . . . The notice forbade me using the railroad going up there and back."[38]

Coal operators recognized the additional benefits derived from the repressive system they had erected to stamp out unionism, and many came to view these benefits as their prerogative. Some coal towns developed into veritable armed camps, and labor organizers were not the only undesirables deliberately barred. George Wolfe described admiringly the arrangements of a fellow coal operator in a 1915 letter to Collins: "Bradley has a five-strand barbed wire fence, ten feet high, around his property, with only one gate and at that gate he keeps someone day and night. . . . Works absolutely non-union and controls the situation and people come for miles to work for him. His net profits on the store are 12 percent and there are no outside teams delivering anything on his job."[39]

However, some mining officials had a different attitude, seeing local retailers not as pesky interlopers but as junior partners in coalfield development. These officials promoted local commerce and worked cooperatively with merchants. In fact, many independent towns arose because corporate landowners or their coal subsidiaries sold chunks of property to real estate developers to build business and residential districts that would exist side by side with coal operations. In Pocahontas, the region's first large coal company sold its land in the top half of the town and maintained ownership of the bottom half. The company's power plant served all local businesses and its store, located on the main downtown street, engaged in friendly competition with the independent stores ranged alongside it. The massive U.S. Coal and Coke Company in McDowell County offers another model of coexistence. Though it retained ownership of many towns, company officials looked benevolently on the small merchants who existed on or near its property, perhaps seeing them as conducive to keeping a productive labor force. Similarly, in the New River Company town of Scarbro, miners lived at the top of the hill while at the bottom could be found the company store, the post office, and some privately owned homes and stores, including those of a few Jewish families.[40]

In small ways, direct economic relationships developed between coal companies and local merchants. Company stores in Mingo County sold tickets to Hyman Bank's Williamson movie theater—at a 10 percent commission. Local tailors came into company stores to fit customers. Occasionally coal companies invested in local enterprises. In 1912, U.S. Coal and Coke planned to sell vacant lots in Welch to Jewish businessman Joseph Lopinsky, who wanted to build a hotel. "Col. O'Toole, the manager of this big corporation, is heartily in favor of the proposition and his company will subscribe liberally to the stock," a newspaper article reported. In later years, some Jewish merchants even ran concessions inside company stores.[41]

Yet the benign attitude of some coal operators could not alleviate the systemic problems the company store posed for independent retailers. The use of scrip offers a prime example. Like the company store itself, scrip began as a necessity. Currency fabricated by individual coal companies (in coins or paper) helped offset the shortage of cash in a region that, at first, lacked financial institutions. Although using scrip to pay wages soon became illegal, says historian Glenn Massay, "there was nothing to prevent employers from issuing scrip" as an *advance* on pay, "and this became a common practice." While miners received their wages in cash if they waited until payday, scrip advances were often unavoidable: not only did they need to purchase job supplies such as tools and blasting powder before they started work but also, until the 1920s, most were paid only once per month.[42]

Once enmeshed in the scrip system, it was difficult for miners to break away. Company officials quickly realized that scrip offered a way to boost store purchases. Coal companies, as historian Crandall Shifflett notes, "encouraged easy credit." Analysts differ on how indebted the average miner was to the company store, though they agree that immigrant miners tended to have less debt, and relied less on scrip, than native whites or blacks. Immigrants were more likely to be single, without local families to support (and if they were sending money to families back home, they needed their pay in cash). But whether or not miners became indebted, the use of scrip greatly reduced the amount of cash they received. And because scrip could be redeemed at full value only at the company store, it served as a powerful disincentive for them to shop elsewhere, regardless of whether their employer pressured or coerced them.[43]

That was not the only problem scrip caused local merchants. The system put pressure on the entire retail economy to operate on a credit basis by contributing to the lack of cash in general circulation. As one Jewish man explained, his family's Northfork store had no choice but to offer credit, because "miners had scrip in their pockets." Miners and their families became accustomed to relying on credit.

The company stores surveyed by the Coal Commission in 1922 made up to 88 percent of their sales on a noncash basis. Independent stores had to do likewise if they wanted to compete.[44]

Yet unlike company stores, shielded from losses by their ability to deduct from their workers' pay, independent stores were vulnerable to bad debts. Miners generally paid their bills as soon as they could, but for small businesses trying to make it through hard times, that was often not soon enough. The boom-and-bust coal economy posed particular risks for the easily overextended small coalfield retailer, noted the commission: "He must do most of his business on a credit basis. . . . As a consequence a number of independently owned stores come into existence when the mines begin work and go out of business when the mines are not operating." When customers who normally settled part or all of their accounts on payday suddenly could not do so, the consequences could be "quite difficult," recalled one Jewish retailer. Merchants continued to "carry" their customers through these periods and hope that good times would soon return. "We just had to wait 'em out," he explained.[45]

Aside from offering credit, many independent retailers made another accommodation to the scrip system: they accepted scrip in lieu of cash or credit. Far from being usable only at company stores, scrip in fact circulated throughout the coalfields, aided by the activities of local scrip dealers who exchanged it for cash—though not at full value. Peddlers, coalfield stores large and small, theaters, and other businesses took in coal company currency in their daily course of operation. Before midcentury, its impact was so widespread that, commented one Jewish merchant, scrip was "a way of life in those days." A former coal camp car peddler confirmed, noting that "to us, scrip was just like money."[46]

It is unknown how many retailers accepted scrip, though it would be safe to say that county-seat stores were less likely to take it than stores located nearer the mines. Shopkeepers and peddlers accepted scrip at anywhere from 60 to 90 percent of its face value (the typical discount was probably 75 to 80 percent). Faced with the task of disposing of the currency, they either turned to scrip dealers or took it themselves to the company store. Coal companies maintained various policies on how they redeemed their scrip. Many demanded the purchase of goods. Others exchanged it for cash, though often at a discount. In this manner, company stores could profit from competitors who accepted scrip.[47]

In West Virginia until the mid-1920s, the law required coal companies to redeem their scrip in cash, at full value, to anyone who brought it to the company store. But penalties for noncompliance were minor and enforcement was lax, so the law was universally disregarded. As George Wolfe remarked to Justus Collins, redeeming scrip in cash "would give the nine competitive stores at Davy the chance of their lives," but "as the matter is only a misdemeanor and at the most would not cost us over $100," he felt safe in ignoring the law.[48]

Merchants forced to deal with scrip tried to profit off the system in creative ways. Some used the company store as a sort of wholesaler: they would accept scrip from customers at significantly less than face value (say, 65 percent), then use it (at full value) to purchase large quantities of cigarettes, candy, or other goods at the company store. They would then sell these goods in their own stores. Then, too, to small entrepreneurs accustomed to extending credit, scrip at least did not present the risk of uncollectible debts. Some peddlers in the coal camps were even willing to accept scrip at full value from their customers and exchange it at a loss to scrip dealers—the markup on their goods was high enough to enable them to make a profit anyway.[49]

Miners who drew scrip were at an automatic disadvantage if they wanted to spend it outside the company store; clearly the system offered opportunities for abuse by scrip dealers and small retailers as well as coal companies. The region's overreliance on credit also invited abuse, as some retailers worked to convince people to buy things they could not afford. But such tactics could easily backfire. One Jewish man who worked the southern West Virginia coal camps observed, "It was easy to sell to [miners] . . . but sometimes you'd have trouble collecting." His method of collection shows how independent entrepreneurs became enmeshed in the system of exploitation. He used the enforcement powers of local justices of the peace, who typically kept for themselves a portion of the monies collected on his behalf. "It was nothing for me to have two or three justices of the peace to turn over my accounts to," he commented. "Of course, sometimes we had trouble collecting from the justice of the peace!"[50]

Conversely, scrip offered possibilities for savvy coalfield residents to manipulate the system as well. It was not uncommon for miners' families to *purchase* scrip from scrip dealers—at marked-down prices—and use it in local company stores, in effect receiving a discount on their purchases. Also, prudent use of scrip could work to their advantage in the same way that consumers today can benefit from careful credit card use. Crandall Shifflett asserts that "miners brought to their dealings with the company store the same realism and practicality they exhibited elsewhere, and in doing so, they limited the hegemony of the store and the operators over their lives." Certainly without this agency, the independent retail sector would have been considerably smaller than it was. Nevertheless, in the context of the dominant position coal companies held over employees and retail competitors, scrip overwhelmingly worked to benefit the region's reigning power, at the expense of the rest of the population.[51]

The company store presented so many difficulties for independent retailers that some interviewees asserted that until the post–World War II era, their families' stores actually served only the nonmining population—a narrow slice of the overall demographic. They explained that miners did not become a substantial part of their customer base until unionization, the gradual elimination of scrip, and improved transportation loosened the grip of the coal companies and enabled coal camp residents to come to the county seats to shop. However, other interviewees maintained that merchants had always vied with company stores for the trade of miners and their families. Certainly businesses based in smaller towns, closer to the mines, had no choice but to compete directly with company stores.[52]

Aside from maneuvering around the scrip system, independent retailers had other ways to hold their own with company stores. Many foreign-born miners preferred to trade at stores "conducted by members of their own race," reported the U.S. Immigration Commission in 1911. Though Jews did not share the ethnicity of the region's Eastern European miners, they did share languages and customs. Hungarian-born Rudy Eiland's ability to speak several languages helped him compete with the company stores around Logan. Immigrants felt more comfortable trading with him since "he could talk to them, they couldn't," his son observed. Some Jewish-owned stores displayed signs reading "Hungarian spoken here," while others sold steamship tickets in a bid for the trade of fellow immigrants. Jewish merchants sometimes helped non-English-speaking miners in encounters with American bureaucracy, for example, by acting as interpreters in court. This role hearkened back to Eastern Europe, where part of the relationship Jews had with their peasant neighbors included helping them deal with officialdom. Max Roston's old-country style gained him customers in the coal town of Wilcoe. "Our customers knew that if they made a large purchase they could haggle with Uncle Max," his nephew writes. "Bargaining was part of the fun." This popular old-country custom was definitely not an amenity offered by the company store.[53]

More important, Roston's nephew recalls, "We had the lower prices." The famously high prices charged by company stores provided independents with their greatest leverage in drawing trade away from coal companies. Some historians rebut the accusation that coal companies overcharged their workers, citing the 1922 Coal Commission study, which found company store prices not significantly higher than those at other coalfield stores. The commission, though, noted "a universal belief among miners' families that prices are higher in company stores," a complaint that remained constant through the decades. (Accompanying this belief, it must be stated, was a general consensus that company stores stocked better-quality goods than other stores.) In the 1930s, James Laing found a bigger gap between independent and company store prices than had the commission. Apparently, much variation in pricing existed among coal companies.[54]

One reason for this variation is clear: independent retailers, by their very existence, curbed the worst abuses of company stores. The Immigration Commission in 1911, the Coal Commission in 1922, and Laing all found that company store prices tended to be lower in areas where local merchants vied for trade. The Coal Commission further reported that "quality of merchandise, upkeep of merchandise and store, and business methods were better where company stores and independent stores were in direct competition." The sole interviewee for this study who insisted that company store prices matched other store prices lived in Pocahontas, where independent competition thrived.[55]

Their dependency on high store profits to overcome an unforgiving coal market led some operators to see independent retailers as more than simply annoying. George Wolfe's frequent, indeed, obsessive, diatribes against the "nine competitive stores" in Davy reflected his frustration at the effect these small stores had on his bottom line. As he explained to Collins, "If we attempted to meet all of this competition, we would wind up selling the whole shooting match at cost. . . . The merchants of Davy have cut our Powder profits from three thousand dollars per year to eight hundred dollars and if they have their way, they will make a serious dent in our store business and profits."[56]

Wolfe's displeasure with the dampening effect local merchants had on store prices led him to offer a revealing analysis of his competitors and how they managed to survive a difficult business environment. "This is the way these outside merchants figure," he told Justus Collins. If they can earn even a modest amount, "they claim that they are getting rich." As he saw it, their willingness to accept low profits gave *them* an unfair advantage, not the coal company. "We have nine competitive stores in Davy and each one of them make a leader out of something and sell it at cost. . . . Most of the merchants in business here own their own property and are satisfied with very small profits, as their store provides them with a job and their families with eatables, so they are satisfied. Then some of them do not mind failing and beating their creditors."[57]

Wolfe's comments provide a glimpse into the marginal nature of independent coalfield retailing. The Coal Commission offered a similar assessment in analyzing why company store prices were often higher than the competition's: while coal companies had to show a profit to shareholders, "many of the independent stores are operated as family concerns with no salaries to pay and only the family living to get."[58] Given the pitfalls surrounding local enterprise, especially outside the county seats, it is not surprising that independent stores tended to be small, dependent on family labor, and low in capital outlay and profitability.

The observations of Wolfe and the Coal Commission echo descriptions of Jewish businesses that for centuries had perched precariously on the edge of whatever economy they found themselves in. In Davy at the time Wolfe wrote, heirs to this tradition of economic marginality included general store owner Sam Masil, clothing store owners Meyer and Israel Sneider, and the three Michaelson brothers, who had a tailoring shop. The town also had two Jewish saloonists, and other Jewish merchants came and went during the 1910s. A few managed to remain in Davy into the 1920s (Meyer Sneider's widow, Lillian, even outlasted Wolfe, operating the family store into the 1950s), while others left to pursue opportunities elsewhere in the coalfields. Most, however, vanished from the historical record.[59]

The relatively stable and prosperous merchant-based Jewish communities in larger coalfield towns offer a contrasting image to the scrappy Jewish contingent of Davy, but in reality they were two sides of the same coin. From the standpoint of the region's retail economy, the problem with coal company stores was that they promoted the marginality of all other businesses, whether they intended to or not. They did not have to be guilty of the most egregious practices in their power to have a negative impact. Scrip, for example, hurt competitors whether meant as an accounting convenience or a deliberate snare. Though various factors restrained their monopolistic tendencies, their overall effect was to subdue commerce and narrow its scope. Their impact was greatest, of course, in towns located closest to the mines. Company stores inhibited the development of these towns, providing ample incentive for merchants to relocate to the county seats at their earliest opportunity. But even the county seats, those "good business towns," suffered from the loss of a major portion of the region's potential customer base.

For decades independent stores served as a secondary shopping site for miners' families, after the company store. It is impossible to know what the economy would have looked like had that not been the case. (And stores were not the only businesses affected, since coal companies operated theaters, barber shops, saloons, pool rooms, and other enterprises.) But some things we do know. By taking for themselves a large share of the retail trade, coal companies not only made life difficult for small businesses but also drained financial resources from the economy. Their store profits, unlike the profits of local merchants, traveled straight out of the region. And when extracting coal proved unprofitable, companies relied upon their stores to prop up unsuccessful mining operations, thus contributing to the overproduction that plagued the coal industry and caused economic distress for the population generally. Company stores therefore constituted an integral part of a single-industry order that proved unable to sustain a healthy economy.

Jewish entrepreneurs attracted to the region by its growing population and its shortage of merchants found, upon their arrival, that the very industry responsible for this opportunity had developed a formidable system to take advantage of it, to the detriment of others. Because they became absorbed into a coalfield middle class that supported the coal industry and rooted for its success, they accepted the situation without protest. They simply went about the business of establishing their own niche in the coal economy, attempting to transform themselves from marginal shopkeepers in coal towns such as Davy into county-seat business leaders.

Before leaving the topic of the coal industry's impact on Jewish economic life, one remaining aspect deserves scrutiny. Sources revealed only thirty-six coalfield Jews with a direct connection to the coal industry. Though small, this group sheds light on the Jewish coalfield experience. Sixteen businesspeople invested in coal mining, while six people worked as company doctors and four held office positions. One young man clerked in the Pocahontas company store before opening a furniture store of his own. A few people dealt in coal sales or supplied equipment to coal companies.[60]

Precisely seven Jewish coal miners were identified. They included a recently arrived immigrant who became a prominent Welch businessman (Sam Polon) and a formerly prominent Kimball merchant who fell on hard times. In the early 1910s, Isadore Tobin owned a saloon and five-and-dime store while serving as Kimball's sergeant and treasurer. Prohibition and a fire that destroyed his store left him bankrupt. He became a store clerk in Williamson and then a coal miner in Logan County, where his brother owned a pharmacy. Two sons of local shopkeepers worked as miners. The 1920 census listed twenty-year-old Alex Leventhal as a coal mine laborer who lived with his parents, owners of a Welch dry-cleaning shop. Isadore Ofsa grew up helping in his family's Keystone grocery store but worked most of his adult life in the mines, rising to become a mine electrician. His success at his chosen career was lost on his family, who considered him something of a failure.[61]

The actual number of Jewish coal miners was undoubtedly higher than the sources reveal. Although their networks and background dictated that the number of Jews working in the coal industry would be small, prevailing assumptions about Jews may have led people to believe that the number was even smaller than it actually was. Interviews with Jews and non-Jews elicited many variations of the phrase "I never heard of any Jewish coal miners" or, perhaps more telling, Jews "wouldn't work in the coal mines." The universal belief (shared by many Jews themselves) that Jews could not or would not engage in manual labor, a charge that originated in Europe as a demeaning way to account for their middleman role, may have influenced interpretations of reality.

Even census records may contain a human bias. Miners with Jewish-sounding names such as "Sam Weisman" and "Joe Solomon," for example, who in 1910 resided in McDowell County boardinghouses for immigrant miners, were listed along with the others as speaking "Magyar" or "Slovak" rather than "Yiddish" or "Hebrew" (the languages often ascribed to immigrant Jews). Not expecting to find Jews in such places, census takers may have simply grouped Jewish coal miners in with their fellow miners. For town Jews, other sources (synagogue records, interviews, local history books) confirmed the Jewish identity of people listed in the census.[62] The lack of such corroboration for miners such as the two men mentioned here indicates that either they were not Jewish or if they were, they were not connected to the local Jewish community. This in itself would be an interesting finding, if it could be verified. It would not only say something about class dynamics among Jews but also shed light on the process of ethnic stereotyping. If Jewish coal miners tended to stay uninvolved with local Jewish communities, invisible to other Jews and to townspeople in general, it is no wonder that stereotypes remained so strong.

Annual reports from West Virginia and Kentucky state mining departments provide another way to get at the issue, though the information they contain is puzzling. In publishing statistics on the ethnicity of their states' coal miners, in some years the reports listed one or two "Hebrew" miners in southern coalfield counties. However, during a few isolated years in the 1920s, the numbers suddenly took a considerable jump. It seems unlikely that eighty-five Hebrew miners worked in Harlan County in 1924 and none at all the following year, though that is what the Kentucky reports indicate. And it seems only slightly more probable that the number of Hebrew miners in Logan and McDowell Counties went from one in 1927 to twenty-eight in 1928 to thirty-eight in 1929 to zero in 1930, as reported in West Virginia statistics. The scarcity of Jewish miners revealed by other sources would suggest that these listings should be dismissed as inexplicable error, yet given the biases of those other sources, and lacking an adequate way to assess the data collection methods of state mining departments, it would be premature to reject them completely. They remain a possible, if mysterious, corrective to the perception that Jewish coal miners were virtually nonexistent.[63]

A discussion of other kinds of Jewish coal industry connections can be conducted on firmer ground. Some businessmen had passive investments in coal companies or coal lands. Former miner Sam Polon, a real estate developer, contracted with coal companies to sell off their houses when the companies decided to shed their residential holdings.[64] Several men attempted to play an active role in the mining business. Leo Schaffer, whose mayoral exploits were noted in chapter 1, leased seven hundred acres from local land baron Thomas McKell to start the Dunglen Coal Company in 1904. One of the smaller coal enterprises in Fayette County (in terms of tonnage mined), the company lasted until about 1910, with Schaffer as general manager or superintendent for most of those years. The mayor evidently brought his usual mode of conduct to his role as coal operator: in 1909, he and partner H. Lyon Smith were indicted for fraud, having attempted to secure a bank loan by claiming their company owned twelve hundred acres of land (it owned no land at all). The case was dismissed in 1913.[65]

The dubious Schaffer notwithstanding, Jewish businessmen who ventured into coal mining included some of the most prominent merchants in the coalfields. Many were tempted into the business during the World War I coal boom; some of these were saloon owners forced out of business by prohibition. I. L. Shor of Keystone bought an abandoned mine near Iaeger, West Virginia, in 1915. Wolf Bank and Israel Totz joined with the superintendent of Keystone's leading coal company to form the Rock Pocahontas Coal Company in 1917. That same year, Wolf's brother Harry and other relatives incorporated the Kimball Coal Company. Jake Levine and Adolph Goodman started up a Mingo County coal company the following year. By coal industry standards, all these firms were insignificant; their outputs placed them among the smallest mines in their counties. Rock Pocahontas never extracted any coal at all, at least none that showed up in state mining reports. And none of the companies lasted very long: Shor got out of the business in 1918, Harry Bank dissolved his company in 1920, and Jake Levine's mine operated until about 1924.[66]

This questionable record bears out the memories of interviewees who recalled their elders' forays into the coal business as less than successful. One man noted that his grandfather had made "a good bit of money" as a Pocahontas saloon owner and

then went into the coal business and "pretty much lost all he had." Another asserted that these normally astute businessmen, lacking knowledge of the coal industry, were destined to fail. "They saw people making money, and they thought
they could do it too," he remarked. "It didn't last very long because they didn't
know what they were doing." However, I. L. Shor claimed that his three-year stint
as coal company owner was a success, yielding him a profit of more than thirty
thousand dollars. "It was not because I was smart," he told an interviewer from a
Cincinnati Jewish newspaper in the 1940s. "I was just ready to work and G-d helped
me." One wonders whether divine intervention also helped Shor succeed in his
other real estate interests, which included accommodating some of the more wide-
open activities that took place at the height of Keystone's boomtown years.[67]

The most (perhaps only) lasting legacy of Jewish participation in the coal industry consists of the town of Totz, Kentucky. Harry Totz, whose parents brought
him and his siblings from Lithuania to Keystone in the 1890s, owned a Northfork
general store in 1921 when he acquired coal land in Harlan County. He and his
younger brother Abe moved to Kentucky and oversaw the construction of a mining complex and a town complete with post office and rail link. According to a
Harlan Enterprise retrospective, "After making their fortune and feeling content
with the fact they had started a community, the Totz brothers moved back to West
Virginia" in the mid-1920s, selling out to "an entrepreneur named Billips." However, a Totz descendant recalled that the brothers' Kentucky venture went bust. The
newspaper article indeed notes that "it wasn't until 1930 that Totz began to flourish," several years after Harry Totz had settled back into his role as a leading Northfork merchant. The town of Totz exists today, its mine recently in operation.[68]

Given their surroundings, it was inevitable that at least some Jews would be
drawn into coal mining. Their participation, though minuscule compared to others in the region and far from satisfactory, was more substantial than has generally been discerned. A 1936 *Fortune* magazine survey of American Jewish economic activity expressed a commonly held view: "It is doubtful whether the roster of
the leading twenty-five [coal] companies would show a single Jew from miner to
manager on up to the board of directors."[69] But their almost total invisibility is
misleading, as other local studies of Jewish communities also suggest. Robert
Levinson writes that despite the local stereotype that Jews would not work as miners, Jews in the California gold rush "did participate in the mining economy as
miners and prospectors," though they soon "turned to merchandising almost exclusively." Like coalfield Jews, they realized that their networks, experience, and
skills, not to mention their lack of knowledge of the mining industry, made them
more likely to achieve success in a subordinate sector of the economy.[70]

Resources for Survival, Strategies for Success

For coalfield retailers, success would not come easily. They faced other perils in addition to the difficulties created by the region's coal dependency. The two most

important were summed up in I. L. Shor's declaration: "Fire and Water were my only enemies."[71] With many coalfield towns ranged along creeks and rivers in narrow mountain valleys, floods were a major, potentially ruinous hazard. Meanwhile, the rapid growth of these towns resulted in slipshod building practices and inadequate infrastructures, so that fires easily turned into fast-spreading conflagrations.

Coalfield newspapers offered frequent accounts of fires and floods that devastated downtown business districts. The great Elkhorn Valley flood of June 1901 crippled businesses in many McDowell County towns, from marginal concerns such as Bessie Zaltzman's grocery store (a five-hundred-dollar loss) to Louis Totz's well-established "booze joint" (a fifteen-thousand-dollar loss). The Keystone conflagration of May 1917, "the biggest fire that ever visited the coal field," wiped out several Jewish businesses. As the *McDowell Recorder* pointed out, "Many of the buildings were frame and the fire swept so rapidly that nothing was saved from its path." The town's most prominent merchant suffered the most. One article estimated I. L. Shor's losses at more than one hundred thousand dollars. Shor recalled this fire as his "greatest financial set back . . . a total loss," as "no fire insurance was available in Keystone at that time." This was not surprising, since the town had seen at least seven major fires over the previous two years.[72]

Alternatively, some Jewish businesses succumbed to an entirely man-made calamity: the prohibition laws that struck West Virginia in 1914, Virginia in 1916, and Kentucky in 1919. Louis Schuchat had made "good money" in the liquor business in McDowell County, according to his daughter. "In prohibition [he] lost the whole bit," she related. "That's when my family started moving."[73] The three towns most dependent on the liquor trade, Keystone, Pocahontas, and Middlesboro, had the region's largest number of Jews in the 1910s. All businesses in these town suffered when prohibition caused them to languish.

The combination of floods, fires, prohibition, national recessions, and the chronic problems of the coal economy meant that coalfield merchants faced economic disaster on a regular basis, with one type of catastrophe often compounding another. After the McDowell County flood of 1901, Bessie Zaltzman managed to rebuild her grocery store and began purchasing residential real estate. She went on to lose three of her buildings in a 1914 fire (including her own home and all her household goods) and once again endured a blaze that destroyed her home in 1917. Pioneering Keystone merchant Wolf Bank had seen his business interests diminished by prohibition more than a decade before the Depression all but finished him off. In Middlesboro, shopkeepers caught in the devastating flood of 1929 were just starting to sort out their losses when the stock market crashed. Louis Sturm's store was one of many ruined in the deluge. He struggled for years to pay off his debts while reestablishing a store in nearby LaFollette, Tennessee, in the Depression-ravaged 1930s.[74]

Between 1929 and 1932, one historian states, "the industrial economy of West Virginia collapsed." The state's economy was "among the worst in the entire country" and conditions were most dire in the coalfields. A 1933 government

survey determined that 63 percent of Mingo County families qualified as "destitute," while percentages in other coalfield counties ranged from 22 to 59 percent.
Store closings left "gaping holes" in Harlan's business district, a local historian
notes. Interviewees recounted the travails of leading Jewish businessmen. Eugene
Lopinsky "lost everything." Wolf Bank's brother Harry was "ruined." Rudy Eiland's grocery business went under. Adolph Goodman lost his bank, and the
savings of the immigrant workers he catered to, in the stock market crash, while
Sam Polon and Louis Fink lost their own fortunes the same way. With the most
prominent businesses in trouble, smaller enterprises faced even more desperate
circumstances.[75]

Clearly, success in the coalfields was hard-earned—and once achieved was not
entirely secure. Bankruptcies struck Jewish merchants large and small. Though
the early Depression years saw a disproportionate share, the region's reliance on
credit meant that any downturn in the coal economy, any uninsured fire loss,
could sink a retail business. In 1889, Pocahontas merchant pioneer Michael Bloch
and his partner Lena Baach placed their property under trusteeship because
"pressing demands against them" left them "unable further to carry on their said
business in justice to their creditors, as well as to themselves." Their court petition
stated, "It is desirous that the services of their clerks, who are in indigent circumstances, shall be paid," including Lena Baach's twenty-year-old son Sol, owed
$381.33 in back wages. The business also owed money to Lena's husband Jacob, "a
very poor man." After securing a loan from local developer Alexander St. Clair to
pay its debts, Bloch and Company went on to become the most prominent department store in Pocahontas.[76]

Despite their trials and tribulations, there is little evidence of poverty among
coalfield Jews. Occasionally congregations stepped in to aid local families. The
Welch Hebrew Ladies Aid Society sent five dollars to "a family reported in need"
in 1916, and a few years later sent fifteen dollars to "a Jewish man in Welch, who
is in destitute circumstances." The Beckley B'nai B'rith chapter established an
emergency fund to assist "people in the community who didn't have money,"
stated one interviewee, "and believe it or not there were a few." The fund helped
pay funeral or medical expenses and meet other emergency needs. Interestingly,
however, most charity doled out to coreligionists went to "out-of-town Jewish
beggars" passing through the area rather than local families. In a 1926 speech,
communal leader Ida Bank noted that the Williamson Jewish Ladies Guild had
been founded in 1913 largely "to take care of the needy Jewish traveling poor who
were very numerous at that time." It is unknown why the town attracted transient
Jews; perhaps its position on the Norfolk and Western main line played a role. In
1941, Williamson's B'nai B'rith, having "been bothered lately with schnorrers
[Jewish beggars]," established a schnorrers fund to aid "the stranded people who
are often visiting our community and are in need of help." The Beckley emergency fund also aided transient Jews who "got stuck" in town.[77]

The paucity of local Jews needing charity suggests that destitution within coalfield Jewish communities was uncommon even during hard times. A survey conducted by Hebrew Union College in 1935, after the worst of the Depression had passed, found the economic state of coalfield Jews ranged from "fair" in Middlesboro and Williamson to "moderate" in Beckley to "good" in Logan, with no Jews on public relief in any of the towns. Yet until the World War II era, the standard of living for middling Jewish shopkeepers was not high. Most families lived above or behind their stores and many took in boarders. Extended families often lived together in crowded conditions, as suggested by this 1915 newspaper brief about a Pocahontas fire: "Joe Matz and L. Magrill had trunks, refrigerators, and groceries on their back porches and these were ruined. Mr. Ferimer's mother was sleeping in a room on the rear end of the house with the head of the bed next to the wall, also a little child of Mr. Magrill was in the same room."[78]

Frequent moves from town to town contributed to a less than comfortable life-style. One interviewee recounted the following family history: his father sold his Mount Hope, West Virginia, business in the early 1930s after a fire, moved back to Baltimore and opened a restaurant, went broke and returned to Mount Hope, opened a clothing store and went broke, removed to Charleston, returned to the New River region and opened a furniture store in Beckley just as the region emerged from the Depression.[79] Rather than poverty, instability and insecurity characterized life for many coalfield Jewish families.

While the coalfield economic scene offered its own special challenges, instability marked Jewish enterprise in both Europe and America. Small family businesses— undercapitalized, credit-driven, relying for their customer base on rural or lower-income groups—lived on the economic edge, vulnerable to the larger forces that swirled around them. As one example among many, Jewish businesses in mid-nineteenth-century Buffalo manifested an impressive 57 percent failure rate.[80] Yet while the overarching narrative of American Jewry as ethnic success story memorializes the hardships suffered in the sweatshops and tenements of teeming urban neighborhoods, it glosses over the long history of setbacks family businesses endured on their way to middle-class (and upper-middle-class) prosperity.

The lack of attention paid to the small business struggle conceals a significant cultural resource immigrant Jews brought with them from Europe. With generations of commercial experience behind them, Jewish families were familiar with life on the economic fringe and well acquainted with business failures caused by forces beyond their control. In the old country, they had contended with rural poverty, discriminatory laws, and flare-ups of antisemitism that provoked economically calamitous pogroms, forced expulsions, and boycotts. In the United States, they confronted recessions, fires, and natural disasters. Though the problems had changed, their response remained the same. Jewish entrepreneurs "did not lose spirit when they lost their business," says Ewa Morawska. "They remained hopeful that, if they 'kept at it,' they would stand back on their feet." Their acceptance of "the possibility of frequent failure and relocation" enabled Jews to become risk takers who might well be considered "exemplary American capitalists," states David Gerber. Comparative historian Walter Zenner finds that both the cycle of success and failure and the ability to persist in an unstable commercial environment are common to ethnic groups with historical experience as middleman minorities.[81]

Everywhere, Jewish entrepreneurs relied on similar strategies to cope with hostile economic conditions, uncertainty, and defeat. Their networks were their most important asset, providing job opportunities, information, and the all-important credit needed to start a business, expand, or outlast hard times. For their work force, they relied on members of the immediate family as well as extended kin. While these strategies were common among immigrant groups, Jews had evolved other approaches as well. Flexibility was a key attribute of Jewish businesses. Most needed little start-up capital and could be easily moved or altered as conditions changed. A related trait was creativity, the ability to improvise, popularly expressed by Jewish immigrants in a phrase brought from Europe, "a *yiddishe kop*." As the ethnography *Life Is with People* explains, "*Shtetl* folk feel that 'head,' *kop*—and especially '*yiddishe kop*'—is the chief capital in any enterprise, and sometimes the only one. . . . It is characterized by rapidity of orientation and grasping of a problem, intuitive perception, and swift application to the situation."[82]

Coalfield Jews inherited these economic survival mechanisms and employed them to good effect. The networks and kinship ties that brought them to the region continued to support them as they made their way through the coal economy, helping them advance during the booms and persevere during the busts. The move from peddler or clerk to store owner was rarely accomplished without assistance from family, other local Jews, or distant Jewish wholesalers with liberal credit policies. More often than not, those who offered assistance benefited as much as those who received help—the "aid" was decidedly "mutual." Wholesalers enlarged their markets; merchants got low-cost labor and the opportunity to expand their businesses. Many county-seat shopkeepers sent relatives out to peddle in the coal camps or open branches in smaller towns. Some set up relatives in business and profited as silent partners. When the time came to retire, the first generation sold out to the second. As such arrangements proliferated, Jewish-owned stores in coalfield towns formed an interconnected web of people directly or indirectly related to one another. In the 1930s, for example, Goldie Scott Jaffe and her husband bought a store in Cumberland, Kentucky, from one of her uncles, just down the street from a store owned by another uncle, who had purchased his from her father.[83]

Partnerships offered an expeditious way to achieve the all-important goal of self-employment. Often, but not always, they involved relatives. One interviewee recalled that after his father's Mount Hope business failed in the 1930s, father and sons worked as traveling salesmen for an out-of-town firm. "From there we would all pool our money, my father, my brother, and I," eventually saving enough to go back into business. When Williamson pioneer merchant David Brown's store declined about 1914, "in desperation," he offered his new son-in-law Harry Schwachter "a fifty-fifty deal partnership" that saved the business. Brothers frequently banded together. The Liebman brothers, Michaelson brothers, Euster brothers, and Sneider brothers were just some of the sibling business alliances that existed through the years.[84]

Outside the family, local Jewish communities provided timely financial aid. One retired merchant recalled that it was common for Jews in the New River area to "set each other up" in business by making small loans. During hard times this support took on more significance. Although "going broke" constituted a family crisis, he acknowledged, "there was a pretty good size Jewish community. They were all very close knit . . . they would loan money to each other." These internal lending activities reflected a self-help tradition that extended back to the mutual-aid societies of Eastern Europe. Coalfield Jewish aid societies were fairly small, so most mutual aid took place between individuals, outside of the formal communal structure. As Ewa Morawska notes, small communities did not have the organizational resources of Jews in large cities, and relied on less systematized ways to fulfill their communal obligations.[85]

The support coalfield Jews offered each other withstood considerable internal conflict. Jewish merchants were competitors in a tough business climate, and their rivalries ranged from friendly to bitter. One man recalled that shop owners in Beckley used to watch each other carefully on Saturday nights to see when to close: no one wanted to be the first. Evidently this practice got a bit out of hand in Williamson, because in 1911 the local newspaper announced that merchants had agreed on a policy to close at 8:30 P.M. every evening except "payday night and the three nights following and Saturday night," so that their clerks could "have some evenings to themselves." The local courts frequently arbitrated internal Jewish disagreements over partnerships gone awry, real estate disputes, failure to pay debts, and other matters.[86]

One case shows how seriously some Jewish merchants took competition from their coreligionists. In the 1910s, David Klein operated a store in Mullens, West Virginia, in newly opened coal territory that few other merchants had discovered. After deciding to move his store into a larger space, he was horrified to learn that his landlord had rented the spot he was vacating to Eugene Lopinsky, one of the region's leading merchants. He offered to pay the landlord double the rent to keep his old space, but the contract with Lopinsky had been signed. When four of Lopinsky's employees arrived to unload their merchandise, Klein locked them out of the building. The landlord gave them permission to break in, and after they did so, Klein had them arrested for breaking and entering with intent to steal. After extricating themselves from the charge, one of the employees sued Klein for malicious prosecution—and the West Virginia Supreme Court concurred.[87]

Yet even fierce competition did not break the bonds that connected Jewish families. And beyond family and community, Jews were linked to acquaintances and even strangers through business ties and cultural affinities. Though Kentuckian David Scott brought numerous relatives to the coalfields, he acquired his own business from a stranger. In 1918, while passing through Pineville, he spotted a clothing store called the Baltimore Bargain House. Guessing that the store was Jewish owned, he went in to see if he knew anyone. The owner had just been drafted into the army and needed to sell out. Although Scott had no savings, the man liked him and, as a fellow Jewish entrepreneur, trusted him. He sold him the store entirely on credit. In 1910s McDowell County, the Jewish business presence was so strong that one job seeker felt confident enough to place this ad in the *McDowell Recorder:* "Young Man, (Hebrew,) good education, business abilities, knowledge of shorthand, bookkeeping and typewriting, desires position in store or office. Excellent reference."[88]

Jewish wholesalers assiduously cultivated relationships with small-town shopkeepers. The region's major supplier to Jewish businesses, the Baltimore Bargain House, strove to keep a personal connection with its customers despite its vast size. A 1906 catalogue urged merchants to make themselves "perfectly at home" on its premises when they came to buy, offering "free desk room and the services of a stenographer if you desire them." The catalogue, filled with chatty news and advice, even promised, "We'll Take Your Photograph Free of Charge." A coalfield native who accompanied his father on buying trips as a child recalled that Jacob Epstein himself gave him a twenty-dollar gold piece for his bar mitzvah.[89]

Close ties between wholesalers and retailers contributed to retailers' ability to recover quickly from misfortune. Just two weeks after the massive Keystone fire of May 1917, Harry Budnick announced in a *McDowell Times* ad, "Burned Out But Still In The Ring. Just Returned From Market With A Select Line Of Goods To Start Anew." He immediately began doing business across from the site of his old store. Shortly after a 1922 fire in Yukon, West Virginia, destroyed the Hyman Underselling Store, the firm placed an ad in the *McDowell Recorder* stating, "Arrived in Yukon with car loads of goods to re-establish business."[90]

The support that coalfield Jewish merchants derived from local and distant networks made success possible, but that doesn't mean it made it easy. Small family businesses required long hours of work to be even marginally successful. Stores opened early and stayed open late. Common closing times were 10:00 P.M. on weekdays and midnight on Saturdays. Jews who grew up in the region recalled the endless hours put in by their fathers, from early morning to well into the night, six days per week. But not just their fathers: as one person stated, both parents "were so busy with the business, they never had time for anything else." And not just their parents: Marilou Schwachter Sniderman recalled that she and her siblings worked at the family store "as soon as we could see over the counter."[91]

Coalfield Jewish businesses were true family concerns, with wives working alongside husbands to help make ends meet. At the very least, wives "helped out" in the store, especially on all-important payday Saturdays, when the stores were crowded with shoppers. But "helping out," though the accepted term to describe a wide range of women's economic activity, greatly understates the contributions to the household economy made by women. Motivated by varying combinations of family need and personal fulfillment, they often took on significant responsibilities in the family business. Some wives functioned as their husbands' business partners in decision making and division of labor. The division was often based on personality, with the more outgoing partner serving customers and the more reserved one handling behind-the-scenes tasks such as bookkeeping. Husband-and-wife teamwork did not necessarily diminish with increased prosperity; if the family owned more than one store, the wife sometimes managed a store.[92]

Women carried out their business activities with confidence derived from a cultural tradition that had long recognized them as important economic contributors. While many immigrant groups had a history of married women helping to earn the family income, for Jewish women, religious custom made a major economic role even more acceptable. In Eastern Europe, the cultural ideal for Jewish men was a life devoted to religious study. A woman who operated a business to support the family while her husband pursued his scholarship earned respect and praise. Although old-country economic realities made this ideal possible for few families, the concept of married woman as breadwinner was ingrained in traditional culture. Jews who grew up in the coalfields recounted instances of grandmothers operating small shops in Eastern Europe, New York, or Baltimore, and their daughters built on their example.[93]

Some female entrepreneurs started their own ventures; others inherited businesses as widows and daughters. Coalfield directories from 1900 to 1920 listed married Jewish women as proprietors of clothing stores, dry-goods stores, and confectioneries. In later years, they owned pharmacies, jewelry stores, and even an auto supply business. Bertha "Mother" Horr operated a popular café in Middlesboro in the 1920s and 1930s while her husband William ran a hotel. Blanche Sohn owned a Williamson confectionery and then a dry-goods store while her husband Eli operated a saloon and then a clothing store. When the couple went into business together, she did the buying, according to a newspaper item that informed readers: "Mrs. Eli Sohn is in the markets purchasing spring millinery. . . . Mr. Eli Sohn is painting the front of his store building in a very handsome style." Widowed in 1912 at age twenty-seven, Mollie ("M. V.") Gaskell became a respected merchant and communal leader as proprietor of the Williamson Bargain House.[94]

Women involved in business nevertheless retained sole responsibility for maintenance of the household. One interviewee remarked that for her mother, the family store "was her life." She spent long hours in the store and enjoyed it—and could often be found cleaning the house at 2:00 A.M.. Another woman recalled that her mother "worked every day, worked hard" in their small family dry-goods store, doing everything from serving customers to altering clothing to traveling with her husband to New York on buying trips. She saw her mother as a role model of strength and ability, proudly calling her a "tremendous buyer." Yet torn between work and home duties, her mother had "no social life" (though she enjoyed splurging on the opera during buying trips). Her mother's activities caused some hardship for the family; as the daughter put it, "We were latchkey kids." Single mothers, of course, faced the most difficult time. One man recalled that he and his widowed mother were "poor as church mice" in the 1910s. She took in boarders and worked in a grocery store to keep them going.[95]

Women's economic activities were respected by both the Jewish community and the broader society. A 1920 obituary made special note that Pauline Josephy of Welch had been "active in business and charitable circles" and had "assisted her husband in the conduct of a flourishing store."[96] Yet the story of Bessie Zaltzman of Keystone reveals it was possible to overstep the boundaries of accepted female behavior. This strong-willed Russian immigrant arrived in Keystone in 1896 and divorced her husband about 1905. She managed to acquire a cow and scraped together a living for herself and her three children, selling butter and milk. Eventually she had a few cows and a small shop to sell her wares. She became a landlady, owner of small residential properties, overcoming crises that included floods, fires—and lawsuits. Her skirmishes with Jewish businessmen occupied the local courts for years, and a hint of moral disapproval on the part of her opponents runs through court records. One man, whom she had sued over a business transaction, advised her that she needed to get herself a husband. Her classic retort: "I don't have to have no husband. I have got good children and I have got good property." Bessie prevailed in the end: at her death in 1949, her assets totaled more than eighty-four thousand dollars.[97]

Certainly the Jewish tradition of female entrepreneurship ran up against the modern middle-class notion that a woman's place was in the home. East European Jews in America (especially men) soon adopted middle-class norms that restricted married women to the domestic sphere.[98] While nationally this transformation began as early as the 1920s, it apparently occurred later in the coalfields, given the amount of economic activity demonstrated by Jewish women in the 1920s and 1930s. After the immigrant generation passed away, it became less common for married women to be heavily involved in business. Martha Albert of Williamson helped run the family store into the 1990s. She enjoyed the business world, she explained, because "I grew up in it." Yet she saw herself as an exception. More typical was Annie Fink of Beckley, described by her son as "99 percent a homemaker" whose ambition "was to be a good hausfrau." Since she left school in the sixth grade in Baltimore to work in the needle trade, the middle-class ideal might have come as welcome relief from a life of toil. (But she did continue to "help out" in the store on Saturdays.) Single daughters in the post–World War II era continued to work, increasingly as teachers, stenographers, nurses, and social workers rather than store clerks. Alice Shein, daughter of a pioneering coalfield family, managed a Williamson radio station in the 1940s and 1950s. Jewish female doctors and dentists worked in the region as early as the 1930s, when Bertha Horr's daughter Goldie, a divorced mother, set up a Middlesboro podiatry practice.[99]

Jewish families needed the economic contributions of women to survive and thrive, given the ups and downs of the coal economy. Yet women tended to be dismissive of their own efforts. Asked to describe how she had gained the skills to become a successful businesswoman, one woman said deprecatingly, "All you have to do is make one trip to New York and you're a buyer." Women used the phrase "helping out" to cover everything from an occasional Saturday turn at the cash register to major responsibilities. Esther Baloff, not one to hide behind false modesty, stated that she "helped" in the family business "when they needed me," especially during World War II, when a shortage of clerks and a rise in business drew her into the store. Only as an aside did she reveal, "Also I did the bookwork and correspondence." Perhaps the women internalized societal attitudes toward women's work even as their cultural background, family necessity, and drive for personal fulfillment led them to enter fully into the world of small business. Interestingly, Jews who grew up in the region, men and women in their seventies and eighties looking back on their childhood, revealed a sense of pride in their mothers' strength, capability, and resourcefulness in the economic realm. One man summed up the feelings of many when he stated approvingly, "My mother had a good business head on her."[100]

A good business head certainly came in handy, whether possessed by male or female. Jewish store owners prided themselves on their mercantile abilities. A longtime Williamson merchant, discussing how Jewish families managed to thrive in a rocky economic landscape, exclaimed, "They were good merchants! You know the old saying it takes a *yiddishe kop*." When asked to elaborate on what made them "good merchants," she offered that Jews did well because they "had to survive." Her seemingly circular explanation makes sense in the context of a long history of surmounting obstacles. Rather than calling attention to particular traits, she instinctively reached back for the underlying motivation: Jews developed successful business strategies because they had to.[101]

Some coalfield Jews pinpointed specific attributes they believed helped Jewish merchants succeed. Salesmanship was at the top of the list. "Jews were always great salesmen," observed the son of a leading Welch businessman. "It didn't require great capital, all you needed was something to sell." A retired Beckley store owner noted, "In their businesses they were great. They could call all their customers by name." The merchants drew on a tradition of regard for the art of selling. A former eastern Kentucky peddler was merely repeating a familiar boast in Jewish folklore when he told his son-in-law, "I sold women curtain goods who didn't even have a window!" Most Jewish merchants took pride in their interpersonal skills and their cordial relationships with customers and genuinely enjoyed the sociable give and take of buyer-seller interaction.[102]

Marilou Sniderman's portrayal of the partnership between her father and grandfather shows that not all Jewish merchants were great salesmen—and that there was more to salesmanship than knowing your customers' names. Her grandfather David Brown had little skill as a merchant. His "drab emporium" in Williamson was going downhill until son-in-law Harry Schwachter joined him. Schwachter's first move was to change the name of the store and put up a "big new sign." He then took out a bank loan to remodel, causing Brown to "run around wringing his hands, 'the boy's gone crazy altogether, we'll go bankrupt yet.'" But the risk paid off, as the younger man's marketing methods rejuvenated the failing business. Recognizing the importance of an attractive shopping environment, and being willing to take financial risks to achieve it, was part of astute retailing. Not that Schwachter neglected the personal side of salesmanship. Says his daughter, "Dad made every customer feel like a queen." His shoppers "floated out the doorway with their packages with a sense of well-being."[103]

A good business head involved creativity, openness to innovation, and ability to improvise during bad times and good. In the 1950s, a car peddler in the New River coal camps started to have problems collecting on his accounts as mining layoffs increased. His business suffering along with the local economy, he walked into a hardware store one day and saw a fabrics display. He bought his wife some fabric to make herself a dress—and then realized that other families were probably resorting to the same tactic to stretch their household budgets. He promptly threw out his old stock and went into the fabric business. Borrowing one thousand dollars from a family member, he spent three hundred on material and seven hundred on advertising. His idea worked, and soon he expanded into the upholstery business, reasoning that people would sooner re-cover their old furniture than buy new. Another former car peddler explained how small retailers scrambled to take advantage of good times. "We'd sell anything we could possibly get our hands on," he said, from watches to pots and pans, lamps, end tables, mattresses—whatever could fit inside or on top of a car.[104]

The tendency of coalfield Jewish merchants to move into different lines of business as the economy dictated, their ability to bounce back from failure, and their propensity to take on low capital enterprises all denote the flexibility needed to negotiate the region's fluctuating economic conditions. Many entrepreneurs pursued multiple ventures to get ahead. Between them, Max Ofsa, I. L. Shor, and Wolf Bank engaged in twenty businesses in Keystone before 1930. Ofsa, a real jack-of-all-trades, worked variously as a bicycle repairman, mechanic, plumber, concrete block manufacturer, oil and coal dealer, and owner of a steam laundry, restaurant, and grocery store. Jews owned several of the region's theaters, a business that involved relatively small capital risk (movies were rented cheaply from distributors, who got a percentage of the box office) and offered a low-cost product, two characteristics that facilitated survival during inevitable downturns. Even so, the son of one Jewish theater owner recalled that during the Depression his father "worked like hell to survive, and thank God for bank night" (a lottery promotion used at that time by theaters around the country). "It saved the theater."[105]

Some merchants applied their business acumen to finding just the right niche that would allow them to avoid competition with company stores and other retailers. After suffering a Depression-induced bankruptcy, James and Naomi Pickus of Beckley decided to aim for the "high fashion" market with their next venture; Pickus's two brothers already catered to lower-income groups. Other families responded to overcrowded retail conditions with the time-honored strategy of moving to another town. Though the trend was to relocate from smaller towns to county seats, circumstances sometimes required a move in the opposite direction. When Milton Gottlieb took over his father's clothing store in the early Depression years, "things were rough in Welch, too much competition," his brother recalled. The business failed and the Gottliebs moved to War, a mining town, where a coal industry upswing enabled their new store to flourish.[106]

While some merchants chose to set themselves apart by specializing, others competed to meet the basic consumer needs of the region's large working class. Their survival strategies echoed methods their ancestors had employed in Eastern Europe. Explains historian Andrew Heinze, the "success of Jewish commerce was based on the tendency to sell . . . at a low margin of profit in order to achieve a rapid turnover of merchandise."[107] Immigrants transplanted this "Jewish style of selling" to New York City's Lower East Side—and to the coalfields, where low pricing was the most effective way to compete with company stores. Car peddlers exemplified the style, with what one man referred to as a "scattershot approach" based on a high volume of small transactions. The region's numerous discount or "underselling" stores were invariably owned by Jews, while other Jewish-owned stores also strove to keep prices low and turnover high. The use of family members as employees kept costs down. Buying wares at the end of the season, when wholesalers slashed their prices, also helped. Rapid turnover could also be achieved by offering credit, in which case a low pricing strategy did not apply: credit transactions always involved a high markup on goods. High default rates, however, meant that profit margins often remained slim.

Reliance on a high turnover meant that these low capital enterprises devoted a large portion of their resources to promoting their wares. The fabrics entrepreneur who started his business by investing 70 percent of his funds in advertising offers a striking example. Coalfield Jewish retailers believed in the power of promotion and put much of their creativity into convincing people to buy. Their ads may have lacked subtlety, but they got their point across. A 1900 ad for Hurvitz and Lopinsky's Great Eastern Bargain House plainly spelled out their retailing strategy: "Our aim is to sell our groceries so as to keep selling, and the only way to do that is to sell at low prices." There were attempts at topical humor, as in a 1902 ad that proclaimed "THE STRIKE! In the Hard Coal Region Will Not Be as Hard on the Miners as our Cheap Prices Are on our Competitors." More common were hackneyed protestations of distress. A 1911 double-page ad for J. Levine's Williamson dry-goods store offers a particularly exuberant (if not quite convincing) sample of the genre: "Face to Face with Trouble: My creditors are clamoring for their money.... I am forced to sacrifice my stock.... No such sale of such gigantic proportions has ever been held in Mingo County.... A tremendous slaughter of modern merchandise ... no fake, but a bonofide [*sic*] sale to save my good name.... My customers will profit from my misfortune. Everything will be on sale as advertised, and is backed up by my honorable business career in Mingo County."[108]

Such hyperbole suggests that the quest for sales could result in overly aggressive marketing tactics. Some Jewish merchants pursued somewhat questionable methods to achieve success, and a few developed reputations that conformed to negative stereotypes about Jews. The recollections of both Jews and non-Jews include less-than-rosy memories of certain hard-driving Jewish businessmen. One former customer recalled a leading merchant as "gracious to me and my family, as long as you paid your bills." Trying to avoid making a derogatory comment, she continued, "He just wanted his money when he wanted it. He never did bother my family." As civil court records show, relations between Jewish merchants and their customers were not always pleasant. Some lawsuits involved charges of fraud against the merchant, though mostly they involved merchants suing to recover debts.[109]

Generally, however, Jewish merchants got along well with their coalfield clientele and gained the respect of the local populace through their comportment of their businesses. Beyond the obvious motivation that good customer relations were good for trade, they also saw themselves as contributing members of their communities. In small towns, work and social life were intertwined; being a good neighbor and conducting business honorably were one and the same thing. Moreover, they were inheritors of a Jewish ethical tradition that offered explicit precepts regarding the proper performance of trade. "Acknowledging the importance of commerce in Jewish life," notes Andrew Heinze, "the Talmud had set forth a series of injunctions to maintain a high standard of conduct.... The revered texts of Jewish law insisted on honest representation of merchandise and on generosity toward consumers." He asserts, "These points of commerce would not be unanimously upheld, but they shaped the method of Jewish merchants in both Europe and America."[110]

While coalfield merchants were not necessarily learned in the fine points of Jewish law, they recognized this aspect of their tradition. As a Beckley businessman explained, it was part of Judaism "to be fair in your dealings." Upholding the standards of the religion was "a way of life" as well as a source of satisfaction to him and, he believed, many of his fellow Jewish merchants. "Most of us were fairly upright and honest people," he concluded. A Welch Jewish native agreed that "it was a part and parcel of their religion" for Jews to conduct themselves with "honesty and integrity.... That's why there was strong respect for Jewish merchants."[111]

Newspaper articles and obituaries offer evidence of high public regard for Jewish businesspeople, from the "square dealing" Joseph Lopinsky to Middlesboro's Sam Weinstein, "very popular with the boys at the mines." Recollections of Jews and gentiles reveal the same for less-well-known merchants. Esther Baloff related how her family earned the good will of the people of LaFollette. When the local mines shut down in the early 1920s, the Baloffs' store started issuing credit and accepting scrip, giving cash back in return. Later, she claimed, people said they "would have starved to death" if not for the Baloffs. Harry Berman grew up in his family's Matewan store and recalled plenty of hard times: "People that needed things and they didn't have the money you know, . . . my father he helped a lot of 'em out. I guess he lost a lot of money, but that's alright. But you make it back someway or another."[112]

Jews seemingly suffered from a major disadvantage compared to many of the region's merchants. Their small numbers and lack of a working-class base meant that they could not build their businesses on the consumer needs of their own particular group. But this was a familiar position for them. In fact, because of their background as members of a minority that had provided commercial services to others, Jewish immigrants were likely to be more comfortable dealing with people from different cultures than other merchants. This could well have given them a competitive edge in establishing good customer relations and gaining trade in the multicultural coalfields. While most of the region's ethnic groups relied on kinship networks and family labor to develop their own commercial contingents, the background of coalfield Jews furnished them with a variety of resources others may have lacked.[113] These resources enabled them to not only meet the challenges of the coal economy but also develop and sustain a retail niche that lasted into the late twentieth century.

Within this niche, individual families struggled, survived, maintained, and prospered. Those who played pioneering roles in their towns had especially notable careers. Overall, almost 60 percent of Jews in the occupational sample attained the status of business proprietor at some point in their lives (see table 3). Thirty-five percent of clerks and 77 percent of peddlers went on to own stores. Yet assessing Jewish economic mobility is a tricky task. Many of the businesses that Jews established were marginal, so the fact of ownership reveals only so much. The peddler-to-merchant progression occasionally went the other way, with some owners reverting to the status of clerk, salesman, or peddler (and then sometimes reemerging as owners again). Even leading Jewish families did not escape misfortune. Also, those who did not manage to overcome the region's business hazards tended to move away, thus becoming statistically invisible.

The "people who stayed" did indeed develop "thriving businesses," as the Williamson merchant quoted earlier insisted. Yet her generalization masks a complex reality. Economic well-being for many families did not arrive until the second generation came of age, around the time the region recovered from the Depression. A second-generation Beckley merchant acknowledged that his father "never did succeed" until going into business with his sons after World War II: "he sort of plugged along." A native of southeastern Kentucky stated that his father's business career was "sort of an up and down thing," with the family moving around quite a bit. During the boom of the late thirties to early fifties, those who had not yet achieved success, or who had seen once-strong businesses languish in the Depression, now had the opportunity to flourish. It is this period interviewees recall when they describe coalfield Jewish communities as "prosperous."[114]

For the most part, Jewish families found the economic security, stability, and indeed, prosperity they were seeking when they came to the region. Some became wealthy. In the 1920s, the Schwachters were considered by Williamson townspeople to be "just plain rich," while Sam Polon did well enough to lose over half a million dollars in the 1929 stock market crash—yet maintain his position as a leading Welch businessman.[115] Most families did not reach such exalted heights, but they managed to attain a middle- to upper-middle-class life-style that enabled them to live comfortably and send their children to college. In the coalfields, where the structural failings and endemic inequalities of the coal industry caused hardship for a large portion of the population, such middle-class families could be considered part of the elite.

Regional Transformation and the Role of the Middleman

Although the coal and timber industries drove Central Appalachia's transformation from a relatively isolated agrarian back country to a rural-industrial society thoroughly integrated into the national (and international) economy, they were not the only agents of change. Rural historians have long recognized the importance of local retailers in connecting the countryside to the national market system. Merchants, peddlers, and mail-order catalogues disseminated modern products, styles, and sensibilities, spreading a "consumer ethic" through the countryside.[116]

Across the United States (though at different times in different places), consumerism helped forge a national culture out of a polyglot American society. City and country dwellers alike engaged in this "Americanization" process, yet through consumption patterns that reflected and incorporated their own cultural traditions. Parallels can be drawn between scattered country folk and immigrants crowded into cities, between Jewish peddlers in the countryside and Jewish street vendors on New York's Lower East Side. By continuing their old-country strategy of catering to underserved, excluded groups, Jewish retailers helped both the rural and urban masses fashion a modern American life-style and identity through the purchase of inexpensive commodities.[117]

The impact of obscure Jewish retailers in country towns and city neighborhoods can be likened as well to that of their famous *landsmen,* the Hollywood moguls and department store "merchant princes" who had such a marked impact on U.S. society. Indeed, as historian Andrew Heinze points out, all partook of the same "buoyant spirit" of an old commercial tradition transplanted to a society that gave it scope to operate. Given the links that tied small, far-flung Jewish businesses to their sources of supply, the connection might have been more than just figurative. One non-Jewish resident of the coalfields recalled how a local Jewish theater owner made annual trips to Hollywood, where he reportedly hobnobbed with the rich and famous. Another insisted that the Lazarus family of Pocahontas was related to the Columbus-based Lazarus department store dynasty. While neither story can be taken as fact, they surely *could* be true. If nothing else, they reveal the extent to which coalfield Jewish retailers helped their fellow residents see their towns as linked to the larger world.[118]

The coalfield population of the early twentieth century included recently arrived immigrants and native country folk, black and white. They became drawn into the consumer culture as mass produced goods began to flow into the region via peddlers, company stores, and independent merchants. As elsewhere, coalfield residents participated in modern consumerism according to their own needs and desires, guided by their own customary practices. Natives and immigrants alike sought to retain rural customs of self-sufficiency and communal reciprocity while indulging in new consumer activities. Gardening, hunting and livestock keeping, home food preservation and clothes making, bartering and haggling coexisted with modern shopping.[119]

Conversely, the uncertainties of coal mining—the danger of death or disability, the lack of job security—combined with easy credit in the form of coal company scrip to promote an "exaggerated consumptive desire" in mining towns. These factors "served to shape a value of short-term individual interests," states John Gaventa. It was "only rational" for miners to purchase goods while they had the chance. The stereotype of the free-spending coal miner was commonly accepted as fact by inhabitants of the region. As a retired Jewish merchant put it, "One thing about coal miners—they spent their money. They didn't save it."[120]

Scholars have just begun to address the emergence of a burgeoning consumer market in the Central Appalachian mountains. The commercial centers that arose with the timber boom "radiated the expanding consumerism of the modern American economy," states Ronald Lewis. "Where a few years earlier stood a vast wilderness," railroad and telegraph linked the region to the national marketplace and made a plethora of manufactured goods available. The methods retailers employed to import and promote their goods, their decisions concerning what and where and how to sell, helped to shape the contours of modern life in the region.[121]

In the coalfields, as elsewhere, peddlers of varying ethnicities served as the advance guard of consumer culture, and reminiscences of local residents testify to their impact. One woman recalled how peddlers walked for miles from Logan to the coal camps "with huge suitcases strapped to their backs." Descendants of Jewish peddlers offer further detail. Sam Aaron carried "shoe findings" through the mountains about 1900, while Max Soon peddled umbrellas in Mingo County in the 1920s. Sam Abrams peddled on horseback in the New River coalfield in the early 1920s, toting rugs, blankets, bedding, pots and pans, dishes, and other household wares. The presence of peddlers on horseback as late as the 1920s attests to the unevenness of regional development. And some of the items they carried, such as shoe findings, "yard goods," needles and thread, suggest an early stage in the advance of consumerism: people were still repairing their own shoes and making their own clothes, purchasing imported raw materials from itinerants.[122]

Local hubs extended the commercial spirit deep into the back country. Peddlers who traveled into the hinterlands generally lived in the region's larger towns, near the rail lines that linked them to their goods. Town-based Jewish merchants sent employees into the countryside to peddle or take orders for goods. If prospects seemed favorable they opened satellite stores, so that some newly created, seemingly isolated hamlets boasted a Jewish-owned store. For example, the Henry brothers of Keystone operated a branch in Coeburn, Virginia, by 1900, while the Hymans of Keystone had a store in tiny Yukon in the 1920s. From their base in Sewell, Lopinsky and Hurvitz spread their Great Eastern Bargain House chain to several coalfield towns.[123]

Rather than sending employees into the countryside, some retailers encouraged their rural customers to come to them. A 1902 newspaper ad placed by the Weinsteins urged, "The country readers of the *Republican* are advised to give these hustlers a visit. Why let your town cousins reap the benefit of these sales? Come to Middlesboro, visit the stores of H. Weinstein & Bro." Merchants understood that their market extended beyond the boundaries of their bustling towns. By targeting surrounding areas with their advertisements, they purposely contributed to the throngs that gathered in county seats and other hubs on Saturdays. As a Jewish woman who lived in a county seat in timber-rich Pocahontas County, West Virginia, explained, "Our customers came from the area about fifty miles around Marlinton. The roads were not as good as they are now, and a whole family, lumbermen or farmers, would come to Marlinton for a day of shopping. We did a lot of advertising, including a monthly magazine, and while we were in Marlinton [between 1916 and 1930] we doubled the size of the store."[124]

As major advertisers, Jewish merchants became leading conveyors of modern styles and sensibilities. In 1901, the *Fayette Journal* happily announced that the Great Eastern Bargain House had contracted for "3000 inches of advertising" for the coming year, "the largest contract for advertising ever made in Fayette County." Retailers' ads often focused on low prices and appealed to the reader's rational urge to save money—but increasingly they enticed the imagination. They cultivated a taste for the fashionable, associating their products with urban style, sophistication, and excitement. A 1900 Great Eastern Bargain House ad emphasized that the store's milliner was trained in Baltimore and would be "pleased to give the ladies her personal attention," while a 1911 ad for Sohn's men's clothing store of Williamson noted that its "Fabric and Cutter are from the famous House of Schloss Bros." If the ads can be believed, city-trained milliners routinely landed in the coalfields from Baltimore or Cincinnati, bringing "the newest and latest" clothing, "strictly up-to-date in make, style and shades."[125]

The luster of modernity was not limited to clothing. In 1911, theater owner Joseph Lopinsky imported the "latest and best" moving pictures for Welch's new opera house. A 1920 ad for real estate developer Moses Hyman celebrated the town's increasingly metropolitan character: "There is more building going on in Welch at this time than you will find in most towns three times its size. . . . Welch is fastly taking on the appearance of a real city. . . . When you get off the train, your eyes are greeted with a sea of faces—multitudes of people, rushing automobiles and the success of its business and professional people are written on their faces."[126]

Newspaper publishers were delighted with Jewish retailers for the revenues they provided—and because the store owners were engaged in a project dear to their own hearts: bringing modern business trends into the region. Newspapers were not just venues for advertising, they were eager partners in promoting new retailing methods. Often it is difficult to tell the difference between articles and ads. A 1914 *McDowell Recorder* article headlined "A New Way Store" extolled the opening of a Welch department store by "the well-known Eugene Lopinsky who is recognized as a progressive man of business." The store featured innovations such as a "ladies' rest parlor" and a billiard room. "This store," the article further explained, "is not only new in name and in stock, but it also operates the 'New Way' system of displaying goods and waiting on customers. The 'New Way' is the most modern of the up-to-now methods. . . . Goods are kept for display in dust-proof glass cases and wardrobes. Customers can look about and pick and choose, and when a selection is made a salesperson quickly slides back a concealed door and the customer's choice is there, neat and clean." The following year, when Lopinsky installed a "magnificent electric sign" in front of his store featuring 350 multicolored blinking lights that flashed one word at a time, the *Recorder* was moved to declare, "Thus Welch grows more like New York City every day."[127]

Such innovations represented an attempt to elevate the shopping experience. Coalfield Jewish merchants strove to lift their downtown business districts into a realm of modern, middle-class sophistication. Harry Schwachter epitomized their enthusiasm for the up-to-date approach. His store renovations and careful attention to window and merchandise display constituted a deliberate effort to bring the "new way" to Williamson. Writes his daughter, "His ideas were new for the small town, and he was clever enough to introduce them slowly."[128]

Coalfield merchants received encouragement and support for their modernizing project from beyond the region as well. Around the country, turn-of-the-century small-town stores made use of display materials sent out by national manufacturers; perhaps equally important to Jewish store owners was the influence of their favorite wholesaler. The Baltimore Bargain House served as a modernizer in more ways than one. Not only did it supply the goods churned out by urban factories, but its catalogue urged small-town merchants to respond to modern fashions and provided tips on modern retailing methods. One 1906 catalogue exhorted, "No matter how small your town may be—no matter how modest your business may be—it will pay you, and pay you well, to have your establishment touch the limit of up-to-dateness. Modern folks are not content with the sort of stores that served their parents and grandparents. People nowadays . . . keep abreast of the times; they know what is going on outside their own communities." The writer advised retailers to keep their stores clean, bright, and well organized, their stock fresh and "free from dead styles." They were told to put their "best bargains on display" and to train their clerks to be aggressive. "Any clerk can sell what is asked for if he has it in stock," the writer observed. "Selling what is not asked for is where *real salesmanship* comes in. . . . When a customer comes in to buy a half-dozen towels, don't let her leave until she has been told about the 'great 10–cent handkerchief' that you are selling."[129]

By adopting the ideas of manufacturers and wholesalers, small-town merchants built the local infrastructure of consumer culture. Sales techniques strove to boost people's consumption habits. Display techniques served to standardize the shopping experience. Marketing techniques proclaimed the superiority of products and styles flowing in from outside the region. Schwachter's choice of a new name for his spruced-up store is telling: National Department Store. Other Jewish-owned coalfield stores bore names such as the New York Racket Store and the Baltimore Bargain House. Like other small-town merchants, coalfield store owners began to push products with nationally advertised brand names. Such methods advanced "a consumer ethic that equated 'new' with better and 'modern' with improvement," as one scholar has pointed out.[130]

The rapid pace of change in the shopping experience was unsettling as well as exciting. Merchants did not hesitate to indulge in a certain amount of nostalgia if it could be turned into a selling point. As early as 1899, Weinstein and Brothers looked back on a simpler era: "Grown-up people will remember how they used to look forward with pleasure to Christmas time. They felt good whenever they saw a picture of Santa Claus and wondered what they'd find in their stocking in the morning after his visit. Now it's different. The coming of Christmas is considered a matter of dollars and cents. . . . But you ought to cheer up and be happy, for it won't cost near so much to buy presents this year if you buy them at our store."[131]

Jews typically had family and friends in large cities and were more likely to travel outside the region than other coalfield merchants. The buying trips they regularly made to Baltimore, Cincinnati, and New York helped them to transmit urban styles and attitudes. While they did not necessarily return with the *very* latest fashions (it was cheaper to buy at the end of the season), the knowledge they gained on these trips filtered through to their neighbors and customers. After Herman Weinstein returned from a two-week visit to New York in 1903, the Middlesboro newspaper reported that his firm "will make some changes in their manner of running the store, and will also add some new features. . . . Herman took notes while in the metropolis, and these he will bring into play when the proper time arrives." Social columns constantly reported on the business-related comings and goings of Jewish merchants; store owners themselves likely placed the items as a form of free advertising. Perhaps even more than paid ads, these ubiquitous missives accustomed readers to look to the cities as the source of quality and style. Certainly they served as a persistent reminder that the coalfields, far from being isolated, had become firmly tied to mainstream American culture.[132]

Buying trips were not the only way to import merchandise. Store owners combined these forays with ordering from wholesale catalogues and purchasing from drummers who came through the region. National manufacturers did not ignore mountain consumers. As one Logan Jewish merchant recalled, "We used to be flooded with salesmen." With all these sources of supply, the coalfields suffered no lack of manufactured goods. When Rudy Eiland noted in 1952 that "there is hardly anything that a person would wish for or want to purchase, that you could not find in the City of Logan," he was not exaggerating—and his statement had applied for decades.[133]

Although consumers' wishes and manufacturers' designs were important factors in shaping modern consumer culture, local entrepreneurs determined precisely which products would be offered and in what form they would be presented. Jewish merchants contributed greatly to the diversity of coalfield retailing, as general stores gave way to a plethora of specialized stores. Their decisions, influenced by the need to survive in a competitive environment, gave coalfield inhabitants a surprisingly wide range of shopping choices. As one Pocahontas resident recalled, "Anything you wanted you could find somewhere in town, there was such a variety of businesses."[134]

The impact of Jewish retailers varied from place to place. They had a substantial presence in many towns, but were entirely absent from others. Their presence was greatest in McDowell County. In War, for example, Jacob Shore and/or his sons owned the Leader Store, Shore's Department Store, the War Bargain House, the War Theater, and the Grand Theater. Summarized a longtime resident, "He owned the whole town here at one time." Their influence in Welch is revealed by their major presence in local newspapers. Before the high holidays in 1922, the *McDowell Recorder* saw fit to print a special message from the Welch rabbi, notifying "the people of Welch and the surrounding territory . . . that the big Jewish holidays will soon be here and all the Jewish merchants and business men will have their respective stores and businesses closed for three days." The rabbi advised "the purchase of all necessary things in advance."[135]

Jews made up a large percentage of retailers in other coalfield county seats and their stores served as anchors for downtown business districts. They comprised a key element in a town-based merchant class whose collective activities disseminated modern ways through the region. With their direct links to Baltimore, Cincinnati, and New York, their frequent trips back and forth, their devotion to advertising and other modern retailing methods, and an outlook that was more urban oriented than that of other coalfield residents, they had an impact on coalfield consumer culture well beyond their numbers.

To put that impact into perspective, it is helpful to place Jewish merchants within discussions about the role of local elites in the region's transformation. In their study of Clay County, Kentucky, Dwight Billings and Kathleen Blee contend that preindustrial leaders failed to engage in productive efforts to develop the economy, choosing instead to fight over the diminishing returns afforded by an agricultural system eroded by population pressures and external competition. Their role as modernizers consisted of enlisting outside sources of capital to rescue them from the dilemma of a shrinking economic pie. As agents for absentee corporations, elites facilitated the transfer of resources to outside forces who imposed a single-industry economy in exchange for local control over social relations and a share of the profits—consigning large parts of the region to dependency and poverty.[136]

Jews and other newcomers, of course, played no role in events leading up to industrialization. And except perhaps in a couple rare cases, they never attained the power of established elite families to influence local politics or society. Like them, however, they served as boosters for coal-based development and played an important, if ancillary, part in transforming the economy. As emissaries of modern consumerism they contributed to the process of dependency both materially and culturally by encouraging the local population to embrace the goods churned out in the nation's industrial centers and by promoting the superiority of cultural trends emanating from beyond the mountains. They were participants in, and beneficiaries of, a system that proved destructive in many ways.

To some critics of capitalism, the role of the merchant is by definition worthy of censure as inherently wasteful and exploitative. Wilma Dunaway, for example, refers to preindustrial Appalachian merchants as "nonproductive profiteers" who offered no benefit whatsoever to the local economy. This sort of blanket condemnation of people engaged in the circulation and distribution of goods because they do not actually produce anything has been a staple in social commentary (not to mention popular opinion) for centuries.[137] In reality, circulation is a vital economic function that arises as soon as societies reach even a modicum of complexity. By importing goods, rural merchants liberated residents from having to produce everything themselves. They also relieved their neighbors of "certain functions," states Lewis Atherton, such as "the farmer's need to market produce." They introduced laborsaving devices that offered escape from unremitting toil, especially for women. The issue therefore becomes defining the line between helping farmers sell their produce and exploiting them, between freeing people from burdensome work and pushing them into a harmful dependency.[138]

Some historians argue that affordable mass-produced goods not only liberated ordinary people from work but enabled them to find new forms of self-expression. These commentators see the rise of consumer culture as an egalitarian development that allowed working people to enjoy higher standards of living, helped women and minorities challenge patriarchal and racist norms, and obliterated class distinctions. Critics counter that consumerism debased local cultures of all sorts, promoted an extreme form of individualism detrimental to healthy communities, and served to obscure the very real class differences and power imbalances that continued to define American society. The negative view contends that agents of consumerism manipulated people into embracing a mind-numbing materialism that impoverished cultural and intellectual life, while the positive view insists that consumers were not passive victims but active participants guided by self-interest who not only consumed but also shaped mass culture through their influence on its purveyors. Yet these competing characterizations are not mutually exclusive. Many observers see the spread of consumer culture as a complex dynamic involving the interplay of all these factors.[139]

In the coalfields, the dynamic was further complicated by the all-encompassing power of coal companies. The region's history shows that claims of the egalitarian effects of consumerism can be taken too far. Increased ability to purchase material goods did not correlate with an increase in local democracy or equality: even as residents attained access to the products of modern life, the coal industry imposed a socioeconomic system that caused class distinctions to become more pronounced than ever before. The company store served as a place to acquire consumer goods—and a place that reinforced workers' subordination to their employers. John Gaventa suggests that miners' consumption patterns were in fact an expression of their powerlessness: their situation discouraged a sense of long-term control over their lives and encouraged an attitude of living for the moment.[140]

If consumerism did offer a way for workers to exercise agency, it was only because a small but vibrant independent retail sector managed to offer an alternative to the company store. From this standpoint, far from being exploiters and profiteers, merchants added some much-needed balance to the region's economy, providing what little diversity existed. Jewish-owned businesses linked the coalfields to a different set of distribution networks, increased the range of shopping choices, served as an alternative source of consumer credit (especially meaningful during strikes), and hampered the ability of coal companies to engage in monopolistic practices such as price gouging. Certainly there were local business people, Jewish and otherwise, who indulged in exploitative practices. Nevertheless, locally based independent retailers pointed to the possibilities of a healthy economy. And the nostalgia with which the bustling county-seat towns are recalled by coalfield residents suggests that the goods and services found in those commercial centers, the leisure opportunities and social interactions that occurred there, were valued by ordinary people.[141]

But the possibilities exemplified by small retail business could not be realized given the structural realities of the region. In 1940, for example, the retail sector was the second leading source of jobs in McDowell County, employing nineteen hundred people; coal mining employed nineteen thousand. In the 1950s, when mechanization began to permanently decimate the mining work force, other forms of economic development failed to catch hold, as most of the land was controlled by absentee owners and reserved for resource extraction. Over the next few decades more than one million people moved away, among them the bulk of the Jewish population.[142]

It must be noted that despite the peculiarities of the coal economy, the economic and demographic trajectory of coalfield Jews conformed to trends in small-town American Jewry. Changing career aspirations of the third generation and the national transformation of small-town retailing would have caused their retail niche to fade even without the coal industry, if not as quickly nor as completely. Central Appalachia was one of many rural areas that lost population in the late twentieth century, as national trends favored suburbanization over both rural and inner city growth. Not surprisingly, geographers have noted that the decline of small-town Jewish communities across the country correlates with the general decline of small American towns.[143]

The out-migration from Central Appalachia involved descendants of those immigrants, blacks, and native whites who had swelled the population of coalfield towns less than a century earlier. Historian Joe Trotter observes that despite the inequalities of coalfield society, the region provided opportunities and "an upward shift in mobility" for members of all these groups, even mountaineers (who, scholars point out, had experienced a decline in the local agricultural economy before industrialization began).[144] To southern sharecroppers, peasants and traders dislocated from the European countryside, and farmers scratching out a living on small, exhausted mountain plots, the towns and camps of the coalfields were a step up. In pursuing their goals, these people all contributed to the development of the region, even if the coal industry ultimately determined the course of that development.

David Scott arrived in Wilcoe, West Virginia, about 1905 to work for horse trader Jake Shore. Photographer and date unknown. (Courtesy of *Goldenseal*)

David Scott as successful Welch, West Virginia, businessman. Photo by Welch Studio, date unknown. (Courtesy of *Goldenseal*)

The Libby Building in downtown Welch, West Virginia, was constructed by David Scott and named for his wife, Libby. Photo by Michael Keller, 1990. (Courtesy of *Goldenseal*)

The Store upon the Hill, Wilcoe, West Virginia. Max Roston (*pictured, with glasses*) co-owned the store with his brother-in-law, David Scott. Roston's wife Viola is sixth from left. Photographer and date unknown. (Courtesy of *Goldenseal*)

Children of I. L. and Sarah Shor in front of their house in Keystone, West Virginia, c. 1914. (Courtesy of Cynthia Burgin)

Two children of I. L. and Sarah Shor with their nanny in Keystone, West Virginia, c. 1911. (Courtesy of Cynthia Burgin)

Max Matz grew up in Pocahontas, Virginia, where his family owned a saloon. As a Bluefield, West Virginia, hotel owner in the early 1930s, he was president of an antiprohibition organization. (Courtesy of West Virginia and Regional History Collection, West Virginia University Libraries)

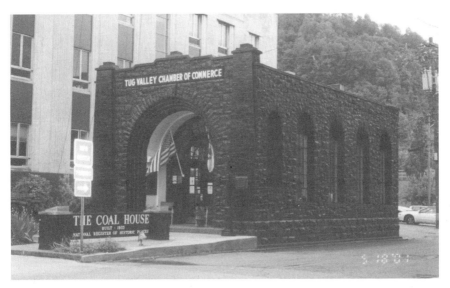

In 1933, the town of Williamson, West Virginia, erected this monument to King Coal. (Photo by Sherry Zander, 2001)

Harry Schwachter of Williamson, West Virginia. (Courtesy of Marilou Sniderman)

CHAPTER 3

Jews in the Coalfield Social Scene

> The figure of "Uncle Joe" Herzbrun is well remembered by thousands of people in the coalfields. This diminutive little man who operated a tailor shop in Welch for a quarter of a century . . . was an outstanding member of his race in the struggling period of McDowell County's growing pains. Uncle Joe knew everyone, and everyone knew him—the age-old type of human being whose sense of moral values tempered business and civic relations at all times.
>
> —Houston Kermit Hunter, "Story of McDowell County," 1940

As in Eastern Europe, Jews in the Central Appalachian coalfields differed from their neighbors in two important realms: religion and economic activity. In the old country, these distinctions reinforced the status of the Jewish population as an often-despised "other." Such would not be the case in the coalfields, where Jews would become stalwart members of a small middle and upper middle class centered in the region's county-seat towns. Though not immune to social tensions related to their ethnic, religious, and economic distinctiveness, they integrated fully into the region's social life. As one second-generation coalfield Jew asserted, Jews "assimilated just about as completely as you could be assimilated" while still remaining Jewish.[1]

Hungarian immigrant Josef Herzbrun offers one example. Owner of Welch's first tailoring establishment, he served on the city council and helped found the chamber of commerce and First National Bank. His sister-in-law Pauline Josephy was equally respected; when she died in 1920, the Welch newspaper eulogized her as "one of the most popular ladies of the city . . . prominent in social, religious, and charitable circles." Charlie Albert came to Williamson with his Russian immigrant parents as a teenager about 1921. For decades he owned Albert's Army-Navy Store and was active in just about every organization imaginable. The town officially recognized his civic leadership with the declaration of Charles Albert Day in 1985, and he even received an award from that supreme arbiter of small-town respectability, the Daughters of the American Revolution.[2]

Beyond the county seats, Jews were also key members of the emerging middle class in boomtowns and smaller independent towns. A 1909 photograph printed in a local history of Pocahontas depicts a mine manager, company doctor, prosperous farmer, town undertaker, and German Jewish merchant Michael Bloch over the caption "Pocahontas Pioneers." Dime-store owner Sam Rosen served as school board member, recorder, and, finally, mayor of Northfork from the 1920s to 1940s. The Weinsteins of Middlesboro received much recognition for their involvement "in every public enterprise and movement . . . for the betterment and improvement of living, social, educational, and civic conditions." The brothers were for some years, "with the exception of the large corporations" (a significant exception), the largest taxpayers in the city.[3]

But it would be misleading to represent Jews only as sober-minded, progressive business people and staid civic leaders. Some engaged in more adventurous activities, such as McDowell County prohibition officer Isadore Katzen, whose daring exploits in pursuit of bootleggers were eagerly chronicled by the local press. Coalfield Jewish communities harbored their fair share of sinners as well. Ike Ginsburg, a Kentucky colonel whose interests ran to bootlegging and gambling, served as mayor of Middlesboro in the mid-1930s. He presided over a "wide open city . . . filled with liquor establishments, gambling joints, and hotels with beautiful prostitutes," with a grand jury accusing his administration of "intentionally allowing such places to continue." Ginsburg's cousin Jake Zuta left town for a career as a Chicago mobster but returned every year to spend the Jewish high holidays with his Kentucky relatives. After his assassination in a 1930 gangland hit, Zuta's body was transported to Middlesboro and laid out at Callison's Funeral Parlor. Ginsburg warned "Chicago hoodlums" to "stay away" from his cousin's funeral, which was conducted according to Orthodox Jewish ritual and was well attended by local townspeople. Zuta was buried in Middlesboro's Jewish cemetery.[4]

From respectable leading citizens to exemplars of the seamier side of coalfield life, Jews played a wide-ranging role in the social scene. Their activities contrasted with the comportment of many small American Jewish communities, North and South, whose members attempted to blend into their surroundings by trying not to be too conspicuous. On the other hand, similar patterns of exuberant participation in social, civic, and political life can be found among Jews in the American West. Regional, demographic, and structural factors all influenced how Jews interacted with the surrounding non-Jewish population.

Jews and the Emerging Coalfield Middle Class

As Central Appalachia industrialized, a rigid class structure developed, based primarily on work hierarchies within the coal industry. While company-owned towns exemplified this new order, the evolving scene in the region's *independent* towns belied the class system solidifying around it. In a milieu where newcomers from many different backgrounds gathered to advance themselves any way they could, relative social fluidity prevailed.

Even writers who have described the extreme imbalance of power in the coal-fields have acknowledged how the coal boom fostered a wide-open atmosphere that implied possibilities for social and economic mobility to people who flocked to the independent towns. John Gaventa offers this description of the founding of Middlesboro: "A boom was created, a period of rapid economic and social change, a time of flux." As a result, "for a brief, critical juncture . . . the social structure appeared fluid," as the town drew an assortment of people "who saw in this venture the chance to make a new start." To Gaventa, this fluidity was more perceived than real: "Within that boom, economic inequalities and monopoly control were also created, though the Zeitgeist of the era may not have brought them into the focus of the thousands of small entrepreneurs, workers and mountaineers who had been attracted to the city. . . . There is no indication that the mobility here was the upward mobility for which frontier boomtowns enjoy a reputation. Rather, it was of a horizontal nature."[5]

Yet the coalfield Jewish experience suggests that county seats and other inde-pendent towns did indeed resemble the boomtowns of other "frontiers."[6] Cer-tainly a clear distinction existed between the towns' large working class and the small but varied middle class of merchants, professionals, white-collar workers, and middle- to upper-level railroad and coal industry employees. Nevertheless, upward mobility would not prove impossible. Moreover, for Jews and other members of the multiethnic coalfield middle class, the period of opportunity lasted longer than the "brief juncture" Gaventa describes, sustained by periodic booms that boosted the region's economic fortunes.

In the popular imagination, boomtowns have been known mostly as places where various forms of vice flourish. But historians have also talked about them as spaces where a freewheeling atmosphere, a diverse populace, and the desire of local boosters for economic development have promoted an unusual degree of tolerance and opportunity for a wide variety of people. For Jews, coalfield towns conformed to a pattern evident in places as far flung as Odessa, Russia, and Wich-ita, Kansas: "fledgling" cities, where entrepreneurial spirit runs high and the social hierarchy is not well fixed, have often proved hospitable. In the nineteenth-cen-tury American West, for example, local elites saw entrepreneurial newcomers as "fellow promoters in an expanding economy rather than as competitors in a static one," writes Earl Pomeroy. Jews were especially well received because their commercial experience and networks, invaluable for importing goods to rela-tively remote areas, seemed to match western economic needs.[7]

The coalfields' preexisting class of merchants, professionals, and public officials sought to promote development, and the local newspaper editors who served as their mouthpiece expressed appreciation for commercially minded Jewish immi-grants loud and clear. A 1900 *Fayette Journal* article enthused that "Hurvitz & Lopinsky, the justly popular proprietors of the Great Eastern Bargain House . . . will shortly open up the largest and best selected line of clothing, dry goods, boots and shoes ever seen in this part of the state. . . . The square dealing and up-to-date methods of this enterprising firm are too well known to need any comment." The *McDowell Recorder* often extolled local Jewish businessmen. When jeweler Henry Millner of Welch, owner of "one of the prettiest and best equipped stores in the state," became certified in optometry in 1915, the *Recorder* found it "another proof of what can be accomplished by a determined young man working under adverse circumstances." The paper soberly noted that Millner, orphaned at age fifteen, was "Hebrew born and reared in the land where the persecution of his race is notorious." A favorite of the *Recorder*'s editor was Sam Polon, described more than once as "our redheaded Jew and all around hustler." Polon, too, had a rags-to-riches tale recounted in a 1913 article, which was summed up, "American boys, take a lesson from this."[8]

The instructive example of such self-made men no doubt held special appeal for local elites intent on transforming a rural mountain society based on communal, agrarian values into a modern society ruled by individualism and an ethic of progress. In addition to bringing needed commercial skills, Jews shared the desire for economic development—a stance that, in a region where capitalist values were not uncontested, local elites found congenial. Many mountain residents maintained a traditional, agrarian-oriented outlook that jarred with elites' plans for the region. The competing visions often took the form of a town-country split, and the town-based promoters of progress welcomed a chance to increase their numbers. As author Mary Beth Pudup puts it, "Longtime residents and newly established families could merge their interests and define an identity as local boosters for capitalist development." Jews and other entrepreneurial newcomers were thus swiftly absorbed into the coalfield middle class.[9]

Charles Midleburg exemplified the values that coalfield elites wished to promote. Born and raised in the region's very first boomtown, Sewell, he and his brother took over the family businesses from their father Arnold, premier merchant of the New River town. The homegrown Midleburgs blended easily into the local elite, and at age twenty-six Charles became justice of the peace. He soon demonstrated his devotion to a new order based on civic authority rather than traditional family and communal norms. According to a 1905 *Fayette Journal* article, "Squire Midelburg [*sic*], at Sewell, tried his first important case this week. Miss Fink . . . found it necessary to whip a Meadows boy for eating peanuts in school. He was given a sound thrashing and his father had the schoolmistress arrested. The trial before Squire Midelburg lasted four hours and resulted in acquital [*sic*] for the schoolmarm, whom the Squire commended for her thorough work."[10]

Town leaders invested in the promise Jewish immigrants represented. Unlike many American locales where Jews suffered from credit discrimination, even recent arrivals to coalfield towns could obtain credit locally. Louis Gottlieb received a bank loan upon arriving in Welch in the 1920s because his brother-in-law had already established himself. Bank financing enabled Hungarian immigrant Rudy

Eiland to recover from a flood that wiped out his four-year-old general store in Logan in 1918. Several McDowell County leaders gave Sam Polon his start in real estate in the 1910s. Their investment yielded results: a local history later referred to the developer as "the man who, so to speak, put Welch 'on the map.'"[11]

Harry Schwachter's brash manner convinced Williamson banker Wells Goody-koontz to finance his first home even though the young man had no money for a down payment. If granted the loan, Schwachter brazenly assured the banker, "I will be glad to see that your bank handles the bulk of my future real estate trans-actions." Goodykoontz's gamble paid off as Schwachter became a prominent businessman and pillar of the community: an organizer of the chamber of com-merce, assistant captain of the volunteer fire department (suffering severe injuries in one blaze), promoter of municipal projects, and speaker at town banquets, where a favorite topic was the progress of his beloved town. In a 1923 speech, Schwachter observed, "Fourteen years ago, when I first came to Williamson, it was the usual, small, busy, hustling mining town, with its rather flexible laws and two or three prosperous saloons. . . . By 1912, things began to boom . . . and the town passed over its primitive stages into the city it is today."[12]

Indeed, a "social and spatial" transformation swept the coalfields as business and civic leaders developed town infrastructures, expanded commercial districts, built residential areas, and promoted the growth of schools and churches.[13] Coun-ty seats became the bastion of the coalfield bourgeoisie, but other independent towns also hosted a small middle class equally concerned with infrastructure, business growth, and social amenities. Boosterism prevailed as well in these towns. Keystone's African American–owned *McDowell Times,* for example, was every bit as strident in promoting development as newspapers in Welch, Logan, William-son, and Beckley.[14]

Throughout their tenure in the region, Jewish men and women enthusiasti-cally contributed to the social and civic life of coalfield towns. Their motivations ranged from enlightened to less-than-enlightened self-interest, to a sense of civic duty rooted in the Judaic principle of *tzedekah,* the same principle that prompted them to assist their fellow Jews and organize their communal institutions. In a 1974 study, Jerome David noted that "Jews are very active in the organizational life of Williamson. They not only give of their time but also of their money. . . . They feel it is their duty as citizens." As one man told him, "I'm involved in everything that pertains to the community in general. This is my home and town and I feel any contribution that will better our town, I will work on."[15]

Their fellow citizens welcomed their participation in civic life. Melvin Sturm returned to the coalfields as a young man in the late 1940s and took over his late father's business in Jellico, Tennessee, near Middlesboro. He soon found himself recruited into the town's civic activities. His college education made him "sort of a rarity," and in short order he became city council member, Kiwanis Club presi-dent, and, not yet thirty years old, mayor. Sturm came from a three-generation tradition of involvement in coalfield affairs. His aunt, Esther Sturm Baloff, had settled with her husband in LaFollette about 1920. During the Depression, she organized what became the school lunch program by cooking soup in a big pot on her stove and having her sons walk it over to the schoolhouse. As she later stated matter-of-factly, "I was head of everything practically that needed help."[16]

Jews participated in local politics, though their activities cannot be described as extensive. They occupied various positions in local government through the years, with at least seven serving as mayors and a handful sitting in the state legislature. Unlike some southern Jewish communities, coalfield Jews did not seem to fear that the public would react negatively to the ethnic background of Jewish candidates or hold all Jews responsible for the actions of Jewish public officials. And, indeed, in two cases of controversy involving Jewish officials, their religion did not become an issue. In the 1930s, Middlesboro mayor Ike Ginsburg's battle with the local utility company plunged the city into chaos, as the utility cut off municipal electric service for weeks at a time. This situation, in addition to corruption charges, doomed Ginsburg's term. As mayor of Jellico, Melvin Sturm became embroiled in controversy after vowing to take action against union-related violence during a United Mine Workers of America (UMWA) organizing drive. "There was a lot of tension," recalled Sturm. "But at no time was there any comment about 'that Jewish mayor.'" After the strike ended, he suffered no repercussions from his stand.[17]

The wide scope for civic involvement enabled some coalfield Jews to earn recognition as public figures. A few even became honorary "colonels." When West Virginia governor Henry Hatfield bestowed the title on Harry Bank in 1914, the *McDowell Recorder* noted that "Mr. Bank's appointment is pleasing his many friends in this section, who think he merits the honor because he is a substantial man of business and was a very ardent supporter of the Governor during his campaign." (The "very ardent" political support was, in fact, the decisive factor.) A second "colonel," Middlesboro's Ike Ginsburg, serves as a reminder that eminence in the coalfields could be achieved under circumstances that were questionable, at best.[18]

Jews as Town Builders

While absentee land corporations and coal companies had little interest in activities that did not directly advance their bottom line, local merchants—at once residents and capitalists—had reason to invest in measures to improve the livability and viability of their towns. Jews helped shape the physical contours of their communities through their town-building activities. Substantial brick buildings adorned with Jewish family names survive to this day in commercial districts across the coalfields: the Schwachter Building in Williamson, the Catzen Building in Northfork, and the Hyman Building in Pocahontas provide just a few examples.

Residential areas such as Logan's Midleburg Addition still bear the name of their Jewish developers. Through the years, Jews worked to establish banks, utility services, parks, libraries, hospitals, and other community institutions.

The town-building activities of Jewish merchants did not always end in success. Leo Schaffer generated some excitement in Sewell in 1901 with his plans to build a bridge across New River. His inability to complete the task probably contributed to Sewell being bypassed as a coalfield center. Other grand plans of coalfield Jewish businessmen also ended in failure, and often in bankruptcy court, because of their own personal misfortunes or shortcomings or because of the vagaries of the coal economy.[19] But Jews nevertheless had an impact on coalfield town development. The following section explores this impact, starting with the smaller towns and concluding with the county seats.

In the smallest towns where they settled, Jewish families constituted a large portion of the merchant class. Sometimes they were the *entire* merchant class. When Ukrainian immigrant Dave Scott arrived in Poor Fork at the opening of the Harlan coalfield about 1910, "there was nothing there," his daughter related. Scott opened a dry-goods store and built the only brick structure in the area. (He started out with a tin building, but it proved too popular as a mark for Saturday-night target shooting by rowdy miners.) After operating the lone store in town, Scott saw Poor Fork grow, aided by its proximity to the U.S. Steel coal mining complex at Lynch. Concerned that the town's name hampered its prospects, he successfully lobbied to get it changed to Cumberland.[20]

Jewish immigrants played a key role in the development of several small McDowell County towns. Russian-born Aaron Catzen came from Baltimore about 1900 and opened a clothing store in Clark. At the time, "the town was a whistle stop on the railway, and it was his hope that [it] would one day serve as a commercial center for the coal mine camps between Bluefield and Welch," a relative later wrote. Catzen soon operated a shoe store, a wholesale store, and a saloon. He developed much of the housing and organized the power company, waterworks, and ice manufacturing company. Clark became somewhat of a fiefdom for the hard-driving businessman. Catzen was the only mayor the town ever had, serving from the 1920s to the 1940s. He also was street commissioner, superintendent of the water plant, and "police judge." His brother-in-law Louis Schwartz served as treasurer and recorder. In 1948, Clark was absorbed into the neighboring town of Northfork, where Sam Rosen presided as mayor.[21]

Nowhere did Jews become more involved in municipal affairs than in Keystone. Today, Hermanson Street is one of the few remaining signs of that involvement. S. L. Hermanson not only developed real estate but also served as town recorder and policeman in the 1910s. Another vestige of Keystone's Jewish legacy is its city hall, which bears a cornerstone listing I. L. Shor and Sol Hyman as two members of the city council that oversaw the building's construction in 1913. At that time, Keystone's five-man city council contained two African Americans and two Jews,

a remarkable configuration for any small American town of the era, and particularly illustrative of Keystone's open social climate. As late as the 1960s, when the
declining town had only two Jewish families, Keystone-born Julian Budnick
served as mayor. His father, merchant and behind-the-scenes power broker
Charles Budnick, had been instrumental in starting the First National Bank of
Keystone decades earlier. I. L. Shor developed much of the town's commercial and
residential real estate. Master mechanic Max Ofsa built the town's new water tank
after the previous tank burst. In the 1920s, his son, butcher Simon Ofsa, served a
term as fire marshal.[22]

Simon Ofsa's post was an important one, since coalfield towns suffered the
common boomtown curse of frequent fires. Jewish men from the lowliest clerks
to the most substantial merchants served in volunteer fire departments that stayed
busy year round. An eyewitness account of a 1921 Pocahontas fire, written by a
former schoolteacher, reveals both the efforts of Jewish businessmen as well as the
primitive fire fighting conditions they worked under: "Pocahontas had very poor
fire protection then, but a most interesting means of alerting the people in case
of a fire. After I had been there only a short time, I was awakened one night by a
rapid succession of shots. Alarmed, I ran to ask . . . what it all meant, and was told
that there was a fire in town. We put on our coats over our night clothes and ran
into the streets in time to see Mr. Sid Block [son of Michael Bloch] pulling a two
wheel cart with some hose on it."[23] The McDowell Times filled its pages with excited accounts of each Keystone fire while complaining bitterly of low water pressure and faulty equipment, not to mention the flimsy construction of many
buildings. In a July 21, 1916, article emblazoned "FIRE! Destroys Three Buildings,
Threatens Half of Keystone," the newspaper reported, "It was only because of the
daring fire fighting of the volunteer fire company led on the Cinder Bottom side
by I. L. Shor and Jake Ofsa [another son of Max] that the fire was confined to the
three buildings mentioned."

The reputation of at least some Keystone Jewish businessmen fluctuated with
the economic fortunes of the town. When the McDowell Times, in full booster
mode, consulted "leading business men in the city" for its 1913 article "Banner
Business Year in Keystone," six out of twelve interviewed were Jewish merchants.
But when the local economy went into decline after passage of West Virginia's
prohibition law, those same people came in for their share of blame. Wrote the
editor in 1916, "The Jews, who are called 'God's chosen people,' are wanted to put
away that usual jealousy that is so characteristic of them in this city, and just start
out on a boosting tour. Any man who prefers to knock, knock, knock rather than
to boost, boost, boost the town ought to be politely [sic] enough to leave the city."
The previous week, the town council had pointedly ordered businessmen Harry
Budnick (Jewish) and A. L. Calhoun (black) to repair their sidewalks. When better times came along with the wartime demand for coal, a typical Times item
praised the "generosity and public-spiritedness" of Wolf Bank for building a

walkway across Elkhorn Creek near his café. "Mr. Bank is the owner of much valuable property in this city and is one of the best and most patriotic citizens," the article observed.[24]

Jews did not play as large a part in the development of county seats as they did in other independent towns. They never made up a numerically significant portion of the population in the county seats, nor did they ever constitute a majority of the merchants. Also, county seats were not as raw as the other towns. Some had existed long before the coal boom and had a fairly entrenched town elite. All, by virtue of their dual role as seat of government and commercial hub, saw the rise of a more broad-based middle class and developed a more traditional small-town social structure led by prosperous, native-born white men.[25]

Nevertheless, Jews became fully involved in county-seat civic life. It helped that they arrived in the early days, when there was plenty to do. And many families stayed long enough to participate in town development for several decades. Joe Herzbrun's son Maurice followed in his civic footsteps, serving on the McDowell County Commission and helping establish the McDowell County Library in the 1950s. The Eusters constructed "the fourth brick building" in Pineville by 1890. In the 1960s, one of Bell County's many Abe Eusters (following Jewish custom, at least four of the original six Euster brothers named a son after their deceased father, Abraham) served as Pineville's mayor. Alex Gergely opened an early Harlan department store. His son Irvin served on the Harlan City Council and as president of the Lions Club, Harlan Country Club, and Red Cross chapter.[26]

Not surprisingly, given their economic niche, Jews participated heavily in local chambers of commerce. These organizations offered a vehicle to directly boost downtown business districts while addressing civic issues. A newspaper account of one "splendid" 1922 chamber meeting in Welch, organized by three men including twenty-seven-year-old Edward Herzbrun, leaves the impression of an organization that was comfortably ecumenical and comfortably middle class, with Jews holding a secure place in the social order. After Reverend Pierce reported on the efforts of the playground committee to secure land, the group discussed providing a rest room for women shoppers and establishing a town cemetery. Leading Jewish citizen Simon Solins, poolroom operator, "called attention to the number of school children who had to cross the railroad tracks daily in order to get to and from school and urged the chamber take some action" to protect children from accidents; a committee was duly appointed. After this "snappy business session," the gathering was treated to a showing of *The Story of Coal,* "the moving picture produced jointly by the National Coal Association and the Department of Interior." Then a "delightful" dinner was served by the Congregation Emanuel Sisterhood, the town's Jewish women's group. The article devoted almost as much space to describing the dinner as it did to the meeting itself, concluding that "the ladies had spared no pains to make this an event long to be remembered." (On the menu:

chicken fricassee, string beans, mashed potatoes, celery, "liver salad," pickles, hot rolls, and French pudding with wine sauce.)[27]

On a chilly day in February 1917, eighteen "young ladies" of Middlesboro treated their friends and relations to a piano recital at the Christian Church. Among them were Pearl Euster, Lillie Weinstein, Irene Weinstein, Rose Mazer, and Rose Liebman, who ranged in age from nine to fifteen years old. This typical small-town event is hardly remarkable, but it does provide clues to life in Middlesboro that are not found in most accounts of the notorious coalfield center. It reveals the ambition of the town's middle to upper classes to bring a measure of "high culture" to the raw atmosphere of the region. It hints that females were disproportionately involved in such attempts. And it suggests that the Jewish population was well integrated into that segment of society concerned with such matters (notwithstanding the venue of that particular event).[28]

Through the years, coalfield newspapers filled many columns with descriptions of similar social affairs, as some towns developed beyond their rough-and-ready beginnings to become modern urban centers with social and physical infrastructures that conformed to small-town American patterns. Yet the more unruly characteristics associated with a boomtown environment never entirely disappeared, especially in towns whose initial contribution to the coal economy consisted of supplying liquor and other distractions to the region's work force. Middlesboro in particular maintained a somewhat schizophrenic personality, with its broad streets, stately homes, substantial business district, plethora of churches and civic clubs—and continued reputation for corruption and wildness. It was the kind of place that a local history book, depicting the 1930s, could refer to as a "gang-controlled city" and (on the very next page) a "nice shopping center" serving the greater Cumberland Gap area.[29]

If coalfield towns had some ground to cover from rawness to refinement (and made the transition to varying degrees), the same can be said of their Jewish contingents. While Jews from Squire Midleburg to the piano-playing young ladies of Middlesboro may have exemplified bourgeois aspects of the new order, Jewish immigrants and some of their descendants partook as well in the less orderly side of life in the region. Each of their incarnations, as participants in boomtown activities and upholders of middle-class ways, grew out of their economic niche and were conditioned as well by the cultural background they brought to their new setting.

At Home in the Boomtowns

The region's first major centers of Jewish population were Keystone, Pocahontas, and Middlesboro, and Jewish immigrants were fully prepared to embrace all the opportunities these wide-open towns afforded. Their involvement in the liquor trade placed them squarely in the center of boomtown affairs, in these and other raucous early coal towns.

Jewish saloonists engaged in an occupation that extended for centuries into the East European countryside, where the Jews' middleman role and job discrimination in other economic sectors made tavern keeping an important means of income. The Jewish-owned tavern was "part of everyday life" in rural areas, with relations between tavern owners and their mostly peasant clients ranging from "fraternal to businesslike to violent." As conditions deteriorated in the eighteenth century, the Jewish innkeeper became a reviled figure, blamed for the "intoxication and impoverishment" of the peasants and especially vulnerable to outbreaks of hostility.[30]

Saloon keeping emerged in many American locales as an important way for immigrant Jews to get a start in their new surroundings.[31] In the coalfields, they made up a relatively small percentage of saloon keepers and there is no indication they came under special disapprobation. Violence did pose a problem, but it had nothing to do with anti-Jewish sentiment. Rapid industrialization produced all the ingredients for mayhem, chief among them an abundance of single men drawn to the region from all over the world. Young men engaged in a perilous occupation, "uprooted from definite expectations of social behavior and placed in a strange and unfamiliar environment," not surprisingly "sought relief in exaggerated and sporadic outbursts of unbridled behavior," observes a coalfield historian. Heavy liquor consumption increased the potential for disorder. The wife of a Pocahontas coal mine superintendent recalled fearful payday nights, "for by that time the men had visited the saloons on the outskirts of town, and were using their firearms in a most reckless way."[32]

If not nearly as dangerous as mining, saloon work offered its own occupational hazards. In 1901, Jewish saloon owner William Henry was shot in the leg while trying to eject an unruly coal miner from his Keystone establishment. The miner had become agitated when Henry's bartender refused to sell him another drink. After the bartender struck the man with a beer bottle and tried to remove him, the man pulled out a pistol and began shooting wildly. The Bluefield newspaper termed the incident an example of Keystone's "usual payday pleasantries." Fellow Keystone saloon owner Israel Totz kept a gun behind his bar for just such emergencies, and many other Jewish business owners in the boomtowns had firearms they occasionally put to use.[33]

An incident in Pocahontas suggests that even though Jews came under no censure for taking part in the saloon business, they were nevertheless sensitive about their image. A (non-Jewish) woman who grew up in the town related that a Chautauqua group came one year to perform at the Pocahontas opera house. The producers sought a local child to appear in their play, and settled on a "pretty little blonde girl" who happened to be Jewish. When members of the Jewish community found out that the production was "Ten Nights in a Bar Room," that its theme was temperance, and that the girl in the play had to go into a bar to look for her father, they at first suspected they were being subjected to an ethnic slur. But after getting together to discuss it among themselves, they decided that no harm was intended and that it was all right for the little girl to appear in the play. Everyone in town attended, "and they were proud of her."[34]

In addition to concern for their image, the Jews of Pocahontas probably did not take well to the theme of the play. They had economic reason: in 1910, 37 percent of the town's Jewish breadwinners owned or worked in saloons or liquor stores. Moreover, cultural mores predisposed Jews to look askance at the temperance movement that swept the nation at the turn of the twentieth century. As one historian notes, "Judaism frowned upon the notion of total self-denial: God's gifts to man were meant to be enjoyed—in moderation—and among those gifts was wine." Rabbinical tradition even considers abstinence from the pleasures of life to be sinful (though overindulgence is discouraged). In addition, wine has always been an integral part of Jewish ritual and celebration.[35]

The Jewish attitude toward prohibition was shared by most coalfield town residents. For decades, the major social event in Pocahontas was the annual Hungarian Grape Festival; Italians in Harlan County maintained a tradition of wine making. The African American–owned *McDowell Times* often mocked prohibition laws, while the liquor-producing activities of "native whites" were achieving mythic status. Although the more reputable saloon owners moved into other lines of business, much of the populace did its best to ignore prohibition. Jews, like others, continued to be consumers. One man who grew up in Welch recalled that the wine for his bar mitzvah was supplied by the county sheriff.[36]

Temperance campaigns within the region were not unknown, however, with local Baptists leading the charge. In Fayette County, crusaders demanded that the county court deny all saloon licenses in 1906. The court session drew a large crowd of "temperance people" and "saloon men," and women temperance supporters took "active part in the discussion." The court compromised, denying licenses only to the most objectionable saloons (one-quarter of the total). Pocahontas witnessed an antisaloon rally in 1909 with well over one hundred demonstrators, mostly women and children, dressed in black and carrying signs ("Saloons Cannot Run Without Boys, Have You One To Spare, Think It Over").[37]

It is likely that most of the participants came not from Pocahontas itself but from the surrounding area. Bell County went through numerous liquor battles through the decades, with residents of Middlesboro consistently defending the "wet" position against their more upright rural neighbors. When the county voted "dry" in 1914, Middlesboro went 639–461 against the majority. In 1937, voters brought liquor back with overwhelming wet support from Middlesboro. But the drys did not give up, and the county continued to swing back and forth between allowing and banning alcohol. In contrast, prohibition garnered little or no support in Keystone's McDowell County. A former West Virginia attorney general contended that the county's politically dominant coal operators insisted on maintaining Keystone as a wide-open town in order to attract and retain labor. The county's large, politically active population of Jews and blacks also may have impeded the movement.[38]

At least a few Jews became involved in prohibition politics. Max Matz was born and raised in Pocahontas, where his family owned a saloon. As a Bluefield hotel owner and active Republican, he served as president of the Association Against the Prohibition Amendment in the early 1930s. In 1955, after Bell County once again went dry, Ike Ginsburg's son Jimmy hung "a mourning wreath on his Indian Rock roadhouse near Dead Man's Curve" near Middlesboro. As supporters and opponents of prohibition gathered outside City Hall one day, tempers flared, and "a fist fight [was] narrowly averted. . . . The argument [was] between a group of local liquor dealers led by Jimmy Ginsburg" and Rev. Wendell Rone of the First Baptist Church.[39]

Aside from saloons, the boomtowns harbored other businesses catering to single men. Illegal gambling parlors abounded. More famously, the demographics offered a flourishing market for prostitution, with Keystone's Cinder Bottom (named for the cinders from nearby coke ovens that covered the ground) the notorious center of the trade. The citizens of Keystone tolerated the goings-on in their vice district; their version of social reform mainly consisted of trying to ensure that Cinder Bottom's licentious activities did not spill over to the rest of the town. A 1914 *McDowell Times* article praised city officials for their attempts to "clean up" Keystone by requiring "women of the underworld to keep off the streets at night . . . [and] to live in Cinder Bottom or leave the city." These measures, the writer commented, along with directives to merchants to "keep chicken coops, boxes, barrels and rubbish off the streets," were giving Keystone "the appearance of a Sunday school . . . and a Puritan of the seventeenth century could not hope to make things better."[40]

In 1915, the *McDowell Times* editor protested the possible denial of restaurant licenses to Cinder Bottom establishments. His words reveal the casual attitude of local leadership: "It has been the understanding here that the County and City authorities segregated that district in order to minimize the evil influence of the class of people who are supposed to contaminate society, that they should be kept off the principal streets of the City and not molest respectable people." As this plan seemed to be working, he argued, it would be hypocritical to move against the district. The *Times* was quick to condemn improprieties that occurred outside the boundaries of Cinder Bottom: in 1917, the editor questioned why denizens of the district "should have such unlimited latitude" and demanded, "Make them scarce. Take them off the streets." Yet the newspaper's moral fervor was equally aroused by other unseemly conditions that made the town look bad. That year an even more outraged article complained of hogs running loose, spreading "dirt and filth . . . all over the town."[41]

Town leaders achieved some success in confining gambling and prostitution to Cinder Bottom. One Jewish man who grew up in Keystone delivered newspapers to the vice district as a boy about 1920. He insisted that "it was like a little town of its own," isolated from the rest of Keystone. Yet Cinder Bottom's reputation, if not its activities, certainly did spill over to the rest of town. In 1912, the anonymous "Virginia lad" contributed to this process with his anti-Keystone booklet, *Sodom and Gomorrah of To-day; or, the History of Keystone, West Virginia.* He put a dark interpretation on the town's seeming normality: "To an ordinary visitor ... it does not appear to be very much different from the ordinary coal mining town. The people are very kind to strangers and visitors are liable to be misled by surface indications. But let us probe beneath the surface a little and what we will find will be rather shocking."[42]

From its vaunted position in the county seat of Welch, the *McDowell Recorder* viewed Keystone with a mixture of disapproval and indulgence. In 1917, the newspaper commented that "there are lots and lots of good people in Keystone, but a lot of them seem indifferent to the town's reputation." As the town went through its ups and downs, so did the newspaper's opinion. In 1922, the *Recorder* observed, "There are many little petty vices holding tenaciously to the one-time unsavory reputation of the city, but ... in the last few years many handsome business and residential structures have been erected in Keystone and the town is really moving along in the right direction."[43]

But despite the geographic isolation of Cinder Bottom, Keystone's respectable and less-respectable sides existed in a symbiosis that often made it hard to differentiate the two. During its heyday from the 1890s to the 1910s, leading citizens, Jewish and non-Jewish, black and white, were involved in the activities that made the town infamous. In 1911, when author Howard Lee asked Keystone's police chief, "Who owns these [Cinder Bottom] dives?" the chief responded: "That is a matter that is never discussed." In fact, between 1905 and 1909 at least two eminent Jewish businessmen were hauled into court for renting buildings to women who ran "houses of ill fame." The court cited one man on at least two separate occasions. The other, one of the town's wealthiest citizens, rented to a woman named Trixie McCloud, who ran "the cleanest and best-conducted house" in Keystone, an ironic compliment coming from the "Virginia lad." The two landlords were fined twenty-five dollars for each offense.[44]

It was common knowledge that local brothels did not cater only to coal miners: McCloud's establishment was "well patronized" by "merchants, clerks, railroad men and a few foreigners." In 1915, a scandalous trial of two well-connected African American madams, accused of forcing an underage black girl into prostitution, threatened to expose Jewish and non-Jewish whites as clients. As the *McDowell Times* noted of one of the pair, "It appears that her patrons were some of the leading white and Hebrew business men and officials of the section and her hold could not be easily broken." Two white patrons were compelled to testify: a non-Jewish coal company bookkeeper and a Jewish pool room employee (and former bartender), who refused to answer questions on grounds of self-incrimination. Ultimately, only blacks were convicted, including the madams and one patron. The bartender was indicted, but there is no record that he ever stood trial. He remained in town and became a prominent pharmacist, which perhaps says something about the forgiving climate of Keystone and its Jewish community.[45]

Keystone was not the only town where Jewish merchants strayed from the letter of the law. Apparently, court fines were considered part of the cost of doing business in the coalfields during the early years of the coal boom. Starting with Arnold Midleburg himself, Jewish saloon owners routinely appeared in court to plead guilty to selling liquor to minors or selling liquor on a Sunday. (Non-Jewish saloonists—black, native white, immigrant—also were often caught for such infractions, including members of leading families.) Midleburg was fined at least fifteen times in the 1880s for selling liquor without a license; why the well-known Sewell merchant did not acquire one in all those years is unknown. In 1890, finally possessed of a license, he was promptly fined for selling to a minor.[46]

Others who became prominent citizens also found themselves in court during their younger days. Wolf Bank, mainstay of the Keystone Jewish community, was even sentenced to a brief jail term in 1897 for not paying a liquor-related fine. In one dramatic 1905 episode, the Middlesboro Distilling Company, owned by Jewish merchant Jake Goodfriend in partnership with non-Jews, became the target of "one of the largest raids known to Kentucky" as revenue officers seized fourteen thousand gallons of whiskey. "It had long been suspected . . . that the local company was disposing of whiskey without paying taxes," stated a newspaper report. Not all offenses concerned liquor. For example, Kimball's Louis Kaufman (later a leading Bluefield businessman) was fined for operating an unlicensed pool room in 1897. And Sam Abel of Mount Hope paid a ten-dollar fine for running a gambling house in 1915.[47]

Clues buried in court records suggest that Jews in the early boomtown era fit well into their surroundings. Arrests on charges such as assault, though not frequent, occurred often enough to suggest that they indulged in the same kind of unruly behavior as their fellow coalfield residents. Arnold Midleburg, apparently, even engaged in a feud with one William D. Stroud. In April 1873, he pled guilty to assault and battery against Stroud, and the following March he was convicted of destroying "a large quantity of medicine and a pair of saddle bags and a bottle of liquor" belonging to the same man. For each misdemeanor he was fined one dollar plus costs, hinting that his actions were not seen as unusual or even all that objectionable.[48]

Nor did Jewish immigrants in the boomtowns seem especially concerned, in their day-to-day lives, about how their neighbors viewed them (notwithstanding occasional sore spots such as the Pocahontas temperance play). Their activities bear out the contention of a Jewish traveler in nineteenth-century South Africa: "It is seldom the most polished part of the population . . . that seek their fortunes" by settling in newly opened territories. Coalfield Jews tangled with non-Jews in the civil courts on a fairly regular basis, mostly over business matters such as property disputes and debt payments. Even more contentious among themselves, they had no qualms about bringing their internal conflicts to the local courts—as when Sam Katzen of Keystone sued Jake Shore for slander for spreading the rumor that he was having an affair with the still-married Bessie Zaltzman. After accusing Shore of "falsely and maliciously" stating he had "taken Mr. Saltzman's wife away from him and [was] living with her," Katzen dropped the suit and paid all court costs, suggesting the rumor had some truth behind it. Bessie Zaltzman subsequently divorced her less-than-upright husband and proceeded to carry on lengthy, heated court battles against her enemies within the Keystone Jewish community.[49]

Depositions from one such lawsuit, from 1909, offer a glimpse into the world of early Jewish coalfield residents. The language they used—rough, broken English inflected with Yiddish and Appalachian constructions—indicates that these were not the most educated of immigrants. (Bessie Zaltzman signed her deposition with a mark, instead of writing her name.) They scrapped and clawed to provide for themselves and their families, sparring with each other and their non-Jewish neighbors if they had to. Pressed by African American businessman A. L. Calhoun to sell her property after her house was destroyed by fire, Bessie refused, later explaining, "I didn't want to sell for no money because I make a living here and I got my customers that I sell my milk and butter and I done got used [to living] here and I will put me up again a little home and live with my children." Meanwhile, her soon-to-be-ex-husband Mose succumbed to the temptations of Cinder Bottom, testified his former employer, the loquacious Jake Shore: "He took my money without my knowing and give it to the womens. I find it out afterwards that he used to pay that womens fifty to seventy-five dollars a night." Since Mose was virtually penniless, Jake tried to recoup his losses by putting a lien on Bessie's property, causing a deep enmity between the two (no doubt exacerbated by Jake's gossiping). As she declared, "I would go a mile around not to see his face."[50]

Fayette County and McDowell County coalfield criminal court indexes from 1890 to 1920 list Jewish names with startling frequency. A close look, however, reveals the vast majority of cases were for a single infraction: violation of the state's Sunday law, which forbade working "at any trade or calling" on the Christian Sabbath. This statute, dating to 1882, nabbed everyone from solid businessmen to struggling peddlers. In 1909 alone, highly respected dry-goods merchants Ben Hurvitz and Joseph Lopinsky were charged at least four different times. On each occasion, they pled guilty and paid a five-dollar fine plus twenty dollars in court costs.

In 1899, one H. or B. Shore, a shopkeeper in Mount Hope, pled not guilty to a Sunday law violation. Although the court record is sketchy, it appears that Shore either doubted the existence of such a law or simply refused to go along with it. In a trial presided over by the town's mayor, Shore, acting in his own defense, proceeded to call the mayor as a material witness (one might speculate that the mayor had been a customer of Shore's on the Sunday in question). His ploy worked: though found guilty by the local court, he won his case on appeal. More often than not, though, Jewish merchants dutifully paid their Sunday law fines. Whether they felt victimized by the law or simply accepted it as part of life in their new homes is unknown. The West Virginia statute, as in some of the thirty-seven states with Sunday laws, did stipulate that people who observed the Sabbath on a different day were exempt from the law "provided that such persons refrain from secular business and labor" on their own Sabbath, but Jewish merchants did not have that option, since Saturdays were the busiest shopping days in the coalfields.[51]

Jewish names appear much less frequently in court records after about 1918. Although Sunday closing laws remained on the books for decades, enforcement became lax in the post–World War I era. By that time, few Jews were involved in the liquor trade, thus removing the other major reason for their entanglement in the criminal court system. Jewish coalfield communities were maturing and passing out of their "frontier" phase. They mirrored the larger society around them: the effect of prohibition, the return of many young, single men to their home countries during World War I, and the maturing of coalfield towns and their populations combined to bring about a new, more settled phase of town life.[52]

Not coincidentally, at that same time, the county seats secured their position as the leading centers of commercial activity and the largest towns in the region. Early Jewish county-seat residents, for the most part, had not pursued the activities of their boomtown counterparts. Few had owned saloons and their appearance in court had always been rare. They had even avoided Sunday law violations, perhaps because shopping on a Sunday was not considered respectable in the county seats—or simply because relatively few Jews operated businesses in these towns before the mid-1910s, when enforcement tapered off. As the bulk of the Jewish population shifted to the county seats, Jews settled into their role as an upstanding component of the town-based middle class.

This chronological and geographic progression had its exceptions, however, and remnants of their rougher edges lingered in various forms. For decades, some businessmen in Keystone and Middlesboro continued to have shady financial interests. Colorful characters did not disappear from the scene. Joe "Jokie" Ofsa, for example, born in Keystone in 1901, became a local high school teacher and coach (a respectable, if not very Jewish, coalfield occupation) but also distinguished himself as "quite a pool shark," who, legend has it, defeated Minnesota Fats in a match in Keystone.[53]

Probably the most conspicuous character was Chicago gangster and erstwhile Middlesboro resident Jake Zuta, who visited through the 1920s in his big black car, bringing lavish gifts to his Ginsburg relatives. Townspeople professed astonishment upon learning of Zuta's involvement with the underworld; until his 1930 murder he had been viewed as a local boy made good in the big city. But they quickly recovered from the shock. As the *Middlesboro Daily News* commented, "In Chicago, a strange, masked career is hidden from the eyes of former friends, near relatives who loved, and old acquaintances. . . . Memory of the beautiful traits of character of Zuta relieves the pain and softens the sorrow." All the Jewish stores in town closed, in memoriam, on the day of his funeral. His obituary noted that he had been a member of the Middlesboro Country Club and the Elks, while an accompanying article reported with tabloidlike relish the details of his last desperate days.[54]

In contrast, the career of Isadore Katzen offers a striking illustration of the passage of coalfield Jews from rough boomtown immigrants to staid county-seat citizens. Katzen came from Hungary with his parents, arriving in Keystone around 1897 at age twelve. His first job, with the A. Goodman Liquor Company of Pocahontas, did not disqualify him from being named prohibition officer for McDowell County in 1915. The *McDowell Recorder* praised the appointment, noting that he was "well acquainted all over the county." The newspaper avidly followed the actions of Katzen and his fellow officer Ben Gay (former saloonkeeper from an old local family), often depicting the pair as "swooping down" on unsuspecting bootleggers (usually "foreigners" or "negroes"). Given their backgrounds, it is unlikely that Katzen or Gay had strong convictions against liquor. But as up-and-coming young men, they enforced the law with gusto. "There is no chance for any person to sell liquor for a very long period in McDowell County and not get caught," an article proclaimed of the duo.[55]

Yet law enforcement had its drawbacks. Isadore Katzen's career as a prohibition officer culminated in a 1916 acquittal for the homicide of a suspected (native white) bootlegger in Deegans, a small coal camp. The jury found that Katzen had acted in self-defense. The *Recorder* ran a detailed account of the "unfortunate" incident, noting, "Mr. Katzen has been a very careful officer in the past. . . . His friends know him to be kind and do not think but that he acted as he deemed right." After the trial, the paper observed, "Mr. Katzen was busy shaking hands with many friends and receiving their congratulations. The verdict seemed to meet with popular approval. Unquestionably Mr. Katzen was the happiest man that ever trod the streets of Welch." He soon turned to a less adventurous occupation, owner of a Welch wholesale grocery concern, which he eventually passed on to his son. Along the way, this relative of alleged adulterer Sam Katzen married Anna Herzbrun, daughter of highly respected merchant tailor Josef Herzbrun. A founding member of Welch's Congregation Emanuel, Isadore became active in civic and fraternal groups, including the Masons and Elks.[56]

Middle-Class Mainstays

Isadore Katzen's move from Keystone to the county seat of Welch, from liquor company employee to lawman to business owner and civic-communal leader, is symbolic of the increased respectability of Jews as they moved away from their immigrant origins, integrated into their social surroundings, and prospered. Yet in the memories of Jews who came of age in the region between the two world wars, it was the neighborliness of small-town life, rather than issues of status, that determined their relations with the non-Jewish majority. Interviews and memoirs echo the same phrases: "We knew just about everyone. I loved Williamson and all my wonderful friends." In Pineville, "all the Jewish people made many Christian friends." Keystone was "a very close community. Everyone was quite friendly."[57]

In Welch, men gathered each evening to talk over the events of the day at the Carter Hotel. A Keystone man related how his older brother, projectionist at their father's theater, turned the projector around on Sundays to show movies on the wall of the neighboring Greek restaurant for the amusement of the townsfolk. As a boy he engaged in the usual activities of Keystone children. "We used to play in the streets [or] sit on the porch of our building and shoot the rats" near the creek with a .22 rifle, he recalled. He and his friends played baseball on a vacant lot or watched the men shoot pool at the American Legion hall. Living in a place where, as a Northfork man put it, "everyone knew everyone else's business" had its advantages and disadvantages. His town's telephone operator kept tabs on everyone; if his mother tried to phone a friend, she might be informed, "I'm sorry Mrs. Koslow, but Mrs. Schwartz went downtown." When he called home from Europe on V-E Day, the operator unabashedly listened to the entire conversation.[58]

Non-Jews also recollect a small-town sociability that characterized relations with their Jewish neighbors. In an obituary, former "voice of the University of Kentucky Wildcats" Cawood Ledford recounted that his close friend Irvin Gergely had "a little basketball court at his parents' home" in 1930s Harlan. "I'd take a group [of children] from my neighborhood and he'd get a group from near his home and we'd play on his court," he related. "We fussed more than we played, I think." A Keystone woman who married a Jewish man in the 1930s stated matter-of-factly, "I'm an Irish girl that married a Jewish boy." She insisted, "We all got along real well. . . . In a little town like Keystone, the Jewish people and the other people loved each other. We didn't think about [religion making people] any different."[59]

While her statement may be a bit of an exaggeration, the multicultural nature of many coalfield towns made ethnic and religious variety an accepted fact of life: unremarkable, even normal. Distinct social circles did exist, revolving around church or synagogue affiliation, while ethnic groups tended to coalesce around their own language and customs.[60] Yet townspeople did not let their diverse backgrounds, or the stereotypes that stubbornly clung to each group, stand in the way of forging close-knit communities. Differences both real and perceived were duly noted and then generally overlooked in the interest of harmony. After reeling off all the groups she could remember from a childhood in Pocahontas (southern whites and blacks, Welsh, Hungarians, Jews, Poles, Russians, "a church of every denomination except Lutheran, and a Jewish synagogue"), a native Virginian who married a Hungarian miner stressed that everyone got along "grand." A non-Jewish woman who grew up in War agreed that nobody "paid any mind" to categories of difference. Of the town's Jewish families, she remarked, "I feel I know them as well as my own family." (Such attitudes did not quite extend to race. See chapter 4 for a more detailed look at ethnic and racial dynamics.)[61]

In towns where everyone was known, people were judged by their behavior, not their group affiliation. Max Ofsa was known for his kindness. When the child of a non-Jewish customer took sick, he appeared at the woman's door bearing "some quinine and some goose grease" from his grocery store, an act the woman never forgot. After a coal train accident, David Scott bought the coal that spilled out into the street and distributed it to the churches of Welch, prompting the congregations to offer prayers on his behalf. "They didn't give a damn what your background was," his son maintained. "There was no social strata. You were either decent society, or you weren't." Of course, the Jewish population did not consist entirely of beloved characters. A non-Jewish woman recalled a family she delicately described as "not very nice people," either in their business or personal lives. They may have been the "only bad apple family" among the Jews in her town, but no doubt they had counterparts in other towns.[62]

Some people stood out for their social graces. A former Pocahontas school-teacher recalled the remarkable appearance of Jenny Baach late one night in 1921 as townspeople gathered outside during a fire: "In minutes the streets were jammed with people in all stages of dress and undress. To our amazement, Mrs. Sol Baach appeared perfectly groomed even to her red carnation in her beautiful hair. That carnation was such a constant companion that I never saw her without it. What a loveable person she was! She came to Pocahontas as a dancing teacher, and her lighthearted spirit and love for her friends was so etched into her magnetic character that everyone loved her. No visitor ever left her home without a gift of some sort. Her hospitality and beautiful parties are still a pleasant memory to me." The Virginia-born daughter of German Jewish immigrants, Jenny Baach presided over Pocahontas social life from her home, the Maples. She "served in style," a 1916 society column remarked, "as everyone familiar with Mrs. Baach's way of entertaining knows." Interestingly, in 1920 Jenny Baach served as the town's census taker. One wonders if she wore her trademark red carnation in her hair as she trooped the streets of her small mining town, recording the residents of homes and boardinghouses.[63]

Not all Jews were comfortable with the coalfield scene. Some attempted to keep their socializing entirely within the Jewish community. Pioneering Williamson merchant Jake Levine once admonished his young clerk Harry Schwachter, "You've got no business fooling around so much with those 'goyim' all the time." This attitude derived from a mix of factors: a longstanding Jewish distrust of gentiles, a reaction to local undercurrents of prejudice, and, conversely, a fear of *too much* acceptance—in the form of intermarriage, an outcome dreaded by most immigrant parents and a very real possibility since their children had such a small pool of fellow Jews from which to draw. Two interviewees related that their mothers tried to discourage their friendships with non-Jews precisely for that reason. Schwachter, in fact, believed that Levine had been urged to speak out by the town's "Yiddisha mamas," who did not want an eligible Jewish male to slip away from them. (They need not have worried. He ended up marrying Levine's niece, Rose Brown.)[64]

To some newly arrived Jewish women, who had lived more insulated lives than the men, their surroundings seemed quite foreign at first and they felt they had little in common with their neighbors. This was especially true for those who settled in the smaller mining towns. As one woman stated, "I can't tell you how my mother reacted coming from Brooklyn, New York, to Scarbro, West Virginia" about 1910. Her mother in fact exclaimed to her husband, "You brought me to a wilderness!" Though she was mostly referring to conditions such as the lack of plumbing and the cows and pigs that coexisted with the hamlet's human inhabit-ants, she also had in mind the lack of Jewish people. That did not stop her daugh-ter from making friends; in later years, she vividly recalled the two hundred hillside steps she had to climb to visit her best friend, the daughter of a Polish coal miner. Her mother, on the other hand, had no social life until the family moved to Beck-ley. Nineteen-year-old Esther Sturm was visiting her aunt in Pineville when her parents decided to move the family there from New York. "When I found out . . . I cried for a week," she later declared. "But then I made the best of it."[65]

The second half of her statement sums up the attitude of most women. On the whole they never found the coalfields as congenial as did the men, who were more likely to find fulfillment as business owners and civic leaders. Yet they adjusted to their surroundings and found ways to involve themselves in town life. Esther Sturm joined a church choir at the invitation of new friends. Goldie Koslow, born in Lithuania, served on McDowell County's Republican Executive Committee. Says her son, "I guess she thought it was part of the Americanization process." One woman, reflecting on her life in Williamson, offered this some-what equivocal statement in the early 1970s: "The town has been good to us. My husband loves his work and that is why we live here. . . . He's happy with what he's doing and I'm happy with what I'm doing. One has to find peace in one's home." Though women were more likely to center their social activities around their local Jewish community, they did not confine their socializing to fellow Jews, as most mixed easily with other residents of coalfield towns.[66]

Pressed to describe the non-Jews they socialized with, interviewees acknowl-edged that when they referred to "everyone" in town, they primarily meant oth-ers in their same class position: merchants, doctors, lawyers, teachers, middle- to upper-level coal company, railroad, and courthouse employees, and the like. This included individual friendships with African Americans in towns with a black middle class, though formal socializing was racially segregated. But it did not usually include the people who formed the bulk of the region's work force.

Since few coal miners lived in the county seats before midcentury, Jews in those towns had little contact with mining families except as customers who came to town on Saturdays. Class differences were compounded by a town-country social dichotomy that had existed before the coal boom and did not disappear with the passage of time. A non-Jew who grew up in Logan in the 1950s and 1960s recalled that all his friends, including his Jewish best friend, were town dwellers and did not associate with youngsters from the coal towns or farms in the surrounding hills. Some town-based members of the middle class, Jewish and non-Jewish, deprecated coal miners (or "mountain people" in general) as violent or ignorant. But most Jews had sympathy and respect for coal miners and their families, an attitude reinforced by the buyer-seller relationship. In interviews, "hard working" and "honest" were the terms most often used to characterize coal miners. Interviewees were especially impressed by the determination of local families to pay off their debts despite frequent economic hard times.[67]

Jews who lived beyond the county seats had a more diverse class acquaintance. Harry Berman grew up in Matewan in the 1910s. His family and the town's one other Jewish family enjoyed close relations with miners and other townspeople. "My father was always . . . in with the union people," Berman stated. "People were nice. They were friendly. . . . They liked us there, and they done a lot of tradin' there, in the store." The town's most famous union man, police chief Sid Hatfield, "used to come and visit quite a bit in the store and talk," Berman said. "He was a likeable fellow." Nevertheless, if a recognizable middle class existed in their small town, Jewish families associated mostly with others who occupied it. Coal-town geography reinforced social separation, since miners usually lived in company housing apart from the other residents, often literally "on the other side of the tracks."[68]

Newspaper articles and society columns provide clues to the position of Jews in the social structure. Jewish residents of the New River area, Middlesboro, Pocahontas, and McDowell County received mention when they entertained out-of-town guests, made buying trips, visited big-city relatives, or simply visited one another. The *McDowell Recorder* kept Welch readers abreast of the news that "Miss Klein Entertains" ("refreshments were served in keeping with the holiday of Passover"), that the Herzbruns were "persuaded to dance a real old time foreign dance" at their anniversary party, and that the "Wagner-Totz Wedding" was "a Brilliant Affair." Jewish communal events prompted glowing reports. In 1911, the *Recorder* noted that Keystone's "Manhattan Social Club has announced its annual Purim Ball" and "all who attend are assured a most enjoyable time" at "the biggest dance of the year." When the Welch Sisterhood hosted a state convention of Jewish women's groups in 1933, the *Welch Daily News* called it "the most brilliant social affair to be held in Welch this season." Though these disclosures offer evidence of Jews' respectability, their meaning is ambiguous: almost all the guests at these various events were Jewish.[69]

At least, their frequent appearance in print confirms that they made up a sizable portion of the middle class in many locales. Some days, they appeared to constitute the *entire* "society set" of their towns. The *Fayette Journal's* "Sewell Notes" of August 8, 1901, had but four items, all featuring Jewish women visiting or being visited by out-of-town relatives. Six of nine "Kimball Items" in the *McDowell Recorder* on January 26, 1912, involved Jews. It would be misleading to characterize such items as coverage of actual society events, at least not in the sense of "high" society. Many were along the lines of this 1919 disclosure about a Jewish butcher: "Sol Kaufman, the well-known meat man from Kimball, was here on business Monday." Even the comings and goings of Jewish clerks received attention. In 1905, for example, the *Middlesboro News* reported that "Sam Zinberg, who has been clerking for the Weinstein boys, is now taking in the money at Dave's."[70]

The inclusion of such plebeian items reveals not only the status of Jews but also the less-than-polished nature of the coalfield social scene. Writing of his experience clerking at his uncle's Wilcoe store in the 1920s, Irving Alexander offers a vivid depiction of the town's leading citizen, J. B. Smith, who lived in "the only really elegant house in town" with a "patrician wife" and two children away at college. J. B. made his living as a railroad agent, scrip dealer, chicken dealer, and unabashed pilferer of coal from the trains that passed through town. Even in the county seats, the society set was a bit rough around the edges: when Harry Schwachter first came to Williamson he boarded with the Stratton family and was surprised to find that the family was considered among the "socially elite" in town, "despite their accommodations for paying guests."[71]

Aside from Welch in McDowell County, the doings of Jews in the county seats were not as well reported as in the boomtowns, reflecting both their smaller proportion in the population, and a more stratified social structure. These towns actually did have a "high society," and Jews were not, for the most part, members. Nor were they absolutely excluded. Though their middle-class position was secure, their status in regard to the elite was less clear. Accepted as town-building contributors, they were not necessarily social equals, especially members of the immigrant generation. In Williamson, the socially ambitious Harry Schwachter became the first Jew "to crash the society set" in the 1910s by flaunting his dancing talent and pursuing a career as "an eligible young white-collar man about town." Says his daughter, other Jews "resented the fact that Dad was invited to all the elite affairs of the 'upper crust.' No Jew had ever attended the dances and parties given by the so-called four hundred—at least not with such regular attendance!"[72]

Later generations too faced some social exclusion by county-seat elites. In Beckley, when the first Jew was nominated for country club membership in the 1950s, the board held a lengthy and heated meeting before accepting him. In Williamson for many years Jews could not join the Elks Club. Then one of the older members died and suddenly they were admitted. (They joined because they wanted to gamble.) As late as the 1970s, it was rumored that the town's Mountain Club had been created so the wealthy could have one club that did not accept Jews. Yet they had little problem joining the town's other fraternal groups, and one year three Jewish men served as president of three clubs at the same time. One Jewish man observed that the town's diversity helped limit small-town prejudice: "Williamson didn't have the problems that a lot of towns have. Because it was settled by so many different ethnic groups, they just wanted to make it a better place to live."[73]

Notwithstanding occasional social discrimination, Jews in county seats as well as other towns joined in the civic, charitable, and recreational activities that characterized small-town middle-class life. Men belonged to fraternal clubs and veterans' groups; women joined their town's Women's Club, PTA, and "female auxiliaries." Both participated in bridge, tennis, music, garden, and book clubs. The smaller the town, the smaller the pool of middle-class people such groups could draw from. The effect was to bring Jews and non-Jews close together, as they constantly encountered each other through volunteer and leisure activities. As a non-Jewish woman observed, "In a small place, you've got the same people working in every organization. . . . It didn't matter about their religion, they all worked together."[74]

Many Jews held leadership positions. The Blochs and Baaches founded the Pocahontas Masonic Lodge in 1883; Harry Kammer of Williamson, Irving Goldstein of Beckley, and Emanuel Katzen of Welch (son of Isadore) served as commanders of their American Legion posts in the 1920s, 1930s, and 1950s. A 1972 study of Williamson Jews recorded that a remarkable 76 percent of men belonged to four or more non-Jewish organizations and 65 percent of women belonged to at least one; 35 percent of both men and women held leadership posts that year.[75]

Their economic niche influenced how Jewish residents contributed to social and cultural life. Small-town merchants were among the more worldly citizens of their towns, since they traveled to large cities on a regular basis. They returned from these trips not only with the latest goods to sell in their stores, but also with news of the latest fashions, music, and dances. As a young man, Harry Schwachter furthered his social ambitions by giving dance lessons to members of the town elite—after visiting relatives in Cincinnati to brush up on the latest popular dances. He also shared his knowledge in local amateur theatricals; one such program featured "Schwachter and Crank" performing "Up-to-Date Society Dances."[76]

Jewish involvement in local culture reflected an interest in typical middle-class pastimes as well as a longstanding Jewish cultural bent toward books, music, and the arts. One of Schwachter's chief enthusiasms was the annual Chautauqua program (a nationwide movement to bring cultural events to small towns). Naturally, he served as president of the local Chautauqua board, and he even offered his own speech to local groups on "Poets from Homer to the Present Age." Jewish parents enthusiastically enrolled their children in music lessons. Ken Bank was sent to Bluefield every week for violin lessons, which no doubt provided a contrast to shooting at rats from his Keystone front porch. Schwachter's children "took piano lessons faithfully," with his son "one of the very few boys who participated in Miss Lovelace's Musicale in 1929." This was no acceptable occupation for a young Williamson male, and he suffered such intense embarrassment that his parents finally allowed him to quit.[77]

Many young people became involved in sports—for boys, a more respectable activity than music. In the 1920s, Charles Sameth captained the Welch high school football team while Bessie Levinson starred on the girl's basketball team. Sam Abrams played on the semipro Middlesboro Allens basketball team in 1947. There weren't enough Jewish boys in Welch in 1921 to form their own basketball team in the Sunday School League, but the "Consolidated" team, made up of miscellaneous congregations, featured a roster that was more than half Jewish, including guard "Punk" Herzbrun. Both the Logan and Beckley congregations fielded basketball teams in their towns' adult church leagues in the 1920s and 1940s.[78]

Coalfield Jewish Social Integration in Larger Context

Immigrant peddler-turned-merchant David Brown of Williamson "was never a great financial success, but was a landmark as one of the pioneers of the community," writes his granddaughter, Marilou Schwachter Sniderman. Though religion was important to him, "his God was most undemanding." When Brown could no longer climb the many steps to the synagogue, he "transferred his diligent and prompt attendance" to the ground-level First Presbyterian Church. "He enjoyed those Sunday services and extolled the praises of the preacher and congregation to all his cronies, who were amused, and to my parents, who were both embarrassed and outraged." But more embarrassed by the social transgression than outraged by the religious one, Sniderman implies:

> "Oh, Papa," mother would fume. "How can you sit there, week after week, when they sing their praises to Jesus? You've always been a good Jew. You know you don't believe in the doctrines of the Presbyterian Church." . . . Papa would answer absent-mindedly, "I like to go there, and they like to have me, too. Why, just last Sunday they had a brand new spittoon for me on the front seat where I always sit." Mother shrieked, "Papa, you didn't spit on the floor in that church!" . . . [My parents] considered . . . tobacco chewing a cardinal sin. "Well now, I useta," Papa answered blithely. "I don't reckon you'd expect me to swallow it. But I don't anymore since I have my own spittoon. And you don't have to worry about me praying to Jesus either, Rosie. He was a right smart Jew and I always thought a lot of him." Mother wailed, "Oh, Papa, the whole town is laughing at you, and I just know the Presbyterians are fit to be tied!" "Nope," he answered, as he

tucked his slightly soiled shirt into the shabby trousers, "they like me just fine.
... Everytime they sing 'Jesus,' I sing 'Moses' or 'Abraham' just as loud as can
be. I tell you, Rosie, the singing is really fine. Nobody seems to mind." And indeed, nobody did, outside of Mother and Dad. Still, I recall that when the new
Presbyterian Church was built, the folks gave a substantial donation.[79]

The contrast between David Brown and his daughter Rose Schwachter encapsu-
lates the contrast between the first generation of respected pioneers and/or
coarse immigrants and the more proper middle-class second generation. It also
illustrates the increasing desire for respectability on the part of Jewish coalfield
residents in response to changing social dynamics and incidentally highlights the
continuing acceptance of difference on the part of larger society.

Jews found diverse ways to fit into the coalfield social scene. Their general trajectory was from rough boomtown immigrant to respectable member of the county-
seat middle class within one or two generations, yet there were plenty of exceptions
to this rule. Perhaps the most accurate generalization that can be made is that they
felt free to follow their inclinations on how to relate to non-Jews. Some, like Jake
Levine, preferred to keep their interaction to a minimum. Others, like Rose
Schwachter's husband Harry, were "determined to crash the society set."

Most fell somewhere in between. They engaged in the social life of their towns
as friends, neighbors, and contributors while their ties to their local Jewish community remained their most vital social connection. As one woman summed up,
referring to Williamson from the 1940s to 1970s, "There was a very active Jewish
social life and there was a very integrated social life [with non-Jews] as well."[80]
That Jews more often socialized among themselves can be attributed to multiple
factors: their own choice, the tendency of the region's ethnic and religious groups
to congregate among their own, class dynamics, and social exclusion in the upper
reaches of society based, in part, on prejudice.

The wide-open atmosphere of the classic coalfield boomtowns, which tolerated all kinds of people and all kinds of behavior, was not completely replicated
in the county seats, where a more traditional small-town social structure developed. Yet the county-seat environment too encouraged Jewish participation in
civic and social life. Town-based elites needed help to achieve "what they were
unable to do themselves, namely the capitalist transformation of the countryside."[81] Though Appalachian scholars have focused on the "help" provided by
absentee investors in coal, the point applies equally to entrepreneurial newcomers, among them Jews, who brought commercial experience and connections,
entrepreneurial ambitions, and a belief in progress—attributes that ensured acceptance into the middle class.

The experience of small Jewish communities across the United States provides a
context for understanding coalfield Jewish-gentile interaction. The open attitude of
coalfield society toward its Jewish minority contrasts with the hierarchical social
structure of Johnstown, Pennsylvania, whose East European Jewish community was

established during the same era. Johnstown's elite tolerated Jews but did not welcome their full participation, states Ewa Morawska. Jews remained socially segregated, their contacts with non-Jews superficial, and their participation in civic life meager. At the other extreme, German Jews in the gold mining town of Eureka, Nevada, in the 1870s were completely absorbed into society and played a leadership role in every area of town life, states Norton Stern. Unlike coalfield Jews, even their communal events were integrated, with the annual Purim Ball serving as a major item on the town's social calendar. The coalfield Jewish experience more closely matches that of the German and East European Jewish community of Wichita, Kansas, as described by Hal Rothman. Jews arrived "before the platting of the town," found a high degree of social and public acceptance, and mixed easily with non-Jews, yet their organized social events tended to be all-Jewish affairs.[82]

Morawska maintains that the economic marginality of Johnstown's Jews (their nonparticipation in the dominant industries of coal and steel), their tendency to immerse themselves in their own social life, the Christian-based culture of the larger society, the ethnic stratification of Johnstown, and the existence of mild antisemitism kept Jews apart from others.[83] Yet each of those factors pertained in the coalfields, with different results. Other variables may perhaps be more salient in accounting for differences in how Jews in small-town America related to the surrounding milieu.

First, the existence of a boomtown atmosphere greatly aided the absorption of Jews into the social sphere. High levels of integration occurred in areas of new settlement and rapid growth, in areas that lacked a rigid social hierarchy, where outsiders were needed to advance elites' notions of progress, and where Jews were present from the beginning as town pioneers. This set of conditions trumped other factors, including region and origins of the Jewish population. In general, German Jews who settled in the growing towns of the West, Midwest, and South benefited from the timing of their midcentury arrival. East European Jews migrated during a later period, after most of the United States had passed out of the "frontier" stage. However, those who ventured to remaining areas of new growth, such as the coalfields, found similar circumstances and showed similar patterns of social interaction.

Second, where ethnic diversity reigned, often the case in boomtowns, the likelihood of Jewish integration was even higher. Jews were more accepted in heterogeneous places where their religion and culture did not stand out as the sole contrast to a prevailing local norm. Such ethnic diversity was more prevalent in the West than in the South, but it characterized the southern coalfields. Heterogeneity inhibited the pressure to conform that often characterized small towns, since there was no well-established single norm with which to conform. Louis Schmier observes that the East European Jews of Valdosta, Georgia, chose to remain separate from the general population in part because they perceived that only total assimilation, resulting in loss of their Jewish identity, would enable

them to win acceptance. The Jews who lived in the coalfields had no such concerns. They remained unselfconsciously Jewish while entering into the larger
society around them.[84]

A third variable is purely demographic: the size of their towns and the proportion of Jews in the population influenced Jewish-gentile interaction. This is clearly demonstrated within the coalfields. Among southern West Virginia county-seat
towns, Jews were most thoroughly involved in the social scene in Welch, where
they made up their largest percentage of the population, followed by Williamson.
In Beckley, where their percentage was smaller, they were less active in civic and
social life and experienced a greater degree of exclusion.

Nationally, Jews in small towns felt more comfortable and experienced less
exclusion than those in small- to medium-sized cities. The smaller the town, the
more members of the middle class relied on each other as friends, neighbors, and
club participants. Jews in cities such as Knoxville and Atlanta experienced a
greater sense of insecurity, concern about gentile perceptions, and need to prove
respectability. They took pains to be inconspicuous and avoid controversy.[85] In
contrast, Jews in the coalfields did not seem bothered about how others viewed
them, especially in the early years. This lack of concern on the part the first generation did give way in later years, as town populations grew, the percentage of
Jews shrank, and the boomtown atmosphere yielded to a more settled and stratified environment in which respectability became increasingly important.

Many historians of American Jewry attribute variations in social integration to
cultural differences between German and East European Jews. German Jewish
immigrants, though they arrived in the United States with the same basic Orthodox Judaism as the Eastern Europeans, came from a culture less insular and less
steeped in religious tradition. They were more comfortable with the process of
assimilation and less foreign in appearance than East European Jewish immigrants.
Even in the coalfields, differences between German and East European Jews can be
discerned. German families such as the Blochs, Baaches, and Midleburgs showed
no interest in Jewish communal activity and blended more thoroughly than others
into the coalfield elite. But most studies posit a far greater dichotomy between
German and Eastern European Jews than was evident in the coalfields. In Valdosta, writes Schmier, German Jews adjusted easily while Eastern Europeans exhibited a "*shtetl* mentality." John Livingston cites the West's "initial cosmopolitanism,
the Jewish pioneer role" and "the absence of large numbers of eastern European
immigrants" as reasons for a high level of integration. The implication is that East
European Jews were less willing because of their cultural predilections, and less
able because of their foreign ways, to mix with non-Jews.[86]

Yet old-country origins may have played a less important role than structural
variables such as town size and stage of development at the time each Jewish
contingent first arrived. Hal Rothman, for one, maintains that East European
Jews, though seeming more foreign, followed generally the same pattern as Ger-

man Jews in integrating into Wichita society. Norton Stern insists that much of the Jewish population in the American West was not actually "German" at all but hailed from Prussian Poland and shared many characteristics of East European Jews. Moreover, as Robert Levinson points out, immigrants who choose to journey to frontiers tend to be "the most adventurous of their people," less bound by tradition than others and more likely to adopt local ways. This would apply just as much to East European as to German Jews.[87]

Certainly the East European Jews of the coalfields belie the view that East European immigrants, by nature, had difficulty assimilating. Rather, timing better accounts for differences in how Jews adapted to their surroundings. In Valdosta, conditions may have changed between the arrival of the Germans and the Eastern Europeans. A more stratified social structure may have developed, and opportunities may have been more along the lines of filling a particular niche or economic gap (catering to black customers in the South or Slavic industrial workers in the North) rather than serving as town pioneers in a relatively open society.

U.S. regional differences too may be overemphasized by historians in explaining variations in Jewish integration. Parallels between the coalfield Jewish experience and that of Jewish communities in the West suggest that "a variety of patterns which transcend region" can be discerned in the adaptation of Jews to their U.S. environments. Such parallels, when applied to Appalachian studies, argue against the myth of Appalachian "exceptionalism."[88]

Although coalfield Jews enjoyed a relatively open environment that allowed them to integrate while feeling free to retain their distinct identity, forces both internal and external created a certain amount of social tension and ambivalence. Within individuals who grew up in the region, questions of self-definition arose. Separated from their neighbors by their families' religion, means of livelihood, and cultural background, many struggled with the implications of being in, but not completely of, their hometowns. Within Jewish families and communities, as integration shaded into assimilation, divisions appeared over how Jewish identity should be expressed: Which cultural practices should be retained, and how? Which should be altered or dropped altogether? Meanwhile, the surrounding society offered its own challenges for the small Jewish population to grapple with: What are the limits of social acceptance? What terms and conditions have been subtly imposed? And of particular concern in the coalfields, how should Jews respond to the conflicts that engulfed the region but did not directly involve them? Periods of intense labor strife and class polarization posed a special dilemma to a people in the middle, whose friends, neighbors, and customers were busy choosing sides. These questions will be explored in the following chapters.

CHAPTER 4

Insiders and Outsiders: Race, Religion, and Politics in the Coalfields

At the 1928 cornerstone-laying ceremony for the Williamson synagogue, congregation president Harry Schwachter directed some of his remarks to the gentiles in the crowd: "The building of this temple will prove to you our permanency. It will show the community that we are not interlopers and we did not come for the purpose of 'filling our bags and baggage,' but rather to live with you, work with you, and serve with you to the end of time. A handful of Jewish people have found a veritable haven in this community." Jews had maintained a presence in Williamson since the town's founding more than thirty years earlier. They had already bolstered Williamson's commercial and civic development and would continue to do so for decades to come. Their decision to build a synagogue showed their confidence that, from an economic, communal, and social standpoint, the town offered them a decent future. As Schwachter's daughter wrote almost forty years after the ceremony, "His words were absolutely true, and were carried out. The same twenty families who started the temple, or their descendants, are still there, building better relations in a struggling community. They have remained loyal to a little town that has had its ups and downs."[1]

And yet Schwachter's words reveal an underlying tension, a hint of insecurity. Why did Jews have something to "prove"? Where and how was it insinuated that they were "interlopers"? Was this an imaginary reproach from imaginary gentiles, part of Schwachter's inheritance of centuries-old Jewish distrust of non-Jews or his absorption of antisemitic stereotypes? Or did it emanate from the coalfield environment? The usually optimistic Schwachter was not the only one to raise doubts about the standing of Jews in coalfield society. Interviews, newspaper articles, and other sources expose ambiguities and contradictions in Jewish-gentile relations and in the attitude of the larger society toward its Jewish minority.

To adequately explore these ambiguities and capture the complexities of Jewish-gentile interaction, it is necessary to consider the dynamics of class, race, and religion that shaped *all* social transactions in the coalfield context. Even within the tolerant boomtown environment, the region's diversity offered scope for ethnic friction. And despite their high degree of integration, despite being one of many different coalfield minorities, Jews occupied ground that can only be described as anomalous: as middle-class, commercial-oriented town dwellers among a predominantly working-class, rural population, as nonparticipants (mostly) in the single industry that employed almost everyone else, and as non-Christians in an overwhelmingly Christian society. These distinctions marked their own sense of identity and the way others viewed them, forming an underlying motif that deeply influenced their relations with non-Jews.

Diversity, Conflict, and Accommodation

Although multicultural cooperation came to characterize coal town life, conflict rather than camaraderie at first marked ethnic relations. The early years of the coal boom were a time of wrenching change exacerbated by harsh living conditions, dangerous working conditions, and fierce labor conflict. This setting offered fertile ground for nativism and racism to flourish, for people from all backgrounds to project their anxieties, confusion, and fear onto an all-to-handy "other." Some coal operators promoted ethnic discord, hoping to "forestall unionism by playing one group off against another," one historian asserts. Cultural differences and misunderstandings intensified ethnic tensions: immigrants "had manners, customs, and languages altogether unfamiliar and often frightening to mountaineers and Blacks." Meanwhile, the American legacy of racism against blacks quickly infected the foreigners. Under the rough-and-tumble conditions that pertained before World War I, these dynamics caused the coalfield melting pot to routinely "boil over into violence."[2]

Institutionalized racism set the tone. Though West Virginia, where most coalfield blacks settled, did not have the full complement of Jim Crow laws, segregation was mandated by law in education and marriage and was customary in other areas. Coal company housing segregated miners into sections with names such as "Niggertown" and "Hunkieville," which expressed the lower status of their residents. Coalfield newspapers often aimed their bigotry at foreigners and blacks, portraying immigrants as "ignorant, dirty, and prone to drinking," says Randall Lawrence. Articles dwelt on the propensity of nonnative white groups to fight among themselves and kill each other for seemingly no reason—or, more threateningly (but less frequently), highlighted the "savage" attacks committed by foreigners against native whites. The African American–owned *McDowell Times,* though biased in its own way, offered an alternative perspective. One 1913 article described a "Near Riot in Anawalt" in which a white mob chased an Italian home after a bar fight. The article castigated "lawless white brutes," neatly echoing the language occasionally directed against blacks in the region's other newspapers.[3]

Ethnic strife, however, soon gave way to accommodation. The immigrant population peaked with the onset of World War I and the federal immigration restrictions of the 1920s. Some stability came to the region with a demographic shift away from young single workers to a more family-based environment. The public schools served as common ground between native whites and foreigners, and marriages between people of different ethnic backgrounds (even between Catholics and Protestants) became increasingly common. The intense, shared experience of coalfield life above and under ground lessened racial hostilities as well. In the early 1930s, researcher James Laing asserted that the conditions of everyday life forged "cordial" black-white relations and a "spirit of cooperation and good will" between the races.[4]

The immigrants, blacks, and native whites who gathered as the coal boom got underway went through a similar process of adjustment to American industrial life as their urbanizing counterparts across the nation. The society that emerged was in many ways a "polyglot culture" that enabled them to retain aspects of their religious and cultural heritage.[5] From houses of worship to foodways, coalfield residents integrated elements of their various cultures into their new homes, and these customs continued to color life in the region. A certain amount of cultural fusion occurred as customs spread beyond each ethnic group to touch a larger circle of neighbors and friends. The Schwachter family enjoyed their "traditional" Sunday breakfast of fried apples and country-cured ham. A gentile woman from Pocahontas recalled how her father's good friend taught him to speak Yiddish. Mary Marsh Ofsa of Keystone, daughter of a Protestant southerner and an Irish Catholic, was raised a Baptist before marrying into a Jewish family. Late into the twentieth century she continued to prepare her mother-in-law's recipe for matzo ball soup, which she sent over to the local Catholic priest when he took ill. A one-woman example of coalfield multiculturalism, for fifty years she played the organ at Baptist, Catholic, Jewish, and Methodist services.[6]

Divisions along class lines emerged as the most potent source of conflict—with the concomitant effect of boosting ethnic and racial unity within each class. Working-class solidarity overcame ethnic and racial animosities among coal miners, and the multicultural middle class melded as well. It is perhaps telling that the Harlan newspapers gave front-page prominence to Jewish communal happenings in the early 1930s, a time of all-consuming labor-management conflict in the Harlan coalfield. On March 5, 1932, the *Harlan Enterprise* even printed a small notice, submitted by Jewish community leader Harry Linden, headlined "Harlan Hebrew Congregation Prays for Safety of Lindbergh Baby."[7]

In the ideological battle between labor and management, the region's power structure began to advance a rosy view of diversity that stressed cooperation among all the various peoples engaged in the capitalist enterprise. Dependent for their profits on a multicultural work force, elites praised foreigners, blacks, and mountain natives as long as they were willing to work hard and celebrated the impact of industrialization in bringing progress, capitalist values, and Americanism to these three benighted groups. In a 1922 speech to fellow coal operators, the fiercely anti-union J. G. Bradley rhapsodized: "One's faith in the 'melting pot' is reestablished upon seeing the children of Jugo-Slavish, Hungarian, and Italian parents leading the schools in the coal fields in regularity of attendance and in concentrated application to their work." The result was a sort of self-serving cosmopolitanism that accepted different kinds of people as long as they did not challenge the structure of economic relations. As a 1912 newspaper article put it, "A person is not questioned as to where he came from. All that is required is that he contains worth, and that he is willing to abide by the provisions of the law."[8]

The transformation of immigrants from alien to acceptable reached its zenith with the United States' entry into World War I, as newspaper articles such as "Our Faithful Italian Friends" and "Syrians Prove Loyal" lauded the Americanism of local immigrants during a time of national need. A coal industry trade journal waxed eloquent on the multicultural nature of a "Patriotic Demonstration at Gary, W. Va." in 1917, carefully listing all the participating immigrant and African American lodges. The event, presided over by the superintendent of U.S. Coal and Coke, included speeches by a Catholic priest, a Methodist minister, and *McDowell Times* editor M. T. Whittico, who "spoke for the colored citizens."[9]

Editor Whittico's participation at the rally was fitting, since his newspaper was the principal cheerleader for harmonious relations between African Americans and the coal industry. As a middle-class black leader, he shared with elite whites a firm belief in the capitalist order. Yet Whittico's devotion also sprang from the fact that the coal industry offered unprecedented opportunity that enabled blacks to come "closer to finding economic equality" than "perhaps anywhere else in America," according to historian Ron Lewis. The region's large black working class provided the basis for vibrant African American communities that supported their own middle class of businesspeople, teachers, and professionals.[10]

Jews, Blacks, and Other Minorities

By 1900, the African American demographic presence was strongest in McDowell County, and Keystone, the most open of all coalfield towns, emerged as the center of black life in the region, the "Mecca of the Coalfields," as the *McDowell Times* often proclaimed. The newspaper enthused that Keystone "always will be famous for its cosmopolitan spirit, its even handed dealing with both races." It could state with confidence that "a man couldn't be lynched in Keystone." Despite its penchant for hyperbole, there is no reason to doubt its claim that "white and colored live more nearly and evenly friends in this city than in any other in the country."[11]

In fact, corroboration comes from an entirely oppositional source: the 1912 anti-Keystone diatribe *Sodom and Gomorrah of Today*. The author (the "Virginia lad") harshly criticized the town's incomplete housing segregation and lambasted its white politicians for "catering to the negro." While his stated purpose was to expose the immoral activities in Cinder Bottom, the true cause of his ire seems to have been the lack of appropriate racial standards, from licentious race-mixing in that infamous red light district to day-to-day cooperation between ordinary blacks and whites. He made sure to point out that the five-member Keystone City Council contained two Jews and two blacks, though he did not comment on the Jews, except to say they were "prominent merchants of the town."[12]

The white residents lauded by the *McDowell Times*, of course, included a large contingent of Jewish immigrants and their families. For many years, Keystone led the region in number and percentage of both blacks and Jews; in 1900, the population was 40 percent black and 10 percent Jewish. *McDowell Times* articles from the 1910s suggest the two groups maintained good relations. An item praising leading businessman Wolf Bank stressed there was "no discrimination between the races" at his café. The *Times* hailed "congenial" theater owner Louis Shore as "public spirited" after he invited a black church to hold services in his theater free of charge until the church could rebuild after a disaster. The newspaper urged readers to patronize Shore's theater because "poor, black or white, they treat you right" and encouraged them to attend Israel Totz's theater because "Mr. Totz has on many occasions proven his friendship" to blacks. Describing Totz as "fair, just, and courteous," the *Times* noted that "one is made to feel welcome" in his theater and, moreover, his pictures "do not tend to incite race hatred" (probably a reference to the film *Birth of a Nation,* which sparked banning campaigns by African American groups across the state). One of Totz's Grand Theater ads promised "courteous and impartial attention," pointing out that "one man's money goes as far as the other."[13]

Jewish-black relations were not restricted to merchant and customer. The black middle class interacted with whites on a more equal footing than elsewhere, leading to friendships between blacks and Jews as well as diverse economic and political relationships. Lacking a professional cohort of their own before the 1930s, Jews retained African American lawyers for legal matters remarkable and routine. Isadore Katzen's defense team at his murder trial included prominent black attorney Arthur Froe. Froe and fellow black attorney Harry Capehart successfully argued for merchant Sigmund Kohn in a civil dispute before the state supreme court. Jews worked with or contended against African American businessmen in real estate deals. The two groups shared a Republican political orientation before the 1930s and actively supported the 1912 gubernatorial campaign of local luminary Henry D. Hatfield. This alliance led the *Times* to endorse McDowell County's sole Jewish lawyer, Sam Solins of Welch, for public office in 1913. The *Times* noted that Solins, "together with some of his influential Hebrew friends, worked untiringly" for Hatfield's election, with the result that "more than two-thirds of the Hebrews of the state" voted for Hatfield. "The colored boys of McDowell have no better friend than Attorney Solins of Welch, and they admire him for his hustling qualities, clean record, and straight Republicanism," the endorsement concluded.[14]

Only a few miles from the border with Jim Crow Virginia, Keystone must have stood as an egregious affront to white supremacists. Yet despite political and civic cooperation, the town's white critics and black supporters probably overstated the degree of interracial social contact. In Keystone and throughout the coalfields, social life remained largely segregated (outside of Cinder Bottom, at least). Clubs and churches were organized along ethnic and racial lines, and society columns show no evidence of black-white interaction. Interviews confirm that the two races got along well—following strict social rules. Certain types of interaction were acceptable: children could play together after school, men could engage in "informal recreational activities," neighbor women could visit one another's homes, and so on. But such exchanges occurred with a clear understanding of the limits involved. Even a *McDowell Times* article extolling Keystone's race relations observed, "Of course there is no social equality here and no one wants nor looks for it. We all get along well without friction."[15]

The 1920s resurgence of the Ku Klux Klan swept the coalfields along with the rest of the nation, confirming that "racial subordination . . . sharply differentiated" the worlds of black and white, as Joe Trotter states. Yet the Klan's popularity was brief and it was generally frowned on by local authorities. In 1923, the Middlesboro City Council banned public speech that "would incite hatred between races and classes" and in 1924 made it illegal to wear a mask in public. The balance of interracial cooperation and segregation, the existence of "cordial" black-white relations and a "spirit of good will" within a framework of racism and discrimination, mark coalfield race relations as particularly complex.[16]

The Klan's displays of native white Protestant chauvinism reminded Jews, Catholics, and indeed all the region's immigrant groups that they had not completely shed their status as outsiders. In fact, trends toward assimilation and intergroup harmony did not completely eliminate racial, ethnic, or religious antagonism. The inclination to label and define people from different backgrounds, to respond to social and economic tensions by ascribing blame to a somehow-alien "other," did not disappear after the coalfields settled down in the post–World War I era. The tendency became muted but remained, affecting relations between people in subtle yet important ways. Each group would take a part in serving as "other" for someone else. African Americans, foreigners, Catholics, Jews, and even native mountaineers were not immune from being thrust into that role.

Some immigrants reacted to their less-than-equal position in the time-honored way of newcomers to America: by seizing on their "superior" status to blacks. A 1930s account of coalfield life asserts that immigrant miners were more racist than native white miners. Jews too were susceptible to absorbing the racist notions prevalent in white society. As one interviewee wryly commented, "Jews can be as prejudiced as any group of people."[17]

The religions brought by Southern and Eastern Europeans furnished a conspicuous difference between natives and immigrants. A deeply held belief in religious freedom had fostered among mountain residents an "ecumenical open-ness" that respected the right of others to practice their own faith. Yet this sensibil-ity vied with nativist influences heightened by some of the more dogmatic tenets of fundamentalist Protestantism. Some locals subscribed to the anti-Catholicism that had long been a prominent feature of American nativism. "Catholic was more hated than Jew," observed a lifelong resident. Catholics were suspected of following the pope rather than the Bible, and the pope, to some, was associated with the antichrist. Margaret Ripley-Wolfe writes that mountaineers had many "false ideas" about Catholic belief and practice, characterizing their stance toward Catholicism as "suspicion and curiosity mixed with a measure of hostility."[18]

All coalfield groups faced the contradictions of acceptance and estrangement, but each group dealt with its own set of contradictions. Jews had been removed from the ethnic-related turbulence that had accompanied the early stage of the coal boom. Their numbers were too small to pose a threat to anyone and they did not compete with other groups for jobs. Having lived in the United States longer than immigrants recruited directly into the mines, most spoke English along with other coalfield languages and thus avoided conflicts based on miscommunication. But they would not be spared the less violent consequences of being perceived as "other."

Sometimes the result was ironic. After West Virginia merchant David Scott lost everything in a 1905 fire that destroyed his home and newly built store in Wilcoe, he decided his only option was to get a job in the mines. He approached U.S. Coal and Coke superintendent Edward O'Toole, who replied, "Dave, the coal mines are no place for a Jew. You get reestablished." O'Toole let the young man occupy a company house and gave him supplies to tide him over while another local leader, Bill Hatfield, lent him funds to rebuild. Because O'Toole subscribed to the stereo-type that Jews were unfit for manual labor, he refused to hire Scott as a miner. The same prejudice would contribute to discrimination against Jews in heavy industry elsewhere in the United States, but for Scott it was entirely beneficial.[19]

Meanwhile, other ethnic groups were being typecast as *only* fit for manual labor, such as Slavs and blacks. Coal operators had even convinced themselves that different ethnic groups were suited by nature for different jobs in the mines (though opinions differed regarding which jobs matched which groups). In one case, Randall Lawrence notes, this too ended up benefiting a local Jewish man:

> In one county seat in West Virginia, a coal company hired a Jewish businessman to meet the trains carrying the immigrants. The Jew, a linguist by reason of his varied life in Europe and America, would meet trains and identify immigrants by nationality and language for the coal companies. Poles, Magyars, Slovaks, Slovenians, Italians . . . arrived by the thousands in the heart of the Appalachian wilderness. Some companies preferred Hungarians as miners, while others might be seeking Italian stone masons. The Jewish businessman was on the spot at the train station to match employer with potential employee.[20]

These two stories show the advantages Jews had over other groups. Both David Scott and the unnamed Jewish businessman were Eastern Europeans, just like the workers whom the latter helped to classify. Unlike the workers, though, they were not "foreigners." Or to be more accurate, they were not *as* foreign, at least not to coal operators and other elites with whom they shared a language—not only English but also the language of capitalism. For this reason, long before Italians were transformed from violent primitives to loyal friends, coalfield newspapers extolled Jews as up-and-coming business leaders and self-made men. Yet the Jewish businessman described by Lawrence spoke the language of the alien "others" as well. Both his foreignness and his middleman status—in this case, as intermediary between coal operators and workers—come through in the story. Jewish-gentile relations would continue to be informed by the paradoxes and ambiguities inherent in the Jews' middleman role and their religious/cultural distinctiveness.

Insiders and Outsiders

The "Pocahontas Pickings" section of the *Bluefield Daily Telegraph* contained two lead items on January 5, 1916. The first described how Pocahontas resident Henry Hicks was badly injured by three "ruffians (Russians)" who attacked him "in a savage manner." Just below this, an article noted that Mr. and Mrs. Sol Baach hosted local Masonic officers at a stylish dinner party, at which their guests presented them with an "elegant silver water pitcher," accompanied by much speechmaking. The juxtaposition of the "savage," unnamed Russians and the "elegant" Baaches offers a striking contrast between the foreign "other" and the civilized local society that coalfield newspapers were determined to promote. The Baaches, second-generation German Jews, serve as just one example that Jews in the coalfields belonged in a different social category than the foreigners: they were insiders, not outsiders.[21]

This status was not limited to the second generation. The stance of local newspapers toward some Jewish immigrants, leading or up-and-coming businesspeople, ranged from admiration to a sort of jocular banter that confirmed their insider standing. They were heartily congratulated and often teased when they got married or had children. When Sam Weinstein's son was born in 1905, the *Middlesboro News* remarked, "Sam takes the event fairly well, though one of the boys says he sold a four dollar pair of pants for a dollar and a half and gave the man eight dollars and a half in change for a five dollar bill. However, this latter may be a 'campaign lie.'" (He was running for city council at the time.) Their travel for business or pleasure was noted and their opinions quoted. When Sam's brother Herman returned from a 1901 visit to the baths at Hot Springs, Arkansas, for example, the paper reported that "he thinks well of the place as a bodily sanitarium but considers it a moral hell on Earth."[22]

The deaths of prominent Jewish immigrants merited sober front page coverage.

The many memorials to Joe Lopinsky included a poem in the *McDowell Recorder* that concluded, "They tell us Heaven's wondrous / And free from earthly guile— / It is brighter now than ever / With Uncle Joe's sweet smile." Welch civic leader Pauline Josephy's passing at age forty-seven caused "a shadow of sincere sorrow to sweep the entire city," in the words of the *Recorder*. The paper published a resolution by the Methodist Women's Missionary Society expressing "its love for and appreciation of [her] life and beautiful character."[23]

Once in awhile, though, a different attitude emerged from the printed page. Jews were not exempt from the stereotypical treatment other coalfield groups received. Such treatment reflected centuries-old gentile attitudes about "the Jew." In the economic realm, Jews embodied capitalist traits and values, good and bad. They could be thrifty, hard working, and ambitious—or stingy, greedy, and prone to cheat non-Jews. In religious discourse, they could be the "Chosen People" or the enemy of Christianity, blamed for killing Jesus and denying his divinity. Pseudo-scientific racial theories that placed Jews lower on the racial scale than Northern Europeans also filtered into the coalfields. European and American "experts" contended that Jews were not "white," as shown by certain physical and behavioral traits. Whether economic, religious, or racial, stereotypes malignant or benign reinforced the idea that Jews were different, a people apart.[24]

Even newspaper articles that commended Jewish merchants occasionally had a subtext that played on ancient aversive images, intentionally or not. The *Mc-Dowell Recorder* frequently reported on the activities of Sam Polon, from his noteworthy real estate deals to his trip to New York to take in a World Series game. One 1913 article noted, "Sam Polin [*sic*], our real estate broker, is back from a trip to Logan where he is also dealing in lands and lots. Our red headed Jew is a hustler. Prithee, what a change has come through the beneficent laws of America. Less than a century ago a Jew wanted no real estate. He couldn't get it in his grip and to have it otherwise meant to be robbed certain, under some form of guise and law." The image of a Jew getting property "in his grip" is hardly favorable; it resonates with the Shylock archetype of the grasping, tightfisted Jew. Yet the editor meant to compliment his friend and to contrast America's enlightened attitude toward Jews with that of Russia.[25]

Both the white-owned *Recorder* and the black-owned *McDowell Times* sometimes ridiculed Jews by reprinting hackneyed ethnic jokes that featured thick Yiddish accents and crafty economic behavior. At times they aimed their derision at specific individuals. In discussing the impact of impending prohibition on Keystone's numerous (multiracial and multiethnic) business owners, the *Times* singled out two Jews, snickering that "Hyman's and Hermanson's faces will look haggard and worn as if they had lost the last relative on earth." The *Recorder* offered this 1913 blurb, headlined "A True One": "This happened Christmas, in McDowell County: He is a little fat Jew, but his wife is a large, handsome, queenly woman. She was visiting his store, and after leaving some of his friends, who were standing by, asked: 'Uncle Jake, who was that fine looking lady?' Replied he, 'dot vas no lady, dot iss mine wife!'" In contrast, a front page article that same day praised "Uncle Joe Lopinsky," who had "caught the New Year spirit in downright earnest" by offering "one of the most unique shows" in the history of the Welch theater. The use of the term "uncle" to describe each man suggests, perhaps, a patronizing attitude toward both. But Lopinsky, in this and numerous other articles, is treated with affection and respect, whereas "Uncle Jake" is mocked as a "little fat Jew."[26]

What was behind the different treatment of the two merchants? Their personal characteristics may have affected gentile attitudes. One clue is Uncle Jake's heavy Yiddish accent. It is likely that this man was not as Americanized as Lopinsky, that his behavior appeared more foreign. In order to be accepted into middle-class coalfield society, in other words, it was necessary to assimilate to some degree, to lose the most obvious trappings of one's ethnicity.

Although there is no way to know for sure, it is likely that the joke refers to Jake Shore, a man who spoke Yiddish (in addition to English) his whole life. Like some Jewish immigrants in the early years of the coal boom, Shore made little attempt to blend into the emerging middle class. His litigious nature involved him in numerous court battles with everyone from struggling Jewish businesswoman Bessie Zaltzman to non-Jewish customers to the mighty U.S. Coal and Coke—and he was known by both Jews and non-Jews for being "tight" with his money.[27] Not only did Shore appear to be more foreign, therefore, but he also seemed to conform to derogatory stereotypes of Jews. Since Lopinsky did not match these negative images, he was looked upon as not as Jewish. His *McDowell Times* obituary paid him this backhanded compliment, noting that "in the presence of his sunny generous disposition one forgot that he was a Jew." Such comments suggest that Lopinsky and other Jewish merchants were embraced to the degree that they did not seem to act "Jewish," meaning they did not fit non-Jews' preconceived notion of how Jews act. This notion combined into one image the Yiddish accent, foreign mannerisms and customs, *and* negative characteristics such as stinginess and greed.[28]

For Jewish immigrants, therefore, the role of merchant did not automatically confer middle-class respectability; one also had to be sufficiently Americanized. But it certainly helped. Another set of contrasting articles reveals how attitudes about Jews were shaped by their position on the economic ladder. A 1901 *Fayette Journal* blurb on the marriage of "Mr. I. Bloom, a leading merchant of Mt. Hope," remarked that "the happy young couple are now enjoying the delights of an extended honeymoon trip.... The best wishes and happiest congratulations of their many Fayette county friends are assured them." Clearly, Bloom was an esteemed member of the community, his Jewish background notwithstanding. Some months earlier, the newspaper had reported on the trial of two local officials who had extorted money from a peddler. The reporter found the incident quite amusing and managed to make fun of all concerned, starting out by noting that the trial "brought to light a way of collecting fines which to say the least, is peculiar and novel and evidently very effective." The article explained,

> Sometime ago, Abraham Joseph, a Jew peddler, appeared at Hill Top with his wares. Mayor Harris gave a "friend" some money and instructed him to make a purchase from Joseph. This was done and the mayor caused Sergeant House to arrest the unsuspecting Israelite [for peddling without a license]. His person secured, court was convened in a convenient saloon and the verdict was "guilty," and the prisoner was fined $5 and the costs. Joseph refused to pay it, thereupon the mayor raised him a dollar. This did not have a producting [sic] effect so the dispensers of justice had him bound hand and foot and placed him on a barrel, under the broiling sun. Abraham endured his torture until he became sick before the shekles [sic] necessary to liquidate were forthcoming.[29]

A vast social distance between "Mr. Bloom" and the "Jew peddler" is apparent. The "Israelite," possessed not of dollars but of shekels, referred to by his first name as if to simultaneously highlight and make light of his Old Testament connection, is a strange and alien presence. Unlike I. Bloom, the familiar and solid man of business, Abraham Joseph is the quintessential wandering Jew who simply "appeared" with his "wares." And his utter lack of status tempted local officials to take advantage of him.

Yet the story offers a number of complications that underscore the complex nature of coalfield ethnic and class relations. The peddler may have been at a disadvantage because of his foreignness and his lowly occupation, but it was Mayor Harris and Sergeant House who were on trial, and a local jury "promptly found them guilty" of robbery. (At the time, there was no law requiring peddlers to be licensed.) A judge set aside the verdict and ordered a new trial, at which another jury found the two men guilty of the lesser crime of assault and battery. They each received a fifty-dollar fine. That not one but three local juries (including the grand jury that issued the indictments) sided with the peddler against local authorities, however corrupt (Harris already had established a dubious reputation), surely indicates something about the ability of coalfield citizens to set aside whatever prejudices they may have had. It would appear that the rule of law enabled justice to be achieved, even for a humble foreigner.[30]

Furthermore, the disparity in social status between Bloom and Joseph obscures the reality that some of the most respected Jewish businessmen in the region started out as peddlers. These articles offer evidence that the newcomers had to travel across economic and social boundaries to become accepted: from peddler to merchant, from foreign to American, from unrespectable to respectable—and this they accomplished to varying degrees. Some never bothered to make the journey at all, content to keep their social lives within the confines of the Jewish community. Most, though, opted for integration into the coalfield middle class.

Abraham Joseph achieved a certain amount of social mobility, himself: he stayed in the area and became a small shopkeeper. Here, however, a greater irony of the story becomes apparent. The Abraham Joseph who resided in Fayette County a few years later was not a Jew but an Assyrian whose store served as "general headquarters for the Assyrian peddlers" in the area. So it appears that the "Jew peddler" was not Jewish at all but, rather, belonged to the one other coalfield ethnic group that followed the same peddler-to-merchant path.[31] Yet the association of "peddler" and "Jew" was entrenched in popular lore, and it is not surprising that the *Fayette Journal* made the link. In fact, it was not unusual for coalfield residents to mistake local Arab merchants for Jews. Though they too occupied a commercial niche—and their contingent was not a small one—in the public mind, the role of peddler or merchant correlated with "Jew." Whether Assyrian or Jewish, the peddler in the story was most definitely foreign, and the fact that his Jewish identity was central to the narrative demonstrates the tendency to look on Jews as "other," despite the insider status of some.[32]

Throughout their tenure in the coalfields, Jews encountered occasional slurs based on their middleman role. During the Depression, a restaurant in Harlan offered a fifteen-cent meal that included as a drink "Jew Pop"—water. The residents of Pineville referred to a local grocer as "Harry the Jew." Perhaps his practice of reading a Yiddish newspaper every day in his store caused him to be singled out in this fashion. The expression "jew him down" was commonplace, although one interviewee noted that people who used the phrase did not always realize its connection to Jews. That all Jews were wealthy, that they were "tight" with their money, that they engaged in "sharp" business practices, that they would not do manual labor were common beliefs among non-Jews irrespective of race or class. Certainly coal operators were no exception. W. P. Tams once referred to a "little shyster Jew lawyer," and Justus Collins complained about the "german-jew controlled" town of Cincinnati.[33]

But even often-malignant stereotypes could be interpreted by coalfield residents in benign ways. One non-Jewish woman explained that Jews were generally perceived as being wealthy, but only some people viewed that as bad (and those people were "just jealous"). She recalled being told that Jews helped each other financially by setting up their coreligionists in business three times, allowing each person two failures. If loan recipients did not succeed by then, their backers "wouldn't fool with them" anymore. "I think it's wonderful if they stick together like that," she offered.[34]

In addition to centuries-old stereotypes, recently developed "scientific" notions of race also influenced how Jews and other minority groups were perceived. Racial theories current in American and European intellectual circles filtered down into popular discourse both nationally and locally, and the notion of an essential Jewish difference was widespread in the pre–World War I years. Other "foreign" groups as well were considered racially distinct from both "whites" (i.e., "Anglo-Saxons") and "blacks." Each of the region's immigrant groups, including "Hebrews," occupied its own separate category somewhere below whites and above blacks on the racial scale. Local newspapers typically referred only to native-born whites as "white," whereas immigrants were referred to as "foreigners" or by their specific "racial" background (such as Italian, "Hebrew," "turk," "Slavish," etc.).[35]

The more foreign a person or group appeared to be, and the lower their economic status, the less "white" they were. As the contrast between the "Israelite" peddler and the respectable merchant suggests, economic mobility and assimilation into coalfield society enabled foreigners to "become" white. In the coalfields, where Jewish entrepreneurship was valued and integration was swift compared to large cities with dense Jewish neighborhoods, the racial status of Jews quickly moved into the white category. Other immigrants also became whiter as they assimilated, and by the second generation, members of all the nonnative groups enjoyed the same advantages of white privilege as their "white" neighbors whose families had lived in the United States for generations. Blacks remained at the bottom of the social hierarchy, forced to serve as the primary "other" against which members of the majority defined themselves.

A 1915 scandal sheds light on the coalfield racial and class hierarchy during a time of transition. When the story of a young black girl forced into prostitution in Keystone and Kimball first broke (see chapter 3), the African American–owned *McDowell Times* reacted to rumors by wondering pointedly "whether anybody other than Jews and Negroes" had been indicted. One of the two African American madams brought to trial was connected with "leading white and Hebrew business men," and there was little doubt that nonblack clients were involved. The *Times* later reported that "eight or nine men, white, Jews, Italians, and Negroes, some of them leading business men and others officers of the law," had been indicted for rape. In contrast, the white-owned *McDowell Recorder* implied that the scandal involved only African Americans. After reporting the testimony of black witnesses, the *Recorder* falsely stated that "this was about the extent of the state's testimony." The *Times,* perhaps limited in how far it could go in covering matters involving whites, abstained from offering details of the court proceedings, stating that "because of the character of the testimony, it will not be published."[36]

In fact, at least two non–African American brothel patrons, a Jewish former bartender and a non-Jewish coal company bookkeeper, were forced to testify. A perusal of court records turned up only one indictment of a non–African American man, the Jewish bartender—hardly one of the "leading business men" cited by the *Times* but conspicuously absent from the *Recorder*'s account. Apparently this man was not quite "white" enough to escape censure, yet he was sufficiently pale to avoid serious penalty: there is no record that he ever stood trial. (In his testimony, he refused to answer questions under grounds of self-incrimination.) The only people convicted were African American, the two madams and one customer.[37]

In general, Jews who settled in the South benefited from the region's racial caste system. Though the racial standing of recent immigrants may have been open to question, "Jews were, first of all, white, or . . . could pass for white," asserts Eli Evans.

In a region where "whiteness" was all-important, this gave southern Jews an advantage over their northern coreligionists in integrating into the social milieu, though Evans adds that their religion and a lingering distrust of "the foreigner" ensured that southern Jews would never quite fit in. This complex dynamic caused southern Jews some confusion and uneasiness (not to mention a certain amount of guilt about the people below them on the racial scale) but came as a relief to people accustomed to serving as their society's "other" in the old country.[38]

While not as rigid or oppressive as in the Deep South, the racial caste system in the coalfields offered similar benefits to whites or those who could "become" white. Coupled with the coalfields' greater receptiveness to outsiders than other parts of the South, the result was a climate that proved favorable to immigrants. When nativism and antisemitism reemerged on a national scale after a brief hiatus during World War I, the gains made by coalfield immigrants were not rolled back. Despite lingering reminders of their "difference," Jews and members of other "foreign" groups had become incorporated into coalfield society.[39]

Apart from the black-white continuum, the belief that Jews were a unique race, distinct from all gentiles, also existed in the coalfields. The source of this belief was much older than the modern racial theories that entered popular discourse. It was expressed most often (but not exclusively) by the less educated and more rural coalfield residents. When the first Jewish child was born in Mingo County about 1903, according to his son, "people came from all over to see the 'Jew-baby'—expecting horns." When Esther Scott arrived in the Harlan County hamlet of Poor Fork about 1912, local women gathered to inspect her, turning her around so they could see her from all sides. A woman who grew up in Lewisburg, West Virginia (just outside the coalfields), recalled that when her father opened a store about 1920, "one of the farmers stuck his head in the door and said, 'I've never seen a Jew, I'm just looking.' He wasn't hostile, just curious. . . . My father was a very social being, he said 'come on in!' and they chatted." Decades later, the tendency to see Jews as exotic specimens had not disappeared. A Williamson woman interviewed in the early 1970s recalled, "When I was in the hospital with my daughter, a nurse came by and said, 'That's the whitest Jew baby I've ever seen!'"[40]

Such experiences were common across the rural South and indicated neither hostility nor denigration, but rather curiosity and fascination. Ancient superstitions about Jews lingered in the countryside. But more important, country folk steeped in the Old Testament relished the opportunity of coming face to face with the descendants of the biblical patriarchs and prophets. To them, Jews indeed belonged to a special race, one whose ancient past they had minutely studied but whose present they knew virtually nothing about.

The Chosen People?

Early-twentieth-century observers described Appalachia as home to intensely religious people whose "remarkable knowledge of the Scriptures" attested to the "primacy of the Bible" in their lives. From the mainstream Protestant denominations found in county-seat towns to the numerous forms of mountain religion rooted in the countryside, a heartfelt Christianity pervaded the coalfields.[41] When Jews appeared on the scene, the emphasis on scriptural study naturally provoked an interest in the modern-day representatives of the Old Testament's chosen people. Jews who were knowledgeable about their religion—or knew even a smattering of Hebrew, as most did—were respected and sought after for theological discussions or demonstrations of the ancient tongue. A Jewish woman from Welch recalled her father "discussing the bible every other day with a colorful preacher, McClure," a highly visible disciple of Christianity who baptized people in the river "in the main part of town" in the 1920s. A rabbi who toured the coalfields in 1926 was struck by the attitude of the Christians he encountered. He spoke at Keystone's Knights of Pythias hall to an appreciative crowd of Jews and non-Jews. Of his train ride to Keystone, he wrote, "Our fellow passengers entertained us in a vivid manner. An aged Christian spoke tenderly, wondrously, of pertinent issues. He had read Josephus's *Antiquities* through more than once. He believed in the prophecies embodied in the Book of Daniel. He was opposed to prohibition, and did not approve of higher education for women."[42]

The extensive newspaper coverage given to Jewish communal events signified a keen interest in the traditions and practices of local Jews. At the dedication of the Pocahontas synagogue in 1913, the guest speaker, a Richmond rabbi, "Thrilled a Large Audience with his Eloquence," enthused the *McDowell Recorder.* The article relayed the rabbi's talk on the history of the Jews and the purpose of a synagogue and noted that the crowd included "a sprinkling of Gentiles." Newspapers routinely informed readers when Jewish congregations celebrated holidays, often providing historical background. A typical Middlesboro article in 1914 disclosed that the high holidays would be "properly observed by the local Hebrew people in their customary manner," with fasting, services, and store closings. When the Jewish women of Williamson conducted Sabbath services one evening in 1926, the *Mingo Republican* printed a lengthy front-page article that quoted the entire invocation.[43]

The *McDowell Recorder* offered the most elaborate coverage. Its articles about Jewish weddings gave an exotic cast to Jewish custom. One item intoned that "the impressiveness and solemnity of the Hebrew ring ceremony was quite pretty," with rituals that "bespoke times long gone by." Holidays received much attention, though the newspaper did not always get the fine points right. An October 1913 front-page story reported, "This has been a week of festivities with our many Jewish friends in this section. It is New Years week according to their calendar and is known as Rosie Sonie. . . . Many and costly have been their arrangements for this celebration which has been greatly enjoyed by them this week. While this is true there has not been a drunk nor a brawl reported among them. Much have we to learn yet from these people—the chosen race of God himself." An April 1915 front-page article educated readers about the festival of Passover: "Monday evening a great many of the Hebrew race in these fields celebrated the anniversary of the 'Passover.' The custom is to meet in family circles or in friendly groups and indulge in social games, etc., and drink four goblets of wine. The Jews today celebrate it in remembrance of their freedom as a race, much the same as we Americans celebrate the Fourth of July. It might in a sense be called the Hebrew Fourth of July. But it is much older than our American institutions as readers of the Bible will recall. It recalls the story of Moses and his marvelous career as a leader of men."[44]

Such articles reflected more than a fascination with Judaism. The small-town progressivism of the county seats also comes through, with coverage serving to promote business-oriented values. The sobriety of the Jewish high holidays was especially meaningful to coalfield employers, who bemoaned the high rate of absenteeism after rowdy holiday celebrations by other groups. The *Recorder* interpreted the business achievements of local merchants as reflecting on the Jews as a people and as inheritors of an ancient civilization that had, through its doctrines, instilled the qualities necessary to get ahead in modern American society. Its articles presented Jews as a civilizing influence and held up for emulation their respect for learning. An article describing a young Jewish immigrant girl dwelt upon her "fluent English," her "Spencerian" penmanship, and her desire to learn shorthand. The writer concluded, "Could not some of our American beauties take a good lesson from this pretty little Russian Jewess?"[45]

The *Recorder*'s items about Jews flaunted a sort of small-town sophistication that implicitly celebrated the growing urbanity of coalfield life. An article with the provocative title "Was Columbus A Jew?" began, "The other night the writer dropped into a local business house to chat and delve a little into Hebrew philosophy with the Jewish manager. It is a sort of mental relaxation we enjoy." While such items served to proudly affirm local broad-mindedness, the newspaper's surprisingly wide-ranging coverage of national and international Jewish issues had a related theme: extolling America as a land of enlightenment and opportunity, in contrast to Europe and, especially, Russia, where "medieval" attitudes prevailed. Stories of local Jewish self-made men typically included a summary of the oppression they had faced in the old country. The newspaper devoted much ink to the 1913 Mendel Beilis trial in Russia, indignantly noting that Beilis was being tried for "ritual murder, a trumped up charge, believed by many, that he murdered Christian children to drink their blood." When Beilis was acquitted, the *Recorder* expressed surprise and relief: "Very few of us have a very exalted opinion of Russian justice when they are dealing with the Jew."[46]

The amount of space devoted to Jewish issues in the *Recorder* reflected, in part, its relatively large Jewish readership. Even obscure topics received attention, such as when it reported in 1915, "Many Jews Enlist with English Army." But newspapers in other coalfield towns also showed an awareness of Jewish issues and a willingness to report on them. In 1920, for example, the *Williamson Daily News* reprinted a *New York Globe* article noting the "astonishing success" of Jewish settlement in Palestine, which deserved the "sympathy and aid" of the United States.[47]

The *McDowell Times*, with a mostly African American readership (but possibly many Jewish readers as well), also reported on Jewish holidays and issues. Much of its coverage related to African American concerns. Articles such as "Hebrew Protective League Calls on Colored and Italian Citizens to Combine Against Race Prejudice" highlighted the commonality of prejudice faced by minorities in the United States. When Jews achieved political milestones (such as the nomination of Louis Brandeis to the Supreme Court and the election of the nation's first Jewish governor), the coverage implied that such progress could bode well for blacks. The *Times* also used Jews as a model of how a minority could relate to the majority. One article noted, "The ability of the Jew to remain a distinct people and yet to support loyally the country of their birth or adoption is one of the marvels of history." The saga of the Ethiopian Jews (known at that time as the "Black Jews of Abyssinia") especially fascinated the *Times*. But distinctions were also drawn, as when an editorial angrily observed that the lynching of a single Jew, Leo Frank, aroused far more national outcry than the lynchings of thousands of southern blacks.[48]

But amid coalfield newspaper articles expounding on Jewish holidays and cheering Jewish efforts to resettle Palestine could be found disturbing treatises on Jewish attitudes toward Christianity. Even the *McDowell Recorder* ran a syndicated religious column that reminded readers that "the brethren of Jesus were the Jews, who crucified Him. . . . It was on account of envy that the Jews called for His crucifixion. His works were good, and theirs were evil." And despite their neighbors' careful reading of the Bible, Jews confronted misconceptions about Judaism and modern Jewish practice on a regular basis. A coalfield rabbi of the post–World War II era noted, for example, that non-Jews often asked him, "Do Jews believe in Jesus?"[49]

Sometimes attitudes toward Judaism went beyond simple ignorance in ways that Jews found offensive or even somewhat threatening. The Christian belief most unsettling, because of its frequent expression, was that Jews bore responsibility for the death of Jesus. As elsewhere in the South, the negative image of Jew as Christ killer persisted alongside the positive view of Jews as the chosen people. One interviewee recalled that his next-door neighbor broadcast a Sunday school class on a local radio station. At Easter, he could hear his neighbor rant over the airwaves that "all Jews had killed Christ." Otherwise, the man was "as nice a neighbor as you could want." The taunt of "Christ killer" was frequently hurled at Jewish children by their peers. Aside from such schoolyard cruelties, the Christ-killer stigma was never directed against Jews personally, or against their communities, and as one man pointed out, insults among children flew in many directions. Nevertheless, encounters with this damning charge against "the Jews" could be disquieting.[50]

The pervasive climate of Christianity fostered an insensitivity toward non-Christians that caused more discomfort than direct anti-Jewish expressions. When a child learned in school that "those who love Jesus have a gold heart, those who don't have a black heart," it did not matter that the comment was not aimed at her as a Jew. Some public schools had daily prayers, and although Jewish children enjoyed sharing holiday experiences with Christian friends, the heavy emphasis on these observances sometimes got to be a bit too much. As one man noted of his Beckley childhood in the 1940s, "I found out at Christmastime I was Jewish." Eventually he came to resent having to participate in his school's annual Christmas play.[51]

Nor were adults immune to feelings of estrangement caused by the weaving of Christianity into the fabric of daily life. Public events invariably began or ended with Christian prayers. "I've found few Christians and Christian ministers who are sensitive to the fact that there are non-Christians around," observed a Jewish native of Logan. A participant in Jerome David's 1974 study of Williamson Jews recounted being at a baccalaureate service where the minister made derogatory remarks about the ancient Jews. To compound this person's dismay, while leaving the event, "people were saying, 'wasn't that a wonderful service.'" Despite active Jewish participation in civic and social clubs, David found, "the clubs have Christian overtones which tend to make many Jews feel like outsiders." One woman was especially bothered, telling him, "I used to belong to Rotary Anns; the meeting ended with a prayer in Jesus' name. The club had no purpose or aim. The thought of going made me sick. I had nothing in common with the people—just too Churchy—that's all they would talk about." Another person flatly stated, "If you're not a Protestant in Williamson, you're a foreigner."[52]

Not all non-Jews were insensitive to the feelings of Jews. A woman who grew up in Pineville in the 1920s as the only Jewish child in her class recalled that her teacher would find some slight errand to send her on every Monday morning. Eventually she discovered that after she left the room, the teacher took the opportunity to instill proper habits of churchgoing in the remaining students by asking those who had attended Sunday school the previous day to raise their hands. "She didn't want to embarrass me," the woman explained.[53]

The teacher's respect for her student's religious beliefs was not uncommon, as most local Christians chose the more tolerant side of their religious tradition when relating to the Jews in their community. Many gentiles simply overlooked the contradictions about Jews inherent in Christian dogma. As one Christian woman stated, "We all believe in the same God." But for Jews the contradictions could not be so easily resolved. The teacher described above, in her very sensitivity and her desire to treat her Jewish student with respect, had singled out the girl and made her feel different from the others. Even with the good will of the majority, the emphasis on religion in coalfield life inevitably set Jews apart and caused them to entertain doubts about their place within society.

Ambiguities and Contradictions

If expressions of respect toward Judaism had paradoxical results, the rare instances when Jews encountered rejection or animosity also were not clear-cut. As
one man put it, "We felt and saw prejudice, but it wasn't overt." At times it surfaced in unthinking comments made by non-Jews. A Jerome David interviewee
recounted, "A fellow businessman told me: 'I always heard Jews were "kikes"—
but you're a good Jew.'" Some of David's respondents believed schools and other institutions practiced subtle discrimination, for example, by passing over their
children for school honors. "There is a quota on the number of Jews allowed to
serve on the Board of Directors of the banks in Williamson—one per bank," one
man told him. While a few social clubs banned Jews, it is difficult to confirm
other charges of bias. The evidence is equivocal, leaving open for interpretation
whether discrimination had indeed occurred and, if so, whether it was one teacher, one club member who stood in the way, a notable minority, or a majority.[54]

The historical record reveals virtually no evidence of aggressive antisemitism or
feelings of hatred against coalfield Jews. Even the 1920s popularity of the Ku Klux
Klan did not signify unadulterated hostility, as the local Klan did not target Jews.
Jews who witnessed the Klan march later expressed some confusion about the
experience. One woman related that as she and her father watched a Klan parade
in Bluefield, a man in the procession waved cheerily at her father as he passed by,
calling out, "Hi, Henry!" A Beckley resident recalled seeing in the marching,
masked throng, identifiable because of his distinctive peg-leg, a man whom his
family had found to be "a wonderful neighbor." One coalfield Jew who played a
brass instrument was asked to march in a Klan parade to fill in for a band member
who was ill (he declined). Echoing a legend that has been told and retold by chroniclers of southern Jewish history, a 1991 Middlesboro library exhibit noted that
Jewish families in the 1920s "were on such good terms with their Christian neighbors that members of the Ku Klux Klan used to buy their sheets at the [Jewish-
owned] Big Store."[55]

Because its members were their cordial neighbors, not the bullies down the
street, Jews felt confident that the Klan meant them no harm. A Logan man asserted that the march he witnessed in 1928 occurred to protest the nomination
of Al Smith, a Catholic, for the presidency—a valid theory, given the Klan's
strident anti-Catholicism. If local Klansmen did harbor antagonism toward Jews,
they focused on the distant, symbolic Jewish capitalist rather than their local
shopkeeper or next-door neighbor. Yet seeing their neighbors and customers join
a group that was known to espouse antisemitism could only have added to the
ambivalence some Jews felt about their relations with gentiles.[56]

Given the ambiguities and contradictions in coalfield society's stance toward
Jews, it is not surprising that Jewish residents expressed a variety of opinions
regarding Jewish-gentile relations. Overall, they emphasized their sense of be-

The B'nai El religious school, Logan, West Virginia. The Logan Jewish community reached its peak in the late 1920s, when this picture was taken. (Courtesy of Edward Eiland)

Logan's Jewish congregation built Temple B'nai El in 1948. The congregation no longer exists. Recently the building has been used as a day-care center. (Photo by Sherry Zander, 2001)

Temple Emanuel in Welch, West Virginia, built in 1922, has not been in use for several years. (Photo by Sherry Zander, 2001)

B'nai Israel synagogue, situated on a steep hill above downtown Williamson, West Virginia. (Photo by Sherry Zander, 2001)

Cornerstone of Temple Beth El in Beckley, West Virginia. (Photo by Sherry Zander, 2001)

The Beckley Jewish community has worshipped at Temple Beth El for more than seventy years. (Photo by Sherry Zander, 2001)

The Middlesboro, Kentucky, Jewish cemetery, founded in 1904. (Photo by Deb Weiner, 2000)

longing. Comments such as "Everybody was friends," "We mixed very well," and "Everybody knew everybody's problems" were typical. Yet beyond this agreement over the neighborliness of their towns and the cordiality of everyday interaction, three different attitudes can be discerned.

Many interviewees flatly stated that they experienced no antisemitism whatsoever, that their relations with non-Jews were uniformly good, that people were judged solely on their behavior and not their background. Their attitude may be summed up by one man's firm comment that "people were people." Others, notably several participants of David's Williamson study, discerned an undercurrent of antisemitism that colored their opinion of all non-Jews. "Even now, with all our non-Jewish friends, I am sure there is underlying hostility," one person remarked. Another went even further: "A lot of Jews in this town are fooled into believing they have non-Jewish friends." These harsh comments reflected a minority viewpoint among the Williamson study participants and even more so among the entire sample of coalfield Jews considered here.[57]

A third group struggled to describe the contradictions emanating from the surrounding environment. They saw their relations with non-Jews as positive, their membership in the coalfield middle class as secure. At the same time, they sensed an estrangement from the majority and recognized that some members of mainstream society, perhaps even society as a whole, looked upon them as "other." They saw themselves, in other words, as both insiders and outsiders. A man who affirmed that his family "never had a difficult time" also mentioned that he made sure people knew of his Jewish identity partly so that he would not be subjected to any unintentional slurs. Another man, whose Presbyterian and Catholic childhood pals remained his best friends throughout his life, nevertheless declared that people who said there was no antisemitism in the coalfields were "liars."[58]

Were instances of prejudice rare exceptions in a climate of acceptance, the tip of the iceberg that revealed the true feelings of the majority, or something in between? Rather than choose among these three viewpoints, it must be recognized that they each contain their own truths, reflecting differences among coalfield Jews in experience, upbringing, and outlook. Some people encountered more prejudice than others. Those raised in McDowell County, home of the most well-integrated Jewish population, had the most positive attitude. Those from the more hierarchical county seats were more ambivalent. (One of David's respondents remarked that "anti-Semitism is more marked among upper-class Christians.") On the other hand, in the more rural, less sophisticated towns, Jews were more of an oddity and sometimes felt their uniqueness in uncomfortable ways.

But even within a single town—Williamson, which offers the most data—perceptions differed.[59] Jerome David notes that those with more positive views tended to be "home-growns" raised in the coalfields, whereas those with more negative views tended to be "imports" who had moved into town as adults in the immediate post–World War II era. (By the time of his study, the immigrant generation had largely died out.) Most of these imports came from urban Jewish neighborhoods and had less experience dealing with a non-Jewish majority. Not surprisingly, they exhibited stronger feelings of alienation. Only an import could have told David, "I'm a 'foreigner' because I'm Jewish. Anyone who is not a mountain person is a 'stranger.'" Jewish coalfield natives saw their coreligionists as paranoid. One commented, "Parents often instill into the child the idea that 'remarks' are anti-Semitic. They misread comments." The perspectives of each group reflected a bias. Home-growns overlooked or downplayed real instances of prejudice, whereas imports saw it where it did not exist.[60]

Meanwhile, traditional Jewish doubts about gentiles crept into the views of both groups. "There are latent hostilities everywhere in the world toward Jews— also here in Williamson," one person philosophically observed. Another offered the sentiment more crudely: "A goy is a goy." References to non-Jews as "goyim" provide a clue that not all the labeling of the "other" came from the Christian majority. A cultural legacy of centuries of unease with gentiles could not be completely shed in one or two generations.[61]

Differences in how Jews interpreted gentile attitudes contributed to differences in how they constructed their social lives, with some people choosing to segregate themselves from non-Jews. This insularity led one Jewish communal leader to complain, "Aside from their business, they didn't take an active part in the community. They were here for one purpose—to make a living." Believing that the less-than-stellar behavior of these people reflected on the entire group and lent credence to antisemitic stereotypes, he and other Jews strove that much harder to become involved in the broader community. In this context, Harry Schwachter's comment that the building of a temple would "prove our permanency" and show that Jews were not "interlopers" concerned only with making money reflected an internalization of antisemitic stereotypes, a recognition of the prejudices in coalfield society, and an awareness that non-Jews tended to judge Jews, as a group, by the actions of their least congenial members.

But even those who integrated into coalfield society had no desire to completely assimilate. Aside from the earliest German Jewish residents, coalfield Jews had an attachment to Jewish culture that led most to look to their coreligionists for their primary social relationships. Almost all found aspects of the dominant culture strange or unappealing, and felt discomfort, even anger, over ways the region's fervent Christianity intruded into their lives. Some people held values and goals they felt were at odds with the mainstream, such as an interest in education and the arts. Others saw their political views as more liberal than those of non-Jews. One person told David, "I have an equal number of Jewish and non-Jewish friends. Yet, Jewish people's viewpoints are more like mine . . . Most non-Jews are non-intellectual, right wing, 'Wallace for President' types. I have to meet them on the level of golf and fun."[62]

A fitting summation of how coalfield Jews perceived their relations with non-Jews comes from a participant in David's Williamson study. "There is an undercurrent of anti-Semitism here," the respondent acknowledged. "It is in every town [in America]. It is not as overt as in other places for Jews take an integral part in the functioning of this community. The Jew in Williamson is a powerful force in terms of what he can do."[63]

Perhaps because of a sense of security derived from playing an "integral part" in coalfield life, Jews were not passive in the face of gentile insensitivity. They could chose to overlook it and focus instead on the positive aspects of their relations with non-Jews. As a Beckley native observed, "My parents' idea of dealing with it was . . . to ignore it, up to a point." But only "up to a point." In numerous ways, coalfield Jews attempted to sensitize their Christian neighbors to their presence and educate them to dispel misperceptions and prejudices. Some individuals took time to educate friends and neighbors about Jewish religion and culture. As Esther Baloff declared, "I explained Jewishness to the people." A Williamson family whose daughter had been called a "Goddam Jew" by a classmate invited the boy and his parents to their home for a chat. This proved highly effective: as they explained how his action had affected their daughter, "a huge tear slowly rolled down the boy's cheek."[64]

Jews also made use of their communal organizations to educate their fellow coalfield residents and promote Jewish-Christian understanding. Their efforts reached a peak in the post–World War II era. At the Williamson Sisterhood's annual Neighbor Night, each member brought a Christian friend to Friday night services. The Welch Sisterhood joined the town's United Council of Churches, though the Williamson Sisterhood bowed out of its branch in 1947, having decided that "we have no place in this organization." Williamson's Jewish youth group sponsored interfaith celebrations of Jewish holidays such as Purim, when "non-Jewish youths were invited to witness the lighting of the candles and an abbreviated reading from the Megillah, followed by a discussion." The Logan congregation purchased subscriptions to a Jewish magazine for "our local ministers and some of the leading gentile citizens of the town for the purpose of promoting a Better Understanding."[65]

Jewish communities enlisted their rabbis and lay leaders as "ambassadors" for Judaism at high school graduation ceremonies, churches, club meetings, and other venues. Pharmacist and rabbi Isadore Wein recalled, "I became a very busy guy, talking to groups" after his arrival in Beckley in the late 1940s. "We had to make ourselves part of this community, and worked at it." In 1950, the Welch student rabbi "gave a most inspiring talk on our local radio for the McDowell Woman's Club," noted the Sisterhood minutes. The Williamson student rabbi even had his own radio program, *Hear, Oh Israel,* in the early 1950s.[66]

Occasionally Jews reacted collectively when they felt their interests threatened. In 1940, the Logan congregation wrote to the public school superintendent protesting the practice of "segregating" children into different religious groups to teach them their respective religions. Drawing on American values of religious freedom and separation of church and state, the letter insisted that religious education should take place in the church, "where it really and properly belongs." When the Williamson Rotary Club in 1947 had a speaker from the Arabian League "who told them the Arabian side of the story on Palestine," the B'nai B'rith decided "it would be a good idea to tell them our side." The lodge's minutes for March 1944 cryptically record that "Sid Goodman reported on some anti-Semitic activities in the county and some in town that were well taken care of."[67]

As this last item suggests, coalfield Jews preferred behind-the-scenes action to public protest. Mindful of their economic vulnerability as merchants who depended on maintaining good relations with their neighbors, they gauged carefully their defense of Jewish rights, believing that a too-aggressive approach could backfire. In discussing the Bluefield public school policy of mandatory Bible classes, one communal leader expressed the dilemma: "We never could have gone to court about Bible in the schools. We would have won, there's no doubt about that, but in the end, what would it have done for us? We'd be stabbing ourselves in the back. Many of us here make our livelihood as businessmen and the majority of our customers are Gentiles. We can't afford to ostracize ourselves from the Gentiles."[68] Jews had to keep in mind that their relationship to non-Jews was not merely an important aspect of social life, it was critical to the economic well-being of their families.

When it came to controversies that did not directly concern them, their actions were similarly guided by their conspicuous economic role. They strove to keep a low profile during divisive situations, to stay away from the extremes to avoid alienating any faction. Of course, this presented problems in a region known for periods of intense class polarization. Yet their middleman economic role pushed Jews toward the middle ground, where, in the coalfields, there often was not a lot of room.

Politics of a Middleman Role

> If you go up to Harlan County / There is no neutral there.
> You'll either be a union man / Or a thug for J. H. Blair.
> —Florence Reece, "Which Side Are You On"

Their lack of involvement in the coal industry did not insulate Jews from the fierce conflict between miners and operators that periodically wracked the region. Aside from the economic consequences of strikes, Jewish merchants, like everyone else, had to face the social and political ramifications of class conflict. Their retail niche ensured that they felt their own special kind of discomfort during times of labor turmoil. On one hand, as self-made businesspeople they had a financial stake in the system. Many had become pillars of their communities. They socialized with other merchants, professionals, and mining officials—the "local elite." On the other hand, their businesses depended on good relations with everyone in the community. In small towns, where everyone knew everyone else, retailers could not afford to offend any segment of the population. As one Jewish merchant put it, "We tried to get along with everyone." During labor disputes, said another, Jews "were caught in the middle. . . . These are your customers, you don't want to antagonize them."[69]

But in the coalfields, labor conflicts tended toward the extreme. Coal operators did not hesitate to use the vast means at their disposal to crush workers' efforts to organize. Unionization attempts were met with everything from injunctions to evictions from company housing to brutality by company security forces and local law enforcement. Faced with this raw exercise of power, miners responded with violence of their own.[70]

The region's sole focus on coal production meant that it lacked a "sizable disinterested middle class to moderate and adjust conflict," as John Hevener puts it. In fact, the middle class was small and completely dependent on coal for its survival. Coal industry hegemony, asserts John Gaventa, enforced "a consensus to the system of industrial inequalities." By depicting insurgent miners as unwitting pawns of outside agitators, coal operators denied the legitimacy of miners' grievances and maintained their vision of a natural and harmonious social order. "The ideology which emerged appealed to the forces of law and order, respectability, and patriotism as opposed to the forces of disorder, anti-religion, and anti-government brought in by the outsider," says Gaventa.[71]

In such an environment, "respectable" opposition to the authority of the coal companies could hardly exist. During the Harlan County battles of the 1930s, the minister of an elite congregation who criticized local employers had to be reassigned and hotel owners were afraid to allow union organizers to stay in their hotels. It is unknown how Harlan's Jewish community reacted to Jewish labor organizers who arrived with the communist-backed National Miners Union. The murder of nineteen-year-old Jewish organizer Harry Simms became a rallying point for labor after he was eulogized in a song made popular by local firebrand "Aunt Molly" Jackson. It is unlikely that local Jews appreciated Simms's activities.[72]

Since stability and order are important preconditions for trade, their centuries-old commercial niche traditionally gave Jews a built-in economic interest in maintaining the status quo. Merchant-based Jewish communities across the United States generally supported measures to advance the rule of law and promote orderly development.[73] The "gun thug" law enforcement methods of coal companies could scarcely be described as the rule of law, but the perceived alternative—lawlessness—hardly beckoned. The coal operators' law-and-order message resonated with business owners worried that escalated levels of violence during strikes, which mostly occurred in coal camps and mining sites throughout the countryside, would eventually penetrate the county-seat towns.

Indeed, during the southern West Virginia mine wars of the early 1920s, the leader of a "public safety force" organized to defeat mobilizing miners claimed that Williamson businessmen "were clamoring for protection" of their property. While he made this statement to justify coal company and governmental repression, it was probably true that the tense climate, combined with propaganda depicting strikers as violent revolutionaries (or dupes of violent revolutionaries), caused townspeople to fear for the public safety. Throughout the region, especially during the pre-1930s era when any attempt by miners to organize was viewed as anarchistic, the coalfield middle class—white and black, Jewish and non-Jewish—dutifully sided with the coal operators, either actively or tacitly, whenever battle lines were drawn.[74]

Sometimes the call to arms was literal. When Mingo County elites formed a volunteer state police contingent at the height of the labor troubles in May 1921, they recruited Williamson businessmen, professionals, and white-collar workers who were "white men and citizens of the State." Some two hundred men joined, mostly former servicemen and American Legion members. Among them were seven Jews. Yet with at least thirty-five Jewish men living in Williamson, virtually all business owners or white-collar workers, seven participants do not indicate overwhelming support. An interviewee from Williamson recalled how "they deputized a lot of people" to go fight the miners. His father refused to participate and later allowed unions to use his theater as a meeting place. (Though when an organizer attempted to unionize his theater employees, he told the man "to get the hell out.") Jews who did join defense efforts were not necessarily enthusiastic. In Welch, after union leaders Sid Hatfield and Ed Chambers were murdered on the courthouse steps in August 1921, rumors that miners planned to march on the town spurred the American Legion to organize a "Home Guard," with a "Merchant's Patrol" to guard the business district. A Jewish Welch native related that his father, along with just about all the other men in town, was deputized and issued a firearm even though he did not volunteer for the job, knew nothing about guns, and had little intention of ever firing one.[75]

Meanwhile, the atmosphere outside the county seats was not as relentlessly anti-union. Business owners in Bluefield apparently did not feel obliged to toe the coal company line. UMWA president John L. Lewis stayed in the Jewish-owned Matz Hotel in 1920, and his associates discussed renting office space from Jewish real estate owner Louis Kaufman. In some of the smaller independent towns, coal miners predominated and fellow residents tended to sympathize with their cause. Some of these places became tiny islands of union support in a coal industry–dominated sea.[76]

Two Jewish families lived in the most controversial independent town of all. The Bermans and Schaeffers owned the only two clothing stores in Matewan at the time of the 1920 Matewan Massacre.[77] According to Harry Berman, his family was well liked, "in with the union people" because his father "carried them on the books" when they were out on strike. The Schaeffers earned the suspicion of the coal operators' unofficial police force, the Baldwin-Felts Detective Agency, for closing their store several hours before the shootout and later fraternizing with union sympathizers. The agency's investigation into the massacre referred to Joe Schaeffer and Jacob Berman as "Jew merchants"; to get information out of Berman, an operative sent "a Jew friend" to question him. But though they may have associated with union supporters, the Bermans and Schaeffers, like Jews in the county seats, were uneasy bystanders to the conflict—if a lot closer to it: sixteen-year-old Harry Berman, loitering on the street, witnessed the shoot-out.[78]

Both families left town shortly afterward, the Bermans settling in Williamson, where they employed union leader Ed Chambers's wife Sallie as a store clerk in the year between the Matewan Massacre and Chambers's murder. They discharged her after suspecting her of theft, but she then went on to work at the National Department Store, owned by Harry Schwachter and his father-in-law, David Brown. While Brown also suspected Chambers of stealing, Schwachter was "rather friendly" with her and refused to talk to Baldwin-Felts agents.[79]

While coalfield historians emphasize the polarized nature of labor disputes, Jews who grew up in the region recalled their families' attempts to remain neutral. "My parents were very careful to try not to be involved," stated a Logan native. "My dad had a business where he was dependent on coal miners." Only one Jewish man was identified who expressed real devotion to the anti-union cause: Sam Solins served as a "captain" in a McDowell County American Legion contingent that traveled to Logan in August 1921 to help Sheriff Don Chafin keep union miners from passing through Logan County. However, he was not a merchant, but possibly the only Jewish lawyer in the coalfields at that time. He was also an aspiring politician.[80]

Although Jews never challenged the elite consensus, they were keenly aware of the exploitative nature of the coal industry. "Coal operators treated coal miners atrociously," one interviewee acknowledged. Harry Berman told an interviewer, "They worked them really like dogs. . . . Fifteen, sixteen hours a day, you know, and didn't pay 'em much. And they laid on their bellies and knees in water, see. You know, you feel sorry for people like that." A former car peddler in the coal camps in the 1930s recalled that coal companies "cheated the hell out of the miners. . . . Most of the time we sympathized with the miners, because the coal companies used to take advantage of them. It was difficult to believe the things they would pull." His own business benefited from unionization since coal companies did not appreciate the presence of peddlers in the camps. "If it wasn't for the United Mine Workers, we couldn't have done anything," he maintained.[81]

The experience of Jewish merchants suggests that even though the county-seat middle class sided with the forces of "law and order" when called upon, its members were in a more ambivalent position than generally has been recognized. Mostly, Jews saw labor conflicts as bad for business and wished them resolved as soon as possible. Although they constituted a small portion of the coalfield middle class, all the region's merchants were in the same basic economic position, and this stance toward labor troubles may have been fairly widespread. An article in the *Williamson Daily News* that appeared just after the Matewan Massacre hints at such a view. Making no reference to either side, it simply stated, "All of our businessmen are deeply concerned over our labor troubles and want to see them quickly ended."[82]

Two Realities

Jews in the coalfields experienced two realities. On a daily level, they lived alongside gentiles as friends, neighbors, classmates, and contributors to their communities. They were the local shopkeeper, the fellow PTA member—a prosaic, everyday, normal part of coalfield life. They blended in as one small group among many, in a region where, for the most part, ethnic differences were not all that important. And yet that other reality occasionally intruded. Jews were different. They were related to the grocer, "Harry the Jew." They listened on the radio or sat in the audience as ministers preached on the faults of their ancestors. They watched from the sidelines as their neighbors marched by wearing the robes of the Ku Klux Klan. And they remained one step removed, uncomfortably so, from the conflicts that periodically consumed their fellow residents.

On the whole, "ambivalence is the appropriate word" to describe Jewish-gentile interaction across America from the nineteenth to the mid-twentieth century, says historian Jonathan Sarna. Yet beyond this broad statement, scholars have drawn contrasting conclusions regarding relations between Jews and non-Jews. Antisemitism in the United States has tended to be insidious rather than open, making it difficult to assess how important it actually has been to the Jewish experience. Social exclusion, economic and educational discrimination, ideological attacks, and physical violence against Jews have all occurred at various times and places. Whether these problems represent aberrations in an overall benign climate or a disturbing pattern that reveals the dark underside of majority attitudes toward Jews has been a matter of fierce debate. This historiographical quandary reflects the quandary faced by coalfield Jews in attempting to characterize their relations with their non-Jewish neighbors. Most came down on the positive side of the issue.[83]

Even as they grappled with these dilemmas, Jews in the coalfields acted from a position of confidence that contrasts with many small-town Jewish communities, North and South. The Jews of Johnstown, Pennsylvania, displayed a "collective insecurity" that caused them to attempt to remain inconspicuous, not just during periods of labor turmoil in the coal and steel industries, but always. Meanwhile, commentators have viewed southern Jewry from opposite extremes. They have emphasized the welcome Jews received and their high degree of participation in civic life (Harry Golden asserted that "this 'most Gentile' section of America has provided the most favorable 'atmosphere' the Jewish people have known in the modern world"), yet as Leonard Dinnerstein points out, these same writers have described southern Jews' powerful fears and anxieties, suggesting that "the fear of antisemitism is pervasive." Some writers maintain, though, that these anxieties arose more from the enormous pressures to conform imposed on everyone in the South than from enmity directed against Jews.[84]

While the coalfields shared many characteristics with the rest of the South (for example, the centrality of religion and, to some extent, racial attitudes), the openness to outsiders that characterized the coal boom, as well as the region's greater diversity, limited the intense obligation to conform that historians have described as endemic to southern society. This atmosphere, combined with the Jews' position as an important segment of the small coalfield middle class, enabled them to confront (or ignore) problems arising from their minority status without the fear or insecurity exhibited by other small-town Jewish communities.

Not that there was no pressure to adhere to the coalfields' prevailing middle-class standards of thought and behavior. Politically, certainly, a strict consensus was enforced on labor issues. Culturally, Jewish immigrants were accepted as long as they did not appear "too Jewish." No doubt, determining what was too Jewish caused bewilderment for some, making opportunities to relax around fellow Jews all the more important. Yet the variety of ways Jews interacted with non-Jews, the choices open to them, and the very differences in how they interpreted their relations with the gentile majority suggest the fluid nature of the coalfield social environment, at least as far as the insiders/outsiders of the middle class were concerned.

CHAPTER 5

Coalfield Jewish Communities

One day late in 1913, several women gathered at the home of Gertrude (Mrs. Jake) Levine to form the Jewish Ladies Guild, the first Jewish organization in Williamson. A terse note in the minutes of the meeting explained, "Purpose, Jewish charity." The women came together to aid the "numerous" Jewish transients passing through town, who "were a perplexing burden indeed to us individually," in the words of Leah Shein. In addition to charity, the guild was started for "social reasons," fellow organizer Ida Bank recalled in a 1926 speech.[1]

It is unclear just what Bank meant by that. Certainly the new group offered the women opportunities to socialize, but soon they embarked on a much more ambitious agenda. In 1916, they started a Sabbath school for the town's five Jewish children, Bank related, "and I was their teacher, with no experience in this work, with no instructions, only with the will and ambition to do something for the children along religious lines and to help them on the path to Judaism." The guild next began to organize communal events and religious services, bringing in a visiting rabbi for the Jewish high holidays. After their efforts led to the founding of the B'nai Israel Congregation, the women (now known as the Williamson Sisterhood) promptly started a temple fund to raise money to build a synagogue.[2]

Ida Bank may not have had experience as a religious teacher, but she had the benefit of an Orthodox Jewish upbringing—in Keystone, where her father Jake Shore and father-in-law Wolf Bank were pioneer merchants. When Ida and her husband Hyman came to Williamson in about 1911, the town's tiny Jewish contingent could not compare to Keystone's thriving Jewish community, which boasted a synagogue and full-time rabbi. But more than just small numbers hindered communal activity in Williamson. According to Bank, the town's Jewish families were so "divided by petty business jealousies" that she considered the first Jewish Ladies Guild meeting to be a significant achievement. Religious disagreements also caused friction among Williamson Jews. Yet the forces pulling them together proved stronger than those keeping them apart. At the time Bank made her remarks at the annual Sisterhood-led Sabbath service in 1926, completion of their synagogue was two years away, but she could look back with satisfaction on a successful endeavor, led largely by women, to forge a close-knit, active Jewish community.[3]

Bank's speech not only captured the early history of the Williamson congregation but also unwittingly summarized the creation of small Jewish congregations across America, outlining a typical progression from charitable activity to children's religious education to forming a congregation and building a synagogue. Coalfield Jewish communities reflected the American Jewish experience in other ways as well. Wherever the Jewish population was too small to split into multiple congregations, community members had to unite despite business conflicts and religious disputes. Moreover, women often played a critical leadership role in communal life. Above all, coalfield Jews shared in what historian Gerald Sorin has termed "the great American balancing act—the need for acculturation on the one side and the desire to retain something of a Jewish world on the other."[4]

Sixty years after the gathering in Gertrude Levine's living room, rabbinical student Jerome David came to Williamson to study "what it means to be Jewish in a small town." By the 1970s the community had shrunk to less than one hundred people (from a maximum of about two hundred) and was in evident decline. But its members, "home-grown" descendants of the original Jewish families and "imports" who had arrived in the post–World War II boom years, remained committed to their congregation. Despite their diverse backgrounds, David concluded, Williamson Jews "have one main goal in common; to provide for the well-being of their children and to transmit a love of Judaism to them." This goal—actually two, economic and spiritual, both seen in the context of transmission to the next generation—also marks Williamson Jews as typical. Historian Jacob Rader Marcus cites economic well-being and "the obligation to be a Jew" as the top two priorities of Jewish immigrants, though he also adds a third: the "fervent wish to become an American," to acculturate and participate in American society.[5]

These three motivating forces shaped the character of Jewish coalfield communities. At times they reinforced each other, and at times they clashed. Family-based economic networks provided a ready-made basis for group solidarity, but the drive to succeed got in the way of religious practice and communal responsibility, not to mention harmony. A desire to perpetuate cultural traditions brought Jews together but generated conflict over how to express Jewish belief and relate to the non-Jewish world. The urge to assimilate encouraged a dilution of traditional practice and threatened group affiliation but served as an impetus to organize communally, because having a congregation conferred legitimacy on the Jewish minority and offered a platform from which to interact with the larger society. By looking at how coalfield Jews integrated these various considerations into the fabric of their communities, the layers of complexity surrounding the "balancing act" begin to emerge.

In the United States, a land of religious freedom where no legal or social caste distinctions have defined Jews as a group, observes sociologist Marshall Sklare, "individual decision is crucial" in "assuming the role of Jew," and the smaller the community, "the clearer it is that the future of Jewish life rests upon the personal decision of each individual." Jewish immigrants who settled in small-town America experienced greater pressure to assimilate, and had far less access to the cultural building blocks of Jewish life, than their relatives in urban neighborhoods. Yet their response sometimes more than made up for these debilities. "Contrary to large city opinion," declared delegates to a 1973 conference of small-town Jews, "the small community offers a richer Jewish life; there is a distinct desire to retain identity which in larger cities is too often lost because it is taken for granted." Williamson Jews offered proof of this assertion. Despite their "limited" exposure to Jewish culture and their immersion in the surrounding society, Jerome David asserted, they showed "a depth of Jewish commitment which is more genuine and sincere than can be found . . . in larger Jewish centers."[6]

Residents of small communities needed a high degree of communal solidarity simply to claim their existence as Jews, which explains why small-town synagogue affiliation rates have always been far higher than in cities, with rates of 80 to 100 percent not uncommon. The need to coalesce brought about a phenomenon unthinkable in large cities: adherents of the various branches of Judaism sharing a single congregation, managing to "tolerate or harmonize differences to maintain communal unity," as Leonard Rogoff states. The synagogue stood as the preeminent symbol of that solidarity, asserts Benjamin Kaplan. "The survival strength of the small-town Jewish community has been in almost direct ratio to the strength of the local synagogue."[7]

Given the difficulties in sustaining small-town Judaism, the 1973 conference delegates concluded that "when all is said and done, the future of small-town Jews is dependent on their own will to survive."[8] Until economic devastation hit their communities, Jews in the coalfields sustained a remarkable number of congregations that provided the basis for a full Jewish life for several generations. This chapter describes how they managed to do it.

Old Country Roots and Three Patterns of Growth

East European Jewish immigrants came from a background "wholly pervaded by Jewishness." For centuries, religious ritual had ordered daily life, and Hebrew schools, aid societies, rabbinical courts, and other community institutions had regulated social interaction. Imperatives such as prayer and study of religious texts (for men), keeping a Jewish home (for women), and communal obligations (primarily for men) set the standard for behavior. Even as society modernized, the new expressions that developed remained grounded in the context of Jewish tradition. Social and religious life continued to be intertwined, especially in the shtetls, where most immigrants to the coalfields originated.[9]

The decision to emigrate was, in part, a decision to leave this insular world behind. And those willing to locate in the vast non-Jewish interior of America, rather than the Yiddish neighborhoods of New York and other cities, were even more prepared than others to give up the all-encompassing Jewish environment in which they had been raised. But this does not mean they contemplated abandoning an identity, religion, and culture so deeply ingrained. Most were internally motivated to retain their Jewishness and find ways to express it.

Moreover, except for the first Jewish pioneers to arrive in an area, the others who joined them through chain migration did not make the same choice to leave their ethnic enclaves to settle in "virgin territory"; they came because they were sent for or because their trail-blazing relatives offered them a job. This included most of the women as well as many male relatives of original Jewish settlers. These people tended to be more traditionally oriented than the pioneers. The recurrent arrival of newcomers, especially those who came straight from Europe to join their relatives, reinforced the Jewish character of Jewish communities and counteracted the assimilatory influences that engaged longer-established residents. In the 1920s, U.S. immigration restrictions put a halt to direct infusions from the old country. This was a turning point; in the years to follow, communities would have to rely on other means to maintain their identity.[10]

Jews in the southern coalfields went to great lengths to transplant their old culture while adapting it to their new home. Their efforts took place on many fronts—at home, at work, through informal socializing. As elsewhere in small-town America, the key to their cultural survival was the creation of local congregations where they could practice their religion, transmit their heritage to their children, and organize the customs that connected them to their tradition. Between 1892 and 1931, coalfield Jews founded nine congregations, each serving as a local center and stimulus for Jewish life (see table 4).

Though small-town Jewish communities may have derived from similar roots, encountered similar challenges, and followed similar stages of development, many variables led each to take on its own character. Demographics, geography, and internal dynamics all played a role. Moreover, the immigrants adapted not to a generalized American experience but to specific social environments that influenced their communities. Even within the coalfields, local congregations exhibited three distinct development patterns. Jews in the boomtowns of Pocahontas, Keystone, and Kimball took one direction, and the West Virginia county-seat towns of Welch, Williamson, Logan, and Beckley took another. In southeastern Kentucky, the Middlesboro and Harlan congregations devised a third way.

The German Jews who arrived in the coalfields in the 1870s and early 1880s were too few to organize communally, leaving the first stirrings of group activity to the East European Jews who came to the boomtowns of the Pocahontas coalfield starting in the mid-1880s. Jews in the town of Pocahontas formed Congregation Aha-

Table 4. Jewish Congregations in the Southern Coalfields

Town	Name of Congregation/ Primary Affiliation	Dates of Operation	Year Synagogue Built or Acquired
Pocahontas, Va.	Ahavath Chesed/Orthodox	1890s–1930s*	1912
Keystone, W.Va.	B'nai Israel/Orthodox	1890s–1940s	1904
Middlesboro, Ky.	Temple of Zion/Orthodox, Conservative	1900s–1930s*	No synagogue
Bluefield, W.Va.**	Ahavath Sholom/Reform	1900s–present	1907, 1949
Kimball, W.Va.	Beth Jacob/Orthodox	1910s–1930s*	1914
Welch, W.Va.	Congregation Emanuel/ Reform	1910s–1980s	1922
Williamson, W.Va.	B'nai Israel/Reform	1910s–present	1928
Logan, W.Va.	B'nai El/Reform	1910s–1980s	1948
Beckley, W.Va.	Beth El/Reform	1920s–present	1935
Harlan, Ky.	B'nai Sholom/Reform, Conservative	1930s–1970s	No synagogue

Sources: Jones, *Early Coal Mining*; Shinedling, *West Virginia Jewry*; Shinedling and Pickus, *History of the Beckley Jewish Community*; "Student Rabbi Survey"; Welch, Williamson, Logan, and Harlan congregation records.

* Precise end date unknown.
** Bluefield, as regional center, included for comparative purposes.

vath Chesed in 1892, and Jews in nearby Keystone soon followed with Congregation B'nai Israel, which hired a rabbi by 1900. Remarkably, Jews in a third small Pocahontas coalfield town also formed a congregation. Kimball, just down the tracks from Keystone and home of Jewish pioneer Harry Bank, hosted Congregation Beth Jacob by 1910. These three congregations reached their prime in the first two decades of the twentieth century, when their Jewish populations were the largest in the region (see table 2).[11]

All the coalfield congregations started out "strictly Orthodox," but only the boomtown congregations remained so throughout their existence. Their synagogues each contained a *mikvah* (ritual bath) and segregated seating for women, two requirements of traditional Judaism.[12] Their Orthodox Judaism was also expressed in their burial arrangements. By 1890, the handful of German Jews in Pocahontas had established a small Jewish section within the town's cemetery that, to this day, is distinguished from the surrounding Christian graves only by the absence of crosses. The sole person from an East European family interred there is Harry Bank's one-year-old son Norris, who died in 1899. The baby's death evidently caught the area's East European Jews by surprise. By 1903, when seven-year-old Arnold Davis of Pocahontas died, his family could bury him in a new Orthodox cemetery located just outside the town of Pocahontas, on land straddling the border of Virginia and West Virginia purchased from an African American farmer. Until the late 1920s, Jews from Keystone, Kimball, and Pocahontas were buried at this site, known locally as Hebrew Mountain. Many of the gravestones are inscribed entirely in Hebrew.[13]

At first, members held prayer services in their homes and rented halls for the high holidays. The rabbis hired by the Keystone congregation "would not stay very long," writes former resident Louis Zaltzman. "The leading Jewish men would conduct the services, [especially] one Kopel Hyman, who was formerly a *schochet* and a rabbi." So far Keystone's experience was typical. A hired rabbi was not needed to lead services since most immigrants were thoroughly familiar with the ritual; all that was required was a *minyan* (quorum) of ten men. For specialized tasks, such as the functions of a *schochet* (ritual slaughterer) or cantor, small congregations across the United States often had in their midst one or two merchants with extensive religious training, like Hyman. Many communities relied entirely on such men because they could not retain rabbis with any sort of permanency. Also, itinerant rabbis with somewhat dubious credentials circulated through small towns and provided temporary services. Their tenures (as Zaltzman notes) tended to be brief.[14]

But the Pocahontas, Kimball, and especially Keystone congregations managed to reach a higher level of organization. For much of their existence they had full-time rabbis who lived in town with their families. These men also served as *schochtim* (ritual slaughterers), enabling their congregants to keep kosher. Rabbi Abraham Davidov arrived in Keystone shortly after the synagogue opened in 1904 and served for sixteen years. He was followed by Moses Borrow, who served from 1921 to about 1940. This record of longevity is striking compared to most small-town Orthodox congregations. Rabbis in Pocahontas and Kimball also exhibited some stability. The Pocahontas congregation supported five full-time rabbis from the 1890s to the 1920s, in addition to those who simply passed through. In 1910, as many as three religious functionaries lived in the little town at the same time: the current and previous rabbis and one J. Rappaport, a Lithuanian immigrant listed in the census as "minister, preaching." In Kimball, Rabbi Nathan Teich served from 1909 to at least 1915, and another rabbi officiated from at least 1919 to 1921.[15]

These rabbis brought their old-country training, and no doubt their old-country styles, with them. Davidov, Borrow, and Teich were all "fresh off the boat," each moving to the coalfields within a year of landing in the United States. The extensive services they provided suggest they were fully ordained, as opposed to the vague qualifications of rabbis of a more itinerant nature. Two Pocahontas rabbis had credentials from respected rabbinical authorities in Lithuania (one received his degree from the famed Rabbi Isaac Elchanan Spector of Kovno). The traditionalism of the congregants was strengthened by having these old-country emissaries on hand to perform all the functions necessary to fill a Jewish community's religious needs: leading prayer services; conducting weddings, funerals, and *brises* (circumcisions); teaching Hebrew; and slaughtering animals in the ritually prescribed manner.[16]

This is not to say that the rabbis were relics of an older or bygone era. Davidov was thirty-six when he came to Keystone, and Borrow, oldest of all the boomtown rabbis at the start of his tenure, was forty-eight. As for Teich, the 1910 census shows the twenty-seven-year-old, non-English-speaking, single rabbi boarding with twenty-five-year-old single butcher Sol Kaufman. His youth mirrored the youth of the Jewish population. In 1910, the average age of Jews in the three communities was only twenty-three. Kimball's forty-five Jews were especially young, with an average age of nineteen (heads of households averaged only twenty-seven years old). At thirty-eight, Harry Bank was the oldest Jewish person in town. Large families with lots of children were the rule: 40 percent of Jews in the three communities were under age seventeen.[17]

Given the youthfulness of the boomtown congregations in their heyday, it is not surprising that Jewish ritual was not their sole preoccupation. Religious observance provided the basis for a lively social scene linking Jews from all three towns. Five years after his arrival, young Rabbi Teich, now married, gave an "impressive" address (in English, no doubt) at the dedication of Kimball's synagogue, an event the *McDowell Recorder* termed "one of the most elaborate affairs ever held among the Hebrews of the Coal Fields." Jews from throughout the area gathered to celebrate their communal progress, and the ladies of Keystone and Kimball presented a twelve-course supper. At the Pocahontas synagogue dedication the previous year, the galleries overflowed, probably with the same people who attended the Kimball event. Keystone's Manhattan Social Club organized festive holiday celebrations that exemplified the intertwining of social and religious functions. Its 1911 Purim Ball was "a decided success," according to the *Recorder,* with the spacious hall "crowded to the limit."[18]

The vitality of the three Orthodox communities did not last beyond the 1920s, however, as the next generation moved to the economically surging coalfield county seats and to Bluefield, the regional hub. Kimball's Beth Jacob folded during the Depression. The Pocahontas congregation sold its synagogue to the town's Women's Club about 1951, but it had ceased to function years earlier. Although Keystone and the adjoining town of Northfork retained enough Jews to keep B'nai Israel going into the 1940s, its role in local Jewish life had diminished. The synagogue was sold in 1952, with the proceeds, as well as the Torah scrolls, donated to a newly established synagogue in Jerusalem. "Until the very end of its existence," B'nai Israel's services "were conducted along strictly traditional, Orthodox lines," states coalfield rabbi and author Abraham Shinedling.[19]

Several factors kept the Keystone, Kimball, and Pocahontas congregations in the Orthodox fold, unlike other coalfield congregations and indeed, unlike most small-town American congregations. First, because much of the second generation moved away, immigrants retained control of communal leadership and saw little reason to relinquish familiar rituals. Keystone-born Ken Bank (Wolf's son) recalled that the synagogue was "too Orthodox for me" and his only choice was to stop attending; there were too few members of his generation in town to press for change.[20] Second, the boomtown atmosphere that prevailed in the three towns exerted less external pressure on Jewish communities to conform to a certain style of behavior. Not that there were no standards at all, but attitudes regarding propriety were distinctly looser than in the county seats. Additionally, Jews constituted a larger percentage of the population and did not experience the feelings of insecurity that caused other Jewish communities to strive to fit in.

Dwelling in these rough little towns were Jews who started out as saloon owners and were often hauled into court in the early years, who squabbled vociferously among themselves and felt free to speak Yiddish in their daily lives. These people felt little urgency to "Americanize" their religious services. Their communal institutions, developed when their numbers were large and growing, continued to serve their purposes. And with full-time rabbis living in their midst, they had the resources and guidance they needed to maintain traditional practices.

This does not mean that Jews in the boomtowns completely retained their old-country ways. They had to make many of the compromises that small-town American Jews had to make, from working on the Sabbath to accepting less-than-rigorous kosher dietary standards. They too were affected by their relative isolation from the larger Jewish world, and they too were drawn into a new and dynamic coalfield society. They did indeed assimilate, but into a milieu that enabled them to keep more of their traditions than Jews in other small communities, including the coalfield county seats.

Though they shared the same region and even the same extended families, Jews in the southern West Virginia county seats faced different circumstances than their coreligionists in the classic boomtowns. By the time their communities began to organize in the 1910s, the second generation—many American-born, others brought to the United States as small children—had begun to make its influence felt. Immigrants shared leadership of their communities with people who had grown up in America, many right in the coalfields. Of the six women who attended the second meeting of Williamson's Jewish Ladies Guild, three came from Europe as young adults. Of the other three, one was born on American soil. Ida Bank and Leah Shein both arrived in America by age three.[21]

While the social milieu in the boomtowns gave Jewish residents little incentive to alter their traditional ways, Jews in the county seats entered a more conventional small-town society, with an emerging middle class that strove for respectability. Though coalfield county seats could hardly be considered staid, clubs and church groups set a tone that was more refined than in neighboring coal towns. County-seat Jews were (for the most part) eager to join in the middle-class social scene, and their neighbors were (for the most part) quite willing to accept them. Forming their own religious congregations, far from isolating Jews, helped them fit into a society in which religious affiliation was all-important. As a Jewish man from Welch put it, "In a small town, *everybody* belongs to a church."[22]

County-seat congregations, therefore, served a dual purpose, as they did throughout the South, as "the agency of Jewish solidarity and survival" and as "a Jewish church which integrated Jews into southern society as citizens and neighbors," as Leonard Rogoff puts it. As a result, they paid more attention to surrounding influences than the boomtown congregations, a phenomenon that showed up in ways large and small. One brief example, for now: in preparing to furnish their new temple in 1922, Welch Sisterhood members visited some of the town's newer churches to see how the Christian women had furnished *their* places of worship.[23]

Their concern that their congregations conform (within certain limits) to mainstream religious expression, coupled with the needs and desires of an American-raised generation, caused county-seat Jews to move away from Orthodox Judaism toward a more Americanized religious practice that one local account described as Reform with "Conservative tendencies."[24] From the beginning, traditional and modern elements mixed, sometimes in easy coexistence, often with underlying tension and occasionally with overt conflict. This does not mean county-seat Jews were less committed to Judaism than their boomtown counterparts; as will be seen, they struggled mightily to keep up traditions and instill a Jewish identity in their children. But their communal institutions took a different form, one more typical of other small-town American Jewish congregations.

Perhaps the most critical difficulty faced by small-town congregations was that they were often too small to afford, and too remote to attract, a full-time rabbi. Unlike the boomtowns, the coalfield county seats solved this problem the way many congregations across the country did: they turned to Hebrew Union College (HUC) for rabbinical support. The Cincinnati-based Reform seminary, for a moderate fee, assigned participating congregations a student rabbi who came on a biweekly basis to lead services, teach the children, and perform other duties. It also offered the option to engage a student for the high holidays only. Eventually, largely as a result of their reliance on the student rabbi program, the southern West Virginia coalfield county-seat congregations all formally affiliated with the Reform movement.[25]

The Welch and Williamson Jewish communities began to organize in the 1910s. As in Williamson, Welch Jews started with mutual aid: men and women founded separate aid societies in 1915. Each town's Jews then rented spaces that they fitted up for services and religious schools. The third floor of City Hall housed Welch's "shul room," while Williamson Jews met in the "dugout," the basement of Hyman Bank's theater. At first, both communities conducted traditional Sabbath services themselves, hiring visiting rabbis for the high holidays. Welch Jews incorporated as Congregation Emanuel in 1918 and built a synagogue between 1922 and 1924. Williamson's B'nai Israel incorporated in 1921 and dedicated its synagogue, still in use today, in 1928.[26]

Despite parallel growth patterns, the two congregations offer contrasting examples of how small-town Jews handled the transition from Orthodox to Reform

Judaism. Welch Jews, slow to convert to modern ways, had a succession of Orthodox rabbis in the early years whom they hired to teach the children and serve as *schochtim*. They were of the itinerant variety, though congregation members intended to employ a permanent rabbi once their synagogue was built. In the meantime, they made do. The (oddly spelled) minutes of a 1918 Ladies Aid Society meeting note that "Mr. Smith the Welch shocet, [asked] the help of the Ladies at the dedication of the new Sefor Thora. . . . [He] then gave a lecture on Jewidism which was enjoyed by everyone present." Welch Jews also had access to the rabbis/*schochtim* in nearby Kimball and Keystone, whereas Williamson, though home to many former Keystoners, was too far away to remain under the influence of those traditionally oriented communities. In 1922, rather than affiliate with the Reform movement's Federation of Temple Sisterhoods, the Welch ladies chose to join the Women's League of the United Synagogue of America because "this league is Orthodox to its utmost." The following year, however, the women changed their minds and joined the Reform group. Pragmatism won out—the federation had a state chapter that offered more in the way of resources.[27]

The religious ritual of Welch's Jews remained Orthodox even as they began to draw on the Reform movement for organizational support. In the early 1920s, they engaged a Bluefield baker and respected Hebrew scholar, Ben Matz, to live in town several days a week to teach religious school and lead services. At a statewide Sisterhood convention in the late 1920s, however, a Welch member assured her Reform cohorts that a process of transition was underway: "We have in Welch a lovely little Temple Building which is filled to capacity on the two most important holidays of the year but during the rest of the year it is hardly used at all. Services are conducted in the Orthodox fashion, under the leadership of a man who has also been teaching the children. . . . [He] is very capable, having modernized his methods to the extent that he teaches Hebrew with the English translation—also Biblical History in English. [The men of the congregation] are thinking of bringing a Modern young leader to Welch, and they have been assured of the hearty support and cooperation of the Sisterhood." The congregation never managed to employ a full-time ordained rabbi, modern or otherwise. Instead, it maintained its arrangement with Matz and services remained Orthodox until "the Reform element came on so strongly" in the early 1940s, according to one member. Around that time, the congregation joined Hebrew Union College's biweekly student rabbi program.[28]

In contrast to the gradual approach in Welch—where bouts of apathy, rather than controversy, appear to have caused occasional problems—some Williamson Jews tried to bring their congregation into the Reform fold shortly after its founding, engaging a Hebrew Union College student for the 1921 high holidays. Other congregation members were not quite ready for this step, as the unlucky eighteen year old found out. In a memoir recalling his first student rabbi experience, Sidney Regner described his attempt to introduce Reform Judaism into

Williamson. On the first night of Rosh Hashanah, the only people paying attention to the services he conducted were family members of the woman who had
engaged him, sitting in the front row:

> They were the only ones who had Union Prayer Books [used by Reform con-
> gregations], and they were the only ones to greet me after the services. The
> following morning they were the only ones *at* the services, except for a man
> who sat there reading a newspaper. The rest were conducting Orthodox ser-
> vices elsewhere. I spent the time between Rosh Hashanah and Yom Kippur
> patching things up. . . . The woman who arranged for the services never told
> the others it would be a Reform service. . . . The experience was so discouraging
> that I almost did not return to the College. To my surprise, they asked for me
> to return the next year, which I would not do.[29]

After this fiasco, the congregation enlisted the help of Abraham Feinstein, the
Reform rabbi in Huntington, West Virginia. By 1923, he was traveling to Williamson monthly to conduct services and assist with the Sisterhood's Sunday school.
He apparently helped B'nai Israel's traditional members adjust to changing times:
by 1924, when the congregation again attempted to hire a rabbinical student for
the holidays, Feinstein could assure HUC officials that the student "will receive
the most cordial treatment, that he will find a community well organized and
prepared to follow any suggestions he may have to make."[30]

Yet tensions remained when the synagogue was built in 1928. Congregation
president Harry Schwachter, an avid member of the Reform camp, tried to placate
the other side by engaging a Conservative rabbi to conduct the first high holiday
services in the new building. "It was a very delicate situation," explains his daughter, "for several of the Jewish families were quite orthodox (and big contributors)
while the remaining families were quite vehemently reform." When Schwachter
informed an official at the Jewish Theological Seminary that the Reform members
were "unanimous in their refusal to wear the traditional skull cap, the yarmulke,"
the official, "aghast," refused to supply a rabbi and Schwachter ended up again
turning to HUC.[31]

Conflict faded as the influence of older members diminished. B'nai Israel entered
HUC's biweekly program in the 1930s. By the 1940s, the congregation had an organ,
a youth choir, and a full slate of activities under the enthusiastic encouragement of
a series of student rabbis. One of these young men later recalled being "impressed
with the whole community set-up. It was a progressive and dynamic community,
isolated yet feeling itself a part of the larger Jewish Community outside."[32]

Logan and Beckley offer two more variations on the county-seat pattern. Logan's Jewish population grew suddenly in the 1910s but then tapered off to remain
the smallest of the four West Virginia county seats. Heavily foreign-born, the community tended toward traditionalism. However, its small size limited its ability to
maintain communal institutions, and its location on a branch of the C&O Rail-

road separated it from the lively Jewish scene that extended along the N&W main line from Bluefield to Williamson. Its leaders realized their best hope for much-needed support came from the Reform institutions in Cincinnati, and so the congregation moved quickly into the Reform camp. As early as 1916, member Edward Coffman wrote to HUC requesting a student rabbi for the holidays. He assured the dean, "Everyone of our Jews in this town are very anxious to have services . . . there are about eighteen to twenty who will attend." Logan's Jews began holding regular services on their own in 1918 and incorporated the B'nai El congregation about 1924. The group met in "a fully equipped temple" on the third floor of the First National Bank building before moving into its own building in 1948.[33]

B'nai El started to engage biweekly student rabbis in 1925, the earliest of the county-seat congregations. The group's request to HUC reveals its concerns. "We are only a handful of families but we would do everything to give our children some Jewish education," emphasized Sisterhood leader Gizella Eiland. Efforts to secure a full-time rabbi had failed, she explained, and the religious school had "come to a deadlock" because "none of us have any experience in teaching." She concluded, "[We are] begging you to assign the student rabbi to us." HUC sent Nahum Friedless, an immigrant whose foreign accent had provoked complaints from some of his other postings. Many small-town congregations placed a high priority on the impression their student rabbi made on gentiles and preferred the all-American type, but Logan Jews expressed no such cares. As immigrants themselves, they were comfortable with Friedless and pronounced themselves "very well pleased" with his tenure.[34]

Yet as much as Logan Jews appreciated the Reform seminary's assistance, they were reluctant "converts" to Reform Judaism. The year before entering the biweekly program, the congregation had arranged for a student to come for the high holidays but canceled at the last minute and hired an Orthodox cantor instead. The Logan student rabbi who participated in a 1935 HUC survey of small-town congregations offered a perceptive answer to the question of whether there was a cleavage between the town's Orthodox and Reform Jews. Although there was no overt conflict, he wrote, the "cleavage is in each member who has orthodox background, and . . . must take part in Reform services." Logan's traditionally oriented Jews "miss the warmth of old-fashioned services," he observed. "On reflection, however, most of them realize HUC will keep religion alive in their children."[35]

Beckley's Jewish population developed later, but as the town grew into a regional center, its Jewish community became the largest in the coalfields. Communal activity began in 1921, when high holiday services took place "in honor of Mrs. Sana Moscovitch Pickus," who had "just arrived from the old country" to be with her three sons. History does not record the reaction of the devoutly Orthodox woman to these services, held in a Presbyterian church and led by a Reform student rabbi. The following year the women started a religious school that met in private homes. In 1925, they formed the Beckley Sisterhood, and for the

next ten years, as Beckley's only established Jewish group, they organized communal events, operated the school, and raised funds for a synagogue. The Beckley
Hebrew Association incorporated in 1935 and built Temple Beth El, which remains
its synagogue today. In 1954, the congregation established a cemetery, the only
county-seat congregation to do so.[36]

From the start, the congregation's formal activities were decidedly Reform. Services in the early years not only took place in a church (or the Woman's Club or
American Legion hall) with a Reform student or visiting rabbi but also featured a
non-Jewish choir. Yet the congregation managed to accommodate "a hodgepodge
of Orthodox, Conservative, and Reform," as one member later put it. "They tried
to blend a little of all of that so everybody was happy." At first, the men gathered
informally for traditional services in private homes, as attested to by "several old
and well-used Orthodox Siddurim (prayer books)" resting on the temple's library
shelves years later. This dual pattern continued after the temple was built. Though
regular Friday night services were "strictly Reform," as late as 1955, "minyan services conducted along slightly more traditional lines, . . . with more Hebrew being
read, and with the use of Hebrew Psalms, were still being held for those members
who requested it."[37]

The congregation showed the same eclectic spirit in regard to its rabbis. For
some years it employed biweekly students, but during its heyday in the 1940s and
1950s, it supported its own full-time rabbis. The first was Conservative, the rest
were Reform. Most stayed only a couple of years (except for Abraham Shinedling,
who served from 1950 to 1956). In the post–World War II years, the congregation
benefited from the leadership of pharmacist and lay rabbi Isadore Wein, a Beckley resident whose Orthodox training, liberal views, and inclusive ways enabled
him to unify a disparate group.[38]

Clearly, the path from an informal collection of traditional-minded Jews to a
small but fairly well established Reform Jewish community could take many
twists and turns. Hebrew Union College and other institutions of Reform Judaism
stand out as a major influence, as all the county seats had Reform-affiliated Sisterhoods and B'nai B'rith chapters. These institutions linked coalfield Jews to the
nation's organized Jewish world while offering a practical solution to the difficulty of finding affordable and reliable religious leaders. Moreover, as the Logan
student rabbi astutely pointed out, even Jews uncomfortable with Reform practice
realized that a Reform affiliation, and the student rabbis themselves, offered the
best chance to accomplish their key goal of getting their children involved in Judaism. Whereas Jewish youth in Keystone found their aging Orthodox rabbi alienating, county-seat congregations were forming youth groups guided by leaders who
were themselves youthful.[39]

The southeastern Kentucky coalfields received fewer Jewish immigrants (or
immigrants of any kind) than other southern coalfields, mostly because the L&N

Railroad did not link to U.S. port cities. Jews who settled there benefited from access to the resources of Knoxville's long-established Jewish community, such as kosher products and rabbis who ventured out to visit their "country cousins," but this may have deterred them from developing their own resources. The scattered nature of the area's Jewish population, spread across towns in Kentucky, Virginia, and Tennessee, also hindered communal organization. These factors set communal development on a trajectory different from that in the other coalfields. Lacking the "critical mass" needed to build a synagogue, Jews in Middlesboro and Harlan reached out to their coreligionists in the broader Cumberland Gap area, creating institutions that enabled a dispersed group to worship on the high holidays, bury their dead, and celebrate life-cycle events together.[40]

The two congregations overlapped in time and space and even attempted to join together at one point. The Middlesboro Jewish community, like those in the other boomtowns, started in the 1890s and peaked in the 1910s. As early as 1891, a local newspaper noted that the town's fifteen or so Jewish families were "discussing the possibility of a synagogue." These plans were dashed by the town's spectacular financial crash, which caused an exodus among all segments of the population. But a core of Jews remained and rebuilt their community, as shown by an 1897 article revealing that Rabbi Winick of Knoxville had recently visited to circumcise the baby son of William and Bertha Horr and "ratify" the marriage of a couple who had eloped: William's seventeen-year-old sister Sadie and twenty-three-year-old Ike Ginsburg, the future mayor. In 1904, the death of Ike and Sadie's six-year-old daughter Rebecca led to the founding of Middlesboro's Jewish cemetery on land donated by Sadie's father Ben, a local fruit store owner. This cemetery served the area's Jews for the next sixty or more years.[41]

The founding of a cemetery precipitated the founding of a congregation, which occurred about 1905. Because it left no records, its history is sketchy, even down to its name, which one source refers to as Temple of Zion. The congregation established quarters in Middlesboro's Masonic hall, where merchant Sam Weinstein led Orthodox services until the 1930s. The congregation later described itself as Conservative, though it also held Reform services led by merchant Louis Sturm. The women were active: the Daughters of Zion functioned in the 1910s, and a Hadassah chapter existed in the 1930s.[42]

Several times in the 1910s and 1920s, Weinstein wrote to Hebrew Union College requesting a student for the high holidays, possibly to conduct Reform services to alternate with his own Orthodox services, since one letter hinted at a growing Reform faction. Often these requests were later retracted, suggesting some ambivalence. Correspondence from 1928 reveals how HUC grappled with the problem of trying to serve traditional congregations. Weinstein informed the dean that his group was Conservative and received a reply warning that student rabbis used the Union Prayer Book, did "no chanting whatsoever," and used "considerable English." (Perhaps the dean recalled that a few years back, Weinstein had

actually asked the Reform seminary to send someone to conduct Orthodox services.) Weinstein said those terms were fine with him, but the dean remained
skeptical and suggested that the group hire an Orthodox cantor. Weinstein persisted, and finally HUC offered to send a young man who was "raised in an orthodox environment" and was willing to chant part of the service. Weinstein
readily agreed and final arrangements were made.[43]

Though serving a population separated by miles of winding mountain roads
posed challenges for both southeastern Kentucky congregations, it gave their high
holiday gatherings a festive air. Out-of-town congregation members often stayed
at the Horr family's hotel. Each meeting was like a family reunion, especially since
many of the far-flung members were actually related to each other.[44]

But Weinstein's move to Nashville in 1933 weakened the Middlesboro congregation, whose numbers had stagnated since the late 1910s. The area's center of
Jewish life shifted to Harlan, where the Jewish population had begun to grow in
the 1920s. Harlan Jews held their first high holiday services in the town's Masonic hall in 1931. A few weeks later, ten men met in Sol Geller's store to organize
Congregation B'nai Sholom of Southeastern Kentucky. The name reflected a deliberate attempt to reach out to Jews in surrounding towns, and the new group
held meetings in Harlan and Pineville to discuss area-wide organization. The first
drew an enthusiastic crowd of more than ninety people, with speakers such as
David Scott of Pineville and Louis Sturm of Middlesboro pledging support. The
new congregation even held its 1932 high holiday services in Middlesboro, perhaps
in deference to the older group. Invitations were extended to all Jewish families
in the area, with the enticement that "housing of visitors and their families at very
reasonable rates have been arranged in the beautiful, clean, and very hospitable
New Middlesboro Hotel." Despite organizational support from the Reform
movement, services were Conservative.[45]

By 1935, the Middlesboro contingent had dropped out, partly out of religious
differences but perhaps also because of the difficult geography. B'nai Sholom now
held services and other events only in Harlan, though it continued to draw from
towns around the Cumberland Gap. A 1935 letter from secretary Harry Miller to
Harry Linden, a founding member who had moved away, shows the do-it-yourself
nature of the services: "We had Services in Harlan, Rosh-Hashonoh. It was not a
very large 'Minion.' But the services were conducted very quietly, and very timely,
just as we had them four years ago, when you were in Harlan. Mr. Rothschild 'Dav-
ent, Shacharith.' Mr. Geller did his 'Musaff.' And I took care of the English reading
and the sermons. We had arranged . . . a communal dinner . . . at which a few
spitches were delivered. . . . Last night, Mr. Geller, Mr. Roodine, and Mr. Bart were
over to my house, and we were practicing the singing of 'Kol Nidrai.'"[46]

The congregation grew beyond this homey description, reaching its high point
in the 1940s. It set up permanent space in Harlan's Masonic hall, with "all the
paraphernalia required for our services," as a member put it. Visiting rabbis came

through, and the Sisterhood organized Purim parties, Bible-reading sessions, and charitable activities to support the war effort and Jewish refugees. The Harlan congregation lasted until about 1970. The Middlesboro group had stopped functioning long before; once it did, the town's remaining Jews traveled to Harlan or Knoxville to participate in organized Jewish life.[47]

The nine coalfield congregations found different ways to organize in response to varying conditions. Yet all exhibited a vibrancy that reflected the strong desire of their participants to experience Jewish communal life and provide that experience to their children, despite group tensions and periods of apathy. On a swing through southern West Virginia in 1926, a rabbi on a lecture tour marveled at the mini-Jewish civilizations he discovered deep in the coalfields of Central Appalachia: "Among the unheralded magnificence of West Virginia's majestic mountains, where the bungalows of the coal miners line the roads . . . there are Jewish congregations. In some of these congregations the men wear hats in the synagogue. In others the members import kosher meat. . . . Keystone, Northfork, and Welch are as well organized as any little city in Ohio, with congregation, sisterhood, and religious school. . . . They are merry folk in Logan, and they talk sweetly of New York, Baltimore, and Cincinnati." His impressions confirm the liveliness of these communities and the determination of their members to forge the group mechanisms necessary for Jewish survival.[48]

As a basis for social life and source of identity and belonging, as well as a locus for Jewish ritual and education, congregations played a central role in the lives of coalfield Jews, even those who were not personally religious. But communal institutions were not the only ways Jewishness was expressed. Issues of religious and cultural identity played out at work, at home, and in society at large—and in turn were reflected back into the communal realm.

Community, Kinship, and Work

Familial and economic networks were the first, if not the most important, factor binding coalfield Jewish communities. With some 90 percent dependent on jobs tied to Jewish sources, it could hardly be otherwise. When asked what held the Beckley Jewish community together before the building of the temple in the 1930s, one woman thought for a moment, then exclaimed, "Work."[49]

The comment of many interviewees that the region's Jews were "one big family" had literal as well as metaphorical truth. Coalfield marriages reinforced the family ties that Jews brought to the region. Given that the communities started with groups of extended families, that these families often had lots of children, and that the imperative to marry within the faith was strong, it was inevitable that links between them would proliferate until many coalfield Jews became somehow related to one another. When the Bank and Totz families, cousins in the old country, each married into the Ofsa family, these three McDowell Coun-

ty clans formed the basis of a network of kin and marital relationships that en-
compassed dozens of families and extended throughout the region.[50]

As kin networks spread, economic connections did likewise. In these merchant-
based communities, there would always be a role for relatives in the common quest
to gain a livelihood. Economic interdependence, in turn, reinforced the close ties of
kinship. And as long as communities were made up of interrelated families, their
communal institutions would themselves be family affairs. At least thirteen of the
twenty-two founding members of the Welch congregation belonged to four extended family groups; three of the five trustees at the 1928 dedication of Williamson's synagogue were close relatives. Four of the ten men at the 1935 founding meeting of the Beckley Hebrew Association were members of the Pickus family.[51]

Familial and economic networks also kept coalfield Jews in close contact with
the major centers of American Jewish life. Despite their location in the heart of
Central Appalachia, they were far from isolated. The rail lines built to transport
coal to metropolitan areas made those areas—New York, Cincinnati, and especially Baltimore—readily accessible. Buying trips to the large Jewish wholesale
houses were not just business matters, they were immersions in Jewish culture, as
they invariably involved visiting kin and spending time in Baltimore's close-knit
Jewish community. Coalfield residents hosted their big-city relatives in turn; guest
lists of Jewish weddings, printed in local society columns, almost always record a
Baltimore contingent on hand to take part in the celebration. Out-of-town connections even provided material support to coalfield congregations, as wholesalers donated to synagogue fund drives. Beckley merchants, for example, entered
into an arrangement allowing each of them to take a 1 percent discount on their
purchases, with proceeds placed in their temple building fund.[52]

These outside relationships did much to shore up Jewish identity and keep
people from feeling cut off from their roots. Even people who spent their lives in
the coalfields may have considered themselves branch members of the Baltimore
Jewish community. Several Keystoners are buried in Baltimore's B'nai Israel Congregation cemetery, and it is probably no coincidence that the Keystone congregation shared the B'nai Israel name. (As did the Williamson congregation, many of
whose founders came from Keystone.) City relatives themselves tended to look
askance at their country cousins; one woman recalled that her Baltimore relatives
"used to call us goyim." But to coalfield Jews, links to the outside world provided
a lifeline that enhanced and lent legitimacy to their efforts to maintain Jewish life
in the mountains.[53]

While networks connected them to the outside world, customs of mutual aid
connected them to their Jewish past. The principles of *tzedekah* that permeated
life in the old country found expression in coalfield aid societies and in the per-
vasiveness of informal loan arrangements. Since the ability of each community
to thrive was dependent upon the economic survival of its members, lending financial support to a fellow Jew meant supporting the community as well. As one

Beckley merchant put it, "Everybody was in competition with each other . . . but there was room for everybody."[54]

The economic realm also bolstered Jewish identity and solidarity by offering a platform for Jews to demonstrate to the surrounding society their loyalty to their religion and culture. This can be seen in newspaper announcements of high holiday business closings. For those businessmen who devoted most of their waking hours to their work, as well as for highly assimilated Jews, store closings served as one of the few means they had to remind themselves and others of their attachment to Judaism. "For some people, that's how they found out you were Jewish," one man explained. The act had communal as well as personal implications. Every high holiday season, David Scott went around to all the Jewish businesses in Welch to make sure recalcitrant merchants fell in line. He thought it was necessary for the entire Jewish community to express its unity during the most holy week on the calendar.[55]

But economic considerations could also work against community. Nationwide, an all-out engagement with U.S. capitalism inevitably caused neglect of religious practice and communal affairs, with the loss of Sabbath observance the most often cited example of how American work patterns disrupted traditional ways. Merchant-based Jewish communities across the country were tied to their stores on Saturdays, the busiest shopping day of the week.[56] Their inability to keep the Sabbath highlighted most sharply the contrast with Eastern Europe, where the very rhythms of daily life were guided by Sabbath preparation and observance.

Jewish coalfield residents can tell this side of the story. A communal leader who often became frustrated by the priorities of his fellow Jews declared that "earning a living was more important to them than anything else." Family businesses consumed men and often women as well. "My parents never attended functions of the Temple," one respondent told Jerome David. "They were so busy with the business, they never had time for anything else." Another explained, "All the stores were open til 10 P.M. every evening and til 12 midnight on Saturday. My parents didn't have time for family rituals." Some people tried to incorporate traditional practices into their work lives as best they could. Esther Baloff lit the Sabbath candles in the store on Friday nights when she was working late, while another person recalled that as a child, "I used to take candles down to the store so my father could say the blessings" during Hanukah. Such makeshift solutions were all that some families were able to do.[57]

And, of course, there were those "petty business jealousies" noted by Ida Bank that sometimes grew into full-blown conflict. Sources on coalfield Jewish life offer plenty of examples. One interviewee grew up in a town with only a few Jewish families who had little to do with one another: "We didn't like each other because we were competitors. . . . We hated them!" Even a cursory perusal of court records shows Jews on opposite sides in numerous lawsuits, from disputes between struggling small shopkeepers to matters of considerable financial import. While Bessie

Zaltzman battled Louis and Esther Crigger over a transaction involving a sick cow, Aaron Catzen and Louis Kaufman's altercation concerned the development of an entire town, Clark. Often the contestants were related, and transcripts suggest that their battles were fierce, as family squabbles often are.[58]

Occasionally congregational records made veiled reference to internal strife. While it is difficult to gauge the impact of such controversies on communal affairs, it would be surprising if they had no effect at all. One clue comes from the 1932 personal jottings of a Harlan communal leader trying to bring people together for Sabbath services: "Hyman Sachs will not attend in Mr. Roodine's home. I have often previously remonstrated with him that it is not a personal affair—attending religious services—but to no avail." Considering the small number of Jewish families in Harlan at that time, and the need to assemble a *minyan* of ten men, Sachs's attitude had implications for the entire group.[59]

Finally, just as favorable economic conditions enabled Jews to build their communities, poor economic conditions would prove their undoing. Attrition occurred even during boom times, as young people with no taste for small-town merchantry could find little else to do in a region dominated by coal mining. But downturns in the coal industry were more detrimental than the lack of nonretail jobs. In the depths of the Depression, members of B'nai El in Logan expressed worries about their "fast depleting congregation." The community managed to limp along until economic recovery in the late 1930s encouraged a spate of inmigration. Ten years after fretting about their dwindling numbers, Logan Jews began to lay plans to build a synagogue.[60]

Unfortunately, by the time their building was completed in 1948, the pendulum was just about to swing back the other way. After the coal economy began its permanent decline in the 1950s, out-migration tore through the region's population. For Jews, whose numbers were small to begin with, this trend constituted an insurmountable blow. While some studies of small-town Jewish life cite the lack of a Jewish environment as the cause of eventual decline, in the coalfields, the loss of the retail niche had a much greater impact.

On balance, the economic realm served as a significant source of strength for coalfield Jewish communities until it dissolved completely, yet from the beginning, economic necessity forced Jews to alter or drop religious practices. The decline of cherished customs was felt as a loss by many. And yet, as they Americanized, they did not expect or desire to preserve their old-country ways intact and unchanged. Like other first- and second-generation Americans, coalfield Jews intended to maintain their connection to their religion and ethnic culture *and* achieve economic success. To the extent that economic networks and community/religious ties reinforced each other, they benefited. To the extent that Jewish practice impeded economic progress, they adapted. Their adaptations did not represent convenient ways to be less Jewish so much as sincere attempts to maintain their religion and culture under difficult conditions.

Community, Religion, and Culture

Discussions of immigrant adaptation generally focus on discontinuity: the loss of tradition or, in positive terms, the embrace of Americanization. Even studies that emphasize continuity with the past (describing immigrants as "transplanted" rather than "uprooted") often see change as dynamic, whereas retention of older cultural elements is viewed as passive. Observes folklorist Barbara Kirshenblatt-Gimblett, "We tend to think of cultural elements surviving, rather than of people choosing to activate" aspects of their tradition. In describing New York's East European Jews, for example, Irving Howe states, "Traditional faith still formed the foundation of this culture, if only by providing norms from which deviation had to be measured. . . . The old persisted, stubborn, rooted in the depths of common memory." But the issue can be viewed from another perspective. As Kirshenblatt-Gimblett asserts, "We may want to distinguish between a reluctance to change and a desire to perpetuate. In either case, continuity must be considered as an active process, as an aspect of traditionalizing."[61]

Coalfield Jews certainly had to take an active approach, as they faced all the problems inherent in trying to maintain Jewish life in a small town. If strict Sabbath observance was impossible, observing the dietary laws was nearly as difficult. Traditional foods were not easily obtainable, and kosher meat ordered from Cincinnati, Baltimore, or Charleston often came spoiled. The small size and diversity of the local Jewish population made it difficult to secure a rabbi or get a *minyan* for services. Resources for imparting religion and culture to the next generation were lacking, while close contact with gentile friends and neighbors exerted a strong influence on young and old. Children became caught up in the preoccupations of their peers—invited to help trim the Christmas tree or color Easter eggs, sharing year-round activities with friends whose families' Christianity was at the forefront of their lives. The assimilatory tendencies that parents fought against on a daily basis come through in this seemingly trivial childhood recollection from Marilou Schwachter Sniderman: "One night I suggested that we clasp hands all around the table and give a nice Presbyterian prayer as my friends did. This was met with such cool disapproval that I dropped the idea immediately."[62]

The realities of daily life in the region led an interviewee to declare, "It's impossible to practice Orthodoxy in a community like Beckley." Immigrants to the coalfields continued to consider themselves Orthodox but did not—could not—follow the all-encompassing traditional way of life. Inevitably, compromise accompanied the very tenacity with which they clung to their customs. A Northfork native recalled that the Northfork Jewish contingent would not ride the train on the high holidays and would walk on the railroad tracks for one mile to the Keystone synagogue dressed in their holiday best. The women would wear sensible shoes for the trek, carrying their fancier shoes with them—a less-than-satisfactory solution, as Jewish law forbids carrying as well as train riding on the Sabbath or Yom Kippur.[63]

Although this particular scenario may have been unique to the southern coal-fields, where steep hillsides and narrow valleys forced pedestrians onto the rail-road tracks, "religiously inconsistent behavior" marked the entire immigrant generation in America. Everywhere, a sort of "eroded Orthodoxy" took the form of nostalgia and an attachment to traditional synagogue ritual while daily practice slipped away. Yet big-city Jewish neighborhoods, with their kosher shops, Yiddish theater, and a shul on every corner, bolstered Jewish identity in ways unavailable to small communities. The lack of a Jewish atmosphere ensured that the most devout Jews who came to the coalfields did not stay long. Even some people who did not consider themselves religious encouraged their children to leave. "They wanted [them] to have more Jewish contact," one woman recalled.[64]

But as the intrepid Northfork Jews demonstrated, those who remained were "committed to retaining as much of traditional Jewish ritual as was possible in their new home," as Hal Rothman writes of Wichita Jews.[65] If the immigrants could not maintain an Orthodox way of life, they could at least draw on their traditions to construct a fulfilling Jewish existence for themselves and their chil-dren centered around the home and their communal institutions. The second generation would take up the same task, though with less emphasis on ritual than their parents and with a shift from nostalgic Orthodox Judaism to practical Re-form.

Observers noticed how coalfield Jews strove to maintain their religious/cul-tural identity and remarked on the "pervasive interpersonal responsibility" this effort called forth. A Logan student rabbi commented that, given the congrega-tion's small size and "physical separation from the rest of the world, . . . I would have predicted twenty years ago that the community would be dead now. But there are eighteen families who keep the temple going." A sociologist who studied three West Virginia Jewish communities in the 1970s marveled at how, in Wil-liamson, "community is sustained in an environment which harbors the attri-butes for its own dissolution."[66]

Many forces encourage Jewish identification and community in the face of erosive tendencies. Among them are religious belief, family loyalty, a desire to preserve cherished traditions, a "common ethic" shared with fellow Jews, and the universal human need to define oneself and achieve a sense of belonging. The impulse to pass the Jewish heritage onto the next generation stands out as a major impetus: American Jews' participation in communal institutions and their retention of certain customs have been driven to a great extent by "child-centered" considerations.[67]

All these motivations spurred coalfield Jews, above all the fear of losing the children to assimilation. The Harlan community's first area-wide meeting in 1931 featured a visiting rabbi speaking on "How Can I Give My Child a Jewish Educa-tion?" In 1926, Williamson communal leader Ida Nabe reminded her congrega-tion that "the guiding of the youth" was the group's "most important mission."

Fifty years later, Williamson Jews still considered children's religious development to be their "top priority." As one person explained, "In a small town, kids have to know they are Jewish." Yet the adults wished to meet their own needs as well. While education might have provided the theme for that first Harlan meeting, the gathering's celebratory air came from the dedication of the Sefer Torah that one member had donated. The acquisition of this central artifact of their tradition signaled to all that the comforts of Jewish religion and culture would not be absent from their home in the mountains.[68]

Women would emerge as prime movers in attempts to maintain Jewish identity and practice both within and outside the home. Their increased involvement in communal affairs defied custom, because women's role in Judaism historically had been confined to the domestic sphere. But in American life in general and small towns in particular, women's role expanded as men became preoccupied with economic advancement. Paradoxically, women's communal leadership disrupted traditional gender patterns—but in the service of preserving traditional ways.[69]

Even as they redefined their role in Jewish life, female immigrants to the coalfields were more prone than the men to remain loyal to their Orthodox upbringing. Many had come to the region at the instigation of husbands, fathers, and brothers and had harbored serious reservations about moving to a place where few Jews lived and where maintaining Jewish practice would not be easy. Interviewees stated that their mothers were "more religious" than their fathers, more attached to Jewish customs, and more determined that their children not intermarry. Even Williamson-raised Rose Schwachter protested her husband Harry's apparent lack of concern when their son began to date gentile girls, exclaiming, "A *shikseh* for a daughter-in-law! Never!"[70]

In their new locale, women vigorously attempted to recreate a Jewish environment for their families. They began in their customary domain, the home. They continued to light candles on the Sabbath and prepare traditional meals. Considering the difficulties, a surprisingly large number in the first generation managed to keep a kosher household. Several interviewees described their childhood homes as "strictly kosher," though more typical was a man who recalled that his mother tried to keep kosher "as much as she possibly could." Keeping kosher, of course, was easier in those communities that had a *schochet* in their midst, whether a rabbi or a local merchant who had undergone training in Baltimore or the old country. Where a *schochet* was not available, the women tried their best. Some of their strategies were ineffective, if sincere. One man related that his mother brought her own knives to the local (non-Jewish) butcher and asked him to use them to carve her cuts of meat.[71]

But even as the women eventually had to give up various practices, the effort in itself made a strong impression on their children and went a long way toward reinforcing a Jewish identity. Members of the second generation pointed to their mothers' example, more than that of their fathers, as being decisive. "My mother instilled a lot of Judaism into us," one person typically stated. "As long as mother was living, I wanted to abide by all the customs," another elaborated. "She was the catalyst that kept things together. She was the guiding influence in our home."[72]

Women were often the last to relinquish strict observance. One man told Jerome David that even after his grandfather acknowledged that keeping kosher "had outlived its day," his mother "would not change." Second and third generation women carried on their mothers' efforts to keep a Jewish home, though they did not keep kosher. As a woman explained to David, "If I lived in a big city, we would not put as much pressure on ourselves to follow tradition. We want the children to have our heritage." Another observed, "The rabbi comes only bi-weekly.... Judaism is home first and then temple." Food played a big role in their strategy, as this comment reveals: "My family knows they're in a Jewish home.... Jewish identity through food. I cook Jewishly all the time." While some may have been more deliberate in their attempts to instill identity than others (who, perhaps, simply preferred to eat Jewish-style cooking), home-centered Jewish customs remained pervasive. As late as the 1970s, David could observe, "On a Friday night in Williamson, one knows it is the Sabbath."[73]

Their concern with Jewish continuity led women out of the home and into the communal realm, causing them to participate in what historian Beth Wenger terms a "new, gender-based reorganization of Jewish communal life" that signified a "radical" alteration in women's place. Yet in the coalfields, as elsewhere, this reorganization was rarely controversial. Women had begun to see themselves as guardians of religion, and men were hard pressed to disagree. Their new role conformed to American patterns: in society at large, men had abdicated religious affairs in full-time pursuit of capitalist success, leading to the "feminization" of religious life. For Jewish men and women anxious to Americanize without abandoning their religion, the emergence of women's communal role served both goals.[74]

Women founded most of the coalfield religious schools and, for the most part, served as the teachers. (Even when a rabbi was present the women played an important educational role—one Welch rabbi relied on them "to make the children be good.") After seeing to their children's education, coalfield women's groups embarked on an ambitious agenda to create full-fledged congregations with regular religious services, programs, and, most important, places of worship. They raised funds to build synagogues. They organized and cooked for the religious/social events that held communities together: Hanukah parties, Purim festivals, community seders. They organized trips to large cities to buy kosher and holiday foods. They made sure that the single men in their midst had a family to go to during Jewish holidays and hosted visiting rabbis in their homes. When new Jewish families moved into town, they immediately visited the wives and applied peer pressure if necessary to get them to join in. They were not above a little arm-twisting in their efforts to maintain group cohesion; members who missed meetings without a valid excuse were assessed a fine.[75]

Despite all this activity, their impact on congregational development was often masked, matching Wenger's description of American Jewish women as "unseen caretakers of communal needs." As long as women did not demand public recognition for their leadership, they did not challenge preexisting notions of gender relations. Wenger's observation that women's groups raised the money "and then allowed male-dominated synagogue boards to allocate the funds" also fits the coalfields. Men were the ones who incorporated Jewish institutions and spoke at ceremonies for newly built synagogues.[76]

In Logan, conflict surfaced when women tried to take a more overt role, asking to be recognized as congregation members entitled to seats on the board. The February 1925 minutes of the congregation relate that Sisterhood members "wanted to become members of our congregation and assist us in our work. They could not state how they could benefit us. This brought up considerable discussion pro and con with the result that it was decided to table this matter . . . until the Sisterhood could bring someone here who would be able to tell us more clearly the benefits of having the ladies of the Jewish community as active members of the B'nai El Congregation." The men's response shows not only that there were boundaries women could not cross but also that their previous contributions, though critical, had gone unrecognized. The women knew what to do about this, however. The next month's minutes note that the community's annual seder had been canceled because "it would work a hardship on the ladies." After that, the minutes record increased consultation with the Sisterhood. The men did not accept their official membership but voted to have joint meetings with them on "matters of importance."[77]

Mostly, though, coalfield Jewish women seemed to accept their behind-the-scenes role. They pragmatically filled in where needed, often prodding the men to take responsibility. In 1919, the Welch Ladies Aid Society voted to help the faltering men's group "[make] their meetings more interesting and get the members to attend . . . better." (This mostly seemed to involve serving meals.) After the synagogue was built, the Welch Sisterhood kept things together, because, as one woman put it, the men "have had no real organization, only a few men taking any interest in Temple matters at all."[78]

No matter how preoccupied with business, men as well as women understood that maintaining Jewish identity and observance required creating and supporting a formal communal structure. As daily religious practice diminished, the synagogue became the focal point for Jewish expression across the United States, especially in small towns. An organized congregation facilitated religious education, worship, mutual aid, and a Jewish-oriented social life. It offered stability in the face of geographic mobility, moral support in the face of assimilation. As

Williamson leader Leah Shein asserted in 1926, "Our congregation gives us our religious background. Even the members who do not attend the services are benefited by keeping in touch with Jewish activities."[79]

In interviews, coalfield Jews emphasized the centrality of the synagogue to communal life. "The temple is the focus. It holds the community together," one respondent told Jerome David. Another person put it more strongly. "I am thankful to God that there is a temple, for without it we would be absorbed in the Christian world.... Jewishness in Williamson would disappear." Achieving a permanent congregational home brought practical and psychological benefits that raised the community to a higher level. As an interviewee recalled, "We flourished after we built the temple."[80]

Coalfield Jews united to support their congregations despite the indifference of some toward religion—and strong disagreements about religion among others. Of the original coalfield pioneers, some showed a notable lack of piety while others were quite devout. Yet even the nonreligious were founders of their congregations. Many nonbelieving Jews attended services regularly, viewing the synagogue as "more of a symbol than anything else" and their participation as an expression of solidarity. Meanwhile, others agreed to disagree. Services in Harlan in 1932 featured both the Union Prayer Book and Adler's Prayer Book; participants designed the liturgy as they pleased, without worrying about inconsistencies or justifications. In Beckley, Jews "all pulled together for the temple" despite their religious diversity, one man recalled. His Orthodox father walked to shul, Reform members drove, and when they arrived, "they would have a little bit of the service from each one." What they shared was an "amazing" amount of pride in their temple. Another Beckley resident stated that his Orthodox parents did not care that the temple was basically Reform. They were just glad it existed.[81]

Communal organizations helped coalfield Jews connect with world Jewry through charitable endeavors that articulated identity. In the early years, they raised money to aid indigent Jews in Europe, Palestine, and the United States. The Welch Hebrew Ladies Aid Society, for example, supported an orphanage in Palestine, the Fund for Rabbis in War-Stricken Countries, and Cincinnati's Orthodox Jewish Home for the Aged. They raised funds to assist local Jews who had received appeals from relatives in the old country, such as the "hunger-suffering" sister of Keystone's Rabbi Davidov. During World War I, coalfield Jews joined a national campaign to alleviate the crisis besetting East European Jewry. The 1916 National Relief Day "was a busy day with our local Israelites. They organized in a business-like manner and went to work quietly and systematically," the *McDowell Recorder* reported. "Their friends and relatives to the extent of nearly ten millions are homeless and starving and driven around like cattle in the snow and rigor of a Polish and Russian winter." As historian Daniel Soyer notes, relief work provided a "concrete ... link between the immigrant and the hometown," a link that meant as much to Jews in the Appalachian mountains as it did to *landsman* groups in New York City.[82]

Although coalfield Jews used the Christian term "charity," their activities reflected the traditional practice of *tzedekah*. Some of their beneficiaries had mutual-aid roots that extended back to Europe, such as the matzo funds of Baltimore and New York, which enabled the Jewish poor to observe Passover. In 1916, the Welch ladies obtained "charity boxes" from Kimball's Rabbi Teich; as in the old country, they probably kept the boxes in their kitchens and dropped in a few coins before each Sabbath. Other communal efforts were more political than charitable. In 1933, the Harlan congregation sent resolutions to President Roosevelt and the U.S. ambassador to Germany protesting "the Haman-like designs of the German Hitler against German Jews." The McDowell County B'nai B'rith participated in a statewide campaign to get the governor to declare "Palestine Day" in 1944. By midcentury, Israel had became the focus of support. The field director of the United Palestine Appeal spoke in Logan in 1938, while Hadassah chapters and youth groups such as the Maccabees flourished in some towns. United Jewish Appeal fund drives had a prominent place on the social calendar.[83]

Their Jewish cultural horizons were enhanced by the rabbinical students who served the region. Coalfield congregants responded favorably to the adult education initiatives of their youthful leaders. In 1950, Welch student rabbi Jakob Petuchowski (who went on to become a prominent theologian at Hebrew Union College) led a discussion series on "Judaism and Christianity" with topics that included, "Do you hesitate to express a difference of opinion or to contradict when you are with Christians?" and "Are Jews more clannish than Gentiles?" and "Someone has said that 'the two religions are truly, basically one.' What is your opinion?"[84]

Student rabbis could be "a powerful and dynamic force" in stimulating congregants far removed from Jewish centers to explore their heritage. They brought the latest in rabbinical trends to the coalfields. As one who served in Welch in 1943 later wrote, "I [was] filled to the brim with Franzblau's ideas on progressive education [and did] a number of things to bring the instruction 'up-to-date' in Welch. One specific project was the building of a model Biblical village." Coalfield residents appreciated the students' energy and ideas. They "helped us . . . keep abreast of what was going on in the world-wide Jewish community," said one. Another recalled students from Istanbul and South Africa. "We were lucky we got 'em. It made it a little more interesting." Petuchowski later remarked on the enthusiasm of the Welch Jewish community. "That small congregation undertook the publication of my Ph.D. thesis, 'The Theology of Haham David Nietho, An Eighteenth Century Defense of the Jewish Tradition.'" The future theology professor dedicated his work to the *McDowell Recorder*'s "red-headed hustler": "To Samuel Polon, lover of Torah, who made the publication of this volume possible."[85]

A "longing for Jewish contact" encouraged travel that further mitigated the remoteness of coalfield Jews. Some parents sent their children away to expose them to Jewish life. Boys made extended visits to Baltimore, where they stayed with relatives while studying for their bar mitzvahs, and girls and boys attended

Jewish summer camps, where they joined children from other small towns whose parents were similarly concerned to "give a Jewish substance to their lives," as Eli Evans puts it.[86] Young people looking to marry within the faith journeyed to Jewish centers—often, in the early years, to enter into arranged marriages. Though some did not return, many brought their new spouses back to live in the coalfields. One young man was packed off to work in the diamond industry in New York and told that "he should come back after he married Jewish," which he did. Some parents sent their children to unlikely places. To expose her sons to a Jewish community that did not exist in LaFollette, Tennessee, Esther Baloff enrolled them in military school in Chattanooga. Both sons ended up finding Jewish brides and bringing them back to LaFollette to live.[87]

Although coalfield congregations benefited from contact with the outside world, their own internal resources were key to creating a Jewish life in their small towns. They kept up a year-round schedule of holiday observances and life-cycle celebrations, buttressed by routine meetings, social gatherings, and Sabbath services. Critical to the communities' "will to survive" was strong leadership: in each congregation were members, male and female, who took responsibility for the whole. Communal activity had its ups and downs, as periods of apathy set in and, more worrisome, periods of economically induced population decline demoralized the remaining residents. But the communities managed to reemerge from these lean times and resume their active pace. An example of their ability to rally comes from Williamson, where one man stated in 1972, "Our B'nai B'rith almost went under a few years ago. We never used to meet and when we did, all we would do was play cards. . . . The national B'nai B'rith sent one of their regional men down from Pittsburgh and he about pleaded with us to keep the thing alive. Everything's going pretty good now, almost every man in the Jewish community belongs."[88]

The impulse to socialize with fellow Jews and the impulse to maintain their religious and cultural identity were mutually reinforcing. A "special closeness between Jewish families" lent a strong dynamic to organizational life. A joy in coming together to share cherished customs comes through in congregation records, interviews, and newspaper articles. Simchas Torah festivities in Harlan celebrated Yiddish culture, with participants enjoying songs, speeches, and readings in their native language. The invitation to the 1932 event announced, "The Joyousest Time of the Year. Gefilte Fish, Roast Chicken, Hot Perakas, Plenty of Ch'rain. A Program of Jolly Good Fun." Guests arrived decked out in ceremonial splendor. Mr. Roodine "wore a brand new satin Kapota which reached to his ankles," donned a long black beard, sniffed imaginary snuff, and "sneezed most heartily and artistically," congregation minutes record.[89]

As the invitation suggests, food was an important part of Jewish togetherness outside as well as inside the home. In Middlesboro, the restaurant run by "Mother Horr" offered matzo ball soup and chopped liver and served as the main gathering place for the town's Jews. Louis Morse, proprietor of the Welch Billiard and Bowling Parlor, evidently considered Jewish food enough of a draw to advertise in a 1922 Welch newspaper, "A Pleasant Retreat for Business Men and for all who seek diversion. Kosher meats by the pound."[90]

Most organized events combined socializing with a more serious purpose. Dances, luncheons, and card parties held to raise money were staples of the social scene. Community seders, Purim festivals, and Hanukah celebrations drew large crowds. One Williamson student rabbi recalled a lively Purim party in the 1940s that "degenerated into a poker game with the officers of the Temple taking a cut from each pot." On the other hand, community members did not need a religious excuse to get together. The Minyan Club, "composed of the Jewish young men of Welch," held parties in its club room for the town's Jewish youth in the 1920s. And on occasions when coalfield Jews wanted a larger pool of Jewish people with which to socialize, they traveled to nearby regional centers such as Bluefield, Charleston, or Knoxville.[91]

Asked to describe how his family maintained a Jewish identity, a man who grew up in Northfork in the 1920s and 1930s summed up, "My mother kept kosher, she made traditional Jewish dishes. We observed the Sabbath, except Dad had to work. We observed the Jewish holidays. We had a synagogue and helped support it. We had other Jewish friends who had varying degrees of *Yiddishkeit*." Such indigenous resources for Jewish survival, along with outside connections actively cultivated, led Jerome David to conclude that coalfield Jews experienced "physical isolation" from Jewish centers but not "social isolation." While their ways of expressing Jewishness changed over time, this combination of resources served their communities well for at least three generations.[92]

Identity, Assimilation, and Communal Organization

Coalfield Jewish communities took shape not simply from the members' desire to remain Jewish. In a variety of contradictory ways, the relationship of Jews to the surrounding society influenced both communal development and individual identity. The region's heavy emphasis on Christianity, along with a subtle sense that they were not completely accepted, encouraged Jews to turn inward to develop their own communal life. Conversely, communal organization served as a bulwark against the attractions of the dominant culture: their high degree of integration posed the possibility that some Jews might blend so thoroughly as to lose their Jewishness altogether. A third factor was more subtle. Communal institutions provided a means to reconcile the two potentially conflicting goals held by most American Jews: to participate in the broader society and yet keep a distinct identity. In small cities and towns, religious institutions conferred respectability, weightiness, and belonging—especially in the religion-soaked atmosphere of the South. As author John Shelton Reed writes, "By participating in organized religious activities, Southern Jews are at the same time more Jewish" *and* "more Southern." The urge to assimilate paradoxically encouraged communal development.[93]

Most coalfield Jews saw themselves as part of the larger community. As a Beckley man explained, although his religion and ethnic heritage were important to him, "being Jewish is not my entire world." Nor did individuals see their identities as Jews and as middle-class coalfield residents as necessarily contradictory. A lifelong Logan resident, describing the highly assimilated nature of his town's Jewish population, added, as if surprised there could be any doubt, "Of course we stayed Jewish." Another coalfield native could remark, "One thing about being Jewish—you're always Jewish" and yet be thoroughly at home in his environment and married to a non-Jew. Interestingly, when Jews who grew up in the coalfields traveled outside the region to go to summer camp or attend college, they discovered that it was the regional aspect of their identity that suddenly became prominent. Marilou Schwachter, for example, found out she had a "southern hillbilly accent" only when she auditioned for a theater role at Ohio State University.[94]

These coalfield residents simply reflected the reality that people are complex beings with multiple facets to their identity. The ultimate form that Jewish communities took expressed the jumble of motivations that existed within their members. While some may have been especially moved by a need to experience Jewish religion or culture, and others chiefly by a desire to separate themselves from gentiles, there were those who cared above all about how the Jewish community interacted with, and was perceived by, society at large. Whatever weight individuals gave to these considerations, membership in the Jewish collective helped them to assert, and to integrate, at least two of their multiple identities: as Jews and as respectable, neighborly, and civic-minded small-town dwellers.[95]

Coalfield Jewish communities offered their members welcome relief from the more alienating, or simply unfamiliar, aspects of coalfield culture. For new arrivals, the opportunity to come together with people of similar background and share in familiar pastimes helped them adjust to a new and strange environment. When Esther Sturm Baloff first moved to the region in the 1910s, despite the friendliness of local townsfolk, "I was lonesome. . . . It was different when you're not among your own kind of people." Even longtime residents found comfort in being around people with whom they felt most compatible. As one person told Jerome David, "Living in a small town, . . . one socializes with non-Jews and Jews. I can feel comfortable either way. I feel *more* comfortable with Jews." Though heavily involved in the larger society, David observed, Williamson Jews "huddle together defensively." This defensiveness must be considered part of the glue holding Jewish coalfield communities together.[96]

On the other hand, communal organization served to guard against the danger that some of their number would disappear into coalfield society and stop being Jews, through either intermarriage or disaffiliation. They feared most, of course, for their own children, and these fears were not unwarranted. Intermarriage began as early as the 1910s, when Celia Ofsa of Keystone married family neighbor Charles Hoover. Her parents, Max and Dena, known for their devout Orthodox beliefs, refused to speak to her for nine years, causing a family breach that never completely healed. As it turned out, half of the Ofsa family's twelve children married within the faith and the other half did not. By the time the youngest, Isadore, took a gentile bride, his parents had become resigned to the situation and welcomed their new daughter-in-law into the family. Isadore's wife Mary later recalled, "They were so good to me it was like they adopted me." While her mother-in-law taught her Jewish cooking, her father-in-law taught her about the Jewish religion. But an accepting family was not enough: Mary and Isadore did not raise their children as Jews because the Keystone synagogue had closed. Instead, they went to church with their friends.[97]

As intermarriage became a coalfield reality, Jewish families responded with a dual strategy in which communal organizations played a key part. First they tried to prevent it through religious education, a focus on child-centered holidays and activities, and exposure to Jewish culture outside the region through youth groups, camps, and other means. This strategy achieved a good deal of success as many who grew up in the coalfields remained committed to finding a Jewish partner. Once an intermarriage did occur, the county-seat congregations accepted mixed couples and encouraged them to raise their children as Jews.

The flexibility of these congregations, made possible by their move to Reform Judaism, enabled them to keep a substantial number of intermarried families within the Jewish fold. The 1935 Hebrew Union College student rabbi survey reported that in Logan and Williamson, all the children of mixed households were being raised Jewish, and in the 1970s most Williamson children of mixed marriages were still being raised as Jews. Non-Jewish women became active members of the Beckley Sisterhood early on. One woman later recalled that after her 1950s marriage, the Sisterhood "accepted me immediately" and she eventually became the group's president. Although she never formally converted to Judaism, she raised her children as Jews and the family attended services devotedly. "I feel like that's my temple," she explained. Meanwhile, the Keystone congregation, which remained Orthodox, had no mechanism for addressing intermarriage: even before the synagogue closed, none of the intermarried Ofsas raised their children as Jews.[98]

There were enough cases such as that of the Ofsas to give coalfield Jews pause. Community members took note of those who stopped practicing their faith after marriage to a gentile. However, they reserved their most disparaging comments for others who, without the impetus of intermarriage, chose to associate only with gentiles or attend church—seeing this as pure social climbing. But Jews who completely turned their backs on their coreligionists were rare.[99]

The handful of German Jews who lived in the region were more likely to disaf-

filiate than the East Europeans. German Jewish pioneer Michael Bloch and his
family belonged to the Methodist church in Pocahontas, and most of the third
generation Blochs and Baaches married and raised their children outside the
faith. Yet other Jews did not view the disaffiliation of German Jewish families in
the same negative light as they viewed the (much rarer) cases of East European
disaffiliation, since the Germans were barely a part of the Jewish community to
begin with. Interestingly, Bloch and his brother-in-law Jacob Baach continued to
consider themselves Jews. Bloch subscribed to the Jewish Publication Society of
America. Baach left money to Jewish charities and made careful mention in his
will to leave his *Jewish Encyclopedia* set to his son Louis.[100]

East European Jews may have been unlikely to disaffiliate, but they were nevertheless thoroughly engaged in the assimilation process even as they began to
organize communally. The Jewish women of Welch actually belonged to the
Methodist ladies aid society before starting their own group.[101] No doubt, the
women had no intention of permanently going over to the Methodists; after all,
the group they started was the most Orthodox of all the county-seat congregations. Probably they joined because their numbers had not yet grown large enough
to support their own organization. But perhaps they also realized that having
their own group would enable them to withstand the temptations provided by a
wide-open society that seemed so ready to include them in.

Certainly they must have felt more comfortable relating to their Methodist
friends from the position of strength afforded by having their own organization,
one that allowed them both to satisfy their longing for Jewish culture and to assert their identity not only as Jews but also as members of the Welch middle class.
Most coalfield Jews saw communal organization as an expression of group pride
and an assertion that the Jewish population had a proper place among the groups
that made up coalfield society. They wanted to fit in and to be recognized as fitting in—as Jews.

Among some, this was a matter of overriding significance. Harry Schwachter,
according to his daughter, was personally insulted by the "unsightly" surroundings of the Williamson congregation's rented quarters in a theater basement. But
"religion had never played much of a part in his busy life," and he did not become
seriously involved in communal affairs until one day in the mid-1920s when he
was chatting with a non-Jewish friend in his store. Two coal miners walked in,
speaking in Hungarian. Schwachter joined their conversation, and "the three men
spoke that wild language with dozens of excited gestures for at least ten minutes."
After the miners departed, his friend turned to him and said, "Harry, I shore owe
you a big apology, ole pal. . . . I allus figured you was a damn Jew!" Schwachter,
"hurt and stunned" by the man's comment, immediately decided it was "time for
Williamson Jewry to be recognized in a more refined way" and threw himself into
the campaign to build a synagogue. "It was a personal crusade," says his daughter,
"for he intended never again to be identified as 'that damn Jew.'" Not one for half

measures, Schwachter became president of the congregation. Presiding over the 1928 dedication ceremony for the new temple with prominent ministers and town leaders as his guests, he saw the fulfillment of his quest to prove the respectability of the Jewish community.[102]

While perhaps not spurred on by a personal slight, others shared Schwachter's concerns. Coalfield Jews recognized that building and maintaining houses of worship, closing their stores on the high holidays, and other public expressions of their faith were important not only as symbols of solidarity within the Jewish community, but as a statement to their fellow citizens, a declaration that Judaism had a place alongside the many Christian denominations. Isadore Scott, son of Welch community leaders David and Libby Scott, explained, "The idea was to maintain the synagogue as a symbol of Jewish life" in the eyes of the public. "My family thought you must show the [larger] community your respect for your religion . . . your self-respect." Scott and Schwachter illustrate Leonard Rogoff's observation that erecting a synagogue enabled small-town Jews to "stake out civic space."[103]

In order to occupy that civic space, it helped to conform to a certain standard of religious behavior. Yet this did not mean dilution of belief. If anything, the religious fervor characteristic of the region encouraged Jews to express their own religiosity. In the Scott family, the importance of upholding public decorum and self-respect went hand in hand with religious conviction and expression. More than fifty years after moving away from the region, Isadore Scott affirmed, "I still *daven* [pray] every day. . . . It's the way Welch taught me to be." While high synagogue affiliation rates owed much to the resolve of members to ensure Jewish survival, no doubt the high church affiliation rates among Christians confirmed them in their actions. Meanwhile, the tendency for social groups to form around church affiliation could only help but serve Jewish communal aims. Jews could not be considered "clannish" or unduly prone to associating among themselves when members of every church were busy doing the same thing.[104]

Moreover, some traditional Jewish organizational forms (aid societies, for example) had close counterparts in Christian organizational life. By recreating these old-style groups, coalfield Jews could address Jewish concerns, yet in ways similar to their churchgoing neighbors. Along with providing the framework for an internal Jewish social and cultural life, these organizations provided a bridge to the surrounding society. They served an important role in shaping the interaction between Jews and non-Jews in the civic and social arenas.

Though Jews readily joined civic groups as individuals, they were most active in their own aid societies, Sisterhoods, and B'nai B'rith lodges. In addition to raising funds for Jewish causes, these groups engaged in extensive local charitable and civic work, supporting causes that ranged from flood relief in Williamson to the tuberculosis hospital in Beckley. The women held bazaars and rummage sales, ran booths at carnivals, and coordinated activities with women's church groups. The men took a more masculine approach: the Beckley B'nai B'rith's popular fund-raising event, a wrestling show with national stars, attracted some four thousand people to the high school stadium annually in the 1940s and 1950s. The wrestlers "put on one wild show," recalled a former member.[105]

Civic and charitable work involved engaging with the pervasive Christianity of the region. Having their own organizations actually helped Jews participate in Christian-oriented activities, as they could contribute in a spirit of interfaith co-operation without regarding their involvement as compromising their identities or beliefs. Thus when a Welch fraternal lodge presented a check to Pamela White "to help her become a missionary," three of the six smiling men in a photo of the event were leaders of Temple Emanuel. Sisterhoods raised funds for the Salvation Army and distributed Christmas baskets to the poor (in Williamson in 1931 they donated fifty sacks of cornmeal, two hundred pounds of beans, and forty-five pounds of bacon). Welch men belonged to Santa's Helpers. In Bluefield, Jewish civic leaders concerned with strengthening their city's institutional base did not let religion stand in their way. The dean of the local Baptist junior college later recalled that "two of the three men who were instrumental in getting Bluefield College located in Bluefield were men who belonged to the Jewish synagogue . . . and served on the committee to go to the Virginia Baptist General Association when it was known that Baptists were going to build a school somewhere in this area."[106]

Jewish groups were especially active in the civic realm during and after World War II, reflecting both the patriotism and inclusive Americanism characteristic of the time. Women rolled bandages and volunteered at USOs. Congregations conducted paper drives and held patriotic programs with their Boy Scouts. The Logan B'nai B'rith lodge presented an American flag to the county's African American high school, and local black and Catholic leaders spoke before the Mc-Dowell County B'nai B'rith. After the war, the Beckley B'nai B'rith Americanism committee offered citizenship classes to "aliens in Raleigh County, both Jewish as well as non-Jewish." Other lodges followed suit; a 1955 B'nai B'rith newsletter noted that a Welch member's "coaching and sympathetic understanding" enabled 186 aliens to become citizens.[107]

The spirit of cooperation worked both ways, as gentiles aided projects impor-tant to their Jewish neighbors. In 1916, McDowell County's Jewish Relief Fund for destitute Jews in war-torn Europe received donations from non-Jews, black and white, and included non-Jews on its board. In later decades, non-Jews duly con-tributed to United Jewish Appeal campaigns. Christians generously supported local synagogues, supplying one-quarter of the funds to build Williamson's. In 1918 the *McDowell Recorder* urged readers to support the newly formed Welch congregation, noting, "It is well known that [local Jews] are always ready to help in everything that will benefit our hustling town. Whenever called upon to con-tribute . . . they have always responded with a spirit that has won the respect of all our citizens."[108]

Adaptation, Continuity, and Identity

Historians differ in regard to how much American Jewish communal structures drew on old-country traditions versus how much they were shaped by the new world milieu. On the whole, notes Marshall Sklare, Jews tended to keep customs that "accorded with the religious culture of the larger community while providing a 'Jewish' alternative," whereas customs that "demanded social isolation or the adoption of a unique life style" tended to be dropped. In the coalfields, as elsewhere, traditions that did not conform to mainstream religious practice fell by the wayside.[109]

The construction of a permanent house of worship was a pivotal moment in this process, with many congregation members seeing the event as an opportunity to modernize services. The increased respectability symbolized by the outward face of the new edifice was to be accompanied by increased decorum inside. A Williamson congregant recalled that "at the dugout [the theater basement] it was more Orthodox, they wore Yarmulkas, prayer-shawls, and *davened*"—practices not followed after the move to the synagogue. Perhaps most emblematic, the new buildings erected by county-seat congregations all featured family seating, an affirmation that the traditional male *minyan* was on its way out. As the communities turned their focus from contributing to Jewish causes to maintaining a temple, the old-style (though perfectly presentable) aid societies gave way to the more Americanized auxiliary model for women (the Sisterhood) and fraternal club model for men (B'nai B'rith).[110]

The evolution of coalfield congregations from Orthodoxy to Reform came about in part because the older ways seemed less relevant to an American-raised generation. However, little generational conflict accompanied this shift. In fact, while Irving Howe documents "unbearably fierce" generational battles within New York City Jewish families as children Americanized, chroniclers of small-town Jewish life rarely describe overt defiance among the young. The pressures of being a small minority, of having to show solidarity with the group, made them less inclined to rebel.[111]

Also, unlike Howe's immigrant tenement dwellers, most first-generation coalfield parents modified their views to be more in line with the society in which they found themselves. Their beliefs were not at odds with those of their Americanized children. Meanwhile, others who did remain attached to the old ways, such as the immigrant parents described earlier by the Logan student rabbi, accepted change as a sacrifice they were prepared to make in order to transmit Judaism to their children. A Williamson Jew who moved to town in the post–World War II years acknowledged, "What turned me toward Reform was that my son liked Reform so much. . . . It was nice to see my children appreciate what was going on in Temple, unlike when we were children in shul. It's nice to sit all together on a Friday night."[112]

Some changes did provoke conflict, as each congregation struggled to find its own balance between tradition and acculturation. But as the years went on, influences from the surrounding society seeped in often unnoticed, as suggested by an offhand note in the 1935 minutes of the Williamson Sisterhood that "the flowers in the temple on Easter Sunday were sent by Mr. Hammond of the Mark Russell Seed Co." While a special display of flowers on Easter may have struck some of the older members as incongruous, to others it was probably just a minor example of the congregation's success in establishing itself as a presence amidst the other religious organizations in town.[113]

Women exemplified the contradictory and uneven process of modernization. Even though they showed a greater loyalty to tradition than men, they were the first to perceive the practical benefits of Reform Judaism. Their increased communal role led them to support family seating, and their guardianship of children's education caused them to promote involvement with the student rabbi program. Nevertheless, they continued to embrace tenets of traditional Judaism that felt right to them. The Williamson Sisterhood sponsored an annual women-led religious service in the 1920s, an event that surely would have been considered ridiculous in Eastern Europe, if not dangerously revolutionary. Yet these same women focused their educational efforts on boys, to make sure they were prepared for the traditional bar mitzvah. Most telling, women tried their best to keep a kosher home during a time when most adherents of Reform Judaism considered the practice obsolete.[114]

Many interviewees recalled with admiration the struggles of their elders, male and female, to uphold traditional standards—but other members of the younger generation had an opposing view. Ironically, although the modern Judaism adopted in the county seats succeeded in keeping youth in the fold, some later concluded their religious training had not been rigorous enough. A Williamson native described the religious school as "a farce" while another called his bar mitzvah "a sham." A Logan interviewee reported the typical American experience of Hebrew school: "All we learned to do was read it—we didn't understand it." Yet even these criticisms show that parents managed to instill a strong Jewish identity under difficult conditions. One person complained of growing up with a lack of "formal Judaism" but acknowledged that "we had a Jewish consciousness." Another said that because of the family business, "my parents didn't have time for family rituals. I don't remember a Seder at home. Yet I knew when I grew up, I would observe these things." Interestingly, some Williamson natives felt that they had "a stronger Jewish identity than their parents," David found.[115]

Many people could not quite say how their parents managed to pass on the Jewish heritage. Their ruminations made clear that the home and the communal realm both were key spaces for enacting Jewish identity and communicating it to the next generation. "What we learned was through osmosis," said one woman whose family lived beyond reach of the county seats and rarely attended services.

"Definitely a Jewish home. . . . You could be Jewish without going to a synagogue or temple. We just absorbed it." During his childhood, a Beckley man recalled, "a great deal of what we did was Jewish. . . . Family, foods, religious holidays . . . a lot of my religious education was in the home." But the place where his Jewishness was publicly ratified was the temple, site of his bar mitzvah, an important event in his life and, he asserted, in the lives of the other Jewish boys in town. Almost all young people who stayed in the region participated in Jewish groups as adults. Their involvement helped them maintain their Jewish identity, just as it had helped their parents.[116]

The Jewish communities of the coalfields gathered together people in various stages of the assimilation process. Within the immigrant generation, those who had recently entered the United States differed markedly from those who came to the region already acculturated. Among the American born, those who grew up in the coalfields contrasted with those who arrived after spending their childhoods in large cities. And these, of course, were not the only variables that influenced how and why individuals participated in communal life. Differences of gender and of generation stand out as two particularly important determinants. Coalfield congregations absorbed and embodied all these disparate elements, from Keystone's B'nai Israel with its *mikvah* and segregated seating to Beckley's Beth El with its organ and non-Jewish choir. Not to mention the diversity *within* each congregation, exemplified by Welch Congregation Emanuel's Orthodox leanings and Easter flowers.

From a demographic standpoint, coalfield Jewish communities may have been among the smallest in the nation to create full-fledged congregational structures. "Very few places with less than 100 or so Jews supported communal institutions," states Lee Shai Weissbach.[117] Yet organizational efforts in all the coalfield towns began well before the number of Jews reached triple digits, and only in Williamson and Beckley did the Jewish population advance beyond 150. To create and maintain their communal institutions, they had to meet the challenges posed by their environment, their diversity, and their small size.

In his 1957 study *The Eternal Stranger,* Benjamin Kaplan analyzed a small Louisiana community that did not meet those challenges, as Jews there became absorbed completely into local society. The community's demise resulted from not just small numbers but also economic imperatives, the desire of Jews to conform to social norms, a lack of Jewish education, isolation from the outside Jewish world, and a lack of leadership. Community members lost both religious conviction and "group pride."[118]

Coalfield Jews experienced the same economic and social pressures but made sure the other factors did not apply to them. They started religious schools when there were as few as five Jewish children in town. They sent their children everywhere from the diamond industry in New York City to military school in Chattanooga to expose them to Jews and Jewish culture. Leadership played a key role in enabling their communities to resist the forces of dissolution: from Ida Bank stepping forward to teach the children of Williamson, to David Scott making sure the Jewish businesses of Welch all closed on the high holidays, to the Orthodox Jews of Logan deciding against their own desires that Reform Judaism would be more likely to reach their children.

The result impressed the two researchers who ventured into the region to study Jewish life in the 1970s, both, coincidentally, in Williamson. Frank Anthony Fear contrasted the community with the findings of researchers in other small towns, stating that in Williamson, "being a Jew is not a solitary sojourn. . . . The isolated Jew described by [an upstate New York study] hardly exists; they manifest a sense of common identity." Jerome David concluded that Williamsonians were not "marginal" but "rooted" in their Jewishness. Unlike many other American Jews, they did not "possess an uncertainty of belongingness." He noted that while Jewish religious practice nationally was at a low level, this was not the case in Williamson. For comparison he chose the growing body of literature on Jewish suburbanites. He contrasted the "total lack of any sense of community," the "loneliness and alienation" found in portrayals of suburbia with the "keen sense of community" he found in Williamson. He attributed the difference, in part, to a small-town environment that enabled families to remain close (fathers, no matter how busy with work, did not commute and were readily accessible), offered fewer distractions, and exhibited greater persistence rates than the high-turnover suburbs.[119]

The two studies' observations about Williamson can be extended to all the coalfield communities. The region's Jews registered the same broad changes as other American Jews in the first half of the twentieth century, with a shift away from tradition and devout belief toward a Jewish identity defined by Americanized religious observance, loyalty to family heritage, and cultural affinity with other Jews. In other words, ethnicity assumed a stronger role as religion became less salient. But commitment to Judaism and Jewish culture remained firm. Moreover, commitment to their own small congregations, located in their own small towns, remained strong. Through the years, some people moved away to experience the cultural benefits of large cities, but not enough to threaten Jewish communal existence. Thriving businesses, the benefits of small-town life, a secure place in the social order, satisfaction derived from their participation in the surrounding society, and—not least—the fulfillment afforded by communal involvement all combined to ensure the persistence of Jews in coalfield towns.

The decline of coalfield Jewish communities in the late twentieth century occurred for economic reasons. When David arrived in the early 1970s, the process was well underway. "It saddens one to see this flourishing, vibrant Jewish community slowly die," he remarked. "But the age of the small family-owned business is drawing to an end." Parents did not encourage their children to remain. As one person said, "I don't want to push my children away from home, but I don't want them to come back to live in Williamson. They would return to a non-Jewish existence."[120]

Jews found it easier than other coalfield residents to move away. They had connections beyond the region and skills that could be readily transferred. And their roots were not as deep as those whose families had lived in the mountains for many more generations. Despite their commitment to their towns, they remained attached as well to places beyond the mountains. In 1926, Rabbi Michael Aaronsohn noted the ability of small-town Jews to live in two worlds: "When his pioneering days are ended, he is the president of the congregation, he summons a trim, American youth [from HUC] to deliver lectures, he subscribes to the *American Israelite* and the *New York Times,* he 'runs' to New York to shop, . . . his children are enrolled at the leading American colleges, and—presto!—he and his family and all his kin are metropolitans again."[121]

Coalfield Jews had loyalties that at times must have conflicted: to their local Jewish communities, to the towns where they lived, to families and communities of origin outside the region. Their identity as Jews and their identity as residents of their small mountain towns could not always have been easy to reconcile. And there were certainly aspects of the surrounding society that added to the difficulty. The strength and adaptability of the communal life they created for themselves enabled them to overcome such obstacles to small-town Jewish existence and persist for several generations in the coalfields.

Conclusion

This book has situated coalfield Jewish communities within two contexts, Appalachian history and Jewish history, and explored the linkages between the two. One linkage connects the Jews' historical economic role with events taking place on the Central Appalachian plateau in the late nineteenth and early twentieth centuries. By drawing on their heritage to establish a retail niche in the economy, Jews contributed to the transformation of the region from a rural, subsistence-oriented society to a rural-industrial, consumer-oriented society.

Another linkage compares Jewish-gentile relations in the coalfields to the Jewish experience elsewhere, from the American South to places around the world. The closest parallels are not to relatively nearby Jewish populations (in Johnstown, Pennsylvania, or the South) but to far-flung communities in which similar boom-town conditions prevailed. As Bernard Reisman observes, "It is at the margins of countless countries that Jews have interacted and benefited from the exchange with many different cultures." He is referring not only to the benefits Jews derived from participating in the larger society but also to how their interaction with others helped them "clarify the ways in which they are different (distinctive) from non-Jews."[1] Coalfield Jews had the opportunity to do this and took advantage of it. Though they acted from a variety of motivations, collectively they defined themselves through the establishment of congregations that asserted a distinct Jewish identity while embracing an active role in local affairs. Like other boomtown environments, the coalfield milieu gave them scope to do so. Not perfectly, by any means, but to a perhaps surprising degree.

Within the patterns that link coalfield Jews to Jews in other places, however, variations can be found. Even within the coalfields their communities displayed considerable diversity, with some remaining Orthodox and others moving to Reform Judaism, most building synagogues but some managing without. One thing that appears to distinguish coalfield Jews from Jewish populations elsewhere is the sheer number of congregations they created within a relatively small geographic area, especially considering the small size of their towns. In the early 1920s, the nine towns that hosted their congregations averaged less than four thousand inhabitants. In McDowell County alone, three small congregations existed within fifteen miles of one another, serving some three hundred Jewish adults and children. The *combined* population of their three towns (Keystone, Kimball, and Welch) was less than seven thousand. These were truly small-town Jews.

In many ways, Jews in the coalfields occupied a peripheral position in history: marginalized from the main body of American Jewry by their location in the heart of Central Appalachia, marginalized from their fellow residents by their religion and their nonparticipation in the coal industry, and, as inhabitants of a region that has been described as a "periphery" within America, marginalized from mainstream American society. But as many scholars have noted, there are things to be learned from people on the periphery. Although from a historical standpoint their position may have been unusual and their numbers small, they did not necessarily believe themselves to be marginal. Or rather, it would be more accurate to say that they fought against marginality by making a concerted effort to maintain their ties to Jews beyond the region and to participate in the society around them despite their minority status. Their success in doing both not only speaks to their own efforts but also contradicts stereotypes that cling to the Appalachian region: a place typically thought of as isolated, homogeneous, inward, and hostile to strangers was none of those things.

Thomas Bender defines community as "a network of social relations marked by mutuality and emotional bonds." Using this definition, coalfield Jews belonged to at least three communities: their own local Jewish group, the town in which they lived, and a larger Jewish collectivity that involved friends, relatives, and business relationships in Baltimore, New York, and other places beyond the region. These communities were not enclaves separated from each other or the world around them but were engaged in a dynamic process of exchange. Local Jewish communities reacted and adapted to their surroundings. Their larger Jewish networks, meanwhile, influenced the culture of coalfield towns through their economic activities.[2]

In contributing to the modernization of the region, Jews can be seen as allies of the chief modernizer, the coal industry. In fact, the coalfield middle class has often been described as a sort of "junior partner" to the coal industry. This role too has echoes with Jewish life in other places, going back to centuries in Eastern Europe, where Jews acted as agents of the ruling class. The comparison can be carried too far, however, as coalfield Jews were not the representatives of coal companies or absentee land corporations and were never blamed for economic breakdowns, as they were in Eastern Europe.

Yet in both cases the alliance could be described as uneasy, as well as unequal. Like everyone else in the region, Jews were dependent on the coal industry for their economic survival. But contrary to usual depictions of the coalfield middle class, they were not always fervent supporters of the industry and they recognized the

inequalities that existed within it. As competitors of company stores, as small businesspeople who preferred stability and moderation to the coal operators' discord-
producing will to dominate, as retailers who benefited from any gain in their customers' purchasing power, they had an agenda that was not entirely compatible
with coal industry hegemony. They preferred to remain neutral in the labor conflicts that consumed the region, though when forced to choose sides, they sided
with the established order. How representative they were of the middle class as a
whole remains an open question. Because so few Jews were directly involved in the
coal industry, they might have taken a more questioning view of it than others. On
the other hand, most merchants, Jewish and non-Jewish, depended for their livelihood on the patronage of the region's large working class, and this might have
mitigated the general enthusiasm for the side of "law and order."

If not always avid boosters of the coal industry, Jews were certainly avid boosters of their towns. As participants in civic life, they supported parks, libraries,
schools, and hospitals. Remnants of their contributions still exist in the region,
visible to the alert observer. Ultimately, however, the small middle class could
play only a minor role in the course of regional development. With the restructuring of the coal industry in the 1950s, the region underwent a swift economic
decline. Merchant-based Jewish communities, who during the same period experienced national retail trends that devastated downtowns, saw their young
people move away, and many older people decided to spend their retirement
years elsewhere. And so Jewish life in most of the towns disappeared.

Today coalfield residents live in a different world than the one that existed at
the height of the coal boom. Though plenty of coal is still mined, very few people
are needed to mine it. Job growth, as elsewhere in America, is found mainly in the
service sector. Reminders of the past are everywhere, sharing the landscape with
markers of change. Abandoned company stores dot the region and downtown
business districts feature rows of blank storefronts. Old slate dumps have become
sites for suburban-style shopping developments. The innumerable products of
American consumer culture can still be purchased, but now they are to be found
at the Wal-Marts and strip malls on the edges of coalfield towns. Sewell, West
Virginia, the first commercial center of the coalfields and home of the first Jewish
settler, now exists only in the heritage tourism literature of the National Park
Service, which owns the land along New River where the town used to be. Mc-
Dowell County, at the turn of the twentieth century the region's fastest growing
place and home to the largest Jewish population, entered the twenty-first as one
of the most economically distressed sites in the nation, its population having
shrunk to pre-1910 figures.[3]

A boom in tourism has made Beckley southern West Virginia's growth center,
and its small but tenacious Jewish community has survived thanks to the resolve
of a few older families and the influx of a few new ones. The late Isadore Wein,
local pharmacist and lay rabbi, saw the congregation through its leanest years

before a small growth spurt occurred in the 1990s. His determination to keep Temple Beth El going reflected not only a desire for Jewish continuity but also a realization that the Jewish experience in the coalfields was something of significance. "This temple must never disappear from Beckley," he once told an interviewer. "Because we need a temple to say—Jews lived here at one time."

Introduction

1. Shinedling, *West Virginia Jewry*, 986.
2. Salstrom, "Newer Appalachia"; Gilman and Shain, *Jewries at the Frontier.*
3. *West Virginia Gazetteer,* 1898, 1900, 1904; Manuscript Census, McDowell County, 1900.
4. Lane and Schnepf, *Sewell,* 8.
5. In the Appalachian studies literature, the terms "local elite" and "middle class" are not always strictly defined and are often used interchangeably. Here the term "middle class" refers to people who were not industrial or agricultural workers, on the one hand, or the economic powers who owned the region's land and resources and their local representatives, on the other hand. Studies that do consider the Central Appalachian middle class include Gaventa, *Power and Powerlessness;* Billings and Blee, *Road to Poverty;* Lewis, *Transforming the Appalachian Countryside;* and Pudup, "Town and Country."
6. The only full-length published treatment of an ethnic (i.e., nonnative white) or minority group in the southern coalfields is Trotter's *Coal, Class, and Color,* which examines African American life in southern West Virginia. A recent essay collection, Fones-Wolf and Lewis's *Transnational West Virginia,* has begun to fill the gap in this literature.
7. Studies of small-town Jewish communities drawn on here include Levinson, *Jews in the California Gold Rush;* Stern, "Jewish Community"; Rothman, "'Same Horse, New Wagon'"; and Morawska, *Insecure Prosperity.* Eli Evans's *Provincials* continues to serve as a valuable introduction for anyone interested in southern Jewish history.
8. Rabinowitz, "Writing Jewish Community History," 126.
9. Ibid., 127.
10. On Jews and boomtowns, see especially Gilman and Shain, *Jewries at the Frontier,* and Rischin and Livingston, *Jews of the American West.*
11. This aspect of the study draws on works of Appalachian, rural, and Jewish history that focus on the transition to capitalism, often from the perspective of world systems theory. See, for example, Lewis, *Transforming the Appalachian Countryside;* Hahn and Prude, *Countryside in an Age of Capitalist Transformation;* Chirot and Reid, *Essential Outsiders;* and Ashkenazi, *Business of Jews.*

Chapter 1: From Shtetl to Coalfield

1. "Weinstein Brothers," *Middlesborough News,* 21 March 1903, p. 1.
2. Shinedling and Pickus, *History of the Beckley Jewish Community,* 41; Pickus interview.
3. Weinryb, *Jews of Poland.*
4. Zborowski and Herzog, *Life Is with People,* 68, 193.

5. For a good introduction to the middleman minority concept, see Zenner, *Minorities in the Middle* (quote, xii).

6. Hundert, "Some Basic Characteristics," 20–23.

7. Zborowski and Herzog, *Life Is with People,* 67; Kugelmass, "Native Aliens," 39–40. See also Hertz, *Jews in Polish Culture,* 79–83.

8. Zenner, *Minorities in the Middle;* Chirot and Reid, *Essential Outsiders.*

9. Levine, *Economic Origins of Anti-Semitism;* Klier, *Russia Gathers Her Jews.*

10. Rubinow, "Economic Condition"; Mahler, "Economic Background."

11. Rogger, *Jewish Policies;* Berk, *Year of Crisis, Year of Hope.* For a catalogue of anti-Jewish legislation from 1881 to 1917, see Johnpoll, "Why They Left."

12. Kassow, "Communal and Social Change"; Baron, *Russian Jew.*

13. Wischnitzer, *To Dwell in Safety,* 28 (quote); Baron, *Russian Jew.*

14. U.S. Immigration Commission, *Emigration Conditions in Europe,* 272, 361, 351–52. On the era's European mass migration movements, see Nugent, *Crossings.* The Russian Empire supplied 76 percent of Jewish immigrants to America between 1881 and 1914, whereas Austria-Hungary supplied 19 percent, though they contained 69 percent and 27 percent, respectively, of Eastern Europe's Jewish population (the remainder was Rumanian). An average of 1.36 percent of the Russian Empire's Jews migrated to America each year between 1899 and 1914, compared to .4 to .5 percent of the empire's Poles and Lithuanians. Almost 22 percent of the Jewish population left Russia during the era, compared to 6 to 8 percent of other ethnic groups. Russian Jews migrated to America at a higher rate than any other European group except the Irish (Kuznets, "Immigration of Russian Jews," 39, 51; *Encyclopaedia Judaica* 13, "Population").

15. Kuznets, "Immigration of Russian Jews," 83–85; Berk, *Year of Crisis, Year of Hope.* On the draft as impetus for emigration among Jews and non-Jews, see Baron, *Russian Jew,* 67.

16. Howe, *World of Our Fathers;* Gartner, "Jewish Migrants"; Goren, "Traditional Institutions Transplanted."

17. Morawska, *Insecure Prosperity,* 23–26; Kligsberg, "Jewish Immigrants in Business."

18. Kligsberg, "Jewish Immigrants in Business," 293.

19. The following discussion draws on these sources, which revealed the origins of coalfield Jews: Manuscript Census, all coalfield counties, 1900–1920; Fayette, Logan, Mingo, McDowell, and Raleigh Counties, Naturalization Records; Shinedling, *West Virginia Jewry;* Shinedling and Pickus, *History of the Beckley Jewish Community;* Marino, *Welch and Its People; Bell County, Kentucky, History;* and various interviews with the author. The regional origins of 710 individuals and the actual hometowns of 122 were determined. On East European towns, sources include *Encyclopaedia Judaica;* Cohen, *Shtetl Finder Gazetteer;* and Schoenburg and Schoenburg, *Lithuanian Jewish Communities.*

20. Shinedling, *West Virginia Jewry,* 1103.

21. Sniderman, "Diamond in the Rough," 7; Scott and Fink interviews; Shinedling and Pickus, *History of the Beckley Jewish Community.*

22. See, for example, Morawska, *Insecure Prosperity;* Ashkenazi, *Business of Jews;* and Eisenberg, "Argentine and American Jewry."

23. Kuznets, "Immigration of Russian Jews," 39; Rubinow, "Economic Condition," 495.

24. Kuznets, "Immigration of Russian Jews," 39, 47, 119. The year of immigration was ascertained for 456 East European Jewish immigrants to the coalfields (see note 19 for sources).

25. U.S. census statistics suggest that in 1890, up to two-thirds of Russian Jewish immigrants may have lived outside the Northeast. However, the numbers are sketchy, since the "out-migration of Jews from the cities . . . has not been studied. Where they went and what they did for how long are difficult questions to answer." Dubrovsky, "Book Review: *Jewish Farmers,*" 97–98.

26. Bodnar, *Transplanted;* Nugent, *Crossings.* On chain migration and the early settlement of Appalachia, see Mann, "Mountain Settlement."

27. U.S. Immigration Commission, *Emigration Conditions in Europe,* 257; Pickus interview.

28. Pickus interview; Nadell, "Journey to America"; Sniderman, "Diamond in the Rough," 15.

29. Golab, *Immigrant Destinations;* Bodnar, *Transplanted.*

30. Kuznets, "Immigration of Russian Jews"; Sorin, *Time for Building.*

31. Characterizing all Jews who came to America between 1820 and 1880 as "German" is somewhat misleading. Although the majority arrived from the German states, others came from the German-French Alsace-Lorraine, Hapsburg-controlled Bohemia and Moravia, and Prussian Poland.

32. Diner, *Time for Gathering;* Barkai, *Branching Out;* Sorin, *Time for Building.* To Americanize their fellow Jews, German American Jews created organizations to encourage East European immigrants to disperse throughout the country. The most prominent, the Industrial Removal Office, settled thousands of East European Jews in towns across North America. The IRO sent a handful of people to larger Appalachian towns such as Huntington and Charleston, West Virginia, but had no impact on the coalfields.

33. Sorin, *Time for Building;* Howe, *World of Our Fathers;* Selevan, "Jewish Wage Earners in Pittsburgh," 272.

34. Sorin, *Time for Building;* Baum, Hyman, and Michel, *Jewish Woman in America.*

35. Howe, *World of Our Fathers,* 16; Soyer, "Between Two Worlds."

36. Perlmann, "Beyond New York," 369; Morawska, *Insecure Prosperity,* 32–37.

37. Weissbach, *Jewish Life in Small-Town America;* Perlmann, "Beyond New York"; Rischin and Livingston, *Jews of the American West.*

38. "Weinstein Brothers," *Middlesborough News,* 21 March 1903, p. 1; "Col. Jos. M. Lopinsky," *McDowell Recorder,* 12 December 1913; "Sam Polan Goes to School," *McDowell Recorder,* 7 November 1913, p. 1; Fink and Weiner interviews.

39. Naturalization records, census data, and interviews were used to pinpoint the debarkation points and previous American homes of coalfield Jews.

40. Mitchell, *Appalachian Frontiers;* Dunaway, *First American Frontier.*

41. Noe, *Southwest Virginia's Railroad;* Williams, "Class, Section, and Culture," 213 (first quote); Pudup, "Town and Country," 277 (second quote).

42. Lewis, *Transforming the Appalachian Countryside;* Pudup, "Social Class." See also Hsiung, *Two Worlds.*

43. Pudup, "Town and Country"; Lewis, *Transforming the Appalachian Countryside.*

44. The six counties: Fayette, Raleigh, Mercer, McDowell, Wyoming, and Logan. In 1895, Mingo County would be formed from part of Logan. *West Virginia Gazetteer,* 1882–83.

45. *West Virginia Gazetteer,* 1882–83.

46. Ibid.; U.S. Census Bureau, *State Compendium;* Eiland, "Retail Merchant."

47. Lambie, *From Mine to Market.*

48. Thomas, "Coal Country"; Lawrence, "Appalachian Metamorphosis."

49. Thomas, "Coal Country"; Lambie, *From Mine to Market;* Herr, *Louisville & Nashville Railroad.* Under the broad form deed, farmers sold the mineral rights to their land but ostensibly kept their surface rights to live on and farm their properties. However, the deed authorized coal companies to remove the coal "by whatever means necessary," enabling them to take control over the surface as well. See Eller, *Miners, Millhands, and Mountaineers,* 55. His chapter "A Magnificent Field for Capitalists" describes how local promoters and outside capitalists transformed land ownership in Appalachia.

50. Thomas, "Coal Country," 82, 275; Eller, *Miners, Millhands, and Mountaineers,* 242. On the impact of the national coal market on the region's economy, see Simon, "Development of Underdevelopment." On the coal industry's political grip on the coalfields, see Gaventa, *Power and Powerlessness,* and Hevener, *Which Side Are You On?*

51. Thomas, "Coal Country," 83. See also Sullivan, "Coal Men and Coal Towns."

52. In 1870, the five West Virginia counties of this study (Fayette, McDowell, Logan/Mingo, Raleigh) had a total black population of only 236. U.S. Census Bureau, *Census of Population,* 1870–1920; U.S. Immigration Commission, *Immigrants in Industries,* 151–61.

53. U.S. Coal Commission, *Report,* 1467; Sullivan, "Coal Men and Coal Towns"; Gillenwater, "Cultural and Historical Geography."

54. Pudup, "Town and Country," 286.

55. Levy, *Jacob Epstein,* 15.

56. Kahn, *Stitch in Time;* Gail Bank interview (quote); Levy, *Jacob Epstein.* On the Baltimore Bargain House's influence elsewhere in the South, see, for example, Evans, *Provincials,* 81; Besmann, *Separate Circle.*

57. Kenneth Bank, Gail Bank, and Sylvan Bank interviews.

58. Correspondence with Henrietta Szold, 6 February 1899, Szold Papers.

59. Waller, *Feud,* 44; Dietz, "As We Lived," 16 (quote); Schmier, "Hellooo! Peddlerman; Hellooo!"; Jones, "Gender, Race"; Semrau, "Roxie Gore."

60. "Weinstein Brothers," *Middlesborough News,* 21 March 1903, p. 1; Sylvan Bank interview.

61. "Weinstein Brothers," 1; Sylvan Bank interview; Berman and Weiner interviews. On Cincinnati, see Barkai, *Branching Out,* 116. On Knoxville, see Besmann, *Separate Circle.*

62. On the intertwining of *tzedekah* and economic self-interest, see Morawska, *Insecure Prosperity,* 20–21, 58–61, and Barkai, *Branching Out,* 46.

63. Rogoff, *Homelands,* 12.

64. Bernard Gottlieb, Scott, Fink, and Weiner interviews.

65. Manuscript Census, Wise County, 1900, 1910; Ken Bank interview.

66. "I. L. Shor."

67. Ibid.; Pickus interview; various interviews.

68. Koslow, Ira Sopher, and Gorsetman interviews; Shinedling and Pickus, *History of the Beckley Jewish Community.*

69. Sturm interview.

70. Sniderman, "Diamond in the Rough"; Marino, *Welch and Its People,* 232; Betty Gottlieb interview.

71. Sullivan, "Coal Men and Coal Towns."

72. Jean Wein interview; correspondence with Henrietta Szold, 6 February 1899, Henrietta Szold Papers.

73. Sniderman, "Diamond in the Rough."

74. *Routes and Resorts,* 4–5, 26. The figure cited includes the Kanawha coalfield along

with the New River field. In the Kanawha field, a Jewish population formed in the town of Montgomery and grew to around eighty people by 1920. It considered itself part of the nearby Charleston Jewish community and is not included in this study. Shinedling, *West Virginia Jewry*, 1046–56.

75. Lane and Schnepf, *Sewell*, 2–3.

76. Ibid., 7–8.

77. Manuscript Census, Fayette County, 1870, 1880, 1900–1920, Kanawha County, 1870, 1900, and Logan County, 1920; *West Virginia Gazetteer*, 1895, 1900, 1910, 1914; *Logan City Directory*, 1927; *Progressive West Virginians*.

78. Manuscript Census, Fayette County, 1900–1920; "Col. Jos. M. Lopinsky," *McDowell Recorder*, 12 December 1913; *West Virginia Gazetteer*, 1895, 1898, 1900, 1904, 1910, 1914; Shinedling and Pickus, *History of the Beckley Jewish Community*.

79. Lane and Schnepf, *Sewell*, 29; Woods, *Raleigh County*; Thomas, "Coal Country," 63–71.

80. In American popular culture as well as historiography extending back to Frederick Jackson Turner, the term "frontier" has connoted the site where advancing white "civilization" encountered and subdued a wild natural landscape and the "primitive" native people who occupied it. Some recent historians, pointing out the ethnocentricity of this definition, have suggested that its usage be "reconfigured" to retain its powerful meaning as a site where different cultures collided in the context of national expansion. Stephen Aron offers the following definition: "lands where separate polities converged and competed, and where distinct cultures collided and occasionally coincided" during the process of "conquest, colonization, and capitalist consolidation." Although "conquest" of the Indians and "colonization" by Europeans had occurred a century earlier, Appalachia in the late nineteenth century was certainly in the throes of "consolidation" as its landscape was finally being "subdued." It exhibited many qualities associated with advancing frontiers, from the in-migration of diverse groups of people to the integration of local markets, land, and resources into the capitalist system. Aron, "Lessons in Conquest," 126, 128. See also Gilman and Shain, *Jewries at the Frontier*, particularly Gilman's introduction, "The Frontier as a Model," 1–25. On boomtowns in Central Appalachia's timber fields, see Lewis, *Transforming the Appalachian Countryside*. On boomtowns in the coalfields, see Gaventa, *Power and Powerlessness*. On Central Appalachia as a frontier, see Salstrom, "Newer Appalachia."

81. Scott, "Thurmond on the New River," 12, 22; Sullivan, *Thurmond*, 35–36; Bragg, *Thurmond*, 20; *Dunloup Days*, 65. The notorious activities attributed to Thurmond actually took place just across the river on land belonging to Glen Jean, a town controlled by vice-tolerant coal baron Thomas McKell. Schaffer, who adamantly denied newspaper reports that he had fined a dead man, was mayor of Glen Jean.

82. Thomas, "Coal Country," 76; Lambie, *From Mine to Market*. The extent of the N&W's involvement in coal development is hinted at in a dry quote from its 1902 annual report: "The Pocahontas Coal and Coke Company having purchased approximately 295,000 acres of the lands in the Pocahontas Field, your Directors deemed it necessary for the protection of the interests of your Company to purchase all the capital stock of the Pocahontas Coal and Coke Company." *Norfolk & Western*, 11. In 1958, the N&W's holding company owned one-third of the land in McDowell County. McCormick, "McDowell County," 202.

83. Thomas, "Coal Country"; *Virginias* 4 (January 1883): 3.

84. Tazewell County, Deed Index, 1876–1908, and Deed Book 19, p. 67 (quote); *Bluefield City Directory*, 1915–16 (includes Pocahontas); Manuscript Census, Tazewell County, 1920.

85. Manuscript Census, Tazewell County, 1900–1920; Tazewell County, Deed Book 24, p. 272.

86. Tazewell County, Deed Index, 1876–1908; Jones, *Early Coal Mining*, 114; Shinedling, *West Virginia Jewry*, 367, 382–83; Manuscript Census, Tazewell County, 1900, 1910; U.S. Census Bureau, *Census of Population*, 1910.

87. Jones, *Early Coal Mining;* Pendleton, *History of Tazewell County*, 664–65 (quote); Manuscript Census, Tazewell County, 1900, 1910; *Kitts' City and Coalfield Directory*, 1904; *Bluefield City Directory*, 1910–11, 1915–16.

88. *Bluefield City Directory*, 1915–16; Jones, *Early Coal Mining;* U.S. Census Bureau, *Census of Population*, 1900; Shinedling, *West Virginia Jewry*, 363–65. Because Bluefield is situated outside of the coalfields, its Jewish community is not part of this study. However, the regional importance of the city and the ties between its Jewish community and Jews in the coalfields will be cause for further consideration.

89. Manuscript Census, McDowell and Mercer Counties, 1900; *Bluefield City Directory*, 1919–20.

90. U.S. Census Bureau, *Census of Population*, 1870–1910; Gillenwater, "Cultural and Historical Geography"; Byrne, *Handbook*, 88.

91. Gail Bank, Ken Bank interviews; Lambie, *From Mine to Market*. Rail timetables courtesy of Gail Bank and the National Railway Historical Society, Philadelphia.

92. See, for example, Suberman, *Jew Store*.

93. Gillenwater, "Cultural and Historical Geography"; Solins and Jones, *McDowell County History;* Manuscript Census, McDowell County, 1900; U.S. Census Bureau, *Census of Population*, 1900.

94. Marino, *Welch and Its People*, 25, 40; *West Virginia Gazetteer*, 1895, 1898; Shinedling, *West Virginia Jewry*, 986; Manuscript Census, McDowell County, 1900.

95. Anonymous, *Sodom and Gomorrah;* Manuscript Census, McDowell County, 1900–1920.

96. Shinedling, *West Virginia Jewry*, 983–88.

97. *McDowell Times*, 1913–18; Manuscript Census, McDowell County, 1910, 1920; Ken Bank interview.

98. Manuscript Census, coalfield counties, 1900–1920; various interviews; Eiland interview.

99. Gaventa, *Power and Powerlessness;* Eller, *Miners, Millhands, and Mountaineers;* Herr, *Louisville & Nashville Railroad; Bell County, Kentucky, History;* U.S. Census Bureau, *Census of Population*, 1890.

100. Herr, *Louisville & Nashville Railroad*, 96; "Middlesboro as She Stands Today," *Middlesborough News*, 4 October 1902, p. 1; Gaventa, *Power and Powerlessness;* Sturm interview. From "Middlesboro History," 20 January 1990: "In 1894, Receivers Club is organized for all the businesses and businessmen who have gone into receivership (bankruptcy)."

101. "Middlesboro History," 22 February 1990; "New Furniture Store," *Middlesborough News*, 12 May 1900; Ann Matheny to David Weinstein, 11 January 1990, letter in possession of the Weinstein family.

102. DeRosett and Marcum, *Middlesboro;* Manuscript Census, Bell County, 1910, 1920.

103. Herr, *Louisville & Nashville Railroad;* Besmann, *Separate Circle*.

104. "Student Rabbi Survey"; Sturm interview; *Bell County, Kentucky, History*, 261; Manuscript Census, Bell County, 1910, 1920.

105. Herr, *Louisville & Nashville Railroad;* Lambie, *From Mine to Market*.

106. McCormick, "McDowell County," 206. On how county seats became coalfield hubs, see Lewis, *Transforming the Appalachian Countryside,* and Pudup, "Town and Country."

107. U.S. Census Bureau, *Census of Population,* 1900–1930.

108. Hunter, "Story of McDowell County"; Rosenheim, "Williamson," 20; *West Virginia Gazetteer,* 1900.

109. Hatcher and Steele, *Heritage of McDowell County,* 27; Manuscript Census, McDowell County, 1900–1920; Shinedling, *West Virginia Jewry.*

110. "Student Rabbi Survey"; Manuscript Census, Mingo County, 1900–1920; *West Virginia Gazetteer,* 1895; Shinedling, *West Virginia Jewry.*

111. Sparkmon, *Chesapeake & Ohio Railway;* Woods, *Raleigh County;* Herr, *Louisville & Nashville Railroad;* U.S. Census Bureau, *Census of Population,* 1900–1940.

112. Manuscript Census, Logan County, 1910, 1920; *Logan City Directory,* 1927; Shinedling, *West Virginia Jewry.*

113. Manuscript Census, Raleigh County, 1910; Fayette County, Law Order Book 9, p. 272; Shinedling and Pickus, *History of the Beckley Jewish Community; Beckley City Directory,* 1940.

114. Manuscript Census, Harlan County, 1920; Harlan congregation records; *American Jewish Year Book,* 1940; Forester, *Harlan County.*

115. Fink interview; Hickam, *October Sky,* 10.

116. Manuscript Census, Logan, McDowell, Mingo, and Raleigh Counties, 1900–1920; *Logan City Directory,* 1927; *Beckley City Directory,* 1940; *Williamson City Directory,* 1952; Weiner interview.

117. Morawska, *Insecure Prosperity,* 135; Rosen interview.

118. Jean Wein interview.

119. Eller, *Miners, Millhands, and Mountaineers;* Toll, "'New Social History,'" 334. See also Weissbach, "Stability and Mobility."

120. Golab, *Immigrant Destinations,* 143.

121. See, for example, Bodnar, *Transplanted;* Perlmann, "Beyond New York"; Morawska, *Insecure Prosperity;* Evans, *Provincials;* and Levinson, *Jews in the California Gold Rush.*

122. See Pudup, Billings, and Waller, introduction to *Appalachia in the Making.*

123. Bodnar, *Transplanted,* xvi.

Chapter 2: Middlemen of the Coalfields

1. Jaffe interview.

2. Ibid.

3. Zenner, *Minorities in the Middle,* 134.

4. See note 9 below.

5. Lawrence, "Appalachian Metamorphosis," 49–50; U.S. Immigration Commission, *Immigrants in Industries,* 225–28; Drosick interview.

6. Manuscript census schedules from coalfield counties document the prevalence of peddlers and merchants from the Middle East. See also Farley's "To Keep Their Faith Strong" and "One of the Faithful."

7. Evans, *Provincials,* 39 (first quote); Ashkenazi, *Business of Jews;* Morawska, *Insecure Prosperity,* 41 (second quote); Webb, "Jewish Merchants and Black Customers."

8. Rischin and Livingston, *Jews of the American West;* Stern, "Jewish Community"; Levinson, *Jews in the California Gold Rush.*

9. A database was constructed of more than two thousand Jewish residents of the coalfields of southern West Virginia, southeastern Kentucky, and southwestern Virginia from the 1870s to the 1950s. Job information was ascertained for 950 individuals. Sources include Manuscript Census, all coalfield counties, 1900–1920; *West Virginia Gazetteer*, 1895, 1898, 1900, 1904, 1910, 1914; *Kitts' City and Coalfield Directory*, 1904; *Bluefield City Directory*, 1910–11, 1915–16 (includes Pocahontas); *Logan City Directory*, 1927; *Beckley City Directory*, 1932, 1940; *Williamson City Directory*, 1952; *Bell County, Kentucky, History*; Lane and Schnepf, *Sewell*; Marino, *Welch and Its People*; Shinedling and Pickus, *History of the Beckley Jewish Community*; and interviews, newspaper articles, and courthouse records. The following discussion is based on these sources.

10. Mankoff interview.

11. Evans, *Provincials*, 28; Shapiro, *Time for Healing*.

12. Koslow interview; David, "Jewish Consciousness," 7.

13. Martha Albert interview.

14. U.S. Census Bureau, *Census of Population*, 1950, 1970; McCoy and Brown, "Appalachian Migration," 35–36; Weiner interview; Marino, *Welch and Its People*, 517. On the impact of national chain stores, see Sheskin, "Dixie Diaspora," 68.

15. David, "Jewish Consciousness," 98; Shinedling, *West Virginia Jewry*, 336; Sylvan Bank and Pickus interviews.

16. Fink interview.

17. Simon, "Development of Underdevelopment"; Eiland and Isadore Wein interviews.

18. Martha Albert interview; various interviews; Eiland, "Retail Merchant."

19. Thomas, "Coal Country"; Hecker and Ira Sopher interviews.

20. "None Failed with Big Wad," *Bluefield Daily Telegraph*, 19 December 1915, p. 7; Simon, "Development of Underdevelopment."

21. Ira Sopher interview; "The Coal Business Good," *McDowell Recorder*, 9 July 1915; "Dawn of New Era of Prosperity Acclaimed by Welch Merchants," *McDowell Recorder*, 3 November 1922; "Middlesborough: Some of Her Possibilities," *Middlesborough News*, 4 October 1902; "Year 1913: Banner Business Year," *McDowell Times*, 26 December 1913. Many of these articles shared the same theme: the coalfields have recently seen hard times, but a new era has arrived and prospects for the future are excellent.

22. Sullivan, "Coal Men and Coal Towns," 191–93; Laing, "Negro Miner in West Virginia," 309–10; U.S. Immigration Commission, *Immigrants in Industries*, 212.

23. Corbin, *Life, Work, and Rebellion*; Eller, *Miners, Millhands, and Mountaineers*; Hevener, *Which Side Are You On?*

24. "Company and Other Stores," 716; Hevener, *Which Side Are You On?* 22. See also Roden, "Commissary," 240; "Store Checks vs. Thrift," 619.

25. For a more detailed analysis of company stores and independent retailers, see Weiner, "History of Jewish Life."

26. Bennett interview. Another man recalled of 1930s Harlan County, "If they caught you trading, going to Harlan and trading in the store, instead of trading in the commissary, why, they'd run you off from here, they didn't take you back." Portelli, *Death of Luigi Trastulli*, 206.

27. "Discussion by Readers" (1915), 895; Lane, *Civil War in West Virginia*, 28; Laing, "Negro Miner in West Virginia," 311.

28. Fishback, "Did Coal Miners 'Owe Their Souls'?"; Phipps interview; Greene, "Strategies for Survival," 51.

29. Shackelford and Weinberg, *Our Appalachia*, 225; various interviews.

30. Hevener, *Which Side Are You On?* 22; U.S. Coal Commission, *Report*, 1462.

31. Roden, "Commissary," 240–41; "Company and Other Stores," 716.

32. U.S. Immigration Commission, *Immigrants in Industries*, 201; letter from W. J. Francis, Glasscock Papers.

33. U.S. Coal Commission, *Report*, 1462–66, 1514; Lane, *Civil War in West Virginia*, 28.

34. U.S. Immigration Commission, *Immigrants in Industries*, 201; Farley, "One of the Faithful," 52; Lane, *Civil War in West Virginia*, 29.

35. Forester, *Before We Forget*, 25; Eiland interview; "Company Store Seeks to Force Employees to Buy" and "Coercion Still Continues," 22 December 1915, and "Injunction Is Applied for by Coal Company," 24 December 1915, all in *Bluefield Daily Telegraph*.

36. Wolfe-Collins correspondence, 1913–15, Collins Papers.

37. Pickus interview.

38. Jones, *Early Coal Mining*, 135; Gleason, "Company-Owned Americans."

39. Wolfe-Collins correspondence, 28 December 1915, Collins Papers.

40. "Most Stupendous Land Deal Ever Pulled Off in Keystone," *McDowell Times*, 12 January 1917; Hunter, "Story of McDowell County"; Jones, *Early Coal Mining*; Tazewell County, Deed Indexes; Alexander, "Wilcoe"; Drosick, Scott, and Jean Wein interviews.

41. Various interviews; "Big Hotel," *McDowell Recorder*, 3 May 1912.

42. Massay, "Coal Consolidation," 169; U.S. Immigration Commission, *Immigrants in Industries*, 201.

43. Shifflett, *Life, Work, and Culture*, 182; Fishback, "Did Coal Miners 'Owe Their Souls'?"; Laing, "Negro Miner in West Virginia," 312; U.S. Immigration Commission, *Immigrants in Industries*, 202; U.S. Coal Commission, *Report*, 1463.

44. Koslow interview; U.S. Coal Commission, *Report*, 1522.

45. U.S. Coal Commission, *Report*, 1462–63; Gorsetman interview; various interviews.

46. Phipps interview transcript, 31–32; Alexander, "Wilcoe," 29; Greene, "Strategies for Survival," 51; Weiner and Gorsetman interviews; various interviews.

47. Ibid.

48. Lane, *Civil War in West Virginia*, 28; Wolfe-Collins correspondence, 23, 26 March 1915, Collins Papers; West Virginia Code, 1891, 1923, 1927. In the mid-1920s, new legislation allowed companies to make scrip nontransferable so that they could legally refuse to take it from non-employees.

49. U.S. Immigration Commission, *Immigrants in Industries*, 202; Roden, "Commissary," 241; Shifflett, *Life, Work, and Culture*, 184; various interviews.

50. Gorsetman interview.

51. Rakes interview; Shifflett, *Life, Work, and Culture*, 189.

52. Various interviews.

53. U.S. Immigration Commission, *Immigrants in Industries*, 213; Eiland interview; various interviews; Alexander, "Wilcoe," 30.

54. Alexander, "Wilcoe," 30; Monk interview; U.S. Coal Commission, *Report*, 1460, 1463; Laing, "Negro Miner in West Virginia," 309.

55. U.S. Immigration Commission, *Immigrants in Industries*, 201; U.S. Coal Commission, *Report*, 1460, 1463; Laing, "Negro Miner in West Virginia," 308; Drosick interview.

56. Wolfe-Collins correspondence, 25, 28 December 1915, Collins Papers.

57. Ibid.

58. U.S. Coal Commission, *Report*, 1461.

59. Manuscript Census, McDowell County, 1900–1920; McDowell County, Naturalization Records; Hatcher and Steele, *Heritage of McDowell County*, 49; Marino, *Welch and Its People*, 118, 224; Shinedling, *West Virginia Jewry*, 1275; Hecker interview.

60. See note 9.

61. Marino, *Welch and Its People*, 232; Manuscript Census, McDowell County, 1920; *McDowell Recorder*, 29 September 1911, 24 December 1915; McDowell County, Naturalization Records, 1918; various interviews.

62. The census does not gather data on religion, making identification of Jews somewhat tricky. Jewish-sounding names, in the absence of other supporting evidence, were not enough to include individuals in the database of coalfield Jews constructed for this study.

63. *West Virginia Department of Mines Annual Report*, 1906–30; *Kentucky Department of Mines Annual Report*, 1924–26.

64. Marino, *Welch and Its People*, 232.

65. Correspondence with Nell Bannister, 1956, Shinedling Collection; Fayette County, Deed Book 27, Order Book 8, and Criminal Court Index; *West Virginia Department of Mines Annual Report*, 1905–10.

66. "I. L. Shor"; "Keystone Men Organize Big Coal Company, Kimball Likewise," *McDowell Times*, 16 November 1917; *West Virginia Department of Mines Annual Report*, 1917–24; McDowell County, Deed Books 76 and 77; Mingo County, Deed Books 35, 38, and 45; "Notice of Dissolution," *McDowell Recorder*, 3 September 1920.

67. Sylvan Bank, Ken Bank, Goodman interviews; "I. L. Shor."

68. McDaniels, "Totz Experienced Boom"; Manuscript Census, McDowell County, 1920; Oppleman interview.

69. "Jews in America," 133.

70. Levinson, *Jews in the California Gold Rush*, 21. See also Stern, "Jewish Community."

71. "I. L. Shor."

72. "Loss at Keystone," *Bluefield Daily Telegraph*, 25 June 1901; "Blaze Destroys Business Block of Keystone," *McDowell Recorder*, 11 May 1917. For a listing of coalfield newspaper articles about fires, see Weiner, "History of Jewish Life," 229.

73. Betty Gottlieb interview.

74. "Bessie Zolsman versus Louis Totz," 1909–10, McDowell County, Circuit Court Records; "Fifteen Thousand Dollar Fire in Keystone," *McDowell Times*, 26 June 1914, and "Keystone Visited by Another Destructive Fire," *McDowell Times*, 20 April 1917; Sylvan Bank and Sturm interviews.

75. Olson, "Depths of the Great Depression," 214, 221–23; Forester, *Harlan County*, 113; various interviews; Shinedling, *West Virginia Jewry*, 1298.

76. Bankruptcy notices, *McDowell Recorder*, 1911–22; Jean Wein, Sylvan Bank, and Jaffe interviews; Tazewell County, Deed Books 24 and 32.

77. Welch and Williamson congregation records; Pickus interview.

78. "Student Rabbi Survey"; Manuscript Census, all coalfield counties, 1900–1920; "Pocahontas Pickings," *Bluefield Daily Telegraph*, 28 December 1915.

79. Ira Sopher interview.

80. Gerber, "Cutting Out Shylock," 628–29. See also Mostov, "Dun and Bradstreet"; Ashkenazi, *Business of Jews*; Perlmann, "Beyond New York."

81. Morawska, *Insecure Prosperity*, 128; Gerber, "Cutting Out Shylock," 630; Zenner, *Minorities in the Middle*, 134. Studies of Jewries around the world document tendencies toward risk-taking entrepreneurship. See, for example, Gilman and Shain, *Jewries at the Frontier*.

82. Mostov, "Dun and Bradstreet"; Gerber, "Cutting Out Shylock," 627–30; Ashkenazi, *Business of Jews;* Zborowski and Herzog, *Life Is with People.*

83. Jaffe interview.

84. Ira Sopher and Rosen interviews; Sniderman, "Diamond in the Rough," 51; Hatcher and Steele, *Heritage of McDowell County; Bell County, Kentucky, History.*

85. Ira Sopher interview; Tenenbaum, "Immigrants and Capital"; Morawska, *Insecure Prosperity,* 56–57. During the Depression, one informant told Morawska, internal lending was so widespread that "everybody owed everybody" (128). Jewish loan societies and informal lending customs were grounded in the biblical commandment to assist fellow Jews in need by providing interest-free loans (Exodus 22:24, Leviticus 25:35–37, Deuteronomy 23:20–21).

86. Ira Sopher interview; "Merchants to Close," *Mingo Republican,* 21 April 1911.

87. "Jerome Goodman versus D. M. Klein," *West Virginia Supreme Court Report,* 1920, 292–300.

88. Jaffe interview; *McDowell Recorder,* 3 May 1912.

89. Baltimore Bargain House catalogues, 1900, 1906; Levy, *Jacob Epstein;* Fink interview. Not all Baltimore Bargain House clients were Jewish, but Epstein's biography emphasizes the importance of Jewish retailers to the firm's business.

90. *McDowell Times,* 5 June 1917; *McDowell Recorder,* 15 September 1922.

91. Various interviews; David, "Jewish Consciousness," 16; Sniderman, "Diamond in the Rough," 76.

92. Various interviews; Manuscript Census, coalfield counties, 1900–1920. Ewa Morawska asserts that the phrase "helping out" served to maintain "the public image of subordination" of women. In reality, she quotes one respondent, "The men knew how important women were [in business], but in those days you did not come out and say it" (*Insecure Prosperity,* 102).

93. On immigrant attitudes regarding women's work, see, for example, Bodnar, *Transplanted.* On Jewish female entrepreneurship and women's work in Europe and America, see Baum, Hyman, and Michel, *Jewish Woman in America;* Neu, "Jewish Businesswoman in America"; Zborowski and Herzog, *Life Is with People;* and Hyman, *Gender and Assimilation.*

94. See note 9 for sources. Quote is from *Williamson Daily News,* 6 February 1920. A complication in assessing women's business ownership is that men who underwent bankruptcies often put subsequent ventures under their wives' names. Nevertheless, many Jewish businesses were genuinely operated by women. At least twenty-six female proprietors were identified.

95. Rosen, Betty Gottlieb, and Mankoff interviews.

96. *McDowell Recorder,* 3 September 1920.

97. Manuscript Census, McDowell County, 1900–1920; Shinedling, *West Virginia Jewry,* 986; McDowell County, Circuit Court Records (1902, 1909, 1910), Deed Books, and Will Books; "Zolsman vs. Totz," *West Virginia Supreme Court Report,* 1914, 604–6.

98. Baum, Hyman, and Michel, *Jewish Woman in America,* 189–204; Hyman, *Gender and Assimilation;* Neu, "Jewish Businesswoman in America."

99. Martha Albert, Fink, and various interviews; Shinedling, *West Virginia Jewry,* 1007, 1294; Marino, *Welch and Its People;* Shinedling and Pickus, *History of the Beckley Jewish Community; Beckley City Directory,* 1940; *Williamson City Directory,* 1952.

100. Martha Albert, Baloff, Koslow, and Bernard Gottlieb interviews.

101. Martha Albert interview.

102. Scott and Isadore Wein interviews; Besmann, *Separate Circle,* 32.

103. Sniderman, "Diamond in the Rough," 39, 51–52.

104. Ira Sopher, Gorsetman interviews.

105. *McDowell Recorder,* 2 January 1914; *McDowell Times,* 11 August 1916; Manuscript Census, coalfield counties, 1900–1920; *West Virginia Gazetteer,* 1898, 1900, 1904, 1910, 1914; *Logan City Directory,* 1927; *Beckley City Directory,* 1940; *Williamson City Directory,* 1952; Sylvan Bank interview.

106. Pickus and Bernard Gottlieb interviews.

107. Heinze, "Jewish Street Merchants," 208.

108. *Fayette Journal,* 28 June 1900, 12 June 1902; *Mingo Republican,* 20 January 1911.

109. Monroe interview; McDowell County and Mingo County, Circuit Court Records; *West Virginia Supreme Court Report,* 1905–20.

110. Heinze, "Jewish Street Merchants," 208.

111. Ira Sopher and Scott interviews.

112. *Fayette Journal,* 16 April 1900; *Middlesboro News,* 21 March 1903; "Jacob Effron," *Thousandsticks,* 2 January 1913; Baloff interview; Berman interview transcript, 27; various interviews.

113. Local history books such as Marino's *Welch and Its People* cite coalfield businesses owned by Italians, Greeks, African Americans, Hungarians, Poles, and other ethnic groups. See also Farley, "To Keep Their Faith Strong," and Trotter, *Coal, Class, and Color.*

114. Ira Sopher and Sturm interviews.

115. Sniderman, "Diamond in the Rough," 67; Shinedling, *West Virginia Jewry,* 1298.

116. Atherton, *Frontier Merchant,* 9; Schlereth, "Country Stores," 373. See also Barron, *Mixed Harvest.*

117. Cohen, *Making a New Deal,* 157; Whitfield, "Commercial Passions."

118. Heinze, "Jewish Street Merchants," 212; McGuire and Drosick interviews.

119. Greene, "Strategies for Survival"; Lewis, "Appalachian Restructuring"; Alexander, "Wilcoe."

120. Gaventa, *Power and Powerlessness,* 90–91; various interviews.

121. Lewis, *Transforming the Appalachian Countryside,* 190, 202.

122. Semrau, "Roxie Gore," 24; Dietz, "As We Lived"; David, "Jewish Consciousness," 3–4; various interviews.

123. Manuscript Census, Wise County, 1900, and McDowell County, 1920; *McDowell Recorder,* 5 September 1922; Hatcher and Steele, *Heritage of McDowell County,* 40; *Fayette Journal,* 1900–1906.

124. *Bell County Republican,* 2 August 1902; Shinedling, *West Virginia Jewry,* 1020.

125. *Fayette Journal,* 8 August 1901, 12 April 1900; *Mingo Republican,* 17 March 1911, 14 April 1911.

126. *McDowell Recorder,* 15 December 1911, 4 June 1920.

127. *McDowell Recorder,* 16 October 1914, 16, 30 April 1915.

128. Sniderman, "Diamond in the Rough," 41.

129. Baltimore Bargain House catalogue, 1906.

130. Sniderman, "Diamond in the Rough," 51; Schlereth, "Country Stores," 373.

131. *Middlesborough News,* 16 December 1899.

132. "Weinstein Brothers," *Middlesborough News,* 21 March 1903; various issues of the *Fayette Journal, McDowell Recorder, McDowell Times, Mingo Republican, Middlesboro News,* and *Harlan Enterprise.*

133. Weiner interview; Eiland, "Retail Merchant."

134. Weiner, Eiland, and Drosick interviews.

135. McGuire interview; "Attention Called to Jewish Holidays," *McDowell Recorder*, 15 September 1922, p. 3. "Some Things Welch Has," *McDowell Recorder*, 9 July 1915; Marino, *Welch and Its People*, 109.

136. Billings and Blee, *Road to Poverty*. This depiction bears an uncanny resemblance to Hillel Levine's portrayal of the early modern Polish nobility, whose determination to maintain their feudal hegemony led to a "failure to modernize" that doomed their lands to peripheral status. By guiding their region into the world market as a supplier of grain without investing in local economic development, they furthered Poland's economic and political decline. Levine, *Economic Origins of Anti-Semitism*.

137. Dunaway, *First American Frontier*, 233. Critics on both the left and the right have long blamed merchants for the evils of capitalism. Scholars who have explored this animus note the traditional suspicion of traders that rural societies throughout the world have exhibited. They also point out that merchants are the most visible representatives of economic change during the shift to a market-based system. While the middleman position offers opportunities for exploitation that many people have acted upon, the tendency to view merchants in categorically negative terms is at best ahistorical, at worst, dangerous—especially since the middleman role has often been held by minorities, easy scapegoats for economic ills. In much sociological analysis, Daniel Chirot notes, "there is a considerable strain of anti-semitism that takes the form of an attack on, or at least a dismissal of, the utility of petty commerce and usury, which are seen as inherently parasitical and unclean. . . . The hatred of markets and capitalist activity easily lapses into blame of minority entrepreneurs for serving the interests of the oppressive elites." See Chirot and Reid, *Essential Outsiders*, 30, and Zenner, *Minorities in the Middle*.

138. Atherton, *Frontier Merchant*, 17. See also Braudel, *Wheels of Commerce*, 166–67.

139. Jaffee, "Peddlers of Progress"; Cohen, *Making a New Deal;* Barron, *Mixed Harvest;* Jones, "Gender, Race"; Kulikoff, "Transition to Capitalism."

140. Gaventa, *Power and Powerlessness*, 90–91.

141. See, for example, Hickam, *October Sky*.

142. Marino, *Welch and Its People*, 517; McCoy and Brown, "Appalachian Migration," 35–36.

143. Obermiller and Philliber, *Appalachia in an International Context;* Sheskin, "Dixie Diaspora."

144. Trotter, *Coal, Class, and Color*, 16; Billings and Blee, *Road to Poverty*.

Chapter 3: Jews in the Coalfield Social Scene

1. Eiland interview.

2. Marino, *Welch and Its People*, 41; *McDowell Recorder*, 3, 14 September 1920; "No Slowing Down for Veteran Businessman," *Williamson Daily News*, 30 July 1993.

3. Jones, *Early Coal Mining*, 189; *West Virginia Blue Book*, 1924–44; "Weinstein Brothers."

4. *McDowell Recorder* (various issues, 1915–17); Forester, *Harlan County*, 113 (first quote); "Jury Demands City Officers End Gambling," *Middlesboro Daily News*, 22 June 1934 (second quote); "Middlesboro History," 4 August 1990 (third quote). Zuta was the business manager of underworld leader Bugs Moran, bitter rival of Al Capone.

5. Gaventa, *Power and Powerlessness*, 57, 80.

6. See chapter 1, note 80 for a discussion of the term "frontier."

7. Gilman and Shain, *Jewries at the Frontier;* Zipperstein, *Jews of Odessa;* Rischin and Livingston, *Jews of the American West;* Levinson, *Jews in the California Gold Rush;* Pomeroy, "On Becoming a Westerner," 202, 204.

8. *Fayette Journal,* 16 August 1900; "Dr. Millner Now," *McDowell Recorder,* 19 February 1915. "Sam Polan [*sic*] Goes to School" (7 November 1913) reveals disgust at Russia's treatment of Jews along with admiration for Polon: "Born in Russia (Sam says against his will) he was of the hated class that the powers of that mighty monarchy are even now treating with the rank cruelty and inhumanity of medieval times. . . . In this inhospitable and cruel land, an orphaned boy of tender years, and with a sister to support, he decided to go to America and make good. . . . Poor, unlearned, with no knowledge of the English language, he has in ten years, or less, become one of the substantial business men of Welch."

9. Pudup, "Town and Country," 292. See also Pudup, Billings, and Waller, *Appalachia in the Making;* Hsiung, *Two Worlds.*

10. "Schoolmarm Acquitted," *Fayette Journal,* 12 January 1905.

11. Bernard Gottlieb and Eiland interviews; Hatcher and Steele, *Heritage of McDowell County;* Marino, *Welch and Its People,* 232. On credit discrimination against Jews, see Mostov, "Dun and Bradstreet," and Gerber, "Cutting Out Shylock."

12. Sniderman, "Diamond in the Rough," 52–54, 97.

13. Pudup, "Town and Country," 290.

14. Some *McDowell Times* booster articles: "All Trains Should Stop at Keystone," 23 May 1913; "Keystone on Boom," 5 December 1913; and "Boost Keystone, Stop Knocking It," 11 January 1918. On the middle class in non-county-seat towns: "Mt. Hope," *Fayette Journal,* 14 March 1901, and "Northfork Rapidly Coming to Front," *McDowell Recorder,* 12 September 1919.

15. David, "Jewish Consciousness," 52, 55.

16. Sturm and Baloff interviews.

17. *Middlesboro Daily News,* various issues, 1933–37; Sturm interview. On Jewish public officials, see *West Virginia Blue Book; Progressive West Virginians; Bell County, Kentucky, History;* and various newspapers. On southern Jews fearing their coreligionists' forays into politics, see Evans, *Provincials,* 6.

18. "Another 'Colonel'," *McDowell Recorder,* 9 January 1914; *Middlesboro Daily News,* various issues.

19. *Fayette Journal,* 11 April, 11 July, 17 October 1901; Lane and Schnepf, *Sewell;* bankruptcy notices, *McDowell Recorder,* 1911–22.

20. Jaffe interview.

21. Shinedling, *West Virginia Jewry,* 1101–2; *West Virginia Blue Book,* 1916–48; *West Virginia Gazetteer,* 1904, 1910; "Northfork-Clark Is 1200 Town," *McDowell Recorder,* 30 June 1922.

22. Keystone City Hall plaque; *McDowell Times,* 23 January, 6 March 1914; *West Virginia Blue Book,* 1922, 1948, 1960; Marino, *Welch and Its People,* 25, 75.

23. Kiser, *Memories of Pocahontas,* 9.

24. "Banner Business Year in Keystone," 26 December 1913; "Keystone: A Few Things About It and a Few Men," 25 August 1916; "New Walkway on Bridge," 27 September 1918. All *McDowell Times.*

25. Pudup, "Town and Country"; Pudup, "Social Class."

26. Marino, *Welch and Its People,* 41; *West Virginia Blue Book,* 1940, 1944, 1948; *Bell*

County, Kentucky, History, 261; "Irvin Gergely" obituary, *Lexington Herald-Leader,* 27 May 2000.

27. "Splendid Meeting," *McDowell Recorder,* 20 January 1922.

28. *Pinnacle* (Middlesboro, Ky.), 12 February 1917.

29. Forester, *Harlan County,* 233–34.

30. Levine, *Economic Origins of Anti-Semitism,* 143–44, 152.

31. Hertzberg, *Strangers within the Gate City;* Levinson, *Jews in the California Gold Rush.*

32. "Notice of Application for Liquor Licenses," *McDowell Times,* 9 May 1913; Shifflett, *Coal Towns,* 52; Thomas, "Coal Country," 75. See also Lee, *Bloodletting in Appalachia.* Jews received eleven of forty-two licenses granted in a 1913 McDowell County court session, likely a typical percentage in the county's pre-prohibition years. Most Jews who sought licenses that year lived not in Keystone but in Kimball, Northfork, Wilcoe, and Davy.

33. "Pay Day Pleasantries. Two Men Wounded and One in Jail at Keystone," *Bluefield Telegraph,* 2 February 1901; Brant interview; *Middlesboro News,* 29 August 1903.

34. Drosick interview.

35. Manuscript Census, Tazewell County, 1910; Sprecher, "Let Them Drink," 137; *Encyclopaedia Judaica,* "Asceticism."

36. Kiser, *Memories of Pocahontas;* Cantrell, "Immigrants and Community," 129; "Terrible Drought in West Virginia," 3 July 1914, and "Whoopee," 4 June 1915, *McDowell Times;* Scott interview.

37. "Dry Spots Abound," *Fayette Journal,* 5 April 1906; Jones, *Early Coal Mining,* 76.

38. "Middlesboro History," 16 June, 28 September 1990; Lee, *Bloodletting in Appalachia.*

39. *West Virginians of 1934–1935,* 67; "Middlesboro History," 21, 23 November 1990.

40. "They Got What They Asked For," *McDowell Times,* 20 March 1914.

41. *McDowell Times* articles: "Are They Sincere?" 11 June 1915; "What Value Are They to Society?" 2 February 1917; and "Clean Up the Streets of Keystone, Move Those Barrels, Put Up Your Hogs, Law Violated Every Day, Why?" 24 August 1917. "Lid Put on Cinder Bottom," 9 February 1917, describes one cleanup attempt. New rules forbade piano playing from midnight Saturday to 6:00 A.M. Monday, and men were not to be seen entering or leaving the district during those hours. "It is also ordered that the 'Ladies' must not be seen too frequently on porches nor with their heads too conspicuously out of windows," says the article, adding, solicitously, that "these orders, we understand, and have been told, are only for the purpose and to the end that the women and men in Cinder Bottom may become a little more particular, cautious, and common-sense like and in no way mean to inflict a hardship or inconvenience on those who by choice and circumstances live there."

42. Ken Bank interview; Anonymous, *Sodom and Gomorrah.* The booklet achieved a fairly wide distribution; a *McDowell Recorder* article mentions that it was sold on N&W trains ("Hung Jury in Calhoun Case," 5 February 1915).

43. *McDowell Recorder,* 11 May 1917, 20 January 1922.

44. McDowell County, Criminal Court Records, 1894–1918; Anonymous, *Sodom and Gomorrah;* Lee, *Bloodletting in Appalachia,* 205.

45. Anonymous, *Sodom and Gomorrah;* "Mamie Flood Is Convicted," *McDowell Times,* 26 November 1915; "Lucy Cooper Is Convicted," *McDowell Times,* 3 December 1915 (quote); *State of West Virginia vs. Mamie Flood,* 1915, McDowell County, Criminal Court Records; Manuscript Census, McDowell County, 1910, 1920; Brant interview. See chapter 4 on the racial implications of this incident.

46. McDowell County and Fayette County, Criminal Court Records, 1870s to 1920s. On

one occasion, Midleburg's accuser was the straitlaced William D. Thurmond, founder of the town of Thurmond, who testified against him before a grand jury and also, somehow, served as foreman at his trial.

47. McDowell County and Fayette County, Criminal Court Records; "Middlesboro History," 5, 15 December 1990. Goodfriend's vice president was H. P. Ball, whose family engaged in the "Colson-Ball feud" in the 1920s. The Balls were a prominent family with extensive business interests in Middlesboro.

48. McDowell County and Fayette County, Criminal Court Records.

49. Quoted in Simon, "South African Jewish Experience," 76; McDowell, Fayette, and Mingo Counties, Circuit Court Records; *West Virginia Supreme Court Report,* various years; *Katzen vs. Shore,* 1902, and *Zaltzman vs. Totz et al.,* 1909, McDowell County, Circuit Court Records.

50. *Zaltzman vs. Totz et al.,* 1909, McDowell County, Circuit Court Records.

51. McDowell County and Fayette County, Criminal Court Records; West Virginia Code, 1923; Friedenberg, "Jews and the American Sunday Laws." Jews made legal challenges to Sunday laws in many states, with mixed results. However, Robert Levinson asserts that Jewish civic leaders supported these laws because they promoted "civilizing tendencies" in the Wild West (*Jews in the California Gold Rush,* 72).

52. On World War I as a turning point in the coalfields, see Shifflett, *Coal Towns,* 52.

53. "Ashes, Memories Have Settled on Keystone's Cinder Bottom," *Bluefield Daily Telegraph,* 26 May 1975; Marino, *Welch and Its People,* 29; Gail Bank interview.

54. "Middlesboro History," 7 August, 21–23 November 1990; "Simple Jewish Rites for Zuta Funeral Today" and "Blond Man Is Being Sought in Zuta Case," *Middlesboro Daily News,* 7 August 1930.

55. Marino, *Welch and Its People,* 25; McDowell County, Naturalization Records; "Katzen Lands Appointment," 9 April 1915; "Lon Eubanks Shot in Raid on Speakeasy," 3 September 1915; "Officers Capture Liquor," 18 May 1917; "Prohibition Sleuths Make Many Hauls," 13 July 1917, all *McDowell Recorder.* The *McDowell Times* also printed favorable stories about Katzen and Gay but tended to praise their restraint rather than their daring deeds. The *Times* was less than enthusiastic about prohibition enforcement, opting for a tone of heavy irony. Of one Katzen and Gay episode, it stated, "There was weeping, wailing, and gnashing of teeth while the unclaimed booze was being supplied to the fish in the Elkhorn" ("Captured!" 7 July 1916).

56. "Unfortunate Homicide," 6 October 1916, "Katzen Trial," 15 December 1916, and "Katzen Found Not Guilty," 22 December 1916, all in *McDowell Recorder;* Marino, *Welch and Its People,* 25; Katzen interview; Temple Emanuel founders' plaque, McDowell County Public Library, Welch.

57. Sniderman, "Diamond in the Rough," 58; various interviews.

58. Scott, Ken Bank, and Koslow interviews.

59. "Irvin Gergely"; Shell, McGuire, and Ofsa interviews.

60. See Cantrell, "Immigrants and Community"; Wolfe, "Aliens."

61. Drosick and McGuire interviews.

62. Ofsa, Scott, and McGuire interviews.

63. Kiser, *Memories of Pocahontas,* 9; "Masonic Officers Entertained," *Bluefield Daily Telegraph,* 5 January 1916; Manuscript Census, Tazewell County, 1920.

64. Sniderman, "Diamond in the Rough," 46; David, "Jewish Consciousness," 67–69; various interviews.

65. Jean Wein, Baloff, Jaffe, and Weiner interviews.

66. Baloff and Koslow interviews; *West Virginia Blue Book,* 1924, 1928, 1933; David, "Jewish Consciousness," 96.

67. Shell interview; various interviews.

68. Berman interview transcript, 6, 27, 31, 43; various interviews.

69. *McDowell Recorder,* 21 April 1922; 5 December 1919, 17 April 1922, 24 February 1911, 7 March 1911; *Welch Daily News,* 24 October 1933.

70. *Fayette Journal,* 8 August 1901; *McDowell Recorder,* 26 January 1912, 12 December 1919; *Middlesboro News,* 25 November 1905.

71. Alexander, "Wilcoe," 29; Sniderman, "Diamond in the Rough," 44–45.

72. Sniderman, "Diamond in the Rough," 44–46.

73. Ivan Albert interview; David, "Jewish Consciousness," 50, 55; various interviews.

74. McGuire interview.

75. "Reminiscences of Early Days, Pocahontas Masonic Lodge," *Bluefield Daily Telegraph,* 6 March 1924; Shinedling, *West Virginia Jewry,* 338; Marino, *Welch and Its People,* 26; Fear, "Quest for Saliency," 116–17.

76. Atherton, *Frontier Merchant;* various issues, *Fayette Journal, Middlesboro News, McDowell Recorder,* and *Harlan Enterprise;* Betty Gottlieb interview; Sniderman, "Diamond in the Rough," 47–49, 78; theatrical program, Keadle Scrapbook.

77. Sniderman, "Diamond in the Rough," 61, 95–96; Cohen and Ken Bank interviews.

78. Marino, *Welch and Its People,* 48; *McDowell Recorder,* 31 December 1920, 4 March 1921; "Middlesboro History," 30 November 1990; Logan congregation records; Shinedling and Pickus, *History of the Beckley Jewish Community.*

79. Sniderman, "Diamond in the Rough," 34–35.

80. Elaine Bank interview.

81. Pudup, "Town and Country," 292.

82. Morawska, *Insecure Prosperity,* 186–213; Stern, "Jewish Community"; Rothman, "'Same Horse, New Wagon,'" 89–90. Eureka's 1870 Purim Ball was described by the local newspaper as "An Event Never Equaled in the Social History of Eureka." Two non-Jewish women won prizes for best costume.

83. Morawska, *Insecure Prosperity,* 186–208.

84. Hundert, "Some Basic Characteristics"; Schmier, "Jews and Gentiles," 9–10.

85. Besmann, *Separate Circle;* Hertzberg, *Strangers within the Gate City;* Evans, *Provincials.*

86. Schmier, "Jews and Gentiles," 9; Rischin and Livingston, *Jews of the American West,* 22.

87. Rothman, "'Same Horse, New Wagon'"; Stern, "Major Role of Polish Jews"; Levinson, *Jews in the California Gold Rush,* 87.

88. Bauman and Malone, "Directions in Southern Jewish History," 192; Pudup, Billings, and Waller, introduction to *Appalachia in the Making.*

Chapter 4: Insiders and Outsiders

1. Sniderman, "Diamond in the Rough," 93.

2. Bailey, "Judicious Mixture," 157; Lawrence, "Appalachian Metamorphosis," 112; Lewis, *Black Coal Miners,* 131. For background on race relations in the region, see Inscoe, *Appalachians and Race.*

3. Trotter, *Coal, Class, and Color;* Wolfe, "Aliens"; Lawrence, "Appalachian Metamorphosis," 115; "Near Riot in Anawalt," *McDowell Times,* 16 May 1913.

4. Cantrell, "Immigrants and Community," 135; Laing, "Negro Miner in West Virginia," 402, 466.

5. Bailey, "Judicious Mixture," 143; Lewis, "Appalachian Restructuring."

6. Wolfe, "Aliens"; Cantrell, "Immigrants and Community"; Farley, "To Keep Their Faith Strong"; Sniderman, "Diamond in the Rough"; Ofsa, Drosick, and Rakes interviews.

7. Corbin, *Life, Work, and Rebellion;* Harlan congregation records.

8. Bradley, "Coal Operator"; "N&W District Is Grossly Libeled," *McDowell Recorder,* 9 February 1912.

9. "Our Faithful Italian Friends," *McDowell Recorder,* 18 October 1918; "Syrians Prove Loyal," *McDowell Recorder,* 1 November 1918; Kneeland, "Patriotic Demonstration," 826.

10. "Flat Top Coal Field: Advantages Offered Laborers," *McDowell Times,* 30 May 1913; "Operators Know No Color Line," *McDowell Times,* 26 September 1913; Lewis, *Black Coal Miners,* 121; Trotter, *Coal, Class, and Color.*

11. Trotter, *Coal, Class, and Color,* 132; "Boost Keystone, Stop Knocking It," *McDowell Times,* 11 January 1918.

12. Anonymous, *Sodom and Gomorrah.*

13. *McDowell Times:* 27 September 1918; 7 July 1916; 9 February 1917; 24 November 1916; 12 May 1916.

14. Scott and Koslow interviews; McDowell County, Criminal Court Records and Circuit Court Records, 1909, 1911; "Katzen Trial," *McDowell Recorder,* 15 December 1916; *West Virginia Supreme Court Report,* 1918, 492–500; "For Pardon Attorney," *McDowell Times,* 4 July 1913.

15. *McDowell Times* and *McDowell Recorder,* various issues; various interviews; Laing, "Negro Miner in West Virginia," 402, 466, 485; *McDowell Times,* "Boost Keystone, Stop Knocking It."

16. "Middlesboro History," 18 August, 20 July 1990; Trotter, *Coal, Class, and Color,* 125.

17. Laing, "Negro Miner in West Virginia," 472–79; Isadore Wein and Pickus interviews.

18. Leonard, *Christianity in Appalachia,* 266; Rakes interview; Wolfe, "Aliens," 48.

19. Scott interview.

20. Lawrence, "Appalachian Metamorphosis," 49–50.

21. "Attacked by Russians" and "Masonic Officers Entertained," *Bluefield Daily Telegraph,* 5 January 1916.

22. *Middlesboro News,* 15 July 1905, 23 March 1901. See also "Grandpa Herzbrun," *McDowell Recorder,* 24 January 1913; "Col. Bank in Capital City," *McDowell Recorder,* 10 March 1916; "Mannie Shore Says Judge Robinson Will Sure Be Nominated," *McDowell Times,* 5 May 1916.

23. "Taps Are Sounded for Col. J. M. Lopinsky," *McDowell Recorder,* 30 January 1914; *McDowell Recorder,* 3, 24 September 1920.

24. See, for example, Gerber, *Anti-Semitism in American History;* Sacks, "How Did the Jews Become White Folks?"

25. *McDowell Recorder,* 5 August (quote), 3 October, 7 November 1913.

26. "Three Great Days," *McDowell Times,* 15 May 1914; "A True One" and "At the Welch Theater," *McDowell Recorder,* 3 January 1913. The *McDowell Times* in 1917 printed this ditty sent in by a black soldier: "Young men were made to be soldiers / Irishmen were made

to be cops / sauerkraut was made for the Germans / spaghetti was made for the wops / fish were made to drink water / bums were made to drink booze / banks were made to take money / money was made for the Jews" ("What They Were Made For," 13 January 1917).

27. Interviews with Jews and non-Jews elicited stories about Shore. His litigiousness comes through in court records, where his name frequently appears as plaintiff. Though records do not reveal the grounds for Shore's 1911 lawsuit against U.S. Coal and Coke, his zeal for using the legal system is apparent: at one point, "after hearing a part of the evidence, the plaintiff moved the court to permit him to amend his declaration by inserting a new count therein" (the court agreed). Eventually he dropped the suit and each side paid its own costs (McDowell County, Circuit Court Records, 1911–12).

28. *McDowell Times,* 23 January 1914. Paul Baltrop, historian of Australian Jewry, notes the correlation gentiles made between foreign manners and unscrupulous business practices. Anglicized Jews were "good Jews" who "in no way stood out from the great anonymous mass of other Australians. 'Bad Jews' were the opposite. They were foreign, exhibited different customs . . . and had business principles derived from the eastern European village" (Gilman and Shain, *Jewries at the Frontier,* 323).

29. "Marriage of Mr. I. Bloom," *Fayette Journal,* 8 August 1901, p. 1; "A Novel Method," *Fayette Journal,* 24 January 1901, p. 1.

30. "A Novel Method"; Fayette County, Law Order Book 3, 1900–1901. This incident elicited several contradictory accounts. One indictment stated that Harris and House "feloniously" injured Joseph by "cruelly tying the hands and feet of him [and placing] him on the public highway in the hot sun for the space of three hours, to be seen by the persons passing by, and did thereby feloniously extort money from [him]." A *Bluefield Daily Telegraph* article (cited by Randall Lawrence in his retelling of the story) identifies not one but two peddlers as Harris's victims, referring to them as the brothers Solomon and Jacob Ihrig. However, no Ihrigs could be found in Fayette County newspaper accounts or court records. The *Daily Telegraph* added that the peddlers were "taken out of town, tied hands and feet to stakes, and their faces plastered with molasses. In this condition, the sun's rays beating down on their faces, and the molasses attracting flies, ants, etc., they were kept until the torture compelled them to agree to pay." Lawrence, "Appalachian Metamorphosis," 116; "Peddlers Told of Torture," *Bluefield Daily Telegraph,* 25 January 1901.

31. *Fayette Journal,* 20 July 1905.

32. The census actually counted more "Syrian" than Jewish peddlers in coalfield counties. In interviews, non-Jewish residents mistakenly identified merchants of Middle Eastern origin as Jews. One Jewish businessman complained, "There were a lot of Syrian [merchants] too. The Syrians, if they would do something wrong. . . . If someone got a raw deal, they would blame the Jews."

33. Forester, *Harlan County,* 113; Tams and various interviews; David, "Jewish Consciousness," 51, 95; Collins Papers.

34. McGuire and Rakes interviews.

35. Even social reformers believed Southern and Eastern European immigrants belonged to an inferior racial category. See, for example, Jacob Riis's 1890 exposé, *How the Other Half Lives.* See also Higham, *Strangers in the Land;* Sacks, "How Did the Jews Become White Folks?"; and Rogoff, "Is the Jew White?"

36. *McDowell Times,* 12 November 1915, and "Mamie Flood is Convicted," 26 November 1915; "Mamie Flood Found Guilty," *McDowell Recorder,* 26 November 1915.

37. "State of West Virginia vs. Mamie Flood," McDowell County, Criminal Court Records.

38. Evans, *Provincials,* 38. See also Rabinowitz, "Nativism, Bigotry and Anti-Semitism."

39. On the return of nativism and antisemitism after World War I, see Higham, *Strangers in the Land.* Not until World War II did Jews (and other ethnic groups) become considered fully "white" by mainstream U.S. society. Sacks, "How Did the Jews Become White Folks?" 87.

40. David, "Jewish Consciousness," 3, 67–68. Jaffe and Betty Gottlieb interviews. See Evans, *Provincials,* 75; Schmier, "Hellooo! Peddlerman; Hellooo!" 81; and Suberman, *Jew Store,* 146, for similar stories from across the South. On southern philosemitism, see Golden, *Jewish Roots in the Carolinas.*

41. McCauley, *Appalachian Mountain Religion,* 79, 150, 155; Leonard, *Christianity in Appalachia.*

42. Marino, *Welch and Its People,* 49; Shinedling, *West Virginia Jewry,* 75–77.

43. "Pocahontas Synagogue Dedicated on Sunday," *McDowell Recorder,* 4 July 1913; "Middlesboro History," 15 September 1990; "Jewish Women Hold Services," *Mingo Republican,* 3 December 1926, p. 1.

44. "Lipman-Leventhal," 8 January 1915; "Wagner-Totz Wedding a Brilliant Affair," 7 April 1922; "Goodman-Lopinsky," 12 February 1915; "Jewish New Year," 3 October 1913; and "Passover Celebrated," 2 April 1915, all in the *McDowell Recorder.* A 1915 article showed some improvement by referring to "Rosha-Shonnah," though it went on to discuss "the week of atonement, which is called Yom Kippers" ("Jewish New Year," 3 September 1915). The *Recorder* later printed a correction, accurately explaining (and spelling) Yom Kippur ("Wednesday Was Jewish New Year 5676," 10 September 1915).

45. "Hurrah for Welch!" *McDowell Recorder,* 29 May 1914.

46. "Was Columbus a Jew"; "The Jew Acquitted," *McDowell Recorder,* 14 November 1913. The *Recorder* had the details of the Mendel Beilis trial mostly right, though he was accused of murdering only one child. The case provoked international outrage.

47. "The Promised Land," *Williamson Daily News,* 20 January 1920; "Many Jews Enlist with English Army," *McDowell Recorder,* 9 September 1915.

48. "Rosh Hashanah, Great Hebrew Holiday," 3 October 1913; "A Hebrew Philanthropy" (a "splendid project" to "recreate the Holy Land"), 16 January 1914; "Jew to Be Governor of Idaho," 11 December 1914, p. 1; "Jew Nominated," 4 February 1916, p. 1; "Our Adopted Citizens, Jewish People Make Patriotic and Most Desirable Citizens," 19 February 1915, p. 1; and "Black Jews in Abyssinia," 2 July 1915, all in *McDowell Times.* One interesting article concerned an Ethiopian Jew who became an Italian nobleman and then an American citizen ("Jewish Negro Count is Now an American," 30 August 1918).

49. *McDowell Recorder,* 6 June 1913; Isadore Wein interview.

50. David, "Jewish Consciousness," 52; Sturm, Pickus, and Katzen interviews.

51. Cohen, Hecker, and Pickus interviews.

52. Eiland interview; David, "Jewish Consciousness," 53, 55, 70.

53. Jaffe interview.

54. Pickus interview; David, "Jewish Consciousness," 54, 68–69.

55. Cohen, Eiland, Katzen, and Mankoff interviews; *Righteous Remnant;* Middlesboro library exhibit. In Shackelford and Weinberg's *Our Appalachia,* a man from a Perry County, Kentucky, coal camp is quoted as saying, "The Jews were very much hated peo-

ple. They peddled goods and mountain people thought anybody [who] wouldn't get out and work by the sweat of his brow and breath was terrible" (222). Whether these views were shared by a significant number of people is not known. Perry County had no Jewish community, which may help explain the man's attitude; antisemitism is often more apparent in places where Jews are more mythical than actual.

56. Eiland interview. Historian Leonard Dinnerstein notes that 1920s Klan hostility focused primarily on Catholics, blacks, and whites who transgressed moral codes, though he cautions that "no one should think of Klansmen as friends of the Jews" (*Antisemitism*, 96–98). On antisemitism directed against distant rather than local Jews, see Sarna, "'Mythical Jew.'"

57. Various interviews; David, "Jewish Consciousness," 54, 69.

58. Various interviews; Sniderman, "Diamond in the Rough."

59. Six people interviewed for this study lived or grew up in Williamson. Jerome David interviewed eighteen out of Williamson's twenty-four Jewish families in 1974, conducting separate interviews with husbands and wives. Fear's "Quest for Saliency" studied Williamson's Jewish community (along with those of Bluefield and Clarksburg, West Virginia). Also, Marilou Sniderman's memoir of her father, Harry Schwachter, is set in Williamson.

60. David, "Jewish Consciousness," 52–54, 67–73, 79; Fear, "Quest for Saliency," 118.

61. David, "Jewish Consciousness," 52, 68; various interviews.

62. David, "Jewish Consciousness," 52–55, 70, 94–95.

63. Ibid., 70.

64. Baloff interview; David, "Jewish Consciousness," 69.

65. Williamson, Welch, and Logan congregation records; Shinedling, *West Virginia Jewry*, 1596.

66. Isadore Wein interview; Williamson and Welch congregation records; *West Virginia Jewry*, 1292, 1585. On the "ambassadorial" approach to Jewish-gentile relations often taken by small-town Jewry, see, for example, Fear, "Quest for Saliency," 20, 30–31.

67. Logan and Williamson congregation records.

68. Fear, "Quest for Saliency," 119.

69. Various interviews.

70. Lee, *Bloodletting in Appalachia*; Gleason, "Company-Owned Americans"; Lane, *Civil War in West Virginia*; Corbin, *Life, Work, and Rebellion*.

71. Hevener, *Which Side Are You On?* 22; Gaventa, *Power and Powerlessness*, 81, 110–11.

72. "The Murder of Harry Simms," http://aztec.lib.utk.edu/pelton/murder.htm; Hevener, *Which Side Are You On?* 79, 109–10.

73. Weinryb, *Jews of Poland*; Levinson, *Jews in the California Gold Rush*, 60–72; Rischin and Livingston, *Jews of the American West*.

74. U.S. Senate, *West Virginia Coal Fields*, 229, 339; "Flat Top Coal Field: Advantages Offered Laborers," 30 May 1913, *McDowell Times*.

75. U.S. Senate, *West Virginia Coal Fields*, 229–32, 339, 345; *McDowell Recorder*, 2 September 1921; Sylvan Bank and Scott interviews.

76. Jones, *Early Coal Mining*, 129; "Sure We Got Problems," 65.

77. The Matewan Massacre occurred on 19 May 1920, when a gun battle between miners and mine guards from the Baldwin-Felts Detective Agency resulted in the deaths of seven guards, two miners, and the mayor of Matewan, a union sympathizer.

78. Berman interview transcript, 6, 11–16, 25, 28; memorandum, 24 October 1921, Baldwin-Felts Collection.

79. Memorandum, 24 October 1921, Baldwin-Felts Collection.

80. Eiland and Weiner interviews; Solins and Jones, *McDowell County History*, 68.

81. Various interviews; Berman interview transcript, 27.

82. *Williamson Daily News*, 25 May 1920.

83. Sarna, "Anti-Semitism in American History," 44.

84. Morawska, *Insecure Prosperity*, 216, 223; Golden, *Jewish Roots in the Carolinas*, 6; Dinnerstein, "Note on Southern Attitudes," 48; see also Evans, *Provincials*, 187–97; and Rabinowitz, "Nativism, Bigotry and Anti-Semitism."

Chapter 5: Coalfield Jewish Communities

1. Williamson congregation records.

2. Ibid.

3. Williamson congregation records; Regner, "Experiences While Officiating."

4. Sorin, *Time for Building*, 168.

5. David, "Jewish Consciousness," I; Marcus, *United States Jewry*, 207.

6. Sklare, *America's Jews*, 28, 125; Lavender, *Coat of Many Colors*, 31; David, "Jewish Consciousness," i.

7. Sklare, *America's Jews;* Rogoff, "Synagogue," 59; Kaplan, *Eternal Stranger*, 108, 126–27.

8. Lavender, *Coat of Many Colors*, 34.

9. Heschel, "Eastern European Era," 4. See also Kassow, "Communal and Social Change."

10. Hal Rothman describes how one Jewish community was renewed by fresh arrivals from the old country in "'Same Horse, New Wagon,'" 84.

11. Jones, *Early Coal Mining*, 65; Shinedling, *West Virginia Jewry*, 382, 983–90; Manuscript Census, McDowell County, 1900, 1910; "Synagogue Dedication," *McDowell Recorder*, 21 August 1914.

12. Refers to Pocahontas and Keystone; little is known about the Kimball synagogue. Correspondence with Louis Zaltzman, 1956–57, Shinedling Collection; Drosick interview.

13. In the 1930s, the region's Jews began to use a much larger cemetery established by the Bluefield congregation. Drosick, Gail Bank interviews; gravestones, Hebrew Mountain Cemetery, Pocahontas, Va.

14. Shinedling, *West Virginia Jewry*, 986. On the transience of small-town Orthodox rabbis, see Rogoff, "Synagogue"; Weissbach, "East European Immigrants"; and Schmier, "'We Were All Part.'"

15. Manuscript Census, McDowell and Tazewell Counties, 1900–1920; Shinedling, *West Virginia Jewry;* "Dedication of the Jacob Congregation of Kimball," *McDowell Recorder*, 28 August 1914; "Jewish Rabbi Struck by Automobile Thursday," *McDowell Recorder*, 18 April 1919; Welch congregation records.

16. Shinedling, *West Virginia Jewry*, 366–67; Manuscript Census, McDowell County, 1910, 1920; McDowell County, Naturalization Records. Historian Lloyd Gartner writes that Rabbi Spector "exercised patronage in placing numerous rabbis, especially younger men from his *kolel*, in rabbinic positions abroad" ("Jewish Migrants," 37).

17. Manuscript Census, McDowell County, 1910. Figures include Keystone congregation members from the adjoining towns of Northfork and Clark.

18. "Dedication of the Jacob Congregation of Kimball," *McDowell Recorder*, 28 August

1914; "Pocahontas Synagogue Dedicated on Sunday," *McDowell Recorder,* 4 July 1913; *McDowell Recorder,* 24 February, 7 March 1911.

19. Shinedling, *West Virginia Jewry;* Drosick interview.

20. Ken Bank interview.

21. Manuscript Census, Mingo County, 1910, 1920; Logan, Welch, and Williamson congregation records; Shinedling and Pickus, *History of the Beckley Jewish Community.*

22. Scott interview.

23. Rogoff, "Synagogue," 43; Welch congregation records.

24. Shinedling and Pickus, *History of the Beckley Jewish Community,* 83.

25. Logan, Welch, and Williamson congregation records; Shinedling, *West Virginia Jewry;* "Student Rabbi Survey."

26. Williamson and Welch congregation records; "Hebrew Aid Society," *McDowell Recorder,* 12 December 1915; "Jewish Congregation Organized," *McDowell Recorder,* 26 April 1918; "Work Started on Jewish Synagogue," *McDowell Recorder,* 15 September 1922.

27. Welch congregation records; Scott interview; Shinedling, *West Virginia Jewry,* 1272; *McDowell Recorder,* 1922–23.

28. Bernard Gottlieb and Scott interviews; Welch congregation records; Shinedling, *West Virginia Jewry.*

29. Regner, "Experiences While Officiating."

30. Williamson congregation records; correspondence, February 1924, Box B-10, Folder 7, Hebrew Union College Collection; Shinedling, *West Virginia Jewry.*

31. Sniderman, "Diamond in the Rough," 92–93.

32. Williamson congregation records; Shinedling, *West Virginia Jewry,* 1580–1601.

33. Logan congregation records; correspondence, September 1916, Box B-9, Folder 4, Hebrew Union College Collection; "Student Rabbi Survey"; Shinedling, *West Virginia Jewry.*

34. Logan congregation records; correspondence, 1925–28, Boxes B-11 and B-12, Hebrew Union College Collection.

35. "Student Rabbi Survey."

36. Shinedling and Pickus, *History of the Beckley Jewish Community,* 81–86; "Student Rabbi Survey"; Shinedling, *West Virginia Jewry.* The other county-seat congregations used Jewish cemeteries in Bluefield or Charleston.

37. Pickus interview; Shinedling and Pickus, *History of the Beckley Jewish Community,* 127, 82–86, 109.

38. Shinedling, *West Virginia Jewry;* Shinedling and Pickus, *History of the Beckley Jewish Community,* 110; *Righteous Remnant.* Shinedling also served as the Bluefield rabbi from 1947 to 1950.

39. On the "national infrastructure" of Reform Judaism and its impact on small-town congregations, see also Rogoff, "Synagogue," 57.

40. On the Knoxville Jewish community and its links to the coalfields, see Besmann, *Separate Circle.* See p. 43 for a list of Cumberland Gap–area towns where Jews lived.

41. Manuscript Census, Bell County, 1900–1920; "Middlesboro History," 22 February 1990; Sturm interview; "Jewish Cemetery, Middlesboro, Kentucky."

42. "Student Rabbi Survey"; "Middlesboro History," 13 March, 10, 16 November 1990; Sturm interview.

43. "Student Rabbi Survey"; correspondence, Box B-9, Folder 2; Box B-10, Folders 2 and 3; and Box B-11, Folders 4 and 9, all in Hebrew Union College Collection.

44. Jaffe, Sturm, and Baloff interviews.

45. "Student Rabbi Survey"; Harlan congregation records.

46. Harlan congregation records.

47. Harlan congregation records; Sturm, Jaffe, and Baloff interviews.

48. Shinedling, *West Virginia Jewry*, 75–77.

49. Jean Wein interview.

50. Sources used to establish kinship networks include interviews, census records, and newspaper wedding announcements.

51. Temple Emanuel founders' plaque, McDowell County Library, Welch; Williamson congregation records; Shinedling and Pickus, *History of the Beckley Jewish Community*, 84.

52. Various interviews; "Goodman-Lopinsky," *McDowell Recorder*, 12 February 1915; "Wagner-Totz Wedding A Brilliant Affair," *McDowell Recorder*, 7 April 1922; Shinedling and Pickus, *History of the Beckley Jewish Community*, 91.

53. *McDowell Recorder*, 24 February 1911; Hecker interview; "B'nai Israel," Cemetery Files, JMM. On links between small-town Jews and urban centers, see Rogoff, *Homelands;* Rothman, "'Same Horse, New Wagon.'"

54. Ira Sopher interview.

55. "Middlesboro History"; "Attention Called to Jewish Holidays," *McDowell Recorder*, 15 September 1922; Bernard Gottlieb and Scott interviews.

56. See, for example, Hertzberg, *Strangers within the Gate City;* Weissbach, "Stability and Mobility"; and Schmier, "'We Were All Part.'" Jews in large U.S. cities also had to conform to American work patterns, but the existence of an internal Jewish economy enabled many to continue Sabbath observance.

57. Isadore Wein and Baloff interviews; David, "Jewish Consciousness," 16, 34.

58. Various interviews; McDowell County, Circuit Court Records; *West Virginia Supreme Court Report*, 1908–22.

59. Harlan congregation records.

60. Logan congregation records.

61. Kirshenblatt-Gimblett, "Folk Culture," 89; Howe, *World of Our Fathers*, 169, 183.

62. Various interviews; Sniderman, "Diamond in the Rough," 74.

63. Isadore Wein and Koslow interviews.

64. Gurock, "Orthodox Synagogue," 52; Rogoff, "Synagogue," 67; Cohen, Gail Bank, and Jaffe interviews.

65. Rothman, "'Same Horse, New Wagon,'" 94.

66. Fear, "Quest for Saliency," 100, 157.

67. Commentators assign different weight to these various motivations. See, for example, Kaplan, *Eternal Stranger;* Lowi, "Southern Jews"; Marcus, *United States Jewry* (first quote, 200); and Sklare, *America's Jews* (second quote, 115–16).

68. Harlan congregation records; "Jewish Women Hold Services," *Mingo Republican*, 3 December 1926; David, "Jewish Consciousness," 23–24, 94.

69. Baum, Hyman, and Michel, *Jewish Woman in America;* Hyman, *Gender and Assimilation;* Blanton, "Lives of Quiet Affirmation."

70. Various interviews; Sniderman, "Diamond in the Rough," 83. On greater female allegiance to tradition, see also Suberman, *Jew Store;* Hyman, *Gender and Assimilation.*

71. Various interviews; David, "Jewish Consciousness," 34.

72. Bernard Gottlieb interview; David, "Jewish Consciousness," 34.

73. David, "Jewish Consciousness," 34, 93, 23, 36, 35.

74. Wenger, "Jewish Women and Voluntarism," 17; Hyman, *Gender and Assimilation.*

75. Welch, Williamson congregation records; Shinedling and Pickus, *History of the Beckley Jewish Community.*

76. Wenger, "Jewish Women and Voluntarism," 21.

77. Logan congregation records, 1925.

78. Welch congregation records, 1919.

79. Marcus, *United States Jewry;* "Jewish Women Hold Services," *Mingo Republican,* 3 December 1926.

80. David, "Jewish Consciousness," 18–20; various interviews.

81. Various interviews; Fear, "Quest for Saliency," 99; Harlan congregation records.

82. Harlan, Welch, Williamson, and Logan congregation records; "Jewish Relief Fund Gets Results," *McDowell Recorder,* 28 January 1916; "Relief Committee," *McDowell Recorder,* 25 October 1918; Soyer, "Between Two Worlds," 6.

83. Harlan, Welch, Williamson, and Logan congregation records; Pickus interview. On matzo funds and other forms of *tzedekah* derived from Eastern Europe, see Zborowski and Herzog, *Life Is with People,* 193–205.

84. Williamson and Welch congregation records; Shinedling, *West Virginia Jewry.*

85. David, "Jewish Consciousness," 23, 5; Weiner interview; Shinedling, *West Virginia Jewry,* 1283, 1291. Future national leaders who served in the coalfields included Williamson student rabbi Alex Schindler, who headed the Reform movement from the 1970s to the 1990s.

86. David, "Jewish Consciousness," 86; Sniderman, "Diamond in the Rough"; Evans, *Provincials,* 147, 165; various interviews.

87. David, "Jewish Consciousness," 60; various interviews.

88. Harlan, Logan, Welch, and Williamson congregation records; various interviews; Fear, "Quest for Saliency," 99–100.

89. Various interviews; David, "Jewish Consciousness"; Harlan congregation records.

90. Harlan, Logan, Welch, and Williamson congregation records; Sturm interview; *McDowell Recorder,* 4 August 1922.

91. Harlan, Logan, Welch, and Williamson congregation records; Shinedling, *West Virginia Jewry,* 1585; various interviews; *McDowell Recorder* articles: "Minyen Club Entertained Last Sunday," 24 March 1922; "Birthday Party," 17 October 1913; "Gave Delightful Party," 11 August 1911; and "Young Folks Entertained," 20 July 1917.

92. Koslow interview; David, "Jewish Consciousness," 92.

93. Reed, "Shalom, Y'All," 111.

94. Pickus, Eiland, and Ira Sopher interviews; Sniderman, "Diamond in the Rough," 78.

95. On identity construction, see Kirshenblatt-Gimblett, "Folk Culture." On multiple identities of southern Jews, see also Rogoff, *Homelands.*

96. Baloff interview; David, "Jewish Consciousness," 52, 87.

97. Hecker, Gail Bank, and Ofsa interviews; Manuscript Census, McDowell County, 1910.

98. "Student Rabbi Survey"; David, "Jewish Consciousness," 58–62; Shinedling and Pickus, *History of the Beckley Jewish Community; Righteous Remnant;* Mary Jo Sopher and Ofsa interviews.

99. Correspondence with Mrs. Milton Gottlieb, 1956, Shinedling Collection; various interviews.

100. Drosick interview; *American Jewish Yearbook,* 1916–17; Mingo and McDowell Counties, Will Books.

101. Marino, *Welch and Its People,* 41.

102. Sniderman, "Diamond in the Rough," 46, 90–91.

103. Scott interview; Rogoff, "Synagogue," 48.

104. David, "Jewish Consciousness," 48; Scott interview. See also Evans, *Provincials,* and Rogoff, "Synagogue," on the effect of southern religiosity on Jewish religious expression.

105. Welch, Williamson, Logan, and Harlan congregation records; Shinedling and Pickus, *History of the Beckley Jewish Community;* Pickus interview.

106. Marino, *Welch and Its People,* 41; Welch congregation records; Shinedling, *West Virginia Jewry,* 470.

107. Harlan, Logan, Welch, and Williamson congregation records; Pickus interview; Shinedling, *West Virginia Jewry,* 317–18.

108. "Jewish Relief Fund Results," *McDowell Recorder,* 28 January 1916; "Relief Committee," *McDowell Recorder,* 25 October 1918; Shell interview; Sniderman, "Diamond in the Rough," 91; "Jewish Congregation Organized," *McDowell Recorder,* 26 April 1918.

109. Sklare, *America's Jews,* 114. See also Marcus, *United States Jewry;* Goren, "Traditional Institutions Transplanted."

110. David, "Jewish Consciousness," 4; Williamson congregation records. On the transformation of ladies' aid societies into sisterhoods, see, for example, Wenger, "Jewish Women and Voluntarism."

111. Howe, *World of Our Fathers,* 181. See also Marcus, *United States Jewry;* Schmier, "'We Were All Part,'" 57.

112. David, "Jewish Consciousness," 15.

113. Williamson congregation records.

114. Harlan, Logan, Welch, and Williamson congregation records; various interviews.

115. David, "Jewish Consciousness," 16–17, 34, 98; Eiland interview.

116. Betty Gottlieb and Pickus interviews; Harlan, Logan, Welch, and Williamson congregation records.

117. Weissbach, "Small Town Jewish Life," 40.

118. Kaplan, *Eternal Stranger,* 96, 108.

119. Fear, "Quest for Saliency," 157–58; David, "Jewish Consciousness," 11, 30, 92.

120. David, "Jewish Consciousness," 96, 98.

121. Shinedling, *West Virginia Jewry,* 75.

Conclusion

1. Reisman, "Alaskan Jews," 125.

2. Bender, *Community and Social Change,* 7.

3. U.S. Census Bureau. *Census of Population,* 1910, 1990.

REFERENCES

The following repository abbreviations are used in the references.
AJA American Jewish Archives, Cincinnati
JMM Jewish Museum of Maryland, Baltimore
WVRHC West Virginia and Regional History Collection, West Virginia University, Morgantown

Alexander, Irving. "Jewish Merchants in the Coalfields." *Goldenseal* 16 (Spring 1990): 34–35.
———. "Wilcoe: The People of a Coal Town." *Goldenseal* 16 (Spring 1990): 28–35.
American Jewish Yearbook. Philadelphia: Jewish Publication Society, 1910, 1916, 1918, 1940.
Anonymous ("A Virginia lad"). *Sodom and Gomorrah of To-day, or, the History of Keystone, West Virginia.* N.p., 1912. WVRHC.
Aron, Stephen. "Lessons in Conquest: Towards a Greater Western History." *Pacific Historical Review* 63 (May 1994): 125–47.
Ashkenazi, Elliott. *The Business of Jews in Louisiana, 1840–1875.* Tuscaloosa: University of Alabama Press, 1988.
Atherton, Lewis E. *The Frontier Merchant in Mid-America.* Rev. ed. Columbia: University of Missouri Press, 1971.
Bailey, Ken. "A Judicious Mixture: Negroes and Immigrants in the West Virginia Mines, 1880–1917." *West Virginia History* 34 (January 1973): 141–61.
Baldwin-Felts Collection. Eastern Regional Coal Archives, Bluefield, W.Va.
Baltimore Bargain House. Catalogues. 1900 and 1906. JMM.
Barkai, Avraham. *Branching Out: German-Jewish Immigration to the United States, 1820–1914.* New York: Holmes & Meier, 1994.
Baron, Salo W. *The Russian Jew Under Tsar and Soviets.* New York: Macmillan, 1976.
Barron, Hal S. *Mixed Harvest: The Second Great Transformation in the Rural North, 1870–1930.* Chapel Hill: University of North Carolina Press, 1997.
Baum, Charlotte, Paula Hyman, and Sonya Michel. *The Jewish Woman in America.* New York: Dial Press, 1976.
Bauman, Mark K., and Bobbie Malone. "Directions in Southern Jewish History." *American Jewish History* 85, no. 3 (September 1997): 191–93.
Beckley City Directory. Pittsburgh: R. L. Polk, 1932, 1940.
Bell County, Kentucky, History. Paducah, Ky.: Bell County Historical Society, 1994.
Bender, Thomas. *Community and Social Change in America.* New Brunswick, N. J.: Rutgers University Press, 1978.
Berk, Stephen M. *Year of Crisis, Year of Hope: Russian Jewry and the Pogroms of 1881–1882.* Westport, Conn.: Greenwood Press, 1985.

Besmann, Wendy. *A Separate Circle: Jewish Life in Knoxville, Tennessee.* Knoxville: University of Tennessee Press, 2001.

Billings, Dwight B., and Kathleen M. Blee. *The Road to Poverty: The Making of Wealth and Hardship in Appalachia.* New York: Cambridge University Press, 2000.

Blanton, Sherry. "Lives of Quiet Affirmation: The Jewish Women of Early Anniston, Alabama." *Southern Jewish History* 2 (1999): 25–53.

Bluefield City Directory. Pittsburgh: R. L. Polk, 1910–11, 1915–16, 1919–20.

Bodnar, John. *The Transplanted: A History of Immigrants in Urban America.* Bloomington: Indiana University Press, 1985.

Bradley, J. G. "The Coal Operator and the Miner—A Partnership." WVRHC.

Bragg, Melody. *Thurmond, Dodge City of the East.* N.p.: n.p.

Braudel, Fernand. *The Wheels of Commerce.* New York: Harper & Row, 1979.

Byrne, George, ed. *Handbook of West Virginia.* Charleston, W.Va.: Lovett, 1915.

Cantrell, Doug. "Immigrants and Community in Harlan County, 1910–1930." *Register of the Kentucky Historical Society* 86, no. 2 (Spring 1988): 119–41.

Chirot, Daniel, and Anthony Reid, eds. *Essential Outsiders: Chinese and Jews in the Modern Transformation of Southeast Asia and Central Europe.* Seattle: University of Washington Press, 1997.

Cohen, Chester. *Shtetl Finder Gazetteer: Jewish Communities in the Nineteenth and Twentieth Centuries.* Bowie, Md.: Heritage Books, 1989.

Cohen, Lizabeth. *Making a New Deal: Industrial Workers in Chicago, 1919–1939.* New York: Cambridge University Press, 1990.

Collins, Justus. Papers. WVRHC.

"Company and Other Stores." *Coal Age* 8 (October 1915): 716.

Corbin, David Alan. *Life, Work, and Rebellion in the Coal Fields: The Southern West Virginia Miners, 1880–1922.* Urbana: University of Illinois Press, 1981.

David, Jerome Paul. "Jewish Consciousness in the Small Town: A Sociological Study of Jewish Identification." Master's thesis, Hebrew Union College, 1974.

DeRosett, Lou, and Joe Marcum. *Middlesboro at One Hundred, 1890–1990.* Middlesboro, Ky.: Middlesboro Centennial Commission, 1990.

Dietz, Elizabeth Jane. "As We Lived a Long Time Ago." *Goldenseal* (Fall 1981): 16.

Diner, Hasia. *A Time for Gathering: The Second Migration, 1820–1880.* Baltimore: Johns Hopkins University Press, 1992.

Dinnerstein, Leonard. *Antisemitism in America.* New York: Oxford University Press, 1994.

———. "A Note on Southern Attitudes Toward Jews." *Jewish Social Studies* 32 (1970): 43–49.

"Discussion by Readers." *Coal Age* 8 (November 1915): 895.

Dubrovsky, Gertrude. "Book Review: *Jewish Farmers in the Catskills,* by Abraham D. Lavender and Clarence B. Steinberg." *American Jewish Archives* 48, no. 1 (Spring–Summer 1996): 97–102.

Dunaway, Wilma. *The First American Frontier: Transition to Capitalism in Southern Appalachia, 1700–1860.* Chapel Hill: University of North Carolina Press, 1996.

Dunloup Days: Glen Jean to Thurmond, Exciting Times and Precious Memories. N.p.: Glen Jean Historical Society, 1989.

Eiland, Rudy. "The Retail Merchant." In *Centennial Program, City of Logan, West Virginia, 1852–1952,* 98. Logan, W.Va.: Logan Centennial Association, 1952.

Eisenberg, Ellen. "Argentine and American Jewry: A Case for Contrasting Immigrant Origins." *American Jewish Archives* 47 (Spring–Summer 1995): 1–16.

Eller, Ronald D. *Miners, Millhands, and Mountaineers: Industrialization of the Appalachian South, 1880–1930.* Knoxville: University of Tennessee Press, 1982.

Encyclopaedia Judaica. New York: Macmillan, 1971.

Evans, Eli. *The Provincials: A Personal History of Jews in the South.* Rev. ed. New York: Simon & Schuster, 1997.

Farley, Yvonne Snyder. "One of the Faithful: Asaff Rahall, Church Founder." *Goldenseal* 8, no. 2 (Summer 1992): 51–53.

———. "To Keep Their Faith Strong: The Raleigh Orthodox Community." *Goldenseal* 8, no. 2 (Summer 1992): 43–53.

Fayette County. Circuit Court Records, Criminal Court Records, Deed Books, Law Order Books, and Naturalization Records. Fayette County Courthouse, Fayetteville, W.Va.

Fear, Frank Anthony. "The Quest for Saliency: Patterns of Jewish Communal Organization in Three Appalachian Small Towns." Master's thesis, West Virginia University, 1972.

Fishback, Price. "Did Coal Miners 'Owe Their Souls to the Company Store'? Theory and Evidence from the Early 1900s." *Journal of Economic History* 46, no. 4 (December 1986): 1011–29.

Fones-Wolf, Ken, and Ronald L. Lewis. *Transnational West Virginia: Ethnic Communities and Economic Change, 1840–1940.* Morgantown: West Virginia University Press, 2002.

Forester, William D. *Before We Forget: Harlan County, 1920 through 1930.* N.p.: n.p., 1983.

———. *Harlan County—The Turbulent Thirties.* N.p.: n.p., 1986.

Friedenberg, Albert M. "The Jews and the American Sunday Laws." *Publications of the American Jewish Historical Society* 11 (1903): 101–15.

Gartner, Lloyd. "Jewish Migrants en Route from Europe to North America: Traditions and Realities." In *The Jews of North America,* edited by Moses Rischin, 25–43. Detroit: Wayne State University Press, 1987.

Gaventa, John. *Power and Powerlessness: Quiescence and Rebellion in an Appalachian Valley.* Urbana: University of Illinois Press, 1980.

Gerber, David A., ed. *Anti-Semitism in American History.* Urbana: University of Illinois Press, 1987.

———. "Cutting Out Shylock: Elite Anti-Semitism and the Quest for Moral Order in the Mid-Nineteenth-Century Marketplace." *Journal of American History* 69 (December 1982): 615–37.

Gillenwater, Mack. "Cultural and Historical Geography of Mining Settlements in the Pocahontas Coal Field of Southern West Virginia, 1880–1930." Ph.D. diss., University of Tennessee, 1972.

Gilman, Sander L., and Milton Shain, eds. *Jewries at the Frontier: Accommodation, Identity, Conflict.* Urbana: University of Illinois Press, 1999.

Glasscock, Governor Walter G. Papers. Box 3. WVRHC.

Gleason, Arthur. "Company-Owned Americans." *Nation* (1920).

Golab, Caroline. *Immigrant Destinations.* Philadelphia: Temple University Press, 1977.

Golden, Harry. *Jewish Roots in the Carolinas: A Pattern of American Philo-Semitism.* Greensboro, N.C.: *Carolina Israelite,* 1955.

Goren, Arthur A. "Traditional Institutions Transplanted." In *The Jews of North America,* edited by Moses Rischin, 62–78. Detroit: Wayne State University Press, 1987.

Greene, Janet W. "Strategies for Survival: Women's Work in the Southern West Virginia Coal Camps." *West Virginia History* 49 (1990): 37–54.

Gurock, Jeffrey. "The Orthodox Synagogue." In *The American Synagogue: A Sanctuary Transformed,* edited by Jack Wertheimer, 37–84. New York: Cambridge University Press, 1987.

Hahn, Steven, and Jonathan Prude, eds. *The Countryside in an Age of Capitalist Transformation: Essays in the Social History of Rural America.* Chapel Hill: University of North Carolina Press, 1985.

Harlan, Ky. Congregation B'nai Sholom Records, 1931–1962 (Sisterhood, congregation minute book). AJA.

Hatcher, Thomas C., and Geneva Steele, eds. *The Heritage of McDowell County, West Virginia, 1858–1995.* War, W.Va.: McDowell County Historical Society, 1995.

Hebrew Union College Collection. Series B, Faculty and Student Affairs. AJA.

Heinze, Andrew. "Jewish Street Merchants and Mass Consumption in New York City, 1880–1914." *American Jewish Archives* 41 (1989): 199–214.

Herr, Kincaid. *The Louisville & Nashville Railroad.* Louisville: L&N Railroad, 1964.

Hertz, Aleksander. *The Jews in Polish Culture.* Evanston, Ill.: Northwestern University Press, 1988.

Hertzberg, Steven. *Strangers within the Gate City: The Jews of Atlanta, 1845–1915.* Philadelphia: Jewish Publication Society of America, 1978.

Heschel, Abraham Joshua. "The Eastern European Era in Jewish History." In *East European Jews in Two Worlds: Studies from the YIVO Manual,* edited by Deborah Dash Moore, 1–21. Evanston, Ill.: YIVO and Northwestern University Press, 1990.

Hevener, John W. *Which Side Are You On? The Harlan County Coal Miners, 1931–1939.* Urbana: University of Illinois Press, 1978.

Hickam, Homer. *October Sky.* New York: Dell, 1999.

Higham, John. *Strangers in the Land: Patterns of American Nativism, 1860–1925.* New Brunswick, N.J.: Rutgers University Press, 1955.

Howe, Irving. *World of Our Fathers.* New York: Harcourt Brace Jovanovich, 1976.

Hsiung, David C. *Two Worlds in the Tennessee Mountains: Exploring the Origins of Appalachian Stereotypes.* Lexington: University Press of Kentucky, 1997.

Hundert, Gershon David. "Some Basic Characteristics of the Jewish Experience in Poland." In *From Shtetl to Socialism: Studies from Polin,* edited by Antony Polonsky, 20–23. Washington, D.C.: Littman Library of Jewish Civilization, 1993.

Hunter, Houston Kermit. "The Story of McDowell County." *West Virginia Review* 17, no. 7 (April 1940): 165–69.

Hyman, Paula E. *Gender and Assimilation in Modern Jewish History.* Seattle: University of Washington Press, 1995.

"I. L. Shor: His Life as He Told It." *Every Friday* (Cincinnati), 23 September 1949.

Inscoe, John C., ed. *Appalachians and Race: The Mountain South from Slavery to Segregation.* Lexington: University Press of Kentucky, 2000.

"Irvin Gergely." Obituary. *Lexington (Ky.) Herald-Leader,* 27 May 2000.

Jaffee, David. "Peddlers of Progress and the Transformation of the Rural North, 1760–1860." *Journal of American History* (September 1991): 511–35.

"Jewish Cemetery, Middlesboro, Kentucky." Middlesboro, Ky., Folder. Small Collections. AJA.

"Jews in America." *Fortune* (February 1936).

Johnpoll, Bernard K. "Why They Left: Russian-Jewish Mass Migration and the Repressive Laws, 1881–1917." *American Jewish Archives* 47 (Spring–Summer 1995): 17–54.

Jones, Jack M. *Early Coal Mining in Pocahontas, Virginia.* Lynchburg, Va.: Jack M. Jones, 1983.

Jones, Lu Ann. "Gender, Race, and Itinerant Commerce in the Rural New South." *Journal of Southern History* 66, no. 2 (May 2000): 297–320.

Kahn, Philip, Jr. *A Stitch in Time: The Four Seasons of Baltimore's Needle Trades.* Baltimore: Maryland Historical Society, 1989.

Kaplan, Benjamin. *The Eternal Stranger: A Study of Jewish Life in the Small Community.* New York: Bookman, 1957.

Kassow, Samuel. "Communal and Social Change in the Polish Shtetl." In *Jewish Settlement and Community in the Modern Western World,* edited by R. Dotterer, D. Dash Moore, and S. M. Cohen, 56–92. Selinsgrove, Pa.: Susquehanna University Press, 1991.

Keadle, Roy H. Scrapbook. WVRHC.

Kentucky Department of Mines Annual Report. 1924–26. Frankfort: Commonwealth of Kentucky, 1924–26.

Kirshenblatt-Gimblett, Barbara. "The Folk Culture of Jewish Immigrant Communities." In *The Jews of North America,* edited by Moses Rischin, 79–84. Detroit: Wayne State University Press, 1987.

Kiser, Virginia Strange. *Memories of Pocahontas.* Bluefield, W.Va.: H. E. Kiser Jr., 1998.

Kitts' City and Coalfield Directory. Bluefield, W.Va.: City Directory, 1904.

Klier, John Doyle. *Russia Gathers Her Jews: The Origins of the "Jewish Question" in Russia, 1772–1825.* DeKalb: Northern Illinois University Press, 1986.

Kligsberg, Moses. "Jewish Immigrants in Business: A Sociological Study." *American Jewish Historical Quarterly* 56 (March 1967): 283–318.

Kneeland, Frank. "Patriotic Demonstration at Gary, W.Va." *Coal Age* 11, no. 19 (1917): 826.

Kugelmass, Jack. "Native Aliens: The Jews of Poland as a Middleman Minority." Ph.D. diss., New School for Social Research, 1980.

Kulikoff, Allan. "The Transition to Capitalism in Rural America." *William and Mary Quarterly* 46 (January 1989): 120–44.

Kuznets, Simon. "Immigration of Russian Jews to the United States: Background and Structure." In *Perspectives in American History* 9, edited by D. Fleming and B. Bailyn, 35–124. Cambridge: Harvard University Press, 1975.

Laing, James T. "The Negro Miner in West Virginia." Ph.D. diss., Ohio State University, 1933.

Lambie, Joseph T. *From Mine to Market.* New York: New York University Press, 1954.

Lane, Ron, and Ted Schnepf. *Sewell: A New River Community.* N.p.: Eastern National Park & Monument Association, 1985.

Lane, Winthrop D. *Civil War in West Virginia: A Story of Industrial Conflict in the Coal Mines.* New York: Arno Press, 1921.

Lavender, Abraham D., ed. *A Coat of Many Colors: Jewish Subcommunities in the United States.* Westport, Conn.: Greenwood Press, 1977.

Lawrence, Randall G. "Appalachian Metamorphosis: Industrializing Society on the Central Appalachian Plateau, 1860–1913." Ph.D. diss., Duke University, 1983.

Lee, Howard B. *Bloodletting in Appalachia.* Morgantown: West Virginia University Press, 1969.

Leonard, Bill J., ed. *Christianity in Appalachia.* Knoxville: University of Tennessee Press, 1999.

Levine, Hillel. *Economic Origins of Anti-Semitism: Poland and Its Jews in the Early Modern Period.* New Haven, Conn.: Yale University Press, 1991.

Levinson, Robert E. *The Jews in the California Gold Rush.* New York: Ktav, 1978.

Levy, Lester S. *Jacob Epstein.* Baltimore: Maran Press, 1978.

Lewis, Ronald L. "Appalachian Restructuring in Historical Perspective: Coal, Culture, and Social Change in West Virginia." *Urban Studies* 30, no. 2 (1993): 299–308.

———. *Black Coal Miners in America: Race, Class, and Community Conflict, 1780–1980.* Lexington: University Press of Kentucky, 1987.

———. *Transforming the Appalachian Countryside: Railroads, Deforestation, and Social Change in West Virginia, 1880–1920.* Chapel Hill: University of North Carolina Press, 1998.

Logan City Directory. N.p.: n.p, 1927.

Logan County. Deed Books, Naturalization Records, and Will Books. Logan County Courthouse, Logan, W.Va.

Logan, W.Va. Congregation B'nai El Records, 1924–1970 (Sisterhood, B'nai B'rith Lodge #1236, congregation minute book). AJA.

Lowi, Theodore. "Southern Jews: The Two Communities." In *Jews in the South,* edited by Leonard Dinnerstein and Mary Dale Palsson, 265–82. Baton Rouge: Louisiana State University Press, 1973.

Mahler, Raphael. "The Economic Background of Jewish Emigration from Galicia to the United States." In *East European Jews in Two Worlds: Studies from the YIVO Annual,* edited by Deborah Dash Moore, 125–37. Evanston, Ill.: YIVO and Northwestern University Press, 1990.

Mann, Ralph. "Mountain Settlement: Appalachian and National Modes of Migration." *Journal of Appalachian Studies* 2 (Fall 1996): 337–45.

Manuscript Census. Fayette, Kanawha, Logan, McDowell, Mercer, Mingo, and Raleigh Counties, W.Va.; Bell and Harlan Counties, Ky.; Tazewell and Wise Counties, Va. Ninth, Tenth, Twelfth, Thirteenth, and Fourteenth Censuses of the United States. 1870, 1880, 1900, 1910, and 1920.

Marcus, Jacob Rader. *United States Jewry, 1776–1985.* Vol. 2. Detroit: Wayne State University Press, 1991.

Marino, Rose. *Welch and Its People.* Marceline, Mo.: Walsworth Press, 1985.

Massay, Glenn. "Coal Consolidation: Profile of the Fairmont Field of Northern West Virginia, 1852–1903." Ph.D. diss., West Virginia University, 1970.

McCauley, Deborah Vansau. *Appalachian Mountain Religion: A History.* Urbana: University of Illinois Press, 1995.

McCormick, Kyle. "McDowell County Celebrates its Centennial." *West Virginia History* 19 (April 1958): 202–8.

McCoy, Clyde B., and James S. Brown. "Appalachian Migration to Midwestern Cities." In *The Invisible Minority: Urban Appalachians,* edited by William W. Philliber and Clyde B. McCoy, 35–78. Lexington: University Press of Kentucky, 1981.

McDaniels, Jennifer. "Totz Experienced Boom, Bust Often Characterized by Coal Industry." *Harlan Daily Enterprise,* 31 March 1998.

McDowell County. Circuit Court Records, Criminal Court Records, Deed Books, Incorporation Books, Naturalization Records, and Will Books. McDowell County Courthouse, Welch, W.Va.

"Middlesboro History." Column. *Middlesboro (Ky.) Daily News.* 1990.

Mingo County. Circuit Court Records, Deed Books, Incorporation Books, Naturalization Records, and Will Books. Mingo County Courthouse, Williamson, W.Va.

Mitchell, Robert, ed. *Appalachian Frontiers: Settlement, Society, and Development in the Preindustrial Era.* Lexington: University Press of Kentucky, 1991.

Morawska, Ewa. *Insecure Prosperity: Small-Town Jews in Industrial America, 1890–1940.* Princeton, N.J.: Princeton University Press, 1996.

Mostov, Stephen G. "Dun and Bradstreet Reports as a Source of Jewish Economic History: Cincinnati, 1840–1875." *American Jewish History* 72, no. 3 (1983): 333–53.

Nadell, Pamela S. "The Journey to America by Steam: The Jews of Eastern Europe in Transition." *American Jewish History* 71 (1981–82): 269–84.

Neu, Irene D. "The Jewish Businesswoman in America." *American Jewish Historical Quarterly* 66, no. 1 (1976): 137–54.

Noe, Kenneth W. *Southwest Virginia's Railroad: Modernization and the Sectional Crisis.* Urbana: University of Illinois Press, 1994.

Norfolk & Western Railway Company Sixth Annual Report. Philadelphia: N&W, 1902.

Nugent, Walter. *Crossings: The Great Transatlantic Migrations, 1870–1914.* Bloomington: Indiana University Press, 1992.

Obermiller, Phillip J., and William W. Philliber, eds. *Appalachia in an International Context: Cross-National Comparisons of Developing Regions.* Westport, Conn.: Praeger, 1994.

Olson, James S. "The Depths of the Great Depression: Economic Collapse in West Virginia, 1932–1933." *West Virginia History* 38 (April 1977): 214–25.

Pendleton, William C. *History of Tazewell County and Southwest Virginia, 1748–1920.* N. p.: W. C. Hill, 1920.

Perlmann, Joel. "Beyond New York: The Occupations of Russian Jewish Immigrants in Providence, R.I. and Other Small Jewish Communities, 1900–1915." *American Jewish History* 72 (March 1983): 369–94.

Pomeroy, Earl. "On Becoming a Westerner." In *Jews of the American West,* edited by Moses Rischin and John Livingston, 194–212. Detroit: Wayne State University Press, 1991.

Portelli, Alessandro. *The Death of Luigi Trastulli and Other Stories: Form and Meaning in Oral History.* Albany: SUNY Press, 1991.

Progressive West Virginians. Wheeling, W.Va.: *Wheeling Intelligencer,* 1923.

Pudup, Mary Beth. "Social Class and Economic Development in Southeast Kentucky, 1820–1880." In *Appalachian Frontiers: Settlement, Society, and Development in the Preindustrial Era,* edited by Robert Mitchell, 235–60. Lexington: University Press of Kentucky, 1991.

———. "Town and Country in the Transformation of Appalachian Kentucky." In *Appalachia in the Making: The Mountain South in the Nineteenth Century,* edited by Mary Beth Pudup, Dwight B. Billings, and Altina L. Waller, 270–96. Chapel Hill: University of North Carolina Press, 1995.

Pudup, Mary Beth, Dwight B. Billings, and Altina L. Waller, eds. *Appalachia in the Making: The Mountain South in the Nineteenth Century.* Chapel Hill: University of North Carolina Press, 1995.

Rabinowitz, Howard N. "Nativism, Bigotry and Anti-Semitism in the South." *American Jewish History* 77 (March 1988): 437–51.

———. "Writing Jewish Community History." *American Jewish History* 70 (September 1980): 119–27.

Raleigh County. Deed Books, Naturalization Records, and Will Books. Raleigh County Courthouse, Beckley, W.Va.

Reed, John Shelton. "Shalom, Y'All: Jewish Southerners." In *One South: An Ethnic Ap-*

proach to Regional Culture, by John Shelton Reed. Baton Rouge: Louisiana State University Press, 1982.

Regner, Sidney L. "Experiences While Officiating as a Student at the High Holidays." Biographies File. AJA.

Reisman, Bernard. "Alaskan Jews Discover the Last Frontier." In *Jewries at the Frontier: Accommodation, Identity, Conflict,* edited by Sander L. Gilman and Milton Shain, 111–26. Urbana: University of Illinois Press, 1999.

Righteous Remnant: Jewish Survival in Appalachia. Video documentary produced by Maryanne Reed. West Virginia Public Television, 1997.

Rischin, Moses, and John Livingston, eds. *Jews of the American West.* Detroit: Wayne State University Press, 1991.

Roden, B. F. "The Commissary: Its Indispensability." *Coal Age* 4 (1913): 240–41.

Rogger, Hans. *Jewish Policies and Right-Wing Politics in Imperial Russia.* Berkeley and Los Angeles: University of California Press, 1986.

Rogoff, Leonard. *Homelands: Southern Jewish Identity in Durham and Chapel Hill, North Carolina.* Tuscaloosa: University of Alabama Press, 2001.

———. "Is the Jew White? The Racial Place of the Southern Jew." *American Jewish History* 85, no. 3 (September 1997): 195–262.

———. "Synagogue and Jewish Church: A Congregational History of North Carolina." *Southern Jewish History* 1 (1998): 43–81.

Rosenheim, W. S. "Williamson: In the Heart of the Billion Dollar Coal Field." *West Virginia Review* 2 (October 1924): 20–22.

Rothman, Hal. "'Same Horse, New Wagon': Tradition and Assimilation among the Jews of Wichita, 1865–1930." *Great Plains Quarterly* 15 (Spring 1995): 83–104.

Routes and Resorts of the Chesapeake and Ohio Railway. Richmond: Chesapeake & Ohio Railway, 1878.

Rubinow, I. M. "Economic Condition of the Jews in Russia." *Bulletin of the Bureau of Labor* 72 (September 1907): 487–583.

Sacks, Karen Brodkin. "How Did the Jews Become White Folks?" In *Race,* edited by Steven Gregory and Roger Sanjek, 78–102. New Brunswick, N. J.: Rutgers University Press, 1994.

Salstrom, Paul. "Newer Appalachia as One of America's Last Frontiers." In *Appalachia in the Making: The Mountain South in the Nineteenth Century,* edited by Mary Beth Pudup, Dwight B. Billings, and Altina L. Waller, 76–101. Chapel Hill: University of North Carolina Press, 1995.

Sarna, Jonathan D. "Anti-Semitism in American History." *Commentary* 71, no. 3 (March 1981): 42–48.

———. "The 'Mythical Jew' and the 'Jew Next Door' in Nineteenth Century America." In *Anti-Semitism in American History,* edited by David A. Gerber, 57–78. Urbana: University of Illinois Press, 1987.

Schlereth, Thomas J. "Country Stores, Country Fairs, and Mail Order Catalogues: Consumption in Rural America." In *Consuming Visions: Accumulation and Display of Goods in America, 1880–1920,* edited by Simon J. Bronner, 339–75. New York: W. W. Norton.

Schmier, Louis. "Hellooo! Peddlerman; Hellooo!" In *Ethnic Minorities in Gulf Coast Society,* edited by Jerrell H. Shofner and Linda V. Ellsworth, 75–89. Pensacola, Fla.: Gulf Coast History and Humanities Conference, 1979.

———. "Jews and Gentiles in a South Georgia Town." In *Jews of the South: Selected Essays from the Southern Jewish Historical Society,* edited by Samuel Proctor and Louis Schmier. Macon, Ga.: Mercer University Press, 1984.

———. "'We Were All Part of a Lost Generation': Jewish Religious Life in a Rural Southern Town, 1900–1940." In *Cultural Perspectives on the American South,* vol. 5, edited by Charles Reagan Wilson. New York: Gordon & Breach, 1991.

Schoenburg, Nancy, and Stuart Schoenburg. *Lithuanian Jewish Communities.* New York: Garland, 1991.

Scott, Eugene L. "Thurmond on the New River." *West Virginia Review* 23 (March 1946): 20–22.

Selevan, Ida Cohen. "Jewish Wage Earners in Pittsburgh, 1890–1930." *American Jewish Historical Quarterly* 65 (March 1976): 272–85.

Semrau, Ronda G. "Roxie Gore: Looking Back in Logan County." *Goldenseal* 16 (Summer 1990): 23–28.

Shackelford, Laurel, and Bill Weinberg, eds. *Our Appalachia.* New York: Hill and Wang, 1977.

Shapiro, Edward S. *A Time for Healing: American Jewry since World War II.* Baltimore: Johns Hopkins University Press, 1992.

Sheskin, Ira M. "The Dixie Diaspora: The 'Loss' of the Small Southern Jewish Community." *Southeastern Geographer* 40, no. 1 (May 2000): 52–74.

Shifflett, Crandall. *Coal Towns: Life, Work, and Culture in Company Towns of Southern Appalachia, 1880–1960.* Knoxville: University of Tennessee Press, 1991.

Shinedling, Abraham I. Collection. AJA.

———. *West Virginia Jewry: Origins and History, 1850–1958.* Philadelphia: Maurice Jacobs, 1963.

Shinedling, Abraham I., and Manuel Pickus. *History of the Beckley Jewish Community.* Beckley, W.Va.: Biggs-Johnston-Withrow, 1955.

Simon, John. "The South African Jewish Experience." In *Jewries at the Frontier: Accommodation, Identity, Conflict,* edited by Sander L. Gilman and Milton Shain, 67–90. Urbana: University of Illinois Press, 1999.

Simon, Richard M. "The Development of Underdevelopment: The Coal Industry and Its Effect on the West Virginia Economy, 1880–1930." Ph.D. diss., University of Pittsburgh, 1978.

Sklare, Marshall. *America's Jews.* New York: Random House, 1971.

Sniderman, Marilou S. "Diamond in the Rough: A Biography of Harry Schwachter on the Occasion of his Diamond Jubilee." Unpublished manuscript, 1963. Williamson Public Library, Williamson, W.Va.

Solins, Mrs. Samuel, and Mrs. Paul W. Jones. *McDowell County History.* Fort Worth, Tex.: University Supply, 1959.

Sorin, Gerald. *A Time for Building: The Third Migration, 1880–1920.* Baltimore: Johns Hopkins University Press, 1992.

Soyer, Daniel. "Between Two Worlds: The Jewish *Landsmanshaftn* and Immigrant Identity." *American Jewish History* 76 (September 1986): 5–24.

Sparkmon, William R. *The Chesapeake & Ohio Railway in West Virginia.* Charleston, W.Va.: Chesapeake & Ohio Historical Society, 1983.

Sprecher, Hannah. "Let Them Drink and Forget Poverty: Orthodox Rabbis' Reactions to Prohibition." *American Jewish Archives* 43 (1991): 135–79.

Stern, Norton B. "The Jewish Community of a Nevada Mining Town." *Western States Jewish Historical Quarterly* 15 (October 1982): 48–78.

———. "The Major Role of Polish Jews in the Pioneer West." *Western States Jewish Historical Quarterly* (July 1976): 326–44.

"Store Checks vs. Thrift." *Coal Age* 8 (October 1915): 619.

"Student Rabbi Survey, 1935–1936." Series B, Faculty and Student Affairs. Hebrew Union College Collection. AJA.

Suberman, Stella. *The Jew Store.* Chapel Hill, N.C.: Algonquin Books, 1998.

Sullivan, Charles Kenneth. "Coal Men and Coal Towns: Development of the Smokeless Coalfields of Southern West Virginia, 1873–1923." Ph.D. diss., University of Pittsburgh, 1979.

Sullivan, Ken. *Thurmond: A New River Community.* N.p.: Eastern National Park & Monument Association, 1989.

"Sure We Got Problems." *Goldenseal* 20 (Summer 1994): 65.

Szold, Henrietta. Papers. MS 38. JMM.

Tazewell County. Deed Records and Will Books. Virginia State Library, Richmond.

Tenenbaum, Shelly. "Immigrants and Capital: Jewish Loan Societies in the United States, 1880–1945." *American Jewish History* 76 (September 1986): 67–77.

Thomas, Jerry Bruce. "Coal Country: The Rise of the Southern Smokeless Coal Industry and Its Effect on Area Development, 1872–1910." Ph.D. diss., University of North Carolina, 1971.

Toll, William. "The 'New Social History' and Recent Jewish Historical Writing." *American Jewish History* 69 (March 1980): 325–41.

Trotter, Joe William, Jr. *Coal, Class, and Color: Blacks in Southern West Virginia, 1915–1932.* Urbana: University of Illinois Press, 1990.

U.S. Bureau of the Census. *Census of Population.* Washington, D.C.: GPO, 1880–1990.

———. *State Compendium: West Virginia.* Washington, D.C.: GPO, 1925.

U.S. Coal Commission. *Report of the United States Coal Commission.* Washington, D.C.: GPO, 1925.

U.S. Immigration Commission. *Emigration Conditions in Europe: Reports of the Immigration Commission.* Vol. 12. Washington, D.C.: GPO, 1911.

———. *Immigrants in Industries.* Vol. 7. 61st Cong., 2d sess. S. Doc. 633. Washington, D.C.: GPO, 1911.

U.S. Senate. *West Virginia Coal Fields: Hearings before the Committee on Education and Labor.* 67th Cong., 1st sess. Washington, D.C.: GPO, 1921.

Waller, Altina. *Feud: Hatfields, McCoys, and Social Change in Appalachia, 1860–1900.* Chapel Hill: University of North Carolina Press, 1988.

Webb, Clive. "Jewish Merchants and Black Customers in the Age of Jim Crow." *Southern Jewish History* 2 (1999): 55–80.

Weiner, Deborah R. "A History of Jewish Life in the Central Appalachian Coalfields, 1870s to 1970s." Ph.D. diss., West Virginia University, 2002.

Weinryb, Bernard. *The Jews of Poland: A Social and Economic History of the Jewish Community in Poland from 1100 to 1800.* Philadelphia: Jewish Publication Society of America, 1973.

"Weinstein Brothers." In *Picturesque Middlesboro, The Magic City.* Middlesboro, Ky.: *Pinnacle News,* n.d.

Weissbach, Lee Shai. "East European Immigrants and the Image of Jews in the Small-Town South." *American Jewish History* 85 (September 1997): 231–62.

———. *Jewish Life in Small-Town America: A History.* New Haven, Conn.: Yale University Press, 2005.

———. "Small Town Jewish Life and the Pennsylvania Pattern." *Western Pennsylvania History* 83 (Spring 2000): 37–53.

———. "Stability and Mobility in the Small Jewish Community: Examples from Kentucky History." *American Jewish History* 79 (Spring 1990): 355–75.

Welch, W.Va. Congregation Emanuel Records 1921–1959 (Hebrew Ladies Aid Society Sisterhood, McDowell County B'nai B'rith Lodge #1265). AJA.

Wenger, Beth S. "Jewish Women and Voluntarism: Beyond the Myth of Enablers." *American Jewish History* 79 (1989–90): 16–36.

West Virginia Blue Book (Legislative Handbook and Manual and Official Register). 1916–64. Charleston, W.Va.: Clerk of the Senate, 1916–64.

West Virginia Department of Mines Annual Report. 1905–30. Charleston: West Virginia Department of Mines, 1905–30.

West Virginia State Gazetteer and Business Directory. Pittsburgh: R. L. Polk, 1882–83, 1895, 1898, 1900, 1904, 1910, 1914.

West Virginia Supreme Court Report. 1905–22. Charleston, W.Va.: n.p.

West Virginians of 1934–1935. Wheeling, W.Va.: *Wheeling Intelligencer,* 1935.

Whitfield, Stephen J. "Commercial Passions: The Southern Jew as Businessman." *American Jewish History* 71 (1981–82): 342–57.

Williams, John Alexander. "Class, Section, and Culture in Nineteenth Century West Virginia Politics." In *Appalachia in the Making: The Mountain South in the Nineteenth Century,* edited by Mary Beth Pudup, Dwight B. Billings, and Altina Waller, 210–32. Chapel Hill: University of North Carolina Press, 1995.

Williamson City Directory. Chillicothe, Ohio: Mullin-Kille and *Williamson Daily News,* 1952.

Williamson, W.Va. B'nai Israel Congregation Records, 1913–1953 (Sisterhood, B'nai B'rith Lodge #1040). AJA.

Wischnitzer, Mark. *To Dwell in Safety: The Story of Jewish Migration since 1800.* Philadelphia: Jewish Publication Society of America, 1948.

Wolfe, Margaret Ripley. "Aliens in Southern Appalachia: Catholics in the Coal Camps, 1900–1940." *Appalachian Heritage* 6 (1978): 43–56.

Woods, Jim. *Raleigh County, West Virginia.* Beckley, W.Va.: Raleigh County Historical Society, 1994.

Zborowski, Marc, and Elisabeth Herzog. *Life Is with People: The Jewish Little-Town of Eastern Europe.* New York: International Universities Press, 1952.

Zenner, Walter P. *Minorities in the Middle: A Cross-Cultural Analysis.* Albany: SUNY Press, 1991.

Zipperstein, Steven J. *The Jews of Odessa: A Cultural History, 1794–1881.* Stanford, Calif.: Stanford University Press, 1985.

Interviews

All interviews conducted by author unless otherwise specified.

Albert, Ivan. 8 November 1996.

Albert, Martha. 8 November 1996.

Baloff, Esther Sturm. Interview by Barbara Winick Bernstein and Marilyn Jacob Shore.

20 May 1985. Archives of the Jewish Community of Knoxville and East Tennessee, Knoxville Jewish Alliance, Knoxville.

Bank, Elaine. 4 March 1998.

Bank, Gail. 28 September and 4 October 1998.

Bank, Kenneth. 6 November 1998.

Bank, Sylvan. 4 March 1998.

Bennett, Wallace. Interview by Paul Niden. 1 October 1980. WVRHC.

Berman, Harry. Interview by John C. Hennen Jr., 15 and 28 June 1989. Matewan Oral History Project, Matewan Development Center, Matewan, W.Va.

Brant, Nancy. October 1998.

Cohen, Bertie Rodgin. 6 March 2000.

Drosick, Edna Moore. 26 April 1998.

Eiland, Edward. 19 May 1998.

Fink, Sidney. 12 October 1996.

Goodman, Temple. 21 February 1999.

Gorsetman, Isadore. 13 May 1998.

Gottlieb, Bernard. 5 November 1996.

Gottlieb, Betty Schuchat. 18 December 1997.

Hecker, Reva Totz. 5 November 1998.

Jaffe, Goldie Scott. 30 April 2000.

Katzen, Emanuel. Interview by author and Maryanne Reed. 30 May 1996.

Koslow, Milton. 13 May 1998.

Mankoff, Lou. Interview by author and Maryanne Reed. March 1996.

McGuire, Christine Carr. November 1998.

Monk, Herman. Interview by Paul Niden. 17 August 1980. WVRHC.

Monroe, Frances. 27 April 1998.

Monroe, Harry. 27 April 1998.

Ofsa, Mary Marsh. 26 March 1999.

Oppleman, Zelda Totz. 1999.

Phipps, E. H. Interview by Paul Niden. 16 August 1980. WVRHC.

Pickus, Manuel. 18 May 1998.

Rakes, Billie. 12 October 1996.

Rosen, Betty Ofsa. Interview by author and Maryanne Reed. 28 May 1996.

Scott, Isadore. 14 December 1997.

Shell, Craig. E-mail correspondence. October 2002.

Sopher, Ira. 13 October 1996.

Sopher, Mary Jo. 13 October 1996.

Sturm, Melvin. 4 October 1998.

Tams, William. Interview by Richard M. Hadsell. 9 June 1966. WVRHC.

Wein, Isadore. 13 October 1996.

Wein, Jean Abrams. 13 October 1996.

Weiner, Harvey. 8 November 1996.

Weiner, Sam. 8 November 1996.

INDEX

Aaron, Sam, 84
Aaronsohn, Rabbi Michael, 185
Abel family: Harry, 28; Sam, 105
Abrams, Sam, 44, 84
African Americans, 23, 33, 35, 37, 97–98, 104–5, 111, 121–25, 128–29, 132–33, 136; and Jews, 97–98, 104, 111, 123–24, 128, 136, 180, 194n52, 208n26
Albert family: Charlie, 91; Martha, 76
Alexander, Irving, 113
antisemitism and anti-Jewish stereotypes, 18, 120, 128–31, 136–41, 146–47, 208n26, 210–11n55
Appalachia, 6, 20, 45–46, 88, 133–34, 188. *See also* Central Appalachia
Appalachia, Va., 43
Appalachian studies, 4, 116, 119, 187, 191n5
assimilation. *See* Jewish identity
Atherton, Lewis, 88
Atlanta, 118

Baach family, 34, 114, 118, 127, 178; Jacob, 34, 70, 178; Jenny, 110; Lena, 34, 70; Sol, 70, 110
Baldwin-Felts Detective Agency, 59, 145
Baloff, Esther Sturm, 77, 81, 96, 111, 141, 165, 174, 176
Baltimore, 9, 19, 24–30, 35–36, 42–43, 47, 71, 76, 85–86, 164, 169, 173, 188
Baltimore and Ohio (B&O) Railroad, 19
Baltimore Bargain House, 24–26, 35, 74, 86
Baltimore B'nai Israel Congregation cemetery, 164
Bank family, 163; Harry, 25, 35–36, 67, 70, 96, 152, 154; Hyman, 60, 148, 156; Ida Shore, 70, 148–49, 155; Ken, 115, 154; Wolf, 25, 35–36, 67–69, 78, 98, 105, 124, 148
Barbourville, Ky., 43
Beckley, W.Va., 9, 15, 27–28, 32, 40–43, 189; Jewish economic life in, 44, 53, 70–71, 73, 76, 79, 165; Jews in civic/social scene, 111, 113–15, 118, 137–38, 141
Beckley Congregation Beth El (Beckley

Hebrew Association), 159–60, 164, 172, 177, 183, 190
Bell County, Ky., 38–39, 47, 99, 102–3
Bender, Thomas, 188
Berman family, 144–45; Harry, 81, 112, 145; Jacob, 26, 145
Bernstein, Saul, 25, 29–30
Billings, Dwight, 88
Blee, Kathleen, 88
Bloch family, 34, 114, 118, 178; Michael, 34, 70, 92, 178; Sidney, 98
Bloom, I., 129–30
Bluefield, W.Va., 35, 39, 40, 103, 105, 115, 138, 142, 144, 175, 180, 196n88
Bluefield College, 180
Bluefield Daily Telegraph, 54, 101, 127
B'nai B'rith lodges, 179–81; Beckley, 70, 179–80; Logan, 180; McDowell County, 173, 180; Williamson, 70, 142, 174
Bodnar, John, 46
boomtowns, 1, 24, 32–33, 35–39, 50, 98, 100–108, 113, 116, 187; Jewish congregations in, 151–55; social landscape of, 5–6, 91–93, 117–18
Borrow, Rabbi Moses, 153–54
Bowyer, Peter, 30–31
Bradley, J. G., 59, 123
Bramwell, W.Va., 57
Brown, David, 73, 78, 115–16, 145. *See also* Schwachter family
Budnick family: Charles, 98; Harry, 74, 98; Julian, 98

Calhoun, A. L., 98, 106
Capehart, Harry, 124
Caswell Creek Coal Company, 57
Catzen family: Aaron, 52, 97, 166; Ethel Catzen Cohen, 52
Central Appalachia, 6, 10, 45–46, 52, 82–83, 90, 92, 188; history of, 19–24, 194n49; plateau, 1, 2, 32, 187
Chambers family: Ed, 144–45; Sallie, 145
Charleston, W.Va., 29, 30, 31, 71, 175

DEBORAH R. WEINER serves as Research Historian and Family History Coordinator at the Jewish Museum of Maryland in Baltimore. She received a doctorate degree in history from West Virginia University in 2002. Her work has been published in several essay collections, including *Transnational West Virginia, Southern Jewish History: An Anthology,* and *Beyond Hill and Hollow.*

The University of Illinois Press
is a founding member of the
Association of American University Presses.

Composed in 10.5/13 Adobe Minion
with Minion display
by Type One, LLC
for the University of Illinois Press
Manufactured by Thomson-Shore, Inc.

University of Illinois Press
1325 South Oak Street
Champaign, IL 61820–6903
www.press.uillinois.edu